# Canadian Intellectual Property
# Law and Strategy

# Canadian Intellectual Property Law and Strategy

## Trademarks, Copyright, and Industrial Designs

John S. McKeown

OXFORD
UNIVERSITY PRESS

# OXFORD
### UNIVERSITY PRESS

*Oxford University Press, Inc., publishes works that further Oxford University's objective of excellence
in research, scholarship, and education.*

Oxford   New York
Auckland   Cape Town   Dar es Salaam   Hong Kong   Karachi   Kuala Lumpur   Madrid   Melbourne
Mexico City   Nairobi   New Delhi   Shanghai   Taipei   Toronto

With offices in
Argentina   Austria   Brazil   Chile   Czech Republic   France   Greece   Guatemala   Hungary   Italy
Japan   Poland   Portugal   Singapore   South Korea   Switzerland   Thailand   Turkey   Ukraine
Vietnam

Library of Congress Cataloging-in-Publication Data
McKeown, John S., 1948-
  Canadian intellectual property law and strategy : trademarks, copyright,
and industrial designs / John S. McKeown.
     p. cm.
  Includes bibliographical references and index.
  ISBN 978-0-19-536942-7 (pbk. : alk. paper)
  1. Intellectual property—Canada. I. Title.
  KE2779.M353 2010
  346.7104'8—dc22                                                      2009040074

1 2 3 4 5 6 7 8 9

Printed in the United States of America on acid-free paper

**Note to Readers**
This publication is designed to provide accurate and authoritative information in regard to the subject matter
covered. It is based upon sources believed to be accurate and reliable and is intended to be current as of the
time it was written. It is sold with the understanding that the publisher is not engaged in rendering legal,
accounting, or other professional services. If legal advice or other expert assistance is required, the services
of a competent professional person should be sought. Also, to confirm that the information has not been
affected or changed by recent developments, traditional legal research techniques should be used, including
checking primary sources where appropriate.

*(Based on the Declaration of Principles jointly adopted by a Committee of the
American Bar Association and a Committee of Publishers and Associations.)*

You may order this or any other Oxford University Press publication by
visiting the Oxford University Press website at www.oup.com

# Contents

# About the Author

John S. McKeown is a practising lawyer in Toronto, Ontario, Canada. He focuses on providing advocacy and advice concerning intellectual property and related matters, including protecting trademarks, domain names, copyrights, patents, confidential information and misleading advertising and claims under the *Competition Act*. Some of Canada's largest marketers rely on his advice. He is certified by the Law Society of Upper Canada as a specialist in Intellectual Property Law (Trade Marks/Copyright).

# Author's Note

This book has been written to explain to practitioners outside Canada how the Canadian legal system works for trademarks, copyright and industrial designs. A practical approach has been adopted and emphasis has been given to how these laws may be used strategically.

Chapters have also been included relating to actions for infringement since this is the type of information that is vital to enforcing rights.

As a practising lawyer and advocate, I have attempted to present the law in a clear and understandable fashion. The law is stated as of July 2009.

I thank my wife and our sons for their patience while I worked on the text.

# CHAPTER
# 1

# Introduction

# 1. Introduction

The purpose of this book is to explain to practitioners and other interested individuals outside of Canada how Canadian laws relating to trademarks, domain names, copyright, and industrial designs work so they can use this information strategically to their advantage.

Canada's international obligations have an important effect on these laws since Canadian legislation must comply with these obligations. However, despite this impetus towards harmonization, there are significant differences between Canadian laws and the laws of other countries.

# 2. International Obligations

## a) Conventions, Agreements, and Treaties

Canada has ratified a number of international conventions or agreements relating to the protection of intellectual property, which are important to developing an understanding of Canadian law. The Paris Convention for the Protection of Industrial Property, the Agreement establishing the World Trade Organization, North American Free Trade Agreement, and the Berne Convention are of particular importance.

Canada is a member of the Paris Convention for the Protection of Industrial Property.[1] The Convention is designed to strengthen the protection of industrial property among its members mainly relating to patents, trademarks, and industrial designs. National treatment and priority rights are made available to applicants from member countries.

Canada is a party to the Agreement that established the World Trade Organization (WTO) and adopted the Agreement on Trade-Related Aspects of Intellectual Property Rights (TRIPS), including trade in Counterfeit Goods. TRIPS provides for standards or minimum levels of protection and enforcement of intellectual property rights, which member countries must implement. Members are required to enact legislation providing mechanisms for the enforcement of rights,[2] including civil, criminal, and customs procedures.[3]

TRIPS requires, among other things, that Members comply with the Berne Convention (Paris Revision, 1971) and the Paris Convention.[4] One of the fundamental principles of TRIPS is national treatment; Members must make

---

1. Canada has adhered to the Stockholm Revision (1967).
2. TRIPS, Article 41.
3. TRIPS, Articles 42–61.
4. Article 9.

available to the nationals of other Members treatment no less favourable than it accords to its own nationals.

Any Member who feels that a benefit accruing to it directly or indirectly under TRIPS has been nullified or impaired, or that the attainment of an objection was impeded as a result of a failure of another Member to carry out its obligations under TRIPS, may invoke the dispute settlement provisions of the General Agreement on Tariffs and Trade (GATT),[5] and the 1994 dispute settlement arrangements. As a result, a TRIPS dispute-settlement panel can enforce the provisions of TRIPS and the relevant Conventions.

Canada has entered into the North American Free Trade Agreement (NAFTA) between Canada, the United States of America, and the United Mexican States, which was signed on December 17, 1992 and implemented in Canada on January 1, 1994. The treaty is primarily directed to trade between the parties but also contains a model code for the protection and enforcement of intellectual property rights.

Under Chapter 17 of NAFTA, each party agrees to provide in its territory to the nationals of the others, adequate and effective protection and enforcement of intellectual property rights, while ensuring that measures to enforce such rights do not themselves become barriers to legitimate trade.[6] To provide this protection, the parties agreed to give effect to, at a minimum, the provisions of Chapter 17 and the provisions of the Berne Convention (Paris Revision, 1971) and Paris Convention.[7] The provisions of Chapter 17 are very similar to the requirements of TRIPS.

Under NAFTA, the parties have agreed to establish the Free Trade Commission to, among other things, resolve disputes.[8] In addition, the option is available to resolve the dispute under the dispute-settlement provisions of the GATT.

Canada is a member of the International Convention for the Protection of Performers, Producers, Phonograms, and Broadcasting Organizations (the "Rome Convention"). The Convention is concerned with the protection of "neighboring rights" granted to performers, producers of phonograms, and broadcasting organizations.[9]

Canada signed both the WIPO Copyright and WIPO Performance and Phonograms Treaties in December of 1997, signaling a commitment not to derogate from the principles set out in the Treaties. Ratification is still being considered but is currently the subject of considerable political debate.

---

5. TRIPS, Articles 63–64.
6. North American Free Trade Agreement, Article 1701(1).
7. North American Free Trade Agreement, Article 1701(2).
8. Article 2001.
9. See Chapter 19.

Canada does not adhere to the Madrid Protocol for the international registration of trademarks, the Trademark Law Treaty, or the Nice Agreement on the Classification of Goods and Services, although the Canadian Intellectual Property Office issued a request for views concerning whether Canada should adhere. There are divergent views and it remains to be seen what approach the Government will take.

## b) Implementation

In Canada, a treaty or convention must be implemented by domestic legislation.[10] Treaties or conventions do not have any direct effect and do not form part of the domestic law,[11] although a treaty may be referred to in the context of interpreting the provisions of the legislation implementing it.[12]

In Canada, the Federal Parliament has jurisdiction over trademarks, copyright, and industrial designs. The provinces may protect unregistered trademarks and trade secrets under provincial laws or the common law in provincial courts.

A brief overview of the law concerning trademarks, common law rights, domain names, copyright, and industrial designs follows. In some cases overlapping protection is possible; for example, a trademark which incorporates a design element that is original may be protected both as a trademark and under the *Copyright Act*.

## 3. Trademarks

### a) *Trade-marks Act*

Parliament has enacted the *Trade-marks Act*[13] which provides a national public registry system showing proscribed information for each registered trade mark. The *Act* facilitates the protection of trademarks by granting exclusive rights to owners and providing for public notice of those rights. The *Act* implements Canada's international obligations.

---

10. *Pfizer Inc. v. Canada* (1999), 2 C.P.R. (4th) 298 (F.C.), affirmed 250 N.R. 66 (F.C.A.).
11. *De Montigny v. Cousineau*, [1950] S.C.R. 297.
12. *National Corn Growers Association v. Canada (Canadian Import Tribunal)* (1990), 74 D.LR. (4th) 449 (S.C.C.).
13. R.S.C. 1985, c. T-13, as amended.

The use of a mark in Canada or in a country that is a member of the Paris Convention or a member of World Trade Organization creates rights under the *Act*. A non-Canadian trademark owner may file an application for a mark on the basis registration and use in the owner's "country of origin."[14] The *Act* provides that the term "country of origin" means a country of the Union (a member of the Paris Convention or the World Trade Organization) in which the applicant had, at the date of the application, a real and effective industrial or commercial establishment, that was his or her domicile, or was a citizen or national.[15]

Priority rights are also available. The priority date for applications based on a mark registered and used abroad is the date of the filing of the application in Canada or, if specific requirements including requirements relating to timely filing are satisfied, the foreign filing date.[16]

In Canada, in order to be eligible to obtain a trademark registration, the applied-for mark must comply with the provisions of the *Act* relating to registrable trademarks. The *Act* lists a number of matters which may preclude obtaining a registration.[17] The application of these matters can be avoided in part for a mark registered and used abroad.[18]

## b) Common Law Rights

The Canadian trademark registration system co-exists with common law trademark rights.[19] Common law rights are typically acquired through actual use of a common law mark in Canada in association with wares or services. These rights are not affected by any international obligations.

In the case of a well-known mark, it may be not necessary that a person actually use the mark in Canada in order to have goodwill or a reputation which may be protected.[20] As a common law trademark becomes known and goodwill is associated with it, the owner of the mark will be able to assert claims against others who use confusing trademarks in the specific region or area where the common law trademark owner has built up goodwill. This type of claim is referred to as "passing off."

---

14. Subsection 16(2) of the *Trademarks Act* and Chapters 4, part 3 and Chapter 6, part 3.
15. Section 2.
16. See Chapter 6, part 3.
17. See Chapter 3.
18. See Chapter 4, part 3.
19. See Chapter 14.
20. See Chapter 14, part 1(b).

## 4. Domain Names

Domain names and the rights associated with them are not affected by any international obligations. In general terms, the registration of domain names is on a first-come, first-served basis and there is no assessment of registrability or entitlement and no opposition procedure. Some Top Level Domains are restricted and require a local presence or specific legal documentation.[21] Typically domain-name registration agreements require that an applicant submit to an administrative dispute-resolution policy limited to cases of abusive registration of domain names.[22]

In Canada, a domain name that is registrable under the *Trade-marks Act* and is used as a trademark may be protected as a trademark.[23]

## 5. Copyright

In Canada, copyright is purely a statutory right. The Federal *Copyright Act*[24] creates the rights and obligations described in the *Act*. The term "copyright" is a shorthand reference to the exclusive rights conferred by the *Act* on the copyright owner and author. Copyright consists of the sole right to exercise, and to restrain others from exercising, specific statutory rights relating to a literary, dramatic, musical, or artistic work, a performer's performance, a sound recording, or a communication signal. In addition, the author of a work is given exclusive moral rights.

Under the *Act*, in order to obtain protection, "connecting factors" or "points of attachment" relating to the nationality of the author or the place of first publication of the work must be satisfied.[25] These requirements are consistent with Canada's international obligations in that they provide for national treatment.

## 6. Industrial Designs

The *Industrial Design Act*[26] protects designs, defined as meaning features of shape, configuration, pattern, or ornament, and any combination of those

---

21. See Chapter 16, part 2(c).
22. See Chapter 16.
23. See Chapter 16, part 2(d).
24. R.S.C. 1985, c. C-42, as amended.
25. See Chapter 17, part 1(a).
26. R.S.C. 1985, c. I-9, as amended and see Chapter 33.

features that, in a finished article, appeal to and are judged solely by the eye.[27] Despite the generality of the definition, no protection afforded by the *Act* extends to:

- (a) features applied to a useful article that are dictated solely by a utilitarian function of the article, or
- (b) any method or principal of manufacture or construction.

National treatment and priority rights are available for applicants from a country that is a WTO member or a country that by treaty, convention, or law affords a similar privilege to Canadian citizens.[28]

---

27. *Industrial Design Act,* R.S.C. 1985, c. I-9, as amended, section 2.
28. See Chapter 33, part 6(c).

# CHAPTER
# 2

# Protection of Trademarks in Canada

## 1. Trademark Legislation in Canada

### a) Federal Legislation

The *Trade-marks Act*[1] came into force July 1, 1954 and has remained substantially unchanged since that time. The *Act* provides for a national public registry system, showing proscribed information for each registered trademark. A registration of a trademark gives the owner the exclusive right to use the mark throughout Canada.

The Supreme Court of Canada recently observed that the power of attraction of trademarks is recognized as among the most valuable of business assets. Despite their commercial evolution, the legal purpose under the *Act* is their use by the owner ". . . to distinguish wares or services manufactured, sold, leased, hired, or performed by him from those manufactured, sold, leased, hired or performed by others." A trademark is a guarantee of origin or source and inferentially, an assurance to the consumer that the quality will be what he or she has come to associate with a particular trademark. The *Act* is, in this sense, consumer protection legislation.[2]

The Act also rests on principles of fair dealing and is sometimes said to hold the balance between free competition and fair competition. In applying its provisions, the interests of the public and other merchants as well as the interest of the trademark owner must be considered. Care must be taken not to create a zone of exclusivity and protection that overshoots the purpose of trademark law.[3]

The purpose of a trademark is to create and symbolize linkages. A trademark is a symbol of a connection between the source of a product and the product itself. This is reflected in the definition of a trademark contained in the *Act*.[4]

### b) Provincial Legislation

There is no provincial legislation relating to trademarks but business names are typically required to be registered in each province as a result of provincial legislation. Federal and provincial legislation also applies to corporations, including corporate names, and the registration of extra-provincial corporations. In general terms, before an incorporation or registration of an extra-provincial corporation is allowed, evidence must be filed to show that the

---

1. R.S.C. 1985, c. T-13, as amended.
2. *Mattel, Inc. v. 3894207 Canada Inc.*, 2006 SCC 22, 49 C.P.R (4th) 321 at paragraph 2 (S.C.C.).
3. *Mattel, Inc. v. 3894207 Canada Inc.*, 2006 SCC 22, 49 C.P.R (4th) 321 at paragraph 21 (S.C.C.).
4. *Mattel, Inc. v. 3894207 Canada Inc.*, 2006 SCC 22, 49 C.P.R (4th) 321 at paragraph 23 (S.C.C.).

proposed corporate name is not so similar to an existing business name as to be confusing.

The Province of Quebec has adopted the Charter of the French language to promote the status and the use of the French language in that province. The Charter provides that every inscription on a product, on its container or on its wrapping or on a document or objects supplied with it, including the directions for use and the warranty certificates, must be drafted in French. While the French inscription may be accompanied by a translation, no inscription in another language may be given more prominence than the inscription in French. Public signs and posters, as well as commercial advertising must be in French. Signs, posters, and advertising may also be both in French and another language, but the French portion must be markedly predominant.

An exception to the mandatory use of French is extended to "recognized" trademarks. Regulations under the Charter provide that in all printed material used in commerce, including on product inscriptions, public signs, public posters, and commercial advertising, a "recognized" trademark within the meaning of the *Trade-marks Act* may appear exclusively in a language other than French, unless a French version has been registered. At least one case has found that the exception extends to both registered and unregistered trademarks so long as they are recognized by consumers.[5]

## 2. Basic Definitions

### a) Trademark

The *Act* provides that a trade-mark means a) a mark that is used by a person for the purposes of distinguishing or so as to distinguish wares or services manufactured, sold, leased, hired, or performed by him from those manufactured, sold, leased, hired, or performed by others; b) a certification mark; c) a distinguishing guise, or d) a proposed trademark.[6] The key to the definition of a "trade-mark" is that it distinguishes the wares or services of its owner from those of others.

---

5. *Attorney General (Quebec) c. St.-Germain Transport (1994) Inc.*, [2006] J.Q. No. 8429 (C. Q. (Crim. & Pen. Div.)) This interpretation is not currently shared by the Office québécois de la langue française, the body responsible for compliance. In its annotated version of the *Charter of the French Language* they take the position that a "recognized" trademark means only a registered mark.
6. Section 2 of the *Trade-marks Act*.

The words "use" and "distinctive" are also defined by the *Act*.[7] To satisfy the definition, a "trade-mark" must be used or proposed to be used. Similarly, a mark must be distinctive or capable of being distinctive. A trademark is a symbol of a connection between a source of a product and the product itself.[8]

The Canadian Intellectual Property Office[9] (CIPO) has taken the position that a mark must be capable of being seen. As a result, they have refused to register non-traditional marks such as colour alone, animated /moving image marks, sounds, and scents.

A certification mark[10] and a distinguishing guise[11] are included in the statutory definition even though they have different attributes than a typical trademark.

Manufacturers' marks are expressly referred to but there is nothing in the definition to prevent the registration of a trademark by a retailer of a private label product so long as the mark distinguishes the retailer's wares from the wares of others.

A slogan or a tagline can be used as a trademark. In order to determine whether the use of a slogan is subject to the *Act*, consideration must be given to whether the slogan is a "trademark" as defined in the *Act* and whether the use of the slogan is trademark "use" within the meaning of subsection 4(1) of the *Act*.[12]

The *Act* contains a related definition of a "proposed trade-mark."[13] It is possible to file an application based on an intention to use a mark in Canada. When an application is filed on this basis, the owner must actually use the trademark in order to obtain a registration.[14]

## b)  Certification Mark

The *Act* provides that "certification mark" means a mark that is used for the purpose of distinguishing or so as to distinguish wares or services that are of a defined standard with respect to a) the character or quality of the wares

---

7. Sections 2 and 4 of the *Trade-marks Act*.
8. *Kirkbi Ag et al v. Ritvik Holdings Inc.* (2005) 43 C.P.R. (4th) 385 (S.C.C.).
9. The Canadian Intellectual Property Office is a Special Operating Agency associated with Industry Canada, that is responsible for the administration and processing of the greater part of intellectual property in Canada.
10. See part 2(b) of this chapter.
11. See part 2(d) of this chapter.
12. *Governor & Co. v. Sears Canada Inc.* (2002), 26 C.P.R. (4th) 457 (T.M.O.B.).
13. Section 2 of the *Trade-marks Act*.
14. Subsection 40(2) of the *Trade-marks Act*.

or services; b) the working conditions under which the wares have been produced or the services performed; c) the class of persons by whom the wares have been produced or the services performed; or d) the area within which the wares have been produced or the services performed. The certification mark must distinguish the wares or services it is used with from wares or services that are not of the defined standard.[15]

A certification mark is used to distinguish wares or services which comply with a defined standard.[16] A certification mark may be adopted and registered only by a person who is not engaged in the manufacture, sale, leasing, or hiring of wares or performance of services such as those in association with which the certification mark is used.[17]

The owner cannot use the certification mark directly[18] but may license others to use the mark in association with wares or services that meet the defined standard. Use by a licensee is deemed to be use by the owner.[19] For example, the WOOLMARK & design mark is reproduced on product packaging by licensees to indicate the existence of pure merino wool.

The owner of a registered certification mark may prevent its use by unlicensed persons or by licensed persons who use the mark in association with wares or services in respect to which the mark is registered but to which their license does not extend.[20]

A geographical certification mark descriptive of the place of origin of wares or services may be registered by an administrative authority or commercial association for a country, state, province, or municipality including or forming part of the area indicated by the mark, but the owner of such a mark must permit the use of the mark in association with any wares or services produced or performed in the area in which the mark is descriptive.[21]

## c) Distinctiveness

"Distinctive" in relation to a trademark, means a trademark that actually distinguishes the wares or services in association with which it is used by its

---

15. Section 2 of the *Trade-marks Act*.
16. Section 2 and see *Life Underwriters Association v. Provincial Association of Quebec Life Underwriters* [1989] F.C. 570 (F.C.T.D.).
17. Subsection 23(1) of the *Trade-marks Act*.
18. *Wool Bureau of Canada, Ltd. v. Queenswear (Canada) Ltd.* (1980), 47 C.P.R. (2nd) 11 (F.C.T.D.), *Mister Transmission (International) Ltd. v. Registrar of Trade-marks* (1978), 42 C.P.R. (2d) 11 (F.C.T.D.).
19. Subsection 23(2) of the *Trade-marks Act* and see *Wool Bureau of Canada, Ltd. v. Queenswear (Canada) Ltd.* (1980), 47 C.P.R. (2nd) 11 (F.C.T.D.).
20. Subsection 23(3) of the *Trade-marks Act*.
21. Section 25 of the *Trade-marks Act*.

owner from the wares or services of others, or is adapted so to distinguish them.[22] The definition applies to trademarks which are used as well as to a trademark which is proposed to be used. In the latter case, the mark must be adapted to distinguish the wares or services in issue, because the trademark is inherently distinctive.[23]

The concept of distinctiveness is not static since distinctiveness may be acquired as the mark is used. Acquired distinctiveness is also referred to as secondary meaning. Conversely, a mark which was inherently distinctive or which has acquired distinctiveness can lose its distinctiveness. For example, if a trademark owner communicates an inappropriate message to the public, this may result in a loss of distinctiveness.[24]

In the context of determining whether two trademarks are confusing, the court or the Registrar must consider, among other things, the inherent distinctiveness of the trademarks in issue and the extent to which they have become known. A mark which is strongly inherently distinctive will only refer the consumer to the wares or services in issue. Typically, such a mark will be a unique coined word. A mark with less inherent distinctiveness will refer the consumer to other sources.

Distinctiveness is the essence and cardinal requirement of a trademark.[25] The Registrar of Trademarks may not directly refuse an application to register a mark on the basis of lack of distinctiveness but an application may be opposed on the ground that the applied-for mark is not distinctive.[26] The registration of a trademark may be found to be invalid if the trademark is not distinctive at the time that the proceedings bringing the validity of the registration into question are commenced.[27]

Generally, three conditions must be satisfied to show distinctiveness: (1) the mark and a product are associated or linked; (2) the owner uses the association or link between the mark and its product and is selling the product; and (3) the association or link enables the owner of the mark to distinguish its product from that of others.[28] The message actually given to

---

22. Section 2 of the *Trade-marks Act.*
23. *Boston Pizza International Inc. v. Boston Chicken Inc.* (2003), 24 C.P.R. (4th) 150 (F.C.A); *AstraZeneca AB v. Novopharm Ltd.* (2003), 24 C.P.R. (4th) 326 (F.C.A.), leave to appeal to the S.C.C. refused 26 C.P.R. (4th) vi.
24. *Heintzman v. 751056 Ontario Ltd.* (1991), 34 C.P.R. (3d) 1 (F.C.T.D.).
25. *Mattel, Inc. v. 3894207 Canada Inc.* 2006 SCC 22, 49 C.P.R (4th) 321 at paragraph 75 (S.C.C.).
26. Subsections 37(1) and 38(2)(d) of the *Trade-marks Act.*
27. Subsection 18(1) of the *Trade-marks Act.*
28. *Philip Morris Inc v. Imperial Tobacco Ltd.* (1985), 7 C.P.R. (3d) 254 (F.C.T.D.), 17 C.P.R. (3d) 289 (F.C.A.); leave to appeal to the S.C.C. refused 19 C.P.R. (3rd) vi; *AstraZeneca AB v. Novopharm Ltd.* (2003), 24 C.P.R. (4th) 326 (F.C.A.), leave to appeal to the S.C.C. refused 26 C.P.R. (4th) vi.

the public is critical.[29] The name which appears on the address line on prod-uct packaging will be important.[30]

Colour can be an important aspect of the trademark and help to make it distinctive.[31] However, a colour by itself is not distinctive and there must be some additional independent feature in order to obtain a registration.[32]

The use of a trademark notice can assist in maintaining distinctiveness. A trademark owner should use the notification ™ to identify an unregistered trademark and the symbol ® to identify a registered trademark. A trademark owner may also use a trademark legend in conjunction with these symbols such as "® a registered trademark of XYZ Company." The use of such a legend when a trademark has been licensed, combined with a statement that the use is licensed, results in a statutory presumption that the use is in fact licensed and under the control of the trademark owner.[33]

In certain cases, the requirement for distinctiveness is relaxed as a result of Canada's compliance with the Paris Convention[34] for non-Canadian appli-cants. A non-Canadian trademark owner may file an application for a trade-mark and claim the benefit of section 14 to obtain a registration in Canada based on a trademark which has been duly registered in the applicant's country of origin, if, in Canada, among other things, the mark applied for is not without distinctive character, having regard to all of the circumstances including the length of time during which the mark has been used in any country.[35]

## d) Distinguishing Guise

A "distinguishing guise" means a shaping of the wares or their containers or a mode of wrapping or packaging wares, the appearance of which is used by a person for the purpose of distinguishing wares manufactured, sold, leased, or hired by it from those manufactured, sold, leased, hired, or performed by others.[36]

---

29. *Consorzio del Prosciutto di Parma v. Maple Leaf Meats* (2001), 11 C.P.R (4th) 48 (F.C.T.D.) (2002), 18 C.P.R. (4th) 414 (F.C.A.).
30. *Moore Dry Kiln Co. Canada Ltd. v. U.S. Natural Resources Inc.* (1976), 30 C.P.R. (2d) 40 (F.C.A.); *White Consolidated Industries, Inc. v. Beam of Canada Inc.* (1991), 39 C.P.R. (3d) 94 (F.C.T.D.).
31. *Smith, Kline & French v. Reg. T.M. No. 2* (1987), 9 F.T.R. 129 (F.C.T.D.); *Ciba-Geigy Canada Ltd. v. Apotex Inc.* [1992] 3 S.C.R. 120 (S.C.C.).
32. *Re Smith Kline & French Can. Ltd., Application for T.M. for Circle Design* (1984), 10 C.P.R. (3d) 246; affirmed 10 C.P.R. (3d) 287 (F.C.A.); *Novopharm Ltd. v. Bayer Inc.* (2000), 9 C.P.R. (4th) 304 (F.C.A).
33. Subsection 50(2).
34. Article 6*quinquies*.
35. Subsection 14(1)(b) of the *Trade-marks Act* and see Chapter 4, part 3(b).
36. Section 2 of the *Trade-marks Act*.

A distinguishing guise is registrable only if a) it has been used in Canada by the applicant or predecessor in title as to have become distinctive at the date of filing of an application for its registration; and b) the exclusive use by the applicant of the distinguishing guise in association with the wares or services with which it has been used is not likely unreasonably to limit the development of an art or an industry.[37] No registration of a distinguishing guise interferes with the use of any utilitarian feature embodied in the distinguishing guise.[38] The registration of the distinguishing guise may be limited to a defined area of Canada.[39]

The registration of a distinguishing guise may be expunged by the Federal Court of Canada on the application of any interested person if the court concludes that the registration has become likely to unreasonably limit the development of any art or industry.[40]

As mentioned above the definition of "trademark" includes a "distinguishing guise." This ensures that the owner of a distinguishing guise has the same rights as those available to a trademark owner, including the right to bring an action for the infringement pursuant to sections 19 and 20.

Unlike an ordinary application for a trademark, an applicant seeking to register a distinguishing guise must provide evidence to establish that the distinguishing guise has been used in Canada so as to have become distinctive.[41] The onus of showing distinctiveness is on the applicant and has been categorized as a heavy burden similar to that required to show acquired distinctiveness or secondary meaning.[42] If the application is opposed the applicant can rely on the same evidence but must advise the Trade-marks Opposition Board and the opponent that it relies on that evidence.[43]

A distinguishing guise incorporating functional features of a product which relate primarily or essentially to the product itself is not registrable.[44] A plaintiff will be unable to successfully assert rights relating to an unregistered

---

37. Section 13(1) of the *Trade-marks Act*.
38. Section 13(2) of the *Trade-marks Act*.
39. Subsection 32(2) of the *Trade-marks Act*.
40. Subsection 13(3) of the *Trade-marks Act* and see *WCC Containers Sales Limited v. Haul-All Equipment Ltd.* (2003), 28 C.P.R. (4th) 175 (F.C.T.D.)
41. Subsection 32(1) of the *Trade-marks Act*. See the practice notice in the Trade-marks Journal, Volume 47, No. 2408, December 20, 2000 dealing with the Trade-mark Office practice.
42. *Calumet Mfg Ltd. v. Mennen Canada Inc.; Gillette Canada Inc. v. Mennen Canada Inc.* (1992), 40 C.P.R. (3d) 76 (F.C.T.D.); *Molson Breweries v. John Labatt Ltd,.* (2000), 5 C.P.R. (4th) 180 (F.C.A.); *Glaxo Wellcome Inc. v. Novopharm Ltd.* (2000), 8 C.P.R. (4th) 448 (F.C.T.D.).
43.  *Canadian Generic Pharmaceutical Association v. Sanofi-Synthelabo Inc.* (2006), 60 C.P.R. (4th) 74 (T.M.O.B.).
44. *Remington Rand Corp. v. Philips Electronics N.V.* (1995), 64 C.P.R. (3rd) 467, leave to appeal to the S.C.C. dismissed 67 C.P.R. (3rd) vi (S.C.C.); *Thomas & Betts, Ltd. v. Panduit Corp.* (2000), 4 C.P.R. (4th) 498 (F.C.A.).

but functional distinguishing guise in an action for passing off for the same reasons.[45]

Similar considerations relating to functionality apply to regular trademarks. If the functionality relates either to the trade mark itself[46] or to the wares[47] this is inconsistent with registration. However, if the functionality is secondary or peripheral with no essential connection to the wares[48] this will not be a bar to registration.

The functionality concept is intended to ensure that an applicant does not indirectly achieve the status of a patent holder, with an unlimited term of protection, by obtaining a trademark registration. It would be abusive and unfair to the public to allow a person to gain the benefits of a patent by obtaining a trademark registration, especially when a person otherwise could not obtain a patent or when the patent in issue has expired.[49] However, even though a distinguishing guise may be registrable as an industrial design this does not prevent its registration as a trademark.[50]

## e) Prohibited Marks

The adoption, which includes use and application for registration,[51] of a variety of regal, governmental or public words, crests, symbols, marks, or other devices is prohibited.[52] Subsection 9 (1) of the *Act* provides that no person shall adopt in connection with a business, as a trademark or otherwise, any mark consisting of, or so nearly resembling as to be likely to be mistaken for, a prohibited mark.

---

45. *Kirkbi Ag et al v. Ritvik Holdings Inc* (2002), 20 C.P.R. (4th) 224 (F.C.T.D.) appeal dismissed (2003), 26 C.P.R. (4th) 1 (F.C.A.), appeal dismissed (2005), 43 C.P.R. (4th) 385 (S.C.C).
46. See *Imperial Tobacco Co. v. Registrar of Trade-marks* [1939] 2 D.L.R. 65 (Ex. Ct.) which dealt with a transparent moisture proof wrapper for cigarettes; *Parke, Davis & Co. v. Empire Laboratories Ltd.* (1964), 43 C.P.R. 1 (S.C.C.) which considered colored bands encircling capsules containing pharmaceuticals.
47. See *Elgin Handles Ltd. v. Welland Vale Manufacturing Co.* (1964), 43 C.P.R. 20 (Ex. Ct.) where a design accentuated the darker coloring of the grain of the wood of tool handles.
48. See *Pizza Pizza Ltd. v. Canada (Registrar of Trade-marks)* (1989), 26 C.P.R. (3d) 355 (F.C.A.) which involved a telephone number for pizza delivery; and *Proctor & Gamble Inc. v. Colgate-Palmolive Canada Inc,* [2007] T.M.O.B. No. 1 (T.M.O.B.) concerning colored stripes added to toothpaste.
49. *Kirkbi Ag et al v. Ritvik Holdings Inc.* (2005), 43 C.P.R. (4th) 385 (S.C.C.).
50. *Hughes, W.J. & Sons "Corn Flower" Ltd. v. Morawiec* (1970), 62 C.P.R. 21 (Ex. Ct.); *WCC Containers Sales Limited v. Haul-All Equipment Ltd.* (2003), 28 C.P.R. (4th) 175 (F.C.T.D.).
51. Section 3 of the *Trade-marks Act.*
52. Sections 3, 9, 10, 10.1, 11, 11.1, 11.14, 11.15 and subsection 12(1)(e) of the *Trade-marks Act.*

The list of prohibited marks includes

a) the Royal Arms, Crest, or Standard;

b) the arms or crest of any member of the Royal Family;

c) the standard, arms, or crest of His Excellency the Governor General;

d) any word or symbol likely to lead to the belief that the wares or services in association with which it is used have received, or are produced, sold, or performed under, royal, vice-regal, or governmental patronage, approval or authority;

e) the arms, crest, or flag adopted and used at any time by Canada or by any province or municipal corporation in Canada in respect of which the Registrar has, at the request of the Government of Canada, or of the province or municipal corporation concerned, given public notice of its adoption and use;

f) the emblem of the Red Cross as used by the Medical Service of armed forces and by the Canadian Red Cross Society, or the expression "Red Cross" or "Geneva Cross";

g) the emblem of the Red Crescent on a white ground adopted for the same purpose as specified in paragraph (*f*) by a number of Moslem countries;

    g.1) the emblem—commonly known as the "Red Crystal"—referred to in Article 2, paragraph 2 of Schedule VII to the *Geneva Conventions Act* and composed of a red frame in the shape of a square on edge on a white ground, adopted for the same purpose as specified in paragraph (*f*);

h) the equivalent sign of the Red Lion and Sun used by Iran for the same purpose as specified in paragraph (*f*);

    *h*.1) the international distinctive sign of civil defence (equilateral blue triangle on an orange ground) referred to in Article 66, paragraph 4 of Schedule V to the *Geneva Conventions Act*;

i) any territorial or civic flag or any national, territorial, or civic arms, crest, or emblem, of a country of the Union[53] if the flag, arms, crest, or emblem is on a list communicated under article 6*ter* of the Paris Convention or pursuant to the obligations under TRIPS[54] stemming from that, and the Registrar gives public notice of the communication;

---

53. Section 2 of the *Act* provides that "country of the Union" means (a) any country that is a member of the Union for the Protection of Industrial Property constituted under the Convention of the Union of Paris made on March 20, 1883 and any amendments and revisions thereof made before or after July 1, 1954 to which Canada is party; or (b) a Member of the World Trade Organization established by Article I of the World Trade Organization Agreement.

54. See Chapter 1 concerning TRIPS.

*i*.1) any official sign or hallmark indicating control or warranty adopted by a country of the Union, if the sign or hallmark is on a list communicated under article 6$^{ter}$ of the Paris Convention or pursuant to the obligations under TRIPS stemming from that article and the Registrar gives public notice of the communication;

*i*.2) any national flag of a country of the Union;

*i*.3) any armorial bearing, flag, or other emblem, or any abbreviation of the name, of an international intergovernmental organization, if the armorial bearing, flag, emblem, or abbreviation is on a list communicated under article 6$^{ter}$ of the Paris Convention or pursuant to the obligations under TRIPS stemming from that article, and the Registrar gives public notice of the communication;

j) any scandalous, obscene, or immoral word or device;

k) any matter that may falsely suggest a connection with any living individual;

l) the portrait or signature of any individual who is living or has died within the preceding thirty years;

m) the words "United Nations" or the official seal or emblem of the United Nations;

n) any badge, crest, emblem, or mark
   (i) adopted or used by any of Her Majesty's Forces as defined in the *National Defence Act*,
   (ii) of any university, or
   (iii) adopted and used by any public authority, in Canada as an official mark for wares or services,
   in respect of which the Registrar has, at the request of Her Majesty or of the university or public authority, as the case may be, given public notice of its adoption and use;

*n*.1) any armorial bearings granted, recorded, or approved for use by a recipient pursuant to the prerogative powers of Her Majesty as exercised by the Governor General in respect of the granting of armorial bearings, if the Registrar has, at the request of the Governor General, given public notice of the grant, recording or approval;

o) the name "Royal Canadian Mounted Police" or "R.C.M.P." or any other combination of letters relating to the Royal Canadian Mounted Police, or any pictorial representation of a uniformed member thereof.

Nothing prevents the adoption, use, or registration as a trademark or otherwise, in connection with a business, of any mark

(*a*) described above with the consent of Her Majesty or such other person, society, authority, or organization as may be considered to have been intended to be protected by this section; or

(*b*) consisting of, or so nearly resembling as to be likely to be mistaken for
    (i) an official sign or hallmark mentioned in paragraph i.1 above except in respect of wares that are the same or similar to the wares in respect of which the official sign or hallmark has been adopted, or
    (ii) an armorial bearing, flag, emblem, or abbreviation mentioned in paragraph i.3 above, unless the use of the mark is likely to mislead the public as to a connection between the user and the organization.[55]

The Registrar of Trade-marks must, at the request of the relevant interested party, give public notice of the adoption and use of any badge, crest, emblem, or mark set out in paragraphs (e) and (n) in order for subsection 9(1) to apply to such devices.

The reference to "university" in item n(ii) above is unlimited and a university in order to request notice of adoption be given need not be subject to the requirement of public control in Canada.[56]

## f) Prohibited Designations

### (i) General

Section 10 states that where a mark has by ordinary and *bona fide* commercial usage become recognized in Canada as designating the kind, quality, quantity, destination, value, place of origin, or date of production of any wares or services, no person shall adopt it as a trade-mark in association with such wares or services or others of the same general class, or use it in a way likely to mislead.[57] In addition, no one may adopt or so use any mark so nearly resembling that mark as to be likely to be mistaken for it.

The section prohibits the adoption of marks like the hallmark for silver and other well-known marks that designate quality or origin. This type of mark or a mark which closely resembles it should be open for use by anyone.[58] The mark as a whole must be considered, and a compound mark which

---

55. Subsection 9(2) of the *Trade-marks Act*.
56. *Canada Post Corp. v. United States Postal Service* (2005), 47 C.P.R. (4th) 177 (F.C.) appeal dismissed 2007 FCA 10 (F.C.A.).
57. See section 11 of the *Trade-marks Act* which prohibits the use in connection with a business as a trademark or otherwise of any mark adopted contrary to section 9 or 10.
58. See *Benson & Hedges (Canada) Ltd. v. Empresa Cubana Del Tobacco* (1975), 23 C.P.R. (2d) 274 (T.M.O.B.) where the trademark HABANOS in association with cigars was found to be unregistrable since the words "habana" and "habanas" are commonly used in association with cigars in Canada to denote that the cigars are made in Cuba; *Scotch Whiskey Association v. Glenora Distillers International Ltd.* 2008 FC 425, 65 C.P.R (4th) 441, reversed 2009 FCA 16, 76 C.P.R (4th) 1 (F.C.A.) where the word GLEN by itself in association with whiskey was found not to be within the section.

includes a prohibited mark as a component combined with a disclaimer of the component may be acceptable.[59] For similar reasons, a component of previously registered marks will not be protected under the section.[60] The party claiming that any mark has become recognized in Canada as designating the kind, quality, quantity, or the like must prove it by presenting appropriate evidence.[61]

### (ii) Under the *Plant Breeders' Rights Act*

Where a denomination must, under the *Plant Breeders' Rights Act*, be used to designate a plant variety, no one may adopt the denomination as a trademark in association with that plant variety or another plant variety of the same species or use it in a way likely to mislead.[62] In addition, no one may adopt or use any mark so nearly resembling that denomination as to be likely to be mistaken for it.

## g) Protected Geographical Indications for Wines and Spirits

Sections 11.11 to 11.12 of the *Trade-marks Act* set out procedures for obtaining protected geographical indications for wines and spirits. No person shall adopt or use in connection with a business, as a trade-mark or otherwise, a protected geographical indication identifying a wine or a spirit in respect of a wine or a spirit not originating in the territory indicated by the protected geographical indication or a translation in any language of the geographical indication in respect of that wine or spirit.[63] The *Act* also sets out procedures for obtaining protection and asserting objections.[64]

## h) Official Marks

The term "official mark" describes marks adopted and used by a public authority, in Canada, under paragraph 9(1)(n)(iii) of the *Act*, as a mark for wares or services. There are a large number of these marks and many of the

---

59. *Jordan Ste-Michelle Cellars Ltd v. Andres Wines Ltd.* (1985), 6 C.I.P.R. 49 (F.C.T.D.).
60. *Scotch Whiskey Association v. Glenora Distillers International Ltd.* 2009 FCA 16, 76 C.P.R (4th) 1 (F.C.A.).
61. *Scotch Whiskey Association v. Glenora Distillers International Ltd.* 2008 FC 425, 65 C.P.R (4th) (F.C.) reversed 2009 FCA 16, 76 C.P.R (4th) 1 (F.C.A.).
62. Sections 10.1 of the *Trade-marks Act*.
63. Sections 11.14 and 11.15 of the *Trade-marks Act* and see the *Spirit Drinks Trade Act*, S.C. 2005, c. 39 which restricts the use of certain names for spirits.
64. Sections 11.12 and 11.13 of the *Trade-marks Act*.

marks are of a commercial nature. In certain cases their existence can cause significant problems for which there may be no redress.

A request for an official mark may only be filed by a "public authority." This term is not defined by the *Act*. It has been established by case law that in order to come within the definition there must be a significant degree of public control of the entity in Canada[65] and it must not exist for private profit.[66] Public control requires that there be power which enables the government, directly or indirectly though its nominees, to exercise a degree of ongoing influence in the entity's governance and decision-making. The fact that an entity is created by statute, subject to legislative amendment from time to time, is not sufficient.[67]

The only limitations on what constitutes an official mark are the prohibitions set out in the *Act*.[68] It is not necessary that the mark create an impression of being "official" in some way,[69] so long as the mark is sanctioned by a "public authority."

An official mark must have been adopted and used in Canada in association with wares or services before a request for publication is made. There is no definition of "adopted" or "used" in this context but both terms seem to require public display.[70] It is not clear whether the use of an official mark under license will be recognized as adoption and use.[71] The use of an official mark by the licensee of a public authority will not be recognized as adoption and use by the licensee.[72] The failure to adopt or use has resulted in the

65. *Canada Post Corp. v. United States Postal Service* (2005), 47 C.P.R. (4th) 177 (F.C.) appeal dismissed 2007 FCA 10 (F.C.A.).
66. *Registrar of Trade-marks v. Canadian Olympic Association* (1982), 67 C.P.R. (2d) 59 (F.C.A.).
67. *Ontario Assn. of Architects v. Assn. of Architectural Technologists* (2002), 19 C.P.R. (4th) 417 (F.C.A.); *Canadian Jewish Congress v. Chosen People Ministries Inc* (2002), 19 C.P.R. (4th) 186 (F.C.T.D.) affirmed (2003), 27 C.P.R. (4th) 193 (F.C.A.) and see Trade-mark Office Practice Notice, published in the Trade-marks Journal, Volume 53, No. 2677 at p. 203.
68. Sections 3, 9, 10, 10.1, 11, 11.1, 11.14, 11.15 and subsection 12(1)(e) of the *Trade-marks Act*.
69. *Insurance Corporation of British Columbia v. Registrar of Trade-marks*, (1979), 44 C.P.R. (2d) 1 (F.C.T.D.).
70. *See You In-Canadian Athletes Fund Corp. v. Canadian Olympic Committee* (2007), 57 C.P.R. (4th) 287 (F.C.), appeal dismissed 2008 FCA 124, 65 C.P.R (4th ) 421 (F.C.A.).
71. The Canadian Intellectual Property Office Practice Notice, dated August 27, 2007, takes the position that such use will not be "use" for the purpose of section 9 relying on *Canada Post Corp. v. United States Postal Service* (2005), 47 C.P.R. (4th) 177 (F.C.) and *Canadian Rehabilitation Council for the Disabled v. Rehabilitation Council for the Disabled* (2004), 35 C.P.R. (4th) 270 (F.C.) but there are two other Federal Court decisions that reached the opposite result, *Ontario Association of Architects v. Association of Architectural Technologists of Ontario* [2003] 1 F.C 331, 19 C.P.R. (4th) 417 (F.C.A.) and *Magnotta Winery Corporation v. Vintners Quality Alliance* (2001), 17 C.P.R. (4th) 45 (F.C.).
72. *Canadian Rehabilitation Foundation for the Disabled v. Rehabilitation Foundation for the Disabled*, 2004 FC 1357, 35 C.P.R. (4th) 270 (F.C.).

finding that the giving of public notice of the adoption and use of the mark by the public authority was ineffective under section 9 of the *Act*.[73]

When an application under subsection 9(1) of the *Act* is submitted, the Registrar of Trade-marks must be satisfied that the applicant is a public authority and must then give public notice of the adoption and use of the mark by the public authority.[74] The application is not examined on any other criteria, however the Registrar of Trade-marks currently requires that evidence of adoption and use of an official mark, which shows an element of public display, be provided as part of the application.[75] An official mark need not distinguish wares or services and it may be descriptive and confusing with an existing registered mark.[76] An application for an official mark is not subject to opposition proceedings.[77] Once public notice has been given, the official mark is hardy and difficult to expunge.[78]

The decision of the Registrar to publish an official mark is subject to judicial review.[79] The time for action is limited since the application must be made within 30 days of the communication of the decision or such further time as a judge of the Federal Court may allow.[80]

Subsection 9 (1) of the *Act* provides that no person shall adopt in connection with a business, as a trademark or otherwise, any mark consisting of, or so nearly resembling as to be likely to be mistaken for, a mark adopted by a public authority in respect of which the Registrar has given public notice. The public notice of the adoption and use of an official mark does not operate retroactively to prohibit the use of an existing mark.[81] A trademark owner can continue to use a trademark adopted or registered before the publication

73. *Pisticelli v. Liquor Control Board of Ontario* (2001), 14 C.P.R. (4th) 181 (F.C.T.D.); *FileNET Corp. v. Registrar of Trade-marks* (2001), 13 C.P.R. (4th) 385 (F.C.T.D.) affirmed (2002), 22 C.P.R. (4th) 328 (F.C.A.); *See You In-Canadian Athletes Fund Corp. v. Canadian Olympic Committee*, (2007), 57 C.P.R. (4th) 287 (F.C.), appeal dismissed 2008 FCA 124, 65 C.P.R (4th) 421 (F.C.A.).

74. *Stadium Corporation of Ontario Limited v. Wagon-Wheel Concessions Ltd.* [1989] 3 F.C. 132 (F.C.T.D.)

75. See Canadian Intellectual Property Office Practice Notice, dated August 27, 2007.

76. *See You In-Canadian Athletes Fund Corp. v. Canadian Olympic Committee* (2007), 57 C.P.R. (4th) 287 (F.C.), appeal dismissed 2008 FCA 124, 65 C.P.R. (4th) 421 (F.C.A.).

77. *Insurance Corporation of British Columbia v. Registrar of Trade-marks* (1979), 44 C.P.R. (2d) 1 (F.C.T.D.).

78. *Mihaljevic v. British Columbia* (1988), 23 C.P.R. (3rd) 80 (F.C.T.D.).

79. *Ontario Assn. of Architects v. Assn. of Architectural Technologists* (2002), 19 C.P.R. (4th) 417 (F.C.A.) reversing (2001), 9 C.P.R. (4th) 501 (F.C.T.D.); *Canadian Jewish Congress v. Chosen People Ministries Inc*, (2002), 19 C.P.R. (4th) 186 (F.C.T.D.) affirmed (2003), 27 C.P.R. (4th) 193 (F.C.A.).

80. *Federal Courts Act*, R.S.C. 1985, c. F-7, as amended, subsection 18.1(2) and see *College of Chiropodists of Ontario v. Canadian Podiatric Medical Association* (2004), 37 C.P.R. (4th) 219 (F.C.).

81. *Canadian Olympic Association v. Allied Corp.* (1990), 28 C.P.R. (3d) 161 (F.C.A.).

of a similar official mark with impunity. However, public notice of the adoption and use of an official mark will preclude the expansion of an existing registration to additional wares or services[82] or the registration of any pending application which was not registered at the time of the publication of the official mark, even if previously adopted, used, and applied for.[83]

The test of resemblance under section 9 "consisting of, or so nearly resembling as to be likely to be mistaken for" is different from the test for registered trademarks set out in section 6 of the *Act*.[84] The test is restricted to the resemblance between the official mark and the impugned mark and the nature of the respective wares or services is irrelevant.[85] It is not a test of straight comparison and the court will consider whether a person, on first impression having only an imperfect recollection of the official mark, would likely be confused by the impugned mark.[86]

## i) *Olympic and Paralympic Marks Act*

In light of the 2010 Vancouver Olympic Games, the *Olympic and Paralympic Marks Act*[87] was passed to address Olympic mark protection and ambush type marketing activities. The *Act* provides special, time limited protection for Olympic and Paralympic marks,[88] prohibits anyone from misleading the public concerning their approval, authorization or endorsement as an official Olympic sponsor[89] and makes it easier to obtain an interlocutory injunction concerning a breach of the *Act*.[90]

---

82. *Canadian Olympic Association v. Konica Canada Inc.* (1991), 39 C.P.R. (3d) 400 (F.C.A.); *Royal Roads University v. Canada* (2003), 27 C.P.R. (4th) 240 (F.C.T.D.).
83. *Canadian Olympic Association v. Allied Corp.,* (1990), 28 C.P.R. (3d) 161 (F.C.A.).
84. See Chapter 11 concerning the test for registered trademarks.
85. *Canadian Olympic Association v. Allied Corp.* (1990), 28 C.P.R. (3d) 161 (F.C.A.).
86. *Big Sisters Assn. v. Big Brothers of Canada* (1996), 75 C.P.R. (3rd) 177 (F.C.T.D.); *Canadian Olympic Association v. Techniquip Ltd.* (1999), 3 C.P.R. (4th) 298 (F.C.A.).
87. S.C. 2007, c. 27.
88. S.C. 2007, c. 27, section 2 and see schedule 1 and 2.
89. S.C. 2007, c. 27, section 4. Enforcement guidelines have been published at http://www.vancouver2010.com.
90. S.C. 2007, c. 27, section 6.

# CHAPTER
# 3

# Registrable Trademarks

## 1. Characteristics Which May Preclude Registration

In Canada in order to be eligible to obtain a trademark registration, the applied-for-mark must comply with the provisions of the *Trade-marks Act* relating to registrable trademarks. Subsection 12(1) of the *Act* lists a number matters which may preclude obtaining a registration. The subsection provides that a trademark is not registrable if it is

(a) a word that is primarily merely the name or the surname of an individual who is living or has died within the preceding 30 years;

(b) whether depicted, written or sounded, either clearly descriptive or deceptively misdescriptive in the English or French language of the character, or quality of the wares or services in association with which it is used or proposed to be used or of the conditions of or the persons employed in their production or of their place of origin;

(c) the name in any language of any of the wares or services in connection with which it is used or proposed to be used;

(d) confusing with a registered trade-mark;

(e) a mark of which the adoption is prohibited by section 9 or 10;

(f) a denomination under the *Plant Breeders' Rights Act*[1] the adoption of which is prohibited by section 10.1;

(g) in whole or in part a protected geographical indication, where the trade-mark is to be registered in association with a wine not originating in a territory indicated by the geographical indication;

(h) in whole or in part a protected geographical indication, where the trade-mark is to be registered in association with a spirit not originating in a territory indicated by the geographical indication,

(i) subject to subsection 3(3) and paragraph 3(4)(a) of the *Olympic and Paralympic Marks Act*,[2] a mark the adoption of which is prohibited by subsection 3(1) of that *Act*.

The subsection does not apply to a "distinguishing guise" which is dealt with separately in section 13.

---

1. S.C. 1990, c. 20.
2. S.C. 2007, c. 27.

## 2. Primarily Merely a Name or a Surname

Subsection 12(1)(a) of the *Act* provides that a trade mark is not registrable if it is "a word that is primarily merely the name or the surname of an individual who is living or has died within the preceding 30 years." To decide whether the limitation applies it must be determined whether "the primary (chief) (principal) (first in importance) meaning of the word is merely (only) (nothing more than) a surname."[3] The question must be considered from the point of view of a person in Canada of ordinary intelligence and education.[4] It does not matter that the name is rare or in common use, as long as the mark is a name and nothing else,[5] but there must be evidence that an individual bearing that name is living or has died within the preceding 30 years.[6]

If the mark is both a surname and a dictionary word, each of which are of substantial significance, it is not "primarily merely" a surname.[7] The subsection does not prevent the registration of a foreign name that a person in Canada of ordinary intelligence and education would not think of as a surname.[8]

The name of a historical character who has died prior to the preceding 30-year period will be registrable[9] but if there are individuals who currently bear the same name, the reference must be perceived to be to the historical character to avoid the limitation.[10]

The name of a fictitious person is not precluded from registration unless the fictitious name is also the name or the surname of an individual who is living or has died within the preceding 30 years.[11]

If the surname is part of a composite mark, it may be possible to disclaim the surname and obtain a registration if the other elements of the mark are sufficiently distinctive to avoid the limitation.[12]

Despite the limitation concerning name or surname significance, a non-Canadian trademark owner may claim the benefit of section 14 to obtain a registration in Canada based on a trademark which has been duly registered

---

3. *Registrar of Trade-marks v. Coles Bookstores Ltd.,* [1974] S.C.R. 438 (S.C.C.).
4. *Standard Oil Co. v. Registrar of Trade-marks* (1968), 55 C.P.R. 49 (Ex. Ct.).
5. *Forge Moderne Inc. v. Registrar of Trade-marks* (1967), 51 C.P.R. 1993 (Ex. Ct.).
6. *Gerhard Horn Investments Ltd. v. Registrar of Trade-marks* (1983), 73 C.P.R. (2d) 23 (F.C.T.D.).
7. *Elder's Beverages (1975), Ltd. v. Registrar of Trade-marks* (1979), 44 C.P.R. (2d) 59 (F.C.T.D.); *Molson Cos. Ltd. v. John Labatt Ltd.* (1981), 58 C.P.R. (2d) 157 (F.C.T.D.).
8. *Galanos v. Registrar of Trade Marks* (1982), 69 C.P.R. (2d) 144 (F.C.T.D.).
9. *Gerhard Horn Investments Ltd. v. Registrar of Trade-marks* (1983), 73 C.P.R. (2d) 23 (F.C.T.D.).
10. *Baroness Spencer-Churchill v. Cohen* (1968), 55 C.P.R. 276 (T.M.O.B.)
11. *Gerhard Horn Investments Ltd. v. Registrar of Trade-marks* [1983] 2 F.C. 878 (F.C.T.D.).
12. *General Motors of Canada v. Décarie Motors Inc.,*(2000) 9 C.P.R. (4th) 368 (F.C.A.).

in the applicant's country of origin, if among other things, the mark applied for is not without distinctive character in Canada, having regard to all of the circumstances including the length of time during which the mark has been used in any country.[13]

The limitation can also be overcome if it can be shown that the mark has acquired distinctiveness. A trademark that is primarily merely the name or surname of an individual who is living or has died within the preceding 30 years, is registrable if it has been so used in Canada by the applicant or its predecessor in title as to have become distinctive at the date of the filing of an application for its registration.[14]

Paragraph 9(1)(l) of the *Act* prohibits the adoption of a trademark consisting of, or so nearly resembling as to be likely to be mistaken for, the portrait or signature of any individual who is living or has died within the preceding 30 years.[15] This prohibition may be overcome by obtaining the consent of the individual involved[16] but a signature may still be unregistrable by virtue of subsection 12(1)(a).[17]

## 3. Descriptive or Deceptively Misdescriptive Trademarks

Subsection 12(1)(b) of the *Act* provides that a trademark is not registrable if it is, whether depicted, written or sounded, either clearly descriptive or deceptively misdescriptive in the English or French languages of the character, or quality of the wares or services in association with which it is used or proposed to be used or of the conditions of or the persons employed in their production or of their place of origin.[18]

There are two underlying policies associated with this limitation. First, it prevents applicants from monopolizing descriptive words to stop competitors from using those words to describe their products.[19] Second, it prevents the public from being misled by the use of deceptively misdescriptive marks.[20]

---

13. Subsection 14(1) of the *Trade-marks Act* and see Chapter 4, part 3(b).
14. Subsection 12(2) and see *Matol Biotech Labratoriees Ltd. v. Jurak Holdings Ltd.* (2008), 69 C.P.R (4th) 321 (F.C.); *Miranda Aluminum Inc. v. Miranda Windows & Doors Inc.* 2009 FC 669 (F.C.) and part 4 of this chapter.
15. See subsection 12(1)(e).
16. Subsection 9(2)(a).
17. *Murjani International Ltd. v. Universal Impex Co.* (1985), 5 C.P.R. (3d) 115 (T.M.O.B.), (1986), 12 C.P.R. (3d) 481 (F.C.T.D.).
18. See *S.C. Johnson & Son, Ltd. v. Marketing International Ltd.* [1980] 1 S.C.R. 99 (S.C.C.).
19. *General Motors Corp. v. Bellows*, [1948] Ex. C.R. 187 (Ex. Ct.); affirmed [1949] S.C.R.; *Fiber-grid Inc. v. Precisioneering Ltd.* (1991), 35 C.P.R. (3d) 221 (F.C.T.D.).
20. *Atlantic Promotions Inc. v. Registrar of Trade-marks*, (1984), 2 C.P.R. (3d) 183 (F.C.T.D.).

## a) The First Impression

The test for determining whether a trademark is either clearly descriptive or deceptively misdescriptive is the immediate or first impression formed by the ordinary user or purchaser of the wares or services in issue.[21] The determination must not be based on research into or critical analysis of the meaning of the words.[22] The common meaning of words in their ordinary and popular sense must be determined and the perspective of experts or people with special knowledge may not be representative of the average ordinary purchaser.[23]

The addition of design features to a composite mark may not be sufficient to avoid the limitation. A trademark, which when sounded, is clearly descriptive of the character or quality of the ware(s) or service(s) in issue, may not be registrable despite the existence of the design features.[24] In order to determine whether the design features are sufficiently distinctive to result in a registrable mark, the first impression created by the mark must be considered. If the substance of the mark is the design, the prohibition should not apply.[25] If the substance of the mark is a word or words which can be sounded and are clearly descriptive, the mark may not be registrable.

While there is agreement concerning the principles that apply to determine whether a trademark is either clearly descriptive or deceptively misdescriptive, their application in a specific case may not be. There are many reported cases dealing with "clearly descriptive" marks which are difficult to reconcile.

A trademark that is not registrable by reason of this provision is registrable if it has been so used in Canada by the applicant or its predecessor in title as to have become distinctive at the date of filing of an application for its registration.[26] A non-Canadian trademark owner may also claim the benefit of section 14 to obtain a registration in Canada based on a trademark which has been duly registered in the applicant's country of origin, if among other

---

21. *ITV Technologies Inc. v WIC Television Ltd.* (2003), 29 C.P.R. (4th) 182 (F.C.T.D.), (2005), 38 C.P.R (4th) 481 (F.C.A.).

22. *Oshawa Group Ltd. v. Registrar of Trade-marks* (1980), 46 C.P.R. (2d) 145 (F.C.T.D); *ITV Technologies Inc. v WIC Television Ltd.* (2003), 29 C.P.R. (4th) 182 (F.C.T.D.), (2005), 38 C.P.R (4th) 481 (F.C.A.).

23. *John Labatt Ltd. v. Carling Breweries Ltd.* (1974), 18 C.P.R. (2d) 15 (F.C.T.D.); *Consorzio del Prosciutto di Parma v. Maple Leaf Meats* (2001), 11 C.P.R (4th) 48 (F.C.T.D.).

24. *Best Canadian Motor Inns Ltd. v. Best Western International, Inc.,* (2004), 30 C.P.R. (4th) 481 (F.C.). A Canadian Intellectual Property Office (CIPO) Practice Notice, dated February 16, 2005, states that an application for a composite mark will be considered not registrable if it contains clearly descriptive or deceptively misdescriptive words which are the dominant feature of the mark. Factors to be considered include the relative size of the design and the words, the inherent distinctiveness of the design, and the font, style, and layout of the words.

25. *Fiesta Barbecues Ltd. v. General Housewares Corp.* (2003), 28 C.P.R. (4th) 60 (F.C.).

26. Subsection 12(2) and see part 4 of this chapter.

things, the mark applied for is not without distinctive character in Canada, having regard to all of the circumstances including the length of time during which the mark has been used in any country.[27]

## b) Clearly

The word "clearly" in the subsection means "easy to understand, self-evident, or plain." It is not synonymous with "accurately."[28] The limitation will apply only if the trademark is clearly descriptive or deceptively misdescriptive. The concept of "clearness" is an essential element to preclude registration.[29]

## c) Deceptively Misdescriptive

To be deceptively misdescriptive a trademark must first be found to be descriptive and then be found to mislead the public as to the character or quality of the wares or services.[30] The test applied is whether an ordinary consumer in Canada would be misled concerning the wares or services with which the trademark is associated.[31] The trademark SHAMMI applied for use in association with a transparent polyethylene glove, which did not contain any chamois or shammy leather, was found to be deceptively misdescriptive contrary to the subsection.[32]

## d) English or French Language

The reference in the subsection to the English or French languages requires a determination of English or French usage on an international basis and not simply the English or French meanings then current in Canada.[33] A descriptive connotation in a foreign language will not preclude registration unless an

27. Subsection 14(1) of the *Trade-marks Act* and see Chapter 4, part 3(b).
28. *Drackett Co. v. American Home Products Corp.,* [1968] 2 Ex. C.R. 89 (Ex. Ct.).
29. *Thomas J. Lipton Ltd. v. Salada Foods Ltd., (No. 3),* (1979) , 45 C.P.R. (2d) 157 (F.C.T.D.).
30. *Candrug Health Solutions Inc. v. Thorkelson* 2007 FC 411, 60 C.P.R (4th) 35 (F.C.), 2008 FCA 100, 64 C.P.R. (4th) 431 (F.C.A.); *Oshawa Group Ltd. v. Registrar of Trade-marks,* (1980), 46 C.P.R. (2d) 145 (F.C.T.D.).
31. *Atlantic Promotions Inc. v. Registrar of Trade-marks* (1984), 2 C.P.R. (3d) 183 (F.C.T.D.).
32. *Dep. A.G. v. Biggs Laboratories (Can.) Ltd,.* (1964), 42 C.P.R. 129 (Ex. Ct.).
33. *Home Juice Co. v. Orange Maison Ltee.* [1970] S.C.R. 942 (S.C.C.).

ordinary consumer in Canada of the wares or services in issue would understand the mark as being clearly descriptive.[34]

If a word is new to the English or French languages, it may not be clearly
descriptive. However, the word must not be a dictionary word and be without
a clearly discernible meaning.[35]

## e) Character or Quality

The word "character" as used in the subsection means a feature, trait, or characteristic of the wares or services listed in the application.[36] The trademark
should not be considered by itself but rather in relation to those wares or
services.[37]

The reference to "quality" means that laudatory words, which praise or
attribute a quality or value to a product or a service, will likely be clearly
descriptive.[38] The words "Select," "Superior," "Perfect" or "Better" will likely
be found to be clearly descriptive.[39] A laudatory connotation may not be fatal
and the mark must still be considered in its entirety.[40]

## f) Conditions of or the Persons Employed in Production of Wares

A trademark, which is clearly descriptive or deceptively misdescriptive of the
conditions of or of the persons employed in the production of the wares or in
the provision of the services, is not registrable. The trademark KILNCRAFT was
found not registrable in association with tableware since the first impression of

---

34. *Gula v. B. Manischewitz Co.,* [1946] Ex. C.R. 570 (Ex. Ct.); affirmed (1947), 8 C.P.R. 103
    (S.C.C.); *B. Manischewitz Co. of Can. v. Hartstone,* [1953] Ex. C.R. 1 (Ex. Ct.); *Jordan & Ste.*
    *Michelle Cellars Ltd. v. Gillespies & Co.* (1985), 6 C.P.R. (3d) 377 (F.C.T.D.).
35. *Pizza Pizza Ltd v. Reg. TM.* (1982), 67 C.P.R. (2nd) 202 (F.C.T.D.); *Clarkson Gordon v.*
    *Registrar of Trade-marks* (1985), 5 C.P.R. (3d) 252 (F.C.T.D.).
36. *Drackett Co. v. American Home Products Corp.,* [1968] 2 Ex. C.R. 89 (Ex. Ct.).
37. *Thompson J. Lipton Ltd. v. Salada Foods Ltd., (No. 3)* (1979), 45 C.P.R. (2d) 282 (F.C.T.D.);
    *Jordan & Ste. Michelle Cellars Ltd. v. T.G. Bright & Co.* (1984), 81 C.P.R. (3d) 103 (F.C.A.).
38. *Registrar of Trade-marks v. G.A. Hardie & Co.,* [1949] S.C.R. 483 (S.C.C.); *Mitel Corporation*
    *v. Registrar of Trade-marks* (1984), 79 C.P.R. (2d) 202 (F.C.T.D.); *Cafe Supreme F. & P. Ltee. v.*
    *Sons P.G. Can.* (1984), 3 C.I.P.R. 201 (F.C.T.D.).
39. *Mitel Corporation v. Registrar of Trade-marks* (1984), 79 C.P.R. (2d) 202 (F.C.T.D.); *Unilever*
    *Canada Inc. v. Superior Quality Foods, Inc.,* (2007) 62 C.P.R. (4th) 75 (T.M.O.B.).
40. *Nabisco Brands Ltd. v. Perfection Foods Ltd.* (1985), 7 C.P.R. (3d) 468 (T.M.O.B.), (1986),
    12 C.P.R. (3d) 456 (F.C.T.D.).

an ordinary consumer in Canada on seeing the mark would be that the wares were produced by a kiln process.[41]

There are few cases dealing with the reference to "persons employed." However, it has been found that the word "engineer" is not registrable for use in association with services as it would be assumed that the services would be performed by a professional with that designation.[42]

## g)  Place of Origin

A trademark which is clearly descriptive or deceptively misdescriptive of the place of origin of the wares or services it is sought to be registered in association with, is not registrable.[43] It must be shown that wares or services referred to in the application are produced or offered in the geographic area suggested by the mark and an average Canadian consumer would be aware of the connection.[44] The fact that words indicate origin alone does not preclude registration.[45]

## h)  Suggestive Words

A mark which is merely suggestive is not "clearly" descriptive.[46] A mark which creates a covert and skillful allusion to the character or quality of the wares may be registrable.[47]

A mark which describes a condition or manner in which the wares or services are used by consumers may not be clearly descriptive of the character or quality of the wares or services. For example, the trademark KOOL ONE in

---

41. *Staffordshire Potteries Ltd. v. Registrar of Trade-marks* (1976), 26 C.P.R. (2d) 134 (F.C.T.D.); *Lubrication Engineers Inc. v. Canadian Council of Professional Engineers* (1992), 41 C.P.R. (3d) 243 (F.C.A.). CIPO has published a practice note concerning professional designations in the Trade-marks Journal, dated June 13, 2007.

42. *Canadian Council of Professional Engineers v. John Brooks Co.*, 2004 FC 586, 35 C.P.R. (4th) 507 (F.C.) and see CIPO practice note concerning professional designations in the Trade-marks Journal, dated June 13, 2007.

43. *Atlantic Promotions Inc. v. Registrar of Trade-marks* (1984), 2 C.P.R. (3d) 183 (F.C.T.D.).

44. *Consorzio del Prosciutto di Parma v. Maple Leaf Meats* (2001), 11 C.P.R (4th) 48 (F.C.T.D.); but compare with *Sociedad Agricola Teresa Ltda v. Vina Leyda Limitada*, 2007 FC 1301 (F.C.) which found that as far as place of origin was concerned it was not dependent on the knowledge of an average Canadian consumer.

45.  *Great Lake Hotels Ltd. v. Noshery Ltd.* (1968), 56 C.P.R. 165 (Ex. Ct.).

46. *Dep. A.G. v. v. Jantzen of Canada Ltd.* (1964)[1965] Ex. C.R. 227 (Ex. Ct.); *Thomas J. Lipton Ltd. v. Salada Foods Ltd. (No. 3)*, (1979), [1980] 1 F.C. 740, 45 C.P.R. (2d) 282 (F.C.T.D.); *Jordan & Ste-Michelle Cellars Ltd./Les Caves Jordan & Ste-Michelle Ltee. v. T.G. Bright & Co.* (1984), 2 C.I.P.R. 45 (F. C.A.).

47.  *Dep. A.G. v. v. Jantzen of Canada Ltd.* (1964)[1965] Ex. C.R. 227 (Ex. Ct).

association with beer was found to be suggestive and registrable because it did not relate to an intrinsic quality or characteristic of the product.[48]

A trademark that refers to the character or quality of wares or services in an elliptical way may be clearly descriptive.[49] However the reference to "elliptical" does not encompass any indirect reference to the nature or characteristics of a product.[50]

## i) Coined Words

Although the individual words of a composite trademark may be clearly descriptive, the mark as a whole may be registrable if the words do not go together in a natural way and create an impression separate and distinct from its components.[51] Joining together of two descriptive words to form a single word,[52] a short, meaningless addition,[53] or the misspelling of a clearly descriptive word, may not be sufficient to avoid the limitation. In each case, the impression created by the trademark as a whole, whether depicted, written, or sounded, must be considered.

## j) Disclaimer

The Registrar of Trade-marks may require an applicant for registration of a trademark to disclaim the right to the exclusive use of a portion of the trademark which is not independently registrable.[54] The disclaimer does not prejudice or affect the applicant's current rights in the disclaimed matter or the applicant's right to registration on a subsequent application if the disclaimed matter has become distinctive of the applicant's wares or services.

---

48.  *Registrar of Trade Marks v. Frank J. Provenzano* (1978), 40 C.P.R. (2d) 288 (F.C.A.).
49.  *S.C. Johnson & Son, Ltd. v. Marketing International Ltd.* [1980] 1 S.C.R. 99 (S.C.C.).
50.  *Fibergrid Inc. v. Precisioneering Ltd.* (1991), 35 C.P.R. (3d) 221 (F.C.T.D.).
51.  *Pizza Pizza Ltd v. Registrar of Trade-marks* (1982), 67 C.P.R. (2nd) 202 (F.C.T.D).
52.  *General Motors Corp. v. Bellows* [1948] Ex. C.R. 187 (Ex. Ct.); affirmed [1949] S.C.R. 678; *Shell Canada Limited v. P.T. Sari Inco Food Corporation,* 2008 FCA 279, 68 C.P.R. (4th) 390 (F.C.A.).
53.  *Thomson Research Assoc. Ltd. v. Registrar of Trade-marks* (1982), 67 C.P.R. (2d) 205 (F.C.T.D.); affirmed (1983), 71 C.P.R. (2d) 287 (F. C.A.).
54.  Section 35. By Practice Notice, published 2007-08-15 CIPO has indicated that effective immediately the Registrar will generally no longer require an applicant for registration of a trademark to enter disclaimers pursuant to section 35 of the *Act*. Disclaimers will continue to be required for 11-point maple leaf designs which are governed by Order in Council P.C. 1965-1623, dated September 2, 1965. Voluntary disclaimers will continue to be accepted.

A disclaimer of part of a trademark may be used to overcome an objection based on descriptiveness or the use of a name or surname so long as the disclaimed matter is not the dominant feature of the composite mark[55] and the remaining portion of the mark contains distinctive matter.[56] It has been suggested that a disclaimer should not be used in relation to deceptively misdescriptive matter so as to render a mark as a whole registrable when the deceptive matter is the dominant feature of the composite mark.[57]

## 4. Acquired Distinctiveness—Secondary Meaning

### a) Applicability

Subsection 12(2) of the *Act* provides relief for a trademark that is not registrable by reason of the limitations of subsections 12(1)(a), (trademarks that are primarily merely names or surnames) or subsection 12(1)(b) (clearly descriptive or deceptively misdescriptive trademarks). A mark that is not registrable as a result of these subsections, is registrable if it has been so used in Canada by the applicant or its predecessor in title as to have become distinctive at the date of filing an application for its registration.

Subsection 12(2) of the *Act* does not apply to marks subject to the remaining limitations of subsection 12(1) including

(a) a trademark which is the name in any language of the wares or services in connection with which it is used or proposed to be used;
(b) in whole or in part a protected geographical indication, where the trademark is to be registered in association with a wine not originating in a territory indicated by the geographical indication; or
(c) in whole or in part a protected geographical indication, where the trademark is to be registered in association with a spirit not originating in a territory indicated by the geographical indication. [58]

---

55. *Lake Ontario Cement Ltd. v. Registrar of Trade-marks* (1976), 31 C.P.R. (2d) 103 (F.C.T.D.); *Canadian Council of Professional Engineers v. John Brooks Co.*, 2004 FC 586, 35 C.P.R. (4th) 507 (F.C.).
56. *Molson Cos. Ltd. v. John Labatt Ltd.* (1981), 58 C.P.R. (2d) 157 (F.C.T.D.); *Canadian Council of Professional Engineers v. John Brooks Co.*, 2004 FC 586, 35 C.P.R. (4th) 507 (F.C.).
57. *Lake Ontario Cement Ltd. v. Registrar of Trade-marks* (1976), 31 C.P.R. (2d) 103 (F.C.T.D.).
58. Subsection 12(1)(c), (g) and (h).

## b) Evidence Required

An applicant who claims that its trademark is registrable under subsection 12(2) must file with the Registrar evidence by way of affidavit or statutory declaration establishing the extent to which and the time during which the trademark has been used in Canada and any other evidence the Registrar may require in support of the claim.[59] The onus of showing acquired distinctiveness is on the applicant. While this has been categorized as being a heavy burden,[60] recent cases have clarified that the standard of proof remains on the balance of probabilities and reference to a heavy burden refers to the exceptional nature of subsection 12(2).[61]

The requirements of the subsection may be satisfied by evidence of acquired distinctiveness in a defined territorial area in Canada, such as a specific province or provinces. In such a case, the Registrar will restrict the registration to the defined territory in which the trademark has shown to have become distinctive.[62]

## c) The Determination

The issue is whether the mark has been so used in Canada as to have become distinctive at the date of filing of an application for its registration.[63] A claim of acquired distinctiveness depends on all the circumstances relating to the use of the mark. Exclusive use of the mark may be compelling evidence but is not an absolute requirement. A trademark that has acquired distinctiveness in a substantial portion of the relevant market may be registered.[64]

In considering the evidence presented, the methods that were employed in selecting each deponent will be assessed to determine whether or not they are representative.[65] Leading questions or other inappropriate practices must not be used to obtain evidence.[66] Survey evidence, if reliable and valid, may be used to show acquired distinctiveness.[67]

---

59. Subsection 32(1) and see the Trade-mark Examination Manual, paragraph. IV.10.03 for a description of the Registrar's requirements.
60. *Standard Coil Products (Canada) Ltd. v. Standard Radio Corp.* (1971), 1 C.P.R. (2d) 155 (F.C.T.D.), affirmed (1976), 26 C.P.R. (2d) 288 (F.C.A.).
61. *John Labatt Ltd. v. Molson Breweries, a Partnership* (2000), 5 C.P.R. (4th) 180 (F.C.A.).
62. Subsection 32(2).
63. Subsection 12(2) and see *John Labatt Ltd. v. Molson Breweries, a Partnership* (2000), 5 C.P.R. (4th) 180 (F.C.A.).
64. *John Labatt Ltd. v. Molson Breweries, a Partnership* (2000), 5 C.P.R. (4th) 180 (F.C.A.).
65. *Robert C. Wian Enterprises Inc. v. Mady* (1965), 46 C.P.R. 147 (Ex. Ct.).
66. *Registrar of Trade-marks v. G.A. Hardie & Co.* [1949] S.C.R. 483 (S.C.C.).
67. *Canadian Schenley Distilleries Ltd. v. Canada's Man. Distillery Ltd.* (1975), 25 C.P.R. (2d) 1 (F.C.T.D.) and see *Mattel, Inc. v. 3894207 Canada Inc.* (2006), 49 C.P.R. (4th) 321 (S.C.C.) concerning survey evidence.

A registration obtained pursuant to the subsection will be subject to the statutory limitations concerning infringement. No registration of a trademark prevents the *bona fide* use by a person of his or her own name as a trade name or the *bona fide* use, other than as a trademark, of any descriptive or geographical expression, in such a manner as to not likely have the effect of depreciating the value of the goodwill attaching to the registered trademark.[68]

## 5. Names of Wares or Services

Subsection 12(1)(c) provides that a trademark is not registrable if it is the name in any language of any of the wares or services in association with which it is used or proposed to be used. Unlike subsection 12(1)(b) all languages are considered. The mark as a whole must be the name of the wares or services based on the immediate and first impression of the Canadian everyday user of the wares or services in issue.[69]

If a portion of a composite mark is the name of the wares or services and the remaining portion of the mark contains distinctive matter, the mark may be registrable with a disclaimer of the right to the exclusive use of the portion of the trademark which is a name.

If a trademark becomes the name of the wares through popular use of the mark as a generic term, the mark may lose its distinctiveness.[70]

## 6. Confusing With a Registered Trademark

### a)  The Statutory Framework

Subsection 12(1)(d) provides that a trademark is not registrable if it is confusing with a registered trademark. The *Act* provides that "confusing" when applied as an adjective to a trademark or trade name means a trademark or trade name, the use of which would cause confusion in the manner and the circumstances described in section 6.[71] Section 6 provides that the use of a

---

68. Section 20.
69. *ITV Technologies Inc. v WIC Television Ltd.*, (2003), 29 C.P.R. (4th) 182 (F.C.T.D.), (2005) 38 C.P.R (4th) 481 (F.C.A.).
70. *Aladdin Industries Inc. v. Canadian Thermos Products Ltd.*, [1969] Ex. C.R. 80, (Ex.Ct.) affirmed [1974] S.C.R. 845 (S.C.C.).
71. Section 2.

trademark causes confusion with another trademark if the use of both trademarks in the same area would be likely to lead to the inference that the wares or services associated with those trademarks are manufactured, sold, leased, hired, or performed by the same person, whether or not such wares or services are of the same general class.

In determining whether trademarks are confusing, the court or the Registrar, as the case may be, must have regard to all of the surrounding circumstances including:

(a) the inherent distinctiveness of the trademarks and the extent to which they have become known;

(b) the length of time the trademarks have been in use;

(c) the nature of the wares, services, or business;

(d) the nature of the trade; and

(e) the degree of resemblance between the trademarks in appearance or sound or in the ideas suggested by them.[72]

During the course of the prosecution of an application, an examiner may issue a report taking the position that the applied-for mark is unregistrable on the ground that it is confusing with a registered trademark. A third party may also oppose an application on the ground that it is confusing with a registered trademark.

## b) Associated Marks

Section 15(1) provides that confusing trademarks are registrable if the applicant is the owner of all such trademarks. Such marks are known as associated trademarks.[73] To obtain the benefit of the subsection, the applicant for registration of the confusing trademark and the owner of the registered trademark must be the same person. The subsection does not apply to related companies.[74]

Upon the registration of any trademark associated with any other registered trademark, a note of the registration of each trademark is made on the record of the registration of the other trademark.[75]

No amendment of the register recording any change in the ownership or in the name or address of the owner of any one of a group of associated

---

72. Subsection 6(5) and see Chapter 11.

73. Subsection 15(1) and see *Wilkinson Sword (Can.) Ltd. v. Juda* (1968), 51 C.P.R. 55 (Ex. Ct.).

74. *Registrar of Trade-marks v. Aciers* (1978), 40 C.P.R. (2d) 28 (F.C.A.). The term "related companies" is defined in section 2.

75. Subsection 15(2).

trademarks will be made unless the Registrar is satisfied that the same change has occurred with respect to all of the trademarks in such group and corresponding entries are made contemporaneously with respect to all such trademarks.[76] As a result, the Registrar has a duty to refuse to record any assignment or change relating to only one of the associated trademarks.

The *Act* does not preclude an unregistered transfer to a third party of one of the associated marks but such a course action may result in a loss of distinctiveness of the marks.[77]

## 7. Prohibited Marks and Designations

A trademark is not registrable if it is

(a) a mark of which the adoption is prohibited by section 9 or 10;[78]

(b) a denomination under the *Plant Breeders' Rights Act*,[79] the adoption of which is prohibited by section 10.1;

(c) in whole or in part a protected geographical indication, where the trademark is to be registered in association with a wine not originating in a territory indicated by the geographical indication;[80]

(d) in whole or in part a protected geographical indication, where the trademark is to be registered in association with a spirit not originating in a territory indicated by the geographical indication;[81] or

(e) subject to subsection 3(3) and paragraph 3(4)(a) of the *Olympic and Paralympic Marks Act*,[82] a mark the adoption of which is prohibited by subsection 3(1) of that *Act*.[83]

---

76. Subsection 15(3) and see *Philco International Corp. v. Registrar of Trade-marks* (1980), 48 C.P.R. (2d) 86 (F.C.T.D.).

77. Subsection 48(2) and see *Wilkinson Sword (Can.) Ltd. v. Juda* (1968), 51 C.P.R. 55 (Ex. Ct.).

78. Subsection 12(1)(e) and see Chapter 2, part 2(e).

79. S.C. 1990, c. 20.

80. Subsection 12(1)(g).

81. Subsection 12(1)(h).

82. S.C. 2007, c. 27.

83. Subsection 12(1)(i).

# CHAPTER

# 4

# Acquisition of Rights

# 1. Adoption

The *Trade-marks Act* provides that rights in a mark are acquired by adopting it. A trademark is deemed to be adopted by a person when that person or his or her predecessor in title commenced to use it in Canada or make it known in Canada.[1] If the mark has not been used or made known in Canada by the applicant or his or her predecessor in title, it is deemed to be adopted on the filing of an application for registration of a trademark in Canada.[2] These provisions are definitional in nature and are applied in the interpretation of the *Act*.[3]

The term "person" includes any lawful trade union, any lawful association engaged in trade or business or the promotion thereof, and the administrative authority of any country, state, province, municipality, or other organized administrative area.[4]

An application for a mark may be filed on the basis of a) the use the trademark in Canada,[5] b) making the trademark known in Canada,[6] c) registration and use in the "country of origin" of the applicant,[7] and d) proposed use.[8] An application can include multiple grounds as the basis of registration.

The term "country of origin" means:

(*a*) the country of the Union in which the applicant for registration of a trademark had at the date of the application a real and effective industrial or commercial establishment, or

(*b*) if the applicant for registration of a trademark did not at the date of the application have in a country of the Union an establishment as described in paragraph (*a*), the country of the Union where he or she on that date had his or her domicile, or

(*c*) if the applicant for registration of a trademark did not at the date of the application have in a country of the Union an establishment as described in paragraph (*a*) or a domicile as described in paragraph (*b*), the country of the Union of which he or she was on that date a citizen or national.[9]

---

1. Section 3.
2. Section 3.
3. *Enterprise Rent-A-Car Co. v.* Singer (1998), 79 C.P.R. (3d) 45 (F.C.A.).
4. Section 2. The *Interpretation Act*, R.S., 1985, c. I-21, states that in every enactment "person" includes a corporation.
5. Subsection 16(1).
6. Subsection 16(1).
7. Subsection 16(2).
8. Subsection 16(3).
9. Section 2.

The term "country of the Union" is defined to mean a country that is a member of the Union for the Protection of Industrial Property constituted under the Convention of the Union of Paris or any member of the World Trade Organization.[10]

In addition to rights available under the *Act*, common law rights may be available. However, common law rights are only obtained when goodwill or reputation is established in the minds of purchasers in a specific territory by associating the trademark, including product trade dress, with specific goods or services such that the trademark/trade dress is recognized by purchasers as distinctive of the owner's goods or services.[11] Since common law rights are generally tied to trade dress, they are more limited than rights under the *Trade-marks Act* which generally focus on the right to use a mark.

## 2. Making Known

A trademark is deemed to be adopted when a person or his or her predecessor in title made the trademark known in Canada.[12] However, as will be seen, the requirements to establish the making known of a mark are restrictive.

A trademark is deemed to be made known in Canada by a person only if the mark is used by such person in a country of the Union, other than Canada, in association with wares and services and:

(a) the wares are distributed in association with the mark in Canada; or
(b) the wares or services are advertised in association with it in
    (i) any printed publication circulated in Canada in the ordinary course of commerce among potential dealers in or users of the wares or services, or
    (ii) radio broadcasts ordinarily received in Canada by potential dealers in or users of the wares or services

and the mark has become well known in Canada by reason of the distribution or advertising.[13] These requirements are peremptory and are matters of substantive law and not evidence.[14]

---

10. Section 2 of the *Trade-marks Act*.
11. *Ciba-Geigy Canada Ltd. v. Apotex* (1992), 44 C.P.R. (3d) 289 (S.C.C.) and see Chapter 14 for a discussion of these rights.
12. Section 3.
13. Section 5.
14. *Valle's Steak House v. Tessier* (1980), 49 C.P.R. (2d) 218 (F.C.T.D.); *Motel 6 Inc. v. No. 6 Motel Ltd.* (1981), 56 C.P.R. (2d) 44 (F.C.T.D.).

For the purpose of establishing that a mark has been made known it is not sufficient to show circulation of printed publications or radio broadcasts alone. It must be shown that the publications or broadcasts circulated among or were ordinarily received in Canada by potential dealers in or users of such wares or services.[15]

The broadcasts relied upon must be substantial and have a significant impact in Canada.[16] Only reputation acquired as a result of the broadcasts described above can be considered; reputation acquired by word of mouth is not relevant.[17]

For the purpose of establishing that a mark has been made known it is sufficient to show that a substantial area or part of Canada knows the mark as opposed to the entire country.[18]

## 3. Registration and Use in the Applicant's Country of Origin

### a) Applications

A non-Canadian trademark owner may file an application for a mark on the basis of registration and use in the owner's "country of origin."[19] The particulars of the registration and use in the country of origin must be set out in the application.[20] Before such an application will be approved for advertisement, a certified copy of the registration must be filed.[21] In order to obtain a registration it is not necessary to show use in Canada of the applied-for mark,[22] but any registration may be subject to attack if use does not occur.[23]

It is important to be aware that the registration in the country of origin must be accompanied by use. While the Registrar does not require proof of use, the application may be opposed on the grounds that use did not occur.[24]

15. *Marineland Inc. v. Marine Wonderland and Animal Park* (1974), 16 C.P.R. (2d) 97 (F.C.T.D.).
16. *Andres Wines Ltd. & E. & J. Gallo Winery* (1975), 25 C.P.R. (2d) 126 (F.C.A.); *Motel 6, Inc. v. No. 6 Motel Ltd.* (1981), 56 C.P.R. (2d) 44 (F.C.T.D.).
17. *Motel 6 Inc. v. No. 6 Motel Ltd.* (1981), 56 C.P.R. (2d) 44 (F.C.T.D.).
18. *Valle's Steak House v. Tessier* (1980), 49 C.P.R. (2d) 218 (F.C. T.D.).
19. Subsection 16(2).
20. Subsection 30(d).
21. Subsection 31(1).
22. Subsection 40(1).
23. Generally after three years under the summary provisions of section 45 concerning "use" or at any time in the Federal Court under section 18, see Chapter 10.
24. *Allergan Inc. v. Lancôme Parfums and Beauté & Cie* (2007), 64 C.P.R. (4th) 147 (T.M.O.B.).

If an applicant applies to register the same or substantially the same trade-mark in Canada for use in association with the same kind of wares or services, within six months from the date of first filing in a country which adheres to the Paris Convention or is a member of the World Trade Organization, then the date of filing in that country becomes the effective Canadian filing date.[25]

## b)  Registrability of Marks Registered and Used in a Country of Origin

### (i)  Availability

Section 14 of the *Act* provides that notwithstanding section 12, a trade- mark that the applicant or applicant's predecessor in title has caused to be duly registered in or for the country of origin of the applicant is registrable if, in Canada:

(a)  it is not confusing with a registered trade mark;
(b)  it is not without distinctive character, having regard to all the circum-stances of the case, including the length of time during which it has been used in any country;
(c)  it is not contrary to morality or public order or of such a nature as to deceive the public; or
(d)  it is not a trade-mark the adoption of which is prohibited by sections 9 or 10.

Section 14 is only available to an applicant with a country of origin that is a member of the Paris Convention or the World Trade Organization and in relation to a trademark that the applicant or applicant's predecessor in title has caused to be duly registered. The section does not apply to trademarks that have been used but not registered in the country of origin.

A claim to the benefit of the section is not restricted to an application based on registration and use and the section can apply to an application based on use or proposed use in Canada.[26]

An applicant who is entitled to claim the benefit of the section may do so at any time during the application process but the registration relied upon must exist at least until the Canadian registration is granted.[27]

---

25.  Section 34 and see Chapter 6, part 3.
26.  *McDonald's Corp. v. Dep. A.G. Can.* (1977), 31 C.P.R. (2d) 272 (F.C.T.D.).
27.  *W.R. Grace & Co. v. Union Carbide Corp.* (1987), 14 C.P.R. (3d) 337 (F.C.A.).

Compliance with section 14 avoids the requirements set out in section 12 relating to registrability. A trademark which is not registrable because it is clearly descriptive, contrary to subsection 12(1)(b), may still be registrable if the requirements of section 14 are satisfied.[28]

If the trademark applied for differs from the trademark registered in the country of origin only by elements that do not alter its distinctive character or affect its identity in the form under which it is registered, the mark will be considered as the trademark so registered.[29]

### (ii) Substantive Requirements

The requirements of subsections 14(a) and (d) are not different from the requirements of subsection 12(1)(d) and (e), which are applicable to all marks.[30]

Subsection 14(b) sets out a test for registrability which is substantially different than that of subsections 12(1)(a) to (c). The term "distinctive character" means that the trademark must have the qualities characteristic of a distinctive trademark and actually distinguish the wares or services of the owner from the wares or services of others or be adapted to distinguish the wares or services of the owner from the wares or services of others.[31]

Subsection 14(c) provides that the mark must not be contrary to morality or public order or of such a nature as to deceive the public.[32]

An applicant claiming the benefit of section 14 must provide such evidence as the Registrar may require by way of affidavit or statutory declaration.[33] The onus of showing that a descriptive trademark is not without distinctive character is similar to the onus under subsection 12(2).[34] Evidence showing that the mark has become distinctive of the applicant's wares or services in Canada is required.[35]

The fact that an applicant relied on section 14 does not prevent an interested third party from commencing proceedings to attack the validity of

---

28. *Pilkington Brothers (Can.) Ltd. v. International Molded Plastics Inc.* (1957), 27 C.P.R. 79 (Reg. T.M.).
29. Subsection 14(2).
30. See Chapter 3, parts 6 and 7.
31. *Imperial Tobacco Co. v. Philip Morris* (1976), 27 C.P.R. (2d) 205 (Reg. T. M.); *Fairmount Resort Properties Ltd. v. Fairmount Hotel Management, L.P.* (2008), 67 C.P.R. (4th) 404 (F.C.).
32. This may not be substantially different than the requirements of subsection 9(1)(j) which applies to all marks, see Chapter 2 part 2(e).
33. Subsection 31(2).
34. *W.R. Grace & Co. v. Union Carbide Corp.* (1987), 14 C.P.R. (3d) 337 (F.C.A.); *John Labatt Ltd. v. Molson Breweries, a Partnership* (2000), 5 C.P.R. (4th) 180 (F.C.A.).
35. *Canadian Counsel of Professional Engineers v. Lubrication Engineers, Inc.* (1992), 41 C.P.R. (3d) 243 (F.C.A.); *Boston Pizza International Inc. v. Boston Chicken Inc.* (2003), 24 C.P.R. (4th) 150 (F.C.A.).

the registration on the basis of lack of distinctiveness at the time those proceedings are commenced.[36] As a result, a trademark owner who has relied on section 14 may find their registration at risk in such proceedings unless they can show some degree of acquired distinctiveness through use in Canada. Delay in use following registration will work against the registrant.[37]

## 4. Use or Proposed Use in Canada

A trademark is deemed to be adopted when a person or his or her predecessor in title commenced to use the trademark in Canada.[38] An application for a mark may be filed on the basis of use of the trademark in Canada. [39] The requirements of the *Act* relating to use must be satisfied.[40]

If the trademark has not previously been used by the applicant or his or her predecessor in title, the mark is deemed to be adopted on the filing of an application for registration of a trademark in Canada.[41] A proposed trademark means a mark that is proposed to be used by a person for the purpose of distinguishing or so as to distinguish wares or services manufactured, sold, leased, hired, or performed by that person from those manufactured, sold, leased, hired, or performed by others.[42]

An application for such a trademark must contain a statement that the applicant, by itself or through a licensee, or both, intends to use such trademark in Canada.[43] Use must commence after filing the application but must occur before a registration may be obtained.

---

36. Subsection 18 (1)(b).
37. *Boston Pizza International Inc. v. Boston Chicken Inc.* (2003), 24 C.P.R. (4th) 150 (F.C.A.).
38. Section 3.
39. Subsection 16(1).
40. Section 4 and see Chapter 5.
41. Section 3.
42. Section 2.
43. Subsection 30(e).

# CHAPTER
# 5

# Trademark Use

## 1. The Importance of Trademark "Use"

Trademark "use" is of fundamental importance under the *Trade-marks Act* since rights are determined by "use", for example:

a) A trademark is deemed to have been adopted when a person or its predecessor in title commenced to use the trademark in Canada.[1]
b) A registration gives to the owner the exclusive right to the use of the mark in Canada in respect of the wares or services set out in the registration.[2]
c) Use must be shown in order to maintain a registration which is the subject of section 45 proceedings.[3]
d) A plaintiff must show that it has used its mark and the defendant has used this mark or a confusing mark in order to be successful in an action for infringement.

Section 4 provides specific closed definitions of use in association with wares, services, and exported wares[4] which can be restrictive, particularly for wares. Each definition refers to a "trade-mark" and incorporates the requirement that the "trade-mark" be used for the purposes of distinguishing wares or services manufactured, sold, leased, hired, or performed by the owner from those manufactured, sold, leased, hired, or performed by others.[5]

Many cases have considered whether "use" has been shown, particularly in the course of proceedings decided under section 45 or in trademark oppositions.

## 2. Wares

Subsection 4(1) states that a trade mark is deemed to be used in association with wares if, at the time of the transfer of the property in or possession of such wares, in the normal course of trade, it is marked on the wares themselves or on the packages in which they are distributed or it is in any other manner so associated with the wares, that notice of the association is then

---

1. Section 3.
2. Section 19.
3. See Chapter 10.
4. Section 4 and see *Enterprise Rent-A-Car Co. v. Singe,* (1998), 79 C.P.R. (3d) 45 (F.C.A.).
5. *Bombardier Ltd. v. British Petroleum Co. Ltd.,* (1973), 10 C.P.R. (2d) 21 (F.C.A.); *Canadian Olympic Association v. Konica Canada Inc.* (1991), 39 C.P.R. (3d) 400 (F.C.A.); *Coca-Cola Ltd v. Pardhan* (1999), 85 C.P.R. (3d) 489 (F.C.A.).

given to the person to whom the property or possession is transferred.[6] The use of the word "means" in the subsection suggests that the definition is restrictive in nature.

## a)  At the Time of the Transfer of Property or Possession

In order to come within the subsection "use" must occur at the time of the transfer of the property in or possession of such wares. The transfer of property or actual possession must occur in Canada. But if any part of the chain of sale from manufacturer to consumer takes place in Canada this is sufficient.[7] Placing an order or issuing a purchase order by itself is not sufficient to show a transfer for the purpose of the subsection.

## b)  In the Normal Course of Trade

The subsection contemplates the normal course of trade as beginning with a manufacturer and ending with a consumer, with a wholesaler and retailer, or one of them, acting as an intermediary.[8] However, the normal course of trade may vary depending on the facts. For example, it is not necessary to show a transfer to the final consumer and a transfer to an intermediary may be sufficient.[9]

There must be a *bona fide* transaction.[10] Token use such as test shipments will not be sufficient.[11] But sending of samples to develop potential sales, if within the regular course of trade in an industry, may be sufficient.[12]

## c)  Notice of Association

Notice of the association of the mark and the wares will be given to the person to whom the property or possession is transferred if the mark is placed on the packaging in which the wares are sold,[13] or on a label attached to the wares.

---

6. Subsection 4(1); and see *Clairol Int. Corp. v. Thomas Supply & Equipment Co.* (1968), 55 C.P.R. 176 (Ex. Ct.); *Cie generale des establissements Michelin-Michelin & Cie v. CAW-Canada* (1996), 71 C.P.R. (3d) 348 (F.C.T.D.).
7. *Manhattan Industries Inc. v. Princeton Manufacturing Ltd.* (1971), 4 C.P.R. (2d) 6 (F.C.T.D.).
8. *Manhattan Industries Inc. v. Princeton Manufacturing Ltd.* (1971), 4 C.P.R. (2d) 6 (F.C.T.D.).
9. *Lin Trading Co. v. CBM Kabushiki Kaisha* (1988), 21 C.P.R. (3d 417 (F.C.A.)
10. *Molson Cos. Ltd. v. Halter,* (1976), 28 C.P.R. (2d) 158 (F.C.T.D).
11. *Ports International Ltd. v. Reg. Trade-marks* [1984] 2 F.C. 119 (F.C.T.D).
12. *ConAgra Foods, Inc. v. Featherstonehaugh & Co.* (2002), 23 C.P.R. (4th) 49 (F.C.T.D.).
13. *Manhattan Industries Inc. v. Princeton Manufacturing Ltd.* (1971), 4 C.P.R. (2d) 6 (F.C.T.D.).

If the mark is not physically on the wares or their packaging, notice of the association of the mark and the wares may be given by reproduction of the mark on show cards, display units, or in other ways so long as notice of the association is given at the time of the transfer of the property or possession.[14]

The use of a trademark in advertising or promotional material in most cases will not be sufficient to establish use in association with wares.[15] For example, use in a news release or in an advertisement or on a letterhead or envelope has been found to be insufficient.[16]

## 3. Services

A trademark is deemed to be used in association with a service if it is used or displayed in the performance or advertising of the service in Canada.[17] The word "service" is not defined in the *Act* and its meaning depends on the facts of each case.[18] A service is not restricted to those that are independently offered to the public and a service may be ancillary to or connected with wares.[19] For example, when a company makes its coupons available to consumers so they may obtain the company's products at a reduced price, this has been found to be use in association with a service.[20] None of the restrictions relating to the use of a mark in association with wares described above apply to the use of a mark in association with a service.[21]

The service must be performed in Canada. Use is not established by advertising a trademark in Canada when the performance of the service takes place outside of Canada.[22]

---

14. *Nissan Canada Inc. v. BMW Canada Inc.* (2007), 60 C.P.R. (4th) 181 (F.C.A.), *Gen. Mills Can. Ltd. v. Procter & Gamble Inc.* (1985), 6 C.P.R. (3d) 551 (T.M.O.B.).
15. *Canadian Olympic Association v. Konica Canada Inc.* (1991), 39 C.P.R. (3d) 400 (F.C.A.).
16. *Molson Cos. Ltd. v. Halter* (1976), 28 C.P.R. 158 (F.C.T.D.); *Parker-Knoll Ltd. v. Registrar of Trade-marks* (1977), 32 C.P.R. (2d) 148 (F.C.T.D.); *Plough (Canada) Ltd. v. Aerosol Fillers Inc.* (1979), 45 C.P.R. (2d) 194 (F.C.T.D.) affirmed 53 C.P.R. (2d) 62 (F.C.A.).
17. Subsection 4(2) and see *Danjaq Inc. v. Zervas* (1997), 75 C.P.R. (3d) 295 (F.C.T.D.).
18. *Kraft Ltd. v. Canada (Registrar of Trade-marks)* (1984), 1 C.P.R. (3d) 457 (F.C.T.D.).
19. *Gesco Industries Inc v. Sim & McBurney* (2000), 9 C.P.R. (4th) 480 (F.C.A.).
20. *Kraft Ltd. v. Canada (Registrar of Trade-marks)* (1984), 1 C.P.R. (3d) 457 (F.C.T.D.).
21. *Gesco Industries Inc v. Sim & McBurney* (2000), 9 C.P.R. (4th) 480 (F.C.A.).
22. *Porter v. Don the Beachcomber* (1966), 48 C.P.R. 280 (Ex. Ct.); *Marineland Inc. v. Marine Wonderland & Animal Park Ltd.,* [1974] 2 F.C. 558 (F.C.T.D.); *Motel 6 Inc. v. No. 6 Motel Ltd.* (1981), 56 C.P.R. (2d) 44 (F.C.T.D.); *Express File Inc. v. HRB Royalty Inc.* (2005), 39 C.P.R. (4th) 59 (F.C.)

## 4. Wares Exported from Canada

A trademark that is marked in Canada on wares or on packages in which they are contained is, when such wares are exported from Canada, deemed to be used in Canada in association with such wares.[23] The purpose of the subsection is to protect producers who do not make local sales but export their wares. In the absence of the subsection, a producer who subsequently used the mark in domestic sales could sue the exporter for infringement. The subsection is not subject to subsection 4(1).[24]

## 5. Deviating Use

It has been held that the practice of departing from the precise form of a trademark as registered is an objectionable and dangerous course of action,[25] although more recent decisions of the Federal Court of Appeal have tempered this prohibition to some degree. The problem is that it can be difficult to determine how significant the deviation must be in order to destroy the validity of the mark. The Federal Court of Appeal has said that cautious variations can be made without adverse consequences if the same dominant features are maintained and the differences are so unimportant that an unaware purchaser of the wares would not be mislead.[26] Maintenance of the identity and recognizability or commercial impression of the registered mark is of vital importance.

The Federal Court of Appeal has also confirmed that the use of a trademark in conjunction with another trademark or a prefix may not be use of the trademark but use of new mark. In the leading case, it was found that use of the composite trademark CII HONEYWELL BULL did not constitute use of the registered trademark BULL.[27] The Court said that the practical test to resolve a case of this nature is to compare the trademark as registered with the trademark as used, and determine whether the differences are so

---

23. Subsection 4(3); and see *Coca-Cola Ltd. v. Pardhan* (1999), 85 C.P.R. (3d) 489 (F.C.A.).
24. *Molson Companies Ltd. v. Moosehead Breweries Ltd.* (1990), 32 C.P.R. (3d) 363 (F.C.T.D.).
25. *Honey Dew Ltd. v. Rudd* [1929] Ex. C.R. 83 (Ex. Ct.).
26. *Promafil Canada Ltee. v. Munsingwear Inc.* (1993), 44 C.P.R. (3d) 59 (F.C.A.); *Saccone & Speed Ltd. v. Registrar of Trade-marks* (1982), 67 C.P.R. (2d) 119 (F.C.T.D.); *Ivy Lea Shirt Co. v. 1227624 Ontario Ltd.* (2001), 11 C.P.R. (4th) 489 (F.C.T.D.); *Marks & Clark v. Sparkles Photo Limited* [2005] FC 1012.
27. *Registrar of Trade-marks v. Cie Int. pour l'Informatique Cii Honeywell Bull S.A.* (1985), 4 C.P.R. (3d) 523 (F.C.A.); reversing *(sub nom. Cie Int. pour l'Informatique Cii Honeywell Bull S.A. v. Herridge, Tolmie)* 1 C.I.P.R. 231 (F.C.T.D.) and see *Nightingale Interloc Ltd. v. Prodesign Ltd.*, (1984), 2 C.P.R. (3d) 535 (T.M.H.O.).

unimportant that an unaware purchaser would be likely to infer that both, in spite of their differences, identify goods having the same origin.

The use of a variant of a registered mark can provide potential grounds for expungement of the mark.[28] To avoid these problems, a trademark should be used in the form in which it is registered. Alternatively, a separate registration can be obtained for the variant.

A similar sort of problem can occur if a trademark is not used as a "trademark" but is used as the name of the wares or service. If a trademark is widely used by consumers as the generic name of the wares or services in issue, the registration may become invalid on the basis that the trademark is no longer distinctive.[29]

28. See Chapter 10.
29. *Dubiner v. Cheerio Toys & Games Ltd.* [1966] Ex. C.R. 801 *Aladdin Industries Inc. v. Canadian Thermos Products Ltd.,* [1969] Ex. C.R. 80, (Ex.Ct) affirmed [1974] S.C.C. 845 (S.C.C.).

# CHAPTER
# 6

# **Entitlement**

## 1. Entitlement to Registration

The *Trade-marks Act* contains rules for determining who is entitled to the registration of a mark for which an application has been filed. In general terms an applicant, who has filed an application that complies with the *Act* for a mark that is registrable[1] is entitled, subject to the completion of opposition proceedings,[2] to secure a registration for a mark in association with the applied for wares or services, unless at the priority date, the mark was confusing with

    (a) a trademark, whether registered or not, that has been previously used or made known in Canada by any other person;

    (b) a trademark in respect of which an application for registration had been previously filed by any other person; or

    (c) a trade name[3] that had been previously used by any other person.

The rules are applied on the priority date, which varies depending on the basis on which the application is filed. Claims relating to entitlement are considered during examination, in opposition proceedings, or proceedings seeking to expunge a registration.[4]

The right of an applicant to secure registration of a registrable trademark is not affected by the previous filing of an application for registration of a confusing trademark by another person, unless the application for registration of the confusing trademark was pending at the date of advertisement of the applicant's application.[5] As a result, a previously filed application will not be taken into account if it was abandoned at the date of the advertisement of the subsequent application.

The right of an applicant to secure registration of a registrable trademark is not affected by the previous use or making known of a confusing trademark or trade name by another person, if the confusing trademark or trade name was abandoned at the date of advertisement of the applicant's application.[6] As a result, an opponent who relies on such a confusing mark or trade name must establish that it has not abandoned its mark or trade name at the date of advertisement of the application.

---

1. See Chapter 3.
2. See Chapter 12.
3. A "trade name" is defined in section 2 of the *Act* to mean the name under which any business is carried on, whether or not it is the name of a corporation, a partnership, or an individual.
4. See Chapter 10.
5. Subsection 16(4).
6. Subsection 16(5).

## 2. Marks That Have Been Used or Made Known in Canada

An applicant who has filed an application for a trademark that complies with the *Act* for a mark that is registrable and that the applicant or its predecessor in title has used or made known in Canada in association with wares or services, is entitled, subject to the completion of opposition proceedings, to secure its registration, unless at the date on which the applicant or its predecessor in title first used it or made it known, it was confusing with:

(a) a trademark that has been previously used or made known in Canada;
(b) a trademark in respect of which an application for registration had been previously filed in Canada; or
(c) a trade name that had been previously used in Canada;

by any other person.

The priority date for applications based on use or making known in Canada is the date of first use or making known not the date of the filing of the application. The date of first use is stated in the application for each of the general classes of wares or services described. Use of a trademark for the purpose of "making known" must be prior to the date of the application for registration and specified in the application.

The date of first use or making known is the only criteria for determining entitlement to such applications. In a dispute between a principal and agent or manufacturer and distributor concerning entitlement to a trademark, the issue is whether the importer or agent, or the manufacturer or distributor, as the case may be, was the first to use the trademark in Canada.[7]

An application may be opposed or attacked on the basis of previous use or making known only at the suit of the person who first used the trademark or made it known or his or her predecessor in title.[8] In addition, such an opponent must establish that it has not abandoned its mark or trade name at the date of advertisement of the application.

---

7. Subsection 16(1); *CBM Kabushiki Kaisha v. Lin Trading Co.* (1985), 5 C.P.R (3d) 27 (T.M.O.B.); affirmed (1987), 14 C.P.R. (3d) 32 (F.C.T.D.); affirmed (1988), 21 C.P.R. (3d) 417 (F.C.A); *Royal Doulton Tableware Ltd. v. Cassidy's Ltd.* (1984), 1 C.P.R. (3d) 214 (F.C.T.D.).
8. Subsection 17(1).

### 3. Marks Registered and Used Abroad

An applicant who has filed an application for a trademark that complies with the *Act* for a mark that is registrable and that the applicant or the applicant's predecessor in title has duly registered in or for the country of origin of the applicant and has been used in association with wares or services is entitled, subject to the completion of opposition proceedings, to secure its registration in respect of the wares or services in association with which it is registered in that country and has been used, unless at the date of filing of the application it was confusing with

(a) a trademark that had been previously used in Canada or made known in Canada;

(b) a trademark in respect of which an application for registration had been previously filed in Canada; or

(c) a trade name that had been previously used in Canada;

by any other person.[9]

An application should claim this ground only if the trademark was in use in association with all of the applied-for wares or services before the date the claim is filed in Canada.[10] The use of the mark is not limited to the country of origin of the applicant and may occur in any country.

The priority date for applications based on a mark registered and used abroad is the date of the filing of the application or, if specific requirements including requirements relating to timely filing are satisfied, the foreign filing date. The applicant is entitled to obtain a registration and priority over another person who has used or applied for the mark after the filing date.[11]

The term "country of origin" is defined by the *Act* to mean a country of the Union (a member of the Paris Convention or the World Trade Organization) in which the applicant had at the date of the application a real and effective industrial or commercial establishment, his domicile, or was a citizen or national.[12] The name of the country of origin must be specified in the application.

In order to support a claim under subsection 16(2) the trademark shown in the registration in the country of origin of the applicant must be identical in all respects with the mark of the application.

An applicant whose right to registration of a trademark is based on a registration of the trademark in another country of the Union must, before

---

9. Subsection 16(2).
10. *Allergan Inc. v. Lancôme Parfums & Beauté & Cie* (2007), 64 C.P.R (4th) 147 (T.M.O.B.).
11. Subsection 16(2).
12. Section 2.

the date of advertisement of the application, furnish a copy of the registration certified by the office in which it was made, together with a translation thereof into English or French if it is in any other language, and such other evidence as the Registrar may require to establish fully the right to registration under the *Act*. [13]

When an application for the registration of a trademark has been made in a country of the Union other than Canada and an application is subsequently made in Canada for use in association with the same kind of wares or services of the same or substantially the same trademark by the same applicant or the applicant's successor in title, the date of filing of the application in the other country is deemed to be the date of filing of the application in Canada, and the applicant is entitled to priority in Canada accordingly notwithstanding any intervening use in Canada or making known in Canada or any intervening application or registration if

(a) the application in Canada, including or accompanied by a declaration setting out the date on which and the country of the Union in or for which the earliest application was filed for the registration of the same or substantially the same trademark for use in association with the same kind of wares or services, is filed within a period of six months after that date, which period shall not be extended;

(b) the applicant or, if the applicant is a transferee, the applicant's predecessor in title by whom any earlier application was filed in or for any country of the Union was, at the date of the application, a citizen or national of or domiciled in that country or had therein a real and effective industrial or commercial establishment; and

(c) the applicant furnishes, in accordance with any request under the *Act* evidence necessary to establish fully the applicant's right to priority.[14]

## 4. Proposed Use Marks

An applicant who has filed an application for a proposed trademark that complies with the *Act* for a mark that is registrable, is entitled, subject to the completion of opposition proceedings and filing a declaration of use of the trademark, to secure its registration in respect to the wares or services specified

---

13. Section 31(1).
14. Section 34.

in the application, unless at the date of the filing of the application it was confusing with:

(a) a trademark that had been previously used or made known in Canada;

(b) a trademark in respect of which an application for registration had been previously filed; or

(c) a trade name that had been previously used in Canada,

by any other person.[15]

The priority date for applications based on proposed use in Canada is the date of the filing of the application. The applicant is entitled to obtain a registration and priority over another person who has used or applied for the mark after the filing date.[16]

An application based on proposed use in Canada must contain a statement that the applicant, by itself or a licensee, or by itself and through a licensee, intends to use the trademark in Canada. [17] In order to satisfy the requirements of the *Act* concerning "use", a licensee must be an entity that is licensed by or with the authority of the applicant to use the trademark, and the applicant must have direct or indirect control of the character or quality of the wares or services.[18]

A certificate of registration cannot be obtained until receipt of a declaration that the applicant, a successor in title or a licensee has commenced the use of the trademark in Canada in association with the wares or services specified in the application.[19] It is permissible to file a declaration which only refers to some of the applied-for wares or services. The registration will be restricted to the wares and services of the declaration and an additional application must be filed if it is desired to obtain a registration relating to the remaining wares and services.

---

15. Subsection 16(3).
16. Subsection 16(3).
17. Paragraph 30(e).
18. See Chapter 9, part 2 concerning the requirements for licenses.
19. Subsection 40(2).

# CHAPTER
# 7

# Applications

## 1. Content

The *Trade-marks Act* provides that an application must contain proscribed information.[1] As the failure to conform with the requirements of the *Act* may be raised as a ground of opposition[2] it is important that the information is correct. The requirements are set out below.

(a) An application must contain a statement in ordinary commercial terms of the specific wares or services in association with which the trademark has been or is proposed to be used.[3] If the wares or services fall into different general categories they should be grouped by category. Canada has not adopted the *Arrangement of Nice Concerning the International Classification of Goods and Services* which sets out a system for the classification of goods and services.

  The Canadian Intellectual Property Office has developed a Wares and Services Manual[4] to serve as a guide for specifying wares and services in trade mark applications. The Manual contains a representative listing of acceptable wares and services, as well as directions for making "insufficiently specific" wares and services acceptable.

(b) If the trademark has been used in Canada, the application must specify the date of first use by the applicant or its predecessors in title in Canada for each of the general classes of wares or services described in the application.[5] This date will be the applicant's priority date[6] and care should be taken in determining it. If there is uncertainty concerning the date, a phrase such as "as early as," may be used in conjunction with a date which is known with certainty.

(c) In the case of a trademark that has not been used in Canada but has been made known in Canada, the name of a country of the Union in which it has been used by the applicant or its named predecessors in title, if any, and the date from and the manner in which the applicant or named predecessors in title have made it known in Canada in association with each of the general classes of wares or services described in the application.[7]

(d) In the case of a trademark that is the subject in or for another country that is a member of the Paris Convention or the World Trade

---

1. Section 30.
2. Paragraph 38(2)(a).
3. Subsection 30(a).
4. Currently available at the Canadian Intellectual Property Office website at http://www.cipo.ic.gc.ca/epic/site/cipointernet-internetopic.nsf/en/h_wr00002e.html.
5. Subsection 30(b).
6. Subsection 16(1) and see chapter 6, part 2.
7. Subsection 30(c) and see chapter 4, part 2.

Organization, of a registration or an application for registration by the applicant or the applicant's named predecessor in title on which the applicant bases the applicant's right to registration, particulars of the application or registration and, if the trade mark has neither been used in Canada nor made known in Canada, the name of a country in which the trade mark has been used by the applicant or the applicant's named predecessor in title, if any, in association with each of the general classes of wares or services described in the application.[8]

(e) In the case of a proposed trademark, an application must include a statement that the applicant, by itself or through a licensee, or by itself and through a licensee, intends to use the trademark in Canada.[9]

(f) In the case of a certification mark, the application must contain particulars of the defined standard that the use of the mark is intended to indicate and a statement that the applicant is not engaged in the manufacture, sale, leasing, or hiring of wares or the performance of services such as those in association with which the certification mark is used.[10]

(g) The address of the applicant's principal office or place of business in Canada, if any, and if the applicant has no office or place of business in Canada, the address of the principal office or place of business abroad, and the name and address in Canada of a person or firm to whom any notice in respect of the application or registration may be sent, and on whom service of any proceedings in respect of the application or registration may be given or served with the same effect as if they had been given to or served on the applicant or the registrant.[11]

(h) Unless the application is for the registration only of a word or words not depicted in special form, it must include a drawing of the trademark.[12]

(i) An application must include a statement that the applicant is satisfied that it is entitled to use the trademark in Canada in association with the wares or services described in the application.[13]

Where the applicant claims a color as a feature of the mark, the nature of the claim must be described in the application.[14] If the description is not clear, the Registrar may require the applicant to file a drawing lined for color in accordance with the regulations.[15]

---

8. Subsection 30(d) and see chapter 6, part 3.
9. Subsection 30(e).
10. Subsection 30(f) and see chapter, part 2(b).
11. Subsection 30(g).
12. Subsection 30(h).
13. Subsection 30(i).
14. See sections 28(1), *Trade-marks Regulations* SOR/96-195 as amended.
15. See sections 28(2), *Trade-marks Regulations* SOR/96-195 as amended.

## 2. Amendment

An application for the registration of a trademark may be amended either before or after the application is advertised,[16] but there are significant limitations on the matters which may be amended. No application may be amended to change

(a) the identity of the applicant, except after recognition of a transfer by the Registrar;

(b) the trademark, except in respects that do not alter its distinctive character or affect its identity;

(c) the date of first use or making known in Canada of the trademark to an earlier date, except where the evidence proves that the change is justified by the facts;

(d) the application from one not alleging use or making known of the trademark in Canada before the filing of the application to one alleging such use or making known; or

(e) the statement of wares or services so as to be broader than the statement of wares or services contained in the application at the time the application was filed.[17]

After an application has been advertised, it may not be amended to change

(a) the trademark in any manner whatsoever;

(b) the date of first use or making known in Canada;

(c) the application from one alleging use or making known to one for a proposed trademark;

(d) the application from one that does not allege that the trademark has been used and registered in or for a country of the Union to one that does so allege; or

(e) the statement of wares or services so as to be broader than the statement of wares or services contained in the application at the time of advertisement.

Clerical errors in an application may be amended at the request of the applicant.[18]

---

16. See sections 30, *Trade-marks Regulations* SOR/96-195 as amended.
17. See sections 31, *Trade-marks Regulations* SOR/96-195 as amended.
18. See section 33, *Trade-marks Regulations* SOR/96-195 as amended.

## 3. Examination

The date of filing of an application is the date a duly completed application, including a drawing of any design mark and the proscribed fee, is received by the Registrar.[19] The Trade-marks office then carries out a search of the register to identify similar or confusing trademarks. The application and search results are passed to an examiner.

The application is examined and must be refused if

(a) the application does not comply with the requirements of section 30;[20]
(b) the trademark is not registrable;[21] or
(c) the applicant is not the person entitled to registration of the trademark because it is confusing with another trademark for which an application is pending.[22]

The Registrar does not consider the dates of first use or making known in pending applications as a relevant consideration under paragraph (c). The only issue is whether there is confusion between the applicant's trademark and a trademark for which an application is already pending. When pending marks are confusing, the applicant with the earlier filing date or priority filing date will be considered to be the person entitled to registration of the trademark.[23] The owners of pending applications which claim prior use or making known must assert their rights in opposition proceedings.

The Registrar must not refuse an application without first notifying the applicant of the objections and the reasons for such objections and giving the applicant adequate opportunity to answer the objections.[24] This obligation is satisfied by issuing examiner's reports which satisfy these criteria. An appeal lies to the Federal Court from any final decision of the Registrar of Trade-marks.[25]

Where the Registrar, by reason of a registered trademark, is in doubt whether the trademark claimed in the application is registrable, the Registrar must, by registered letter, notify the owner of the registered trade mark of the

---

19. Section 25, *Trade-marks Regulations*, SOR/96-195 as amended.
20. Subsection 37(1)(a) and see part 1 of this chapter.
21. Subsection 37(1)(b) and see Chapter 3.
22. Subsection 37(1)(c) and see Chapter 6.
23. Canadian Intellectual Property Office, Practice Notice dated 2005-05-19 and see *Unitel International Inc. v. Canada (Registrar of Trade-marks)* (1999), 86 C.P.R. (3d) 467 (F.C.T.D.) affirmed (2000), 9 C.P.R. (4th) 127 (F.C.A.); *Attorney-General of Canada v. Effigi Inc.* (2005), 41 C.P.R. (4th) 1 (F.C.A).
24. Subsection 37(2) and see *Mr. Transmission (International) Ltd. v. Reg. T.M.* [1979] 1 F.C. 787 (F.C.T.D.).
25. Section 56.

advertisement of the application.[26] This provision is typically applied when the examiner is in doubt concerning whether the applied for mark is potentially confusing with an existing registered mark.

## 4. Disclaimer

The Registrar may require the applicant to disclaim the right to the exclusive use apart from the trademark of such portion of the trademark as is not independently registrable, but such disclaimer does not prejudice or affect the applicant's rights then existing or thereafter arising in the disclaimed matter. The disclaimer does not prejudice or affect the applicant's right to registration on a subsequent application if the disclaimed matter has then become distinctive of the applicant's wares or services.[27] The absence of a disclaimer in an application is not a ground of opposition.[28]

The Canadian Intellectual Property Office has indicated that the Registrar will generally no longer require an applicant for registration of a trademark to enter disclaimers pursuant to the *Act*.[29] Disclaimers will continue to be required for eleven-point maple leaf designs.[30]

Despite the change of policy, voluntary disclaimers will continue to be accepted. A disclaimer may assist in overcoming an examiner's report asserting that a mark is clearly descriptive contrary to subsection 12(1)(b) or 12(1)(e) of the *Act*.[31] However, a disclaimer will not be accepted concerning an assertion that the mark is deceptively misdescriptive or confusing with a registered mark.[32]

## 5. Advertisement

Registrar will refuse an application if he is satisfied that the application does not conform with section 30 of the *Act*,[33] the trademark is not registrable,[34]

---

26. Subsection 37(3).
27. Section 35.
28. *Sunny Crunch Foods Ltd. v. Reg. T.M.* (1982), 63 C.P.R. (2d) 201 (F.C.T.D.); *T.G. Bright & Co. v. Andres Wines* (1986), 12 C.P.R. (3d) 1 (F.C.A.).
29. Practice Notice, dated 2007-08-15.
30. These designs are governed by Order in Council P.C. 1965–1623, dated September 2, 1965.
31. *T.G. Bright & Co. v. Andres Wines* (1986), 12 C.P.R. (3d) 1 (F.C.A.).
32. *Lake Ontario Cement v. Reg. T.M.* (1976), 31 C.P.R. (2d) 103 (F.C. T. D).
33. See part 1 of this chapter.
34. See Chapter 3.

or the applicant is not entitled to the registration.[35] In the absence of concerns about these matters, the Registrar will approve the application for advertisement.[36] Particulars of the application are advertised in the Trade-marks Journal.[37]

Between the time a mark is scheduled to be advertised and the actual advertisement, the Registrar may reverse the decision to advertise if facts sufficient to warrant a refusal come to the Registrar's attention.[38]

---

35. See Chapter 6.
36. Subsection 37(1).
37. *Trade-marks Regulations*, section 34.
38. *Beaver Knitwear Ltd. v. Registrar of Trade-marks* (1986), 11 C.P.R. (3d) 257 (F.C.T.D.).

# CHAPTER
# 8

# Registration

## 1. Allowance

Under the *Trade-marks Act* when an application has not been opposed or it has been opposed and the opposition has been decided in favor of the applicant, the application will be allowed[1] and the mark, other than a mark based on proposed use, registered.[2]

The Registrar shall not extend the time for filing a statement of opposition with respect to any application that has been allowed.[3] However, if the Registrar has allowed an application without considering a previously filed request for an extension of time to file a statement of opposition, the Registrar may withdraw the application from allowance at any time before issuing a certificate of registration and extend the time for filing a statement of opposition.[4]

When an application for a mark based on proposed use is allowed, the Registrar notifies the applicant and will register the trademark on receipt of a declaration that the applicant, its successor in title, or licensee[5] has commenced the use of the trademark in Canada in association with the wares or services specified in the application.[6] If the applicant for a proposed trade mark fails to file a declaration of use before the later of six months after the notice by the Registrar and three years after the date of filing of the application in Canada, the application will be deemed to be abandoned.[7]

An extension may be sought to extend the three-year period but the request must be justified by objective reasons. Significant and substantive reasons are required which clearly justify an extension that extends beyond three years from the original deadline to file a declaration of use.[8]

---

1. Subsection 39(1).
2. Subsection 40(1). Unless the mark was filed based on proposed use there are no other requirements apart from paying the proscribed fee.
3. Subsection 39(2).
4. Subsection 39(3) and see *Sadhu Singh Hamdard Trust v. Canada (Registrar of Trade-marks* (2006), 47 C.P.R. (4th) 373 (F.C), affirmed on appeal 2007 FCA 355, 62 C.P.R (4th) 245 (F.C.A.).
5. A licensee must be an entity that is licensed by or with the authority of the applicant to use the trademark, and the applicant must have direct or indirect control of the character or quality of the wares or services. See Chapter 9, part 2 concerning the requirements of the *Act*.
6. Subsection 40(2).
7. Subsection 40(3).
8. See *Trade-marks Office Practice Notice* dated July 22, 1998 and *A. Lassonde Inc. v. Registrar of T.M.* (2003), 27 C.P.R. (4th) 316 (F.C.T.D.).

## 2. Registration

Subject to limited restrictions, the registration of a trademark in respect of wares or services, unless shown to be invalid, gives to the owner the exclusive right to the use throughout Canada of such trademark in respect of those wares or services.[9]

The primary restriction relates to the right to make descriptive use under section 20.[10] The other restrictions relate to the concurrent right to use a trade mark under section 21,[11] restrictions imposed under section 32 of relating to marks registered under subsection 12(2)[12] and the special provisions of section 67 relating to trademarks registered or pending in Newfoundland before April 1, 1949.[13]

A copy of the record of the registration of a trademark certified by the Registrar is evidence of the facts set out therein and that the person shown as the owner is the registered owner of the trademark.[14]

## 3. Marking

The *Act* is neutral concerning the use of a trademark notice. There are no provisions of the *Act* that require a trademark owner to use a trademark notice. However the use of a trade is particularly helpful.

A trademark owner may use the notification ™ to identify an unregistered trademark and the symbol® to identify its registered trademarks. In addition the owner may choose to use a trademark legend in conjunction with these symbols such as "®registered trade mark of ABC Company." The use of such a legend when a trademark has been licensed, combined with a statement that the use is licensed and the name of the owner, results in a statutory presumption that the use is licensed and under the control of the owner.[15]

The use of such notices is very common and most sophisticated trademark owners use such notices. This position has probably been influenced by U.S.

---

9. Section 19.
10. See Chapter 13, part 1(a).
11. See part 5 of this chapter.
12. See Chapter 3, part 4.
13. The registration of a trademark under the laws of Newfoundland before April 1, 1949 has the same force and effect in the Province of Newfoundland as if Newfoundland had not become part of Canada, and all rights and privileges acquired under or by virtue of those laws may continue to be exercised or enjoyed in the Province of Newfoundland as if Newfoundland had not become part of Canada.
14. Subsection 54(3).
15. Subsection 50(2).

practice and the fact that in a suit for infringement, if a registrant fails to give notice of registration, no profits and damages shall be recovered unless the defendant had actual notice of the registration. There is no similar provision in the *Trade-marks Act* and an infringer cannot successfully assert lack of notice of the registration as a defence.

There are numerous advantages of using a trademark notice including the following matters:

(a) Consumers will recognize that the trademark being used is a trade-mark, as opposed to some other device such as a business name.

(b) Continuous use of the trademark notice with a trademark has the ten-dency to increase the strength of the link between the registered trade-mark presented to consumers and the source of the goods they purchase. The stronger the link, the more goodwill can be established in association with the mark.

(c) If third parties are aware of a registered trademark, they may be more inclined to avoid infringing it. The use of such notice serves a function similar to a "no trespassing" sign to ward off competitors who may consider the adoption of a similar mark.

(d) The use of the notice provides an additional element of confidence for consumers as they may infer that the trademark thus endorsed carries the weight of statutory approval.

(e) A trademark notice may help educate the public regarding the trade-mark use of a descriptive or suggestive word.

(f) A notice may help prevent a mark from being adopted by customers in a "generic" rather than in a trademark sense.

## 4. Invalidity

Section 18 of the *Act* provides that the registration of the trademark is invalid[16] if:

(a) the trademark was not registrable at the date of registration;[17]

(b) the trademark is not distinctive at the time proceedings bringing the validity of the registration into question are commenced;[18]

(c) the trademark has been abandoned;[19] or

---

16. For a detailed discussion see Chapter 10.
17. Subsection 18(1)(a).
18. Subsection 18(1)(b).
19. Subsection 18(l)(c).

(d)  subject to section 17,[20] the applicant for registration was not the person
entitled to secure the registration.[21]

No registration of a trademark that had been so used in Canada by the registrant or his predecessor in title as to have become distinctive at the date of
registration will be held invalid merely on the ground that evidence of the
distinctiveness was not submitted to the competent authority or tribunal
before the grant of the registration.[22]

## 5.  Registration of Concurrent Rights

Section 21 of the *Act* is directed to protecting the rights of a person who has,
in good faith, used a confusing trademark or trade name prior to the date of
filing of the application for registration of a registered trademark. In proceedings relating to a registered trademark, which has become incontestable by
virtue of the expiration of the five year period referred to in subsection 17(2),[23]
if the Federal Court considers that it is not contrary to the public interest that
the continued use of the confusing trademark or trade name should be permitted in a defined territorial area concurrently with the use of the registered
trademark, the Court may permit the continued use of the unregistered
trademark within that area with an adequate specified distinction from the
registered trademark.[24]

## 6.  Term of Protection and Renewal

Unlike other intellectual property rights, a trademark registration may
be renewed any number of times without limitation and can be extended
indefinitely. A registration is subject to renewal within a period of 15 years
from the day of the registration or last renewal.[25] Apart from the timely
payment of the prescribed renewal fee, there are no other requirements for
renewal. In particular, there is no obligation to show the mark is in use.

The Registrar is required to send a notice to the registered owner and its
representative for service, if any, stating that, if within six months after the

---

20.  See Chapter 10, part 2(d).
21.  Subsection 18(1)(c).
22.  Subsection 18(2).
23.  See Chapter 10, part 2(d).
24.  Subsection 21(1).
25.  Subsection 46(1).

date of the notice the prescribed renewal fee is not paid, the registration will be expunged.[26] If the prescribed renewal fee is not paid within the six-month period, which may not be extended, the registration will be expunged.[27] If the prescribed fee for a renewal is paid within the time limited for the payment, the renewal takes effect as of the day next following the expiration of the 15-year period set out above.[28]

---

26. Subsection 46(2).
27. Subsection 46(3).
28. Subsection 46(4).

# CHAPTER
## 9

## Assignments and Licenses

Under the *Trade-marks Act* it is possible to assign a trademark or to license another person to use a mark. In both situations, care must be taken to ensure that the mark remains distinctive of the trademark owner.

## 1. Assignments

### a) Scope

Subsection 48(1) of the *Act* provides that a trademark, whether registered or unregistered, is transferable, and deemed always to have been transferable,[1] either in connection with or separately from the goodwill of the business, and in respect of either all or some of the wares or services in association with which it has been used.[2] The subsection applies to both registered and unregistered trademarks.[3]

The subsection also applies to the assignment of a trademark that is the subject of a pending application for registration. In this case, the application will be amended to change the identity of the applicant after recognition of the transfer by the Registrar.[4] Nothing in the *Act* prevents the assignment of an application relating to a mark registered and used abroad.

The subsection does not apply to trade names, which are defined by the *Act* to mean "the name under which any business is carried on, whether or not it is the name of a corporation, a partnership or an individual."[5] It appears that a trade name may only be transferred with the goodwill of the business it is associated with.[6]

The *Act* does not permit territorial assignments of trademarks within Canada, since for the purposes of the *Act*, Canada is regarded as an indivisible unit,[7] subject to two exceptions relating to territorially restricted trade marks. First, under section 21, the Federal Court may permit concurrent use of trademarks in a defined territorial area.[8] Second, where a trademark is

---

1. Subsection 48(1) has retroactive effect and validates a trademark whose validity may have been destroyed through an improper assignment in the past prior to the passing of the *Act*.
2. *Cheerio Toys & Games Ltd. v. Dubiner* (1964), 44 C.P.R. 134 (Ex. Ct.); affirmed [1966] S.C.R. 206 (S.C.C.).
3. See *McCurdy Enterprises Ltd. v. Shamrock Spring Water Inc* (2005), 45 C.P.R. (4th) 55 (Nfld and Lab. Sup. Ct. T.D.).
4. Sections 31(a) and 48, *Trade-marks Regulations* SOR/96-195 as amended.
5. Section 2.
6. *Cheerio Toys & Games Ltd. v. Dubiner* (1964), 44 C.P.R. 134 (Ex. Ct.); affirmed [1966] S.C.R. 206 (S.C.C.).
7. *Great Atlantic & Pacific Tea Co. v. Reg. TM.* [1945] Ex. C.R. 233 (Ex. Ct.).
8. Section 21 and see Chapter 8, part 5.

registered on proof of acquired distinctiveness or secondary meaning pursuant to subsection 12(2), the Registrar may restrict the registration to the defined territorial area in Canada in which the trademark is shown to have become distinctive.[9] Nothing in the *Act* prevents the assignment of such territorially restricted trademarks.

## b) Effectiveness

An assignment becomes effective when the assignor ceases to be entitled to the exclusive right to use the assigned mark in association with the wares or services referred to in the registration and such right is vested in the assignee. However, the exclusive right that is vested is the right to use the mark as a "trade mark" and not the right to use it for some other purpose. The right to use it as a trademark is the right to use it for the purpose of distinguishing or so as to distinguish the owner's wares or services from the wares or services of others.[10]

Registration is not necessary to make an assignment of a trademark effective against a third party.[11] In addition, an assignee may commence an action for infringement even though the assignment is not registered.[12] Despite these decisions, registration of an assignment is prudent. In addition registration will help ensure that notice of proceedings[13] or renewal under the *Act*[14] is brought to the attention of the assignee.

The *Act* does not proscribe any form of assignment. A court, in an appropriate case, may infer that an assignment or transfer took place after considering all of the relevant facts without the necessity of a written agreement.[15] In addition, an assignor may be estopped from disputing the validity of the assigned mark on the basis that it cannot derogate for its grant.[16]

The registrar is required to register the transfer of any registered trademark upon being furnished with satisfactory evidence of the transfer and the

9. Subsection 32(2) and see Chapter 3, part 4.
10. *Wilkinson Sword (Can.) Ltd. v. Juda* (1966), 51 C.P.R. 55 (Ex. Ct.).
11. *Marcus v. Quaker Oats Co. of Can./Cie Quaker Oats du Canada* (1985), 4 C.I.P.R. 212 (F.C.T.D.); *White Consolidated Industries, Inc. v. Beam of Canada Inc.* (1991), 39 C.P.R. (3d) 94 (F.C.T.D.); *McCurdy Enterprises Ltd. v. Shamrock Spring Water Inc* (2005), 45 C.P.R. (4th) 55 (Nfld and Lab. Sup. Ct. T.D.).
12. *Wilkinson Sword (Can.) Ltd. v. Juda* (1966), 51 C.P.R. 55 (Ex. Ct.).
13. Section 45 and see Chapter 10, part 1.
14. Section 46 and see Chapter 8, part 6.
15. *Gattuso v. Gattuso Corp. Ltd.*, [1968] 2 Ex. C.R. 609 (Ex. Ct.); *Philip Morris Inc. v. Imperial Tobacco Ltd.* (1985), 7 C.P.R. (3d) 254 (F.C.T.D.) affirmed 17 C.P.R. (3d) 289 (F.C.A.); *White Consolidated Industries, Inc. v. Beam of Canada Inc.* (1991), 39 C.P.R. (3d) 94 (F.C.T.D.).
16. *Cheerio Toys & Games Ltd. v. Dubiner*, (1965), 48 C.P.R. 226 (S.C.C.).

same information concerning the address of the transferee that would be required in an application by the transferee to register such trademark.[17]

## c) Distinctiveness

Subsection 48(2) provides that nothing in subsection 48(1) prevents a trademark from being held not to be distinctive if, as a result of a transfer, there subsisted rights in two or more persons to the use of confusing trademarks and such rights were exercised by such persons. When determining whether the registration of a trademark is invalid on the grounds that it is not distinctive, the determination is made at the time of the commencement of the proceedings, bringing the validity of the registration into question.[18]

Once a mark is assigned, the new owner must take the necessary steps to cause the mark to actually distinguish its wares or services from the wares or services of others, including those of the assignor.[19] If the mark does not become distinctive of the new owner, the validity of the registration may be attacked on the ground that it is not distinctive.[20] The function and the purpose of a trademark is to indicate the source of the goods, and by definition, it must be and remain distinctive of a single source.[21]

Where, as the result of an assignment, a trademark becomes the property of one person for use in association with some of the wares or services specified in the registration and another person for use with other such wares or services and the transfer is registered by the Registrar, each person is deemed to be a separate registered owner and to have a separate registration of the trademark for use in association with the respective wares or services.[22] In such a case, particular attention must be given to maintaining the distinctiveness of the assigned marks. The Registrar will not allow such a partial transfer if the effect of having separate owners would likely cause confusion.

---

17. Subsection 48(3) and see sections 48-50, *Trade-marks Regulations* SOR/96-195 as amended.
18. Subsection 18(1)(b).
19. See Chapter 2, part 2(c).
20. See *Wilkinson Sword (Can.) Ltd. v. Juda*, [1968] 2 Ex. C.R.137 (Ex. Ct.); *Magder v. Breck's Sporting Goods Co.* [1976] 1 S.C.R. 527 (S.C.C.); *Heinzman v. 751056 Ontario Limited* (1990), 34 C.P.R. (3d) 1 (F.C.T.D.); *Cross-Canada Auto Body Supply (Windsor) Limited v. Hyundai Auto Canada*, 2007 FC 580 (F.C.), 60 C.P.R. (4th) (F.C.), 2008 FCA 98, 65 C.P.R. (4th) 121 (F.C.A.).
21. *Cross-Canada Auto Body Supply (Windsor) Limited v. Hyundai Auto Canada*, 2007 FC 580 (F.C.), 60 C.P.R. (4th) (F.C.), 2008 FCA 98, 65 C.P.R. (4th) 121 (F.C.A.).
22. See sections 49–50, *Trade-marks Regulations* SOR/96-195 as amended.

## 2. License

### a) Availability

Both at common law and under the earlier legislation, a license of a trade-mark was fatal to its validity.[23] However, the *Act* currently allows for a license of a trademark subject to the conditions set out in the *Act*.[24]

Section 50 provides that, for the purposes of the *Act*, if an entity is licensed by or with the authority of the owner of a trademark to use the trademark in a country and the owner has, under the license, direct or indirect control of the character or quality of the wares or services, then the use, advertisement, or display of the trademark in that country as or in a trademark, trade name, or otherwise by that entity has, and is deemed always to have had, the same effect as such a use, advertisement, or display of the trademark in that country by the owner. The section applies retroactively.[25]

The use of the words "in a country" allows an applicant for a trademark, based on registration and use abroad, to rely on use by a licensee abroad. The section is not limited to trademark use as described in section 4 and is significantly broader, as it extends to "the use, advertisement or display of the trademark . . . . as or in a trademark, trade name, or otherwise."

For the purposes of the *Act*, use of the mark by the licensee under the control of the owner is deemed to be use by the owner. This deemed use is only for the purpose of the *Act* and the trademark owner is not deemed to have sold the goods or provided the services for other purposes.[26]

The *Act* does not contain any limitation concerning the form of a license other than it must be with the authority of the owner of a trademark, who must have under the license, direct or indirect control of the character or quality of the licensed wares or services.[27] For evidentiary purposes, it is prudent that the license be in writing.

---

23. *Bowden Wire Ltd. v. Bowden Brake Co. Ltd.* (1913), 30 R.P.C. 580; 31 R.P.C. 385 (H.L.).
24. When the *Act* was brought into force in 1954 it provided for the licensing of trademarks through a system of registered users and permitted use. A registered owner could permit the use of a registered trademark by other persons subject to its control. The *Act* was amended in 1993 to terminate the registered user system.
25. *Eli Lilly & Co. v. Novapharm Ltd.* (2000), 10 C.P.R. (4th) 10 (F.C.A.) leave to appeal to the Supreme Court of Canada refused.
26. *Mister Transmission(International) Ltd. v. Registrar of Trade-marks* (1978), 42 C.P.R. (2d) 11 (F.C.T.D.).
27. See *Spiros Pizza & Spaghetti House Ltd. v. Riveria Pizza Inc.* (2005), 39 C.P.R. (4th) 527 (Alberta Q.B.).

## b) Control

Control by the trademark owner of the character or quality of the licensed wares or services is fundamental, since a license without adequate control is not within the section and may result in the invalidity of the mark.[28]

Even though a related company controls another company by virtue of its share holdings, as in a parent and wholly owned subsidiary relationship, such control is not sufficient to comply with section 50. In cases involving such a relationship, there must be evidence of facts from which it can be concluded that a licensing arrangement existed and that the trademark owner had direct or indirect control of the character or quality of the licensed wares or services provided pursuant to that licensing arrangement.[29]

For the purposes of the *Act*, to the extent that public notice is given of the fact that the use of a trademark is a licensed use and of the identity of the owner, it will be presumed, unless the contrary is proven, that the use is licensed by the owner of the trademark and the character or quality of the wares or services is under the control of the owner.[30] This presumption may be rebutted if evidence to the contrary is presented.

The fact that a trademark owner has entered into a license does not by itself result in the licensor owing a fiduciary duty to the licensee. The fundamental hallmark required to establish a fiduciary duty is evidence that one party has relinquished its own self-interest and agreed to act solely on behalf of the other party. On its face, a contractual relationship would not be expected to lead to a fiduciary relationship because it is negotiated and both parties look after their own self-interests and not the interests of the opposite party.[31]

## c) Proceedings for Infringement

Subject to any agreement between the owner of a trademark and a licensee of the trademark, the licensee may call on the owner to bring proceedings for infringement, and, if the owner refuses or neglects to do so within two months after being so called on, the licensee may institute proceedings for infringement in the licensee's own name as if the licensee were the owner, making the owner a defendant.[32] Frequently this right is contractually removed.

---

28. *Bowden Wire Ltd. v. Bowden Brake Co. Ltd.* (1913), 30 R.P.C. 580; 31 R.P.C. 385 (H.L.) but not in all cases; see for example *Imperial Developments v. Imperial Oil Ltd.* (1984), 79 C.P.R. (2d) 12 (F.C.T.D.).
29. *M.C.I. Communications Corp. v M.C.I. Multinet Communications Inc.* (1995), 61 C.P.R. (3d) 245 (T.M.O.B.); *Cheung Kong (Holdings) Ltd. v. Living Realty Inc*, (1999), 4 C.P.R. (4th) 71 (F.C.T.D.).
30. Subsection 50(2).
31. *Bluefoot Ventures Inc. v. Ticketmaster* (2007), CanLII 55363 (On S.C.).
32. Subsection 50(3).

# CHAPTER
# 10

# Expungement

# 1. Section 45 Proceedings

## a) Summary Procedure

The purpose of section 45 of the *Trade-marks Act* is to provide a summary procedure[1] for trimming the register of "dead wood."[2] Frequently, proceedings under the section will be instituted by third parties who are prevented from obtaining a registration for a desired mark by a registration which is perceived not to be in use.

The section provides that the Registrar, at any time and at the written request made after three years from the date of the registration of a trademark by any person who pays the prescribed fee, shall, unless the Registrar sees good reason to the contrary, give notice to the registered owner of the trademark requiring the registered owner to furnish within three months an affidavit or statutory declaration showing with respect to each of the wares or services specified in the registration, whether the trademark was in use in Canada at any time during the three-year period immediately proceeding the date of the notice and, if not, the date when it was last so in use and the reason for the absence of such use since such date.[3]

The Registrar may, in his discretion, issue a notice pursuant to the section at any time. However, under the current practice, the Registrar considers that in order to ensure compliance with Article 19 of the TRIPS Agreement no notice should be issued prior to three years after the date of registration.[4]

There is no prescribed form for the "written request." It can be made by any person as there is no requirement for standing. Frequently, proceedings are instituted by law firms on behalf of clients.[5]

The Registrar should not attempt to resolve any question other than whether the registration is in use. The procedure under the section is not intended to create or rescind substantive rights.[6] For example, difficult questions of interpretation concerning the wares of the registration will not be considered.[7] Requesting that notice be given under the section should not be

---

1. *AnheuserBusch Inc. v. Carling O Keefe Breweries of Can. Ltd.* [1983] 2 F.C. 71 (F.C.A.).
2. *Plough (Canada) Ltd. v. Aerosol Fillers Inc.* (1979), 45 C.P.R. (2d) 194 (F.C.T.D.), affirmed 53 C.P.R. (2d) 62 (F.C.A.).
3. Section 45 and see Practice in Section 45 Proceedings in effect September 14, 2009, currently available at the Canadian Intellectual Property Office website at http://www.cipo.ic.gc.ca/eic/site/cipointernet-internetopic.nsf/eng/h_wr00002.html.
4. See Practice in Section 45 Proceedings, *supra*, part II.2.
5. *Rogers, Bereskin & Parr v. Reg. T.M.* (1986), 9 C.P.R. (3d) 260 (F.C.T.D.).
6. *Rogers, Bereskin & Parr v. Reg. T.M.* (1986), 9 C.P.R. (3d) 260 (F.C.T.D.).
7. *Levi Strauss & Co. v. Registrar of Trade-marks,* (2006), 51 C.P.R. (4th) 434 (F.C.); *Countryside Caners Co. v. Registrar of Trade-marks,* (1981), 55 C.P.R. (2nd) 25 (F.C.T.D.).

seen as an alternative to initiating proceedings in the Federal Court seeking expungement.[8]

The requesting party cannot file evidence or conduct a cross examination on the affidavit or statutory declaration of the registered owner.[9] The requesting party is limited to filing written argument and taking part in an oral hearing to argue that the registration should be expunged or amended.

## b) Evidence

The registered owner has three months[10] within which to furnish an affidavit or statutory declaration showing, with respect to each of the wares or services specified in the registration, whether the trademark was in use in Canada at any time during the three-year period immediately preceding the date of the notice and, if not, the date when it was last so in use and the reason for the absence of such use since that date.[11]

Section 45 requires an affidavit or statutory declaration not merely stating but "showing" sufficient facts to demonstrate trademark use[12] within the meaning of the definition of a "trade mark" in section 2 and of "use" in section 4 of the *Act*.[13] Multiple affidavits can be filed including affidavits sworn by third parties.[14]

The evidence filed must show the use of the registered trademark in issue not a variant of the mark.[15] However, cautious variations may be accepted as use of the registered mark without adverse consequences if the same dominant features are maintained and the differences are so unimportant that an unaware purchaser of the wares would not be mislead.[16]

---

8. *Phillip Morris Inc. v. Imperial Tobacco* (1987), 13 C.P.R. (3d) 289 (F.C.T.D.).
9. *Plough (Canada) Ltd. v. Aerosol Fillers Inc.* (1979), 45 C.P.R. (2d) 194 (F.C.T.D.), affirmed 53 C.P.R. (2d) 62 (F.C.A.).
10. An extension of time may be sought, see See Practice in Section 45 Proceedings, *supra*, part IV.
11. Subsection 45(1).
12. *Plough (Canada) Ltd. v. Aerosol Fillers Inc.* (1979), 45 C.P.R. (2d) 194 (F.C.T.D.), affirmed 53 C.P.R. (2d) 62 (F.C.A.); *United Grain Growers Ltd. v. Lang Michener* (2001), 12 C.P.R. (4th) 89 (F.C.A.).
13. See Chapter 5.
14. *Registrar of Trade-marks v. Harris Knitting Mills Ltd.* (1985), 4 C.P.R. (3d) 488(F.C.A.).
15. *Reg. T.M. v. Cie Int. pour L'Informatique Cii Honeywell Bull S.A.* (1985), 4 C.P.R. (3d) 523 (F.C.A.); *Rogers, Bereskin & Parr v. Reg. T.M.* (1986), 9 C.P.R. (3d) 260 (F.C.T.D.).
16. *Promafil Canada Ltee. v. Munsingwear Inc.* (1993), 44 C.P.R. (3d) 59 (F.C.A.); *Saccone & Speed Ltd. v. Registrar of Trade-marks.* (1982), 67 C.P.R. (2d) 119 (F.C.T.D.); *Ivy Lea Shirt Co. v. 1227624 Ontario Ltd.* (2001), 11 C.P.R. (4th) 489 (F.C.T.D.); *Marks & Clark v. Sparkles Photo Limited* [2005] FC 1012 and see Chapter 5, part 5.

The evidence must also describe the nature of the business and the normal course of trade of the owner of the trademark.[17] The Registrar cannot make assumptions or be expected to know the nature of the registrant's business and its practices.[18]

The majority of cases have found that evidence of a single sale, whether wholesale or retail, in the normal course of trade, can satisfy the requirements of the section, so long as the sale follows the pattern of a genuine commercial transaction and is not seen as being deliberately manufactured or contrived to protect the registration of the trademark in issue.[19] In addition, the provision of samples can in some circumstances be considered use in the normal course of trade.[20]

Use by a licensee may be sufficient if the requirements of the *Act* relating to licensing are satisfied.[21] Control for the purpose of section 50 of the *Act* dealing with a licensed mark will not be inferred and must be expressly referred to.[22]

It is not necessary to provide an over-abundance of evidence of use of the mark. Inferences can be drawn from the evidence as a whole.[23] A registrant must carefully consider what is required to satisfy the requirements of the section. A bald assertion of use is not sufficient and an affidavit must disclose sufficient facts so as to demonstrate trademark use during the three-year period immediately preceding the date of the notice.

Because the evidence is not subject to cross-examination, at the hearing, the Registrar is under a duty to ensure that reliable evidence has been presented.[24] If an affidavit or declaration is ambiguous, an interpretation adverse to the registrant should be adopted.[25] The use must be "in a normal course of trade" as opposed to a fictitious or colorable use.[26]

17. *S.C. Johnson & Son, Inc. v. Reg. T.M.* (1981), 55 C.P.R. (2d) 34 (F.C.T.D.); *Sim & McBurney v. Majdell Manufacturing Co.* (1986), 11 C.P.R. (3d) 306 (F.C.T.D.).
18. *S.C. Johnson & Son, Inc. v. Reg. T.M.* (1981), 55 C.P.R. (2d) 34 (F.C.T.D.).
19. *Guido Berlucchi & C.S.r.l. v. Brouilette Kosie Prince*, 2007 FC 245 (F.C.).
20. *Lin Trading Co. v. CBM Kabushiki Kaisha,* (1988), 21 C.P.R. (3d) 417 (F.C.A.).
21. See Chapter 9, part 2 and *Sim & McBurney v. Netlon Ltd.* (2004), 41 C.P.R. (4th) 455 (T.M.O.B.): *Marks & Clark v. Cristall U.S.A. Inc.*, (2007), 59 C.P.R. (4th) 475 (T.M.O.B.)
22. *Farris, Vaughan, Mills & Murphy v. Kabushiki Kaisha Yaskawa Denki* (2008), 68 C.P.R. (4th) 220 (T.M.O.B.).
23. *Eclipse International Fashions Canada Inc. v. Shapiro Cohen* (2005), 48 C.P.R. (4th) 224 (F.C.A.).
24. *88766 Canada Inc. v. Monte Carlo Restaurant Limited*, 2007 FC 1174, 63 C.P.R. (4th) 391 (F.C.); *Grapha-Holding Ag v. Illinois Tool Works Inc.* (2008), 68 C.P.R. (4th) 180 (F.C.).
25. *Plough (Canada) Ltd. v. Aerosol Fillers Inc.* (1979), 45 C.P.R. (2d) 194 (F.C.T.D.), affirmed 53 C.P.R. (2d) 62 (F.C.A.).
26. *Molson Cos. Ltd. v. Halter* (1976), 28 C.P.R. (2d) 158 (F.C.T.D.); *Plough (Canada) Ltd. v. Aerosol Fillers Inc.* (1979), 45 C.P.R. (2d) 194 (F.C.T.D.), affirmed 53 C.P.R. (2d) 62 (F.C.A.); *Ports International Ltd. v. Reg. T.M.*, [1984] 2 F.C. 119 (F.C.T.D.); *Phillip Morris Inc. v. Imperial Tobacco* (1987), 13 C.P.R. (3d) 289 (F.C.T.D.).

Where the evidence shows the trademark is being used only in respect to some of the wares or services specified in the registration, the registration should be amended and not expunged.[27]

## c) Effect of Non-Use

Where by reason of the evidence furnished or the failure to furnish such evidence, it appears to the Registrar that the trademark, either with respect to all of the wares or services specified in the registration, or with respect to any of the wares or services, was not in use in Canada, and that the absence of use has not been due to special circumstances that excuse the absence of use, the registration of the trademark is liable to be expunged or amended accordingly.[28] The onus is on the registered owner to establish that there are special circumstances justifying non-use.

It has been said that it is impossible to state precisely what circumstances will excuse the absence of use of a trademark. The duration of the absence of use and the likelihood it will last a prolonged period are important factors. However, circumstances may excuse the absence of use for a brief period of time without excusing a prolonged absence of use. It is also essential to know to what extent the absence of use relates solely to a deliberate decision on the part of the owner of the trademark rather than to obstacles beyond the control of the owner. It will be more difficult to justify absence of use due solely to a deliberate decision by the owner of the trademark.[29]

## d) The Hearing

A Hearing Officer authorized by the Registrar[30] will hear representations made by or on behalf of the registered owner of the trademark and by or on behalf of the person who has requested that notice be given. The Registrar

---

27. *John Labatt Ltd. v. Rainier Brewing Co.* (1984), 80 C.P.R. (2d) 228 (F.C.A.), reversing (1982) 68 C.P.R. (2d) 266 (F.C.T.D.); but see *Ridout & Maybee LLP v. Omega SA.* 2004 FC 1703 (FC) where use of certain wares was sufficient evidence of use of an entire category of wares on a plain reading of the registration.
28. Subsection 45(3) and see Practice in Section 45 Proceedings, *supra*, part III.3.
29. *Harris Knitting Mills v. Reg. T.M.* (1982), 66 C.P.R. (2d) 158 (F.C.T.D.); (1985), 4 C.P.R. (3d) 488 (F.C.A.); *Smart & Biggar v. Attorney General of Canada*, 2006 FC 1542 (F.C.), 58 C.P.R (4th) 42, 2008 F.C.A. 129, 65 C.P.R. (4th) 303 (F.C.A.) and see *Bereskin & Parr v. Bartlett* (2008), 70 C.P.R. (4th) 469 (T.M.O.B.) concerning the effect of illness.
30. Subsection 63(3).

will generally invite the parties to file written submissions and an oral hearing may be requested.[31]

When the Registrar reaches a decision as to whether the registration of the trademark should be expunged or amended, notice of the decision together with written reasons must be given to the registered owner and to the person at whose request the notice was given.[32]

The decision must relate only to whether the evidence supplied or the failure to supply evidence shows the mark was in use or the absence of use was due to special circumstances and finally determines nothing else.[33] The doctrine of *res judicata* does not apply to the decision.[34]

The Registrar must act in accordance with the decision if no appeal is initiated within the time limited by the *Act* or, if an appeal is taken, must act in accordance with the final judgment given in the appeal.[35]

## e) Appeal

An appeal may be made to the Federal Court from the Registrar within two months from the date on which notice of the decision was dispatched by the Registrar or within such further time as the Court may allow, either before or after the expiration of the two months.[36] On an appeal, evidence in addition to that which was before the Registrar may be adduced[37] and the Court may exercise any discretion vested in the Registrar.[38]

Due to the nature of section 45 only the registered owner may adduce additional evidence[39] but the requesting party is entitled to cross-examine on new affidavits filed on the appeal.[40] The judgment of the Federal Court on the appeal is filed with the Registrar.[41]

---

31. See Practice in Section 45 Proceedings, *supra,* parts VI and VII.
32. Subsection 45(4).
33. *Broderick& Bascom Rope v. Reg. T.M.* (1970), 62 C.P.R. 268 (Ex. Ct.); *United Grain Growers v. Lang Mitchener,* (2001), 12 C.P.R. (4th) 89 (F.C.A.).
34. *Molson Cos. Ltd. v. Halter* (1976), 28 C.P.R. (2d) 158 (F.C.T.D.).
35. Subsection 45(5).
36. Subsection 56(1).
37. Subsection 56(5) and see *Austin Nichols & Co. v. Cinnabon Inc.* (1998), 82 C.P.R. (3d) 513 (F.C.A.); *Baxter International Inc. v. P.T. Kalbe Frama TBK,* 2007 FC 439 (F.C.).
38. Subsection 56(5) and see *Brouillette Kosie Prince v. Orange Cove-Sanger Citrus Association,* 2007 FC 1229 (F.C.) and *Promotions C.D. Inc. v. Sim & McBurney* 2008 FC 1071 (F.C.) for a discussion of the appropriate standard of review on an appeal.
39. *Plough (Canada) Ltd. v. Aerosol Fillers Inc.* (1979), 45 C.P.R. (2d) 194 (F.C.T.D.), affirmed 53 C.P.R. (2d) 62 (F.C.A.).
40. *House of Kwong Sang Hong International Ltd. v. Borden Ladner Gervais LLP,* 2001 FCA 346 (F.C.A.).
41. Section 61.

## 2. Expungement by the Federal Court

### a) Jurisdiction

The Federal Court has exclusive original jurisdiction, on the application of any person interested, to order that any entry in the register be struck out or amended on the ground that at the date of the application the entry as it appears on the register does not accurately express or define the existing rights of the person appearing to be the registered owner of the mark.[42] An application for expungement is not an appeal under section 56 of the *Act* for which a standard of review should be identified. It is the exercise of original jurisdiction.[43]

In matters concerning the register the Court must consider the "purity of the register"[44] and the public interest.[45] The *Act* rests on principles of fair dealing and is sometimes said to hold the balance between free competition and fair competition. In applying these principles the interests of the public and other merchants as well as the interest of the trademark owner must be considered.[46]

The power to amend the register is only exercised where a trademark is otherwise open to expungement, for example, if a registration is invalid only in respect of some wares it may be amended. There is no jurisdiction to amend an inappropriate description[47] or to order an involuntary substitution of one registrant for another.[48]

The Courts of the provinces have jurisdiction in actions for infringement, but have no jurisdiction to direct that the registration of a trademark be expunged or amended.[49]

---

42. Subsection 57(1) and see section 20 of the *Federal Courts Act*, R.S.C. 1985, c. F-7 as amended.
43. *Emall.ca Inc. v. Cheap Tickets and Travel Inc.*, 2007 FC 243, 56 C.P.R (4th) 82 (F. C.), appeal dismissed, 2008 FCA 50 (F.C.A.).
44. *British Drug Houses, Ltd. v. Battle Pharmaceuticals*, [1944] Ex. C.R. 239 (Ex. Ct.); affirmed [1946] S.C.R. 50 (S.C.C.); *General Motors Corp. v. Bellows*, [1949] S.C.R. 678 (S.C.C.); *Aladdin Industries Inc. v. Can. Thermos Products Ltd.* (1969), 57 C.P.R. 230 (Ex. Ct.), affirmed [1974] S.C.R. 845 (S.C.C.).
45. *British Drug Houses, Ltd. v. Battle Pharmaceuticals*, [1944] Ex. C.R. 239 (Ex. Ct.); affirmed [1946] S.C.R. 50 (S.C.C.), *Aladdin Industries Inc. v. Can. Thermos Products Ltd.* (1969), 57 C.P.R. 230 (Ex. Ct.), affirmed [1974] S.C.R. 845 (S.C.C.).
46. *Mattel, Inc. v 3894207 Canada Inc.*, 2006 SCC 22, 49 C.P.R. (4th) 321 (S.C.C.).
47. *Omega Engineering, Inc. v. Omega SA* (2006), 56 C.P.R. (4th) 210 (F.C.).
48. *Royal Doulton Tableware Ltd. v. Cassidy's Ltée.* (2006), 1 C.P.R. (3rd) 214 (F.C.T.D.).
49. *Canadian Shredded Wheat v. Kellogg*, [1936] O.W.N. 199 (Ont. H.C.).

## b) Procedure

An application for expungement is made to the Federal Court[50] by the filing of an application[51] or by statement of claim in an action claiming additional relief under the *Act*.[52] It is also possible to assert a claim for expungement by way of counterclaim in an action for infringement brought in the Federal Court.[53]

An application is heard and determined on evidence introduced by affidavit unless the Court otherwise directs.[54] Any affidavits filed in support of an application must be confined to facts within the personal knowledge of the deponent[55] and otherwise comply with the usual rules of evidence.

In such proceedings, the Court may order that any procedure permitted by its rules and practice be made available to the parties, including the introduction of oral evidence generally or in respect of one or more issues specified in the order.[56]

The burden of proof in proceedings for expungement lies on the party seeking to expunge.[57] The registrant benefits from a presumption that its registration is valid and the onus remains on the attacking party to show it should be expunged[58] but this presumption has been categorized as weakly worded, adding little to the onus already resting, in the usual way, on the attacking party.[59] Acquiescence or laches may be advanced as a defense.[60]

If the respondent voluntarily cancels its registration, there may be nothing to expunge and the application must be dismissed.[61]

---

50. Subsection 57(1) and see section 20 of the *Federal Courts Act*, R.S.C. 1985, c. F-7 as amended.
51. See Part 5-Applications of the *Federal Court Rules, 1998*, SOR/98–106.
52. Section 58.
53. Section 58.
54. Subsection 59(3) and Rule 306 of the *Federal Court Rules, 1998*, SOR/98–106. It is inappropriate to rely on affidavits of individuals employed by the solicitors for a party concerning contentious matters and such solicitors may be removed from the record, *Cross-Canada Auto Body Supply (Windsor) Limited v. Hyundai Auto Canada* (2006), 53 C.P.R. (4th) 286 (F.C.A.).
55. Rule 81 of the *Federal Court Rules, 1998*, SOR/98-106 and see *Canadian Tire Corp. v. P.S. Partsource Inc.* (2001), 11 C.P.R. (4th) 386 (F.C.A.).
56. Subsection 59(3).
57. *Cheerio Toys & Games Ltd. v. Dubiner* [1965] 1 Ex. C.R. 524 (Ex. Ct.); affirmed [1966] S.C.R. 206 (S.C.C.); *Parke, Davis & Co. v. Empire Laboratories Ltd.* [1964] Ex. C.R. 399 (Ex. Ct.); affirmed [1964] S.C.R. 351(S.C.C.).
58. *Cross-Canada Auto Body Supply (Windsor) Limited v. Hyundai Auto Canada*, 2007 FC 580, 60 C.P.R. (4th) (F.C.), 2008 FCA 98, 65 C.P.R. (4th) 121 (F.C.A.).
59. *Cheap Tickets and Travel Inc. v. Emall.ca Inc.*, 2008 FCA 50 (F.C.A.).
60. *Carling O'Keefe Breweries of Can. Ltd. v. Labatt Brewing Co.* (1982), 68 C.P.R. (2d) 1 (F.C.T.D.); 10 C.P.R. (3d) 433 (F.C.A.).
61. *SC Prodal 94 SR v. Spirits International B/V.* (2009), 73 C.P.R. (4th) 439 (F.C.A.).

## c) Person Interested

The term "person interested" includes any person who is affected, or reasonably apprehends that he or she may be affected by any entry in the register, or by any act or omission or contemplated act or omission under or contrary to the *Act*, and includes the Attorney General of Canada.[62]

In order to have standing as a "person interested," an applicant must be affected or reasonably apprehend that they may be affected by an entry in the register.[63] The entry must stand in the way of the person seeking to expunge it or prejudice that person.[64] Typically trademark "use" is an important factor. A person who alleges they have previously used the registered trademark;[65] a person who was sued or threatened with infringement as result of their use of a mark;[66] or a person who alleges that their agent or distributor wrongfully obtained a registration on the basis of purported use;[67] will have standing.

## d) Limitations

No registration of a trademark shall be expunged or amended or held invalid on the ground of any previous use or making known[68] of a confusing trademark or trade name by a person other than the applicant for such registration or his predecessor in title, except at the instance of such other person or his successor in title.[69] The burden lies on that other person or his successor to establish that he had not abandoned the confusing trademark or trade name at the date of advertisement of the applicant's application.[70]

In proceedings commenced after the expiry of five years from the date of registration of a trademark, no registration shall be expunged or amended or held invalid on the ground of the previous use or making known referred to above, unless it is established that the person who adopted the registered

---

62. Section 2 and see *Aladdin Industries Inc. v. Can. Thermos Products Ltd.* (1969), 57 C.P.R. 230 (Ex. Ct.), affirmed [1974] S.C.R. 845 (S.C.C).
63. *Fairmount Resort Properties Ltd. v. Fairmount Hotel Management, L.P.* (2008), 67 C.P.R. (4th) 404 (F.C.).
64. *Fairmount Resort Properties Ltd. v. Fairmount Hotel Management, L.P.* (2008), 67 C.P.R. (4th) 404 (F.C.).
65. *Sequa Chemicals Inc. v. United Colour and Chemicals Ltd.* (1992), 44 C.P.R. (3d) 371 (F.C.T.D.).
66. *Havana House Cigar & Tobacco Merchants Ltd. v. Skyway Cigar Store* (1998), 81 C.P.R. (3d) 203 (F.C.T.D.).
67. *Citrus Growers Association Ltd. v. William G. Branson Ltd.* (1990), 36 C.P.R. (3d) 434 (F.C.T.D.).
68. See Chapter 4, part 2.
69. Subsection 17(1) and see *Robert C. Wian Enterprises Inc. v. Mady* (1965), 46 C.P.R. 147 (Ex. Ct.).
70. Subsection 17(1).

trademark in Canada did so with knowledge of such previous use or making known.[71] This is the only limitation prescribed by *Act* concerning expungement and there are no other limitation periods for bringing an application to expunge a registered trademark.[72]

No person is entitled to institute any proceeding in the Federal Court calling into question any decision given by the Registrar of which such person had express notice and from which they had a right to appeal.[73] However, a prior decision of the Registrar under section 45 is not a bar to an application for expungement.[74]

### e) Grounds for Expungement

Section 18 lists the grounds under which the validity of a registration of a trademark may be attacked. The section provides that a registration of a trademark is invalid if:

(a) the trademark was not registrable at the date of registration;[75]
(b) the trademark is not distinctive at the time proceedings bringing the validity of the registration into question are commenced;[76] or
(c) the trademark has been abandoned; and
(d) subject to section 17, the applicant for registration was not the person entitled to secure the registration.[77]

Non-statutory grounds of invalidity have been recognized, including misappropriation of a trademark in violation of a fiduciary duty or fraudulent or material misrepresentation for the purposes of registration.[78] Depreciation of the value of the goodwill attached to the mark or deception of the public in

---

71. Subsection 17(2).
72. *Boston Pizza International Inc. v. Boston Market Corp.* (2003), 27 C.P.R. (4th) 52 (F.C.T.D.) but see the case referred in footnote 60.
73. Subsection 57(2) and see *Cafe de Brasil, S.p.A. v. Walong Marketing Inc.*, (2006) FC 1063, 53 C.P.R. (4th) 322 (F.C.).
74. *Noxzema Chemical Co. v. Sheran Manufacturing* (1968), 55 C.P.R. 147 (Ex. Ct.); *Saxon Industries Inc. v. Aldo Ippolito & Co.* (1982), 66 C.P.R. (2d) 79 (F.C.T.D.); *Long v. Tucker* [1985] 2 F.C. 534 (F.C.T.D.).
75. See Chapter 3.
76. See Chapter 2, part 2(c) and *Magder v. Breck's Sporting Goods Co.* [1976] 1 S.C.R. 527 (S.C.C.).
77. See Chapter 6.
78. *Remo Imports Ltd. v. Jaguar Cars Limited*, 2007 FCA 258, 60 C.P.R. (4th) 130 (F.C.A.) but not for an innocent or negligent misrepresentation which is cured by amendment, *Parfums de Coeur, Ltd. v. Christopher Asta* 2009 FC 21, 71 C.P.R. (4th) 82 (F.C.).

the context of a claim for passing off are not grounds of invalidity under section 18 of the *Act*.[79]

### (i) Not Registrable

A trademark that was not registrable at the date of its registration is invalid and may be expunged.[80] When it is alleged a registered trademark was not registrable because it is confusing with a previously registered trademark, a mere possibility of confusion is not sufficient to invalidate a registration.[81]

Where both parties to an action attack the registration of the other a court is entitled to rely on the facts adopted by the unsuccessful plaintiff who alleged that the defendant's mark was confusing with the plaintiff's registered mark and expunge its registration.[82]

### (ii) Not Distinctive

A trademark that is not distinctive at the time proceedings bringing the validity of its registration into question are commenced is invalid.[83] The determination is made at the time when proceedings are issued. If significant time passes, the registrant may be able to make the registration distinctive of it.[84]

A trademark may lose its distinctiveness if the owner allows the widespread use of the mark by rival traders. Widespread infringement of significant duration by just one trader may be sufficient.[85]

---

79. *Remo Imports Ltd. v. Jaguar Cars Limited,* 2007 FCA 258, 60 C.P.R. (4th) 130 (F.C.A.), paragraph 38.
80. Subsection 18(1)(a); and see Chapter 3 and *Adidas (Can.) Ltd. v. Colins Inc.* (1978), 38 C.P.R. (2d) 145 (F.C.T.D.); *Carling O'Keefe Breweries of Can. Ltd. v. AnheuserBusch Inc.; Carling O'Keefe Breweries of Can. Ltd. v. Labatt Brewing Co.* (1982), 68 C.P.R. (2d) 1 (F.C.T.D.); 10 C.P.R. (3d) 433 (F.C.A.).
81. *Remo Imports Ltd. v. Jaguar Cars Limited,* 2007 FCA 258, 60 C.P.R. (4th) 130 (F.C.A.).
82. *Remo Imports Ltd. v. Jaguar Cars Limited,* 2007 FCA 258, 60 C.P.R. (4th) 130 (F.C.A.).
83. Subsection 18(l)(b); and see Chapter 2, part (2)(b) *Consorzio del Prosciutto di Parma v. Maple Leaf Meats Inc.* (2001), 11 C.P.R. (4th) 48 (F.C.T.D.), 18 C.P.R. (4th) 414 (F.C.A.); *Boston Pizza International Inc. v. Boston Chicken Inc.* (2002), 24 C.P.R. (4th) 150 (F.C.A.).
84. See *Cross-Canada Auto Body Supply (Winsdor) Limited v. Hyundai Auto Canada,* 2007 FC 580, 60 C.P.R. (4th) (F.C.), 2008 F.C.A. 98, 65 C.P.R. (4th) 121 (F.C.A.) where the Court considered the considerable period of time that the registrant had to make the registration distinctive of it and factually distinguished the case from previous decisions in *Wilkinson Sword (Canada) Ltd. v. Juda* (1966), 51 C.P.R. 55 (Ex. Ct.) and *Breck's Sporting Goods Co. v. Magder,* [1976] 1 S.C.R. 527 concerning trademarks that had been assigned from foreign parent companies to Canadian subsidiaries.
85. *Auld Philips Ltd. v. Suzanne's Inc* (2005), 39 C.P.R. (4th) 45 (F.C.), affirmed (2005), 46 C.P.R. (4th) 81 (F.C.A.)

If a trademark registration has been obtained by an agent who was using the mark on behalf of a principal, the registration may be invalid as it is not distinctive of the agent.[86]

Subsection 18(2) of the *Act* provides that no registration of a trademark that has been so used in Canada by the registrant or his predecessor in title as to have become distinctive at the date of registration shall be held invalid merely on the ground that evidence of such distinctiveness was not submitted to the competent authority or tribunal before the grant of the registration. The existence of subsection 18(2) does not preclude the responding party from invoking subsection 12(2) during expungement proceedings.[87]

### (iii)  Abandonment

The registration of a trademark is invalid if the trademark has been abandoned.[88]

In order to establish abandonment of a mark, an applicant must prove two elements: the mark is no longer in use in Canada, and an intention to abandon the mark.[89] The abandonment of a trademark is a question of fact to be decided in view of the particular circumstances of each case; non-use is not sufficient to establish abandonment, though an intention to abandon can be inferred from a long period of non-use.[90] The onus of proving abandonment is on the attacking party.[91]

### (iv)  Entitlement

A registration of a trademark may be invalid if the applicant for registration was not the person entitled to secure the registration. This may occur if the applicant did not satisfy the requirements of section 16.[92] In addition a

---

86.  *Turban Brand Products Ltd. v. Khan* (1980), 52 C.P.R. (2d) 71 (F.C.T.D.); *Wilhelm Layher GmbH v. Anthes Industries Inc.* (1986), 8 C.P.R. (3d) 187 (F.C.T.D.); *Citrus Growers Assn. Ltd. v. William D. Branson Ltd.* (1990), 36 C.P.R. (3d) 434 (F.C.T.D.).

87.  *Emall.ca Inc. v. Cheap Tickets and Travel Inc.*, 2007 FC 243, 56 C.P.R. (4th) 82 (F.C.) appeal dismissed 2008 FCA 50 (F.C.A.).

88.  Subsection 18(1)(c).

89.  *Cross-Canada Auto Body Supply (Windsor) Ltd. et al. v. Hyundai Auto Canada* (2007), 60 C.P.R. (4th) 406; *J.A. & M. Cote Ltee v. B.F. Goodrich Co.* (1949), 14 C.P.R. 33 (Ex. Ct.); *Promafil Canada Ltée v. Munsingwear Inc.* (1992), 44 C.P.R. (3d) 59 (F.C.A.).

90.  *Tommy Hilfiger Licensing Inc. v. Produits de Qualite I.M.D. Inc.* (2005), 37 C.P.R. (4th) 1 (F.C.); *Omega Engineering, Inc. v. Omega SA* (2006), 56 C.P.R. (4th) 210 (F.C.).

91.  *Western Clock Co. v. Oris Watch Co. Ltd.* [1931] 2 D.L.R. 775, [1931] Ex. C.R. 64.

92.  Subsection 18(1) and section 17. Also see Chapter 6.

registration may be invalid if it was obtained by the inclusion of a materially false statement of use that was fundamental to the registration[93] or on the basis of a fraudulent misrepresentation.[94]

---

93. *Unitel Communications Inc. v. Bell Canada* (1995), 61 C.P.R. (3d) 12 (F.C.T.D.); *WCC Containers Sales Limited v. Haul-All Equipment Ltd.* (2003), 28 C.P.R. (4th) 175 (F.C.T.D.). In such a case it may not be necessary to show either fraud or intent to deceive. The registration may be void *ab initio* but not in other cases where the registrant is entitled to the benefit of section 19, *Remo Imports Ltd. v. Jaguar Cars Limited,* (2007), 60 C.P.R. (4th) 130, 2007 FCA 258 (F.C.A.).

94. *WCC Containers Sales Limited v. Haul-All Equipment Ltd.* (2003), 28 C.P.R. (4th) 175 (F.C.T.D.).

# CHAPTER
# 11

# Confusing Trademarks

# 1. Introduction

The *Trade-marks Act* provides that the word "confusing," when applied as an adjective to a trademark or trade name, means a trademark or trade name the use of which would cause confusion in the manner and circumstances described in the *Act*.[1] The potential for confusion must be considered in the following situations, among others:

    (a)  when a determination is being made concerning whether a proposed mark is potentially available for use;

    (b)  when an examiner issues an office action asserting that the applied-for mark is confusing with another mark;[2]

    (c)  in opposition proceedings where the opponent alleges that the applicant's mark is confusing with the opponent's mark;[3]

    (d)  in an action for infringement;[4]

    (e)  in proceedings seeking the expungement of a registered trade mark.[5]

# 2. Confusing Trademarks

## a) The Statutory Framework

The *Act* provides that the use of a trademark causes confusion with another trademark if the use of both marks in the same area would be likely to lead to the inference that the wares or services associated with such trademarks are manufactured, sold, leased, hired, or performed by the same person, whether or not such wares or services are of the same general class.[6] The use of a trademark causes confusion with a trade name and the use of a trade name causes confusion with a trademark under corresponding conditions.[7] The concluding phrase "whether or not such wares or services are of the same general class" clarifies that the general class of wares and services, while relevant is not controlling.[8]

---

1. Section 2.
2. See Chapter 7, part 3.
3. See Chapter 12.
4. Section 20 and Chapter 13.
5. See Chapter 10, part 2(e).
6. Subsection 6(2) and see *Mattel, Inc. v 3894207 Canada Inc.* (2006), 49 C.P.R. (4th) 321 (S.C.C.) and applied in *Veuve Clicquot Ponsardin Maison Foneée en 1772 v. Boutiques Cliquot Ltée* (2000), 7 C.P.R. (4th) 189 (F.C.T.D.), (2004), 35 C.P.R. (4th) 1 (F.C.A.), (2006), 49 C.P.R. (4th) 401 (S.C.C.).
7. Subsections 6(3) and (4).
8. *Mattel, Inc. v 3894207 Canada Inc.* (2006), 49 C.P.R. (4th) 321 (S.C.C.).

The purpose of trademarks is to create and symbolize linkages. A trademark is a symbol of a connection between a source of a product and the product itself.[9] Confusion can be seen as mistaken inferences about the source of a product which take place in the marketplace.[10] In this context a mistaken inference can only be drawn if a link or association is likely to arise in the consumer's mind between the source of the wares or services of the senior mark and the source of the wares or services of the junior mark. Establishing the likelihood is a matter of evidence not speculation.[11] If there is no likelihood of a link, there can be no likelihood of a mistaken inference, and thus no confusion within the meaning of the *Act*.[12]

The court or the Registrar, as the case may be, must make a determination of the effect of the marks from the perspective of a mythical consumer who normally makes up the market.[13] The point of view of the average hurried consumer having an imperfect recollection of the marks in issue is applied.[14] The reaction of a "moron in a hurry" or the rash, careless, or unobservant purchaser should not be considered unless there are special circumstances.[15]

Evidence of actual confusion is persuasive and relevant but is not necessary to show confusion.[16] Conversely, an adverse inference may be drawn from the lack of evidence of instances of confusion in circumstances where it would readily be available if the allegation of likely confusion were justified.[17]

The *Act* directs that in determining whether trademarks or trade names are confusing, the court or the Registrar, as the case may be, must have regard to all of the surrounding circumstances, including:

(a) the inherent distinctiveness of the trademarks or trade names and the extent to which they have become known;
(b) the length of time the trademarks or trade names have been in use;
(c) the nature of the wares, services, or business;
(d) the nature of the trade; and

---

9. *Kirkbi AG v. Ritvik Holdings Inc.* [2005] 3 S.C.R 302 (S.C.C.); *Mattel, Inc. v 3894207 Canada Inc.* (2006), 49 C.P.R. (4th) 321 (S.C.C.).
10. *Mattel, Inc. v 3894207 Canada Inc.* (2006), 49 C.P.R. (4th) 321 (S.C.C.).
11. *Veuve Clicquot Ponsardin Maison Foneé en 1772 v. Boutiques Cliquot Ltée* (2000), 7 C.P.R. (4th) 189 (F.C.T.D.), (2004), 35 C.P.R. (4th) 1 (F.C.A.), (2006), 49 C.P.R. (4th) 401 (S.C.C.).
12. *Mattel, Inc. v 3894207 Canada Inc.* (2006), 49 C.P.R. (4th) 321 (S.C.C.).
13. *Alticor Inc. v. Nutravite Pharmaceuticals Inc.* (2005), 42 C.P.R. (4th) 107 (F.C.A.)
14. *Mattel, Inc. v 3894207 Canada Inc.* (2006), 49 C.P.R. (4th) 321 (S.C.C.)
15. *Mattel, Inc. v 3894207 Canada Inc.* (2006), 49 C.P.R. (4th) 321 (S.C.C.).
16. *Mr Submarine Ltd. v. Amandista Investments Limited* (1986), 11 C.P.R. (3d) 425 (F.C.T.D.), reversed (1987), 19 C.P.R. (3d) 3 (F.C.A.); *Mattel, Inc. v 3894207 Canada Inc.* (2006), 49 C.P.R. (4th) 321 (S.C.C.); *Canadian Tire Corp. v. Accessoires D'Autos Nordiques Inc.* 2006 FC 1431 (F.C.) appeal dismissed (2007), 62 C.P.R. (4th) 436 (F.C.A) relating to the use of survey evidence in this context.
17. *Mattel, Inc. v 3894207 Canada Inc.* (2006), 49 C.P.R. (4th) 321 (S.C.C.).

(e)  the degree of resemblance between the trademarks or trade names in appearance or sound or in the ideas suggested by them.[18]

As set out in the *Act*, the statutory factors listed above are not limiting and different circumstances will be given different weight in a context-specific assessment.[19] The totality of the circumstances will dictate how each factor should be treated[20] and in some cases some factors will carry greater weight than others. Each of the factors need not be given equal weight.[21] However, in many cases, the degree of resemblance between the trademarks in appearance, sound, or in ideas suggested by them is the dominant factor.[22]

The perspective of the average Anglophone consumer or the average Francophone consumer, or in special circumstances the average bilingual consumer, should be considered. But, the perspective of the average bilingual consumer is only considered where a trademark consists of unusual or distinct words which would create confusion for someone who knew what they meant in both English and French.[23]

The trademarks or trade names in question must be considered as a whole as they are perceived by a mythical consumer who normally makes up the market. It is not a correct approach to put the trademarks side by side or break them up into components and make a careful comparison in order to observe similarities and differences.[24]

The determination of whether two trademarks or trade names are confusing involves the exercise of personal judgment in light of all the evidence having regard to the totality of the circumstances and statutory factors. This is a judicial determination of a question of fact or question of mixed fact and law[25] not the exercise of discretion.[26]

---

18. Subsection 6(5) and see *Cushman & Wakefield, Inc. v. Wakefield Realty Corp.* (2004), 37 C.P.R (4th) 212 (F.C.A.).
19. *Mattel, Inc. v 3894207 Canada Inc.* (2006), 49 C.P.R. (4th) 321 (S.C.C.); *Veuve Clicquot Ponsardin Maison Foneée en 1772 v. Boutiques Cliquot Ltée* (2000), 7 C.P.R. (4th) 189 (F.C.T.D.), (2004), 35 C.P.R. (4th) 1 (F.C.A.), (2006), 49 C.P.R. (4th) 401 (S.C.C.).
20. *Veuve Clicquot Ponsardin Maison Foneée en 1772 v. Boutiques Cliquot Ltée* (2000), 7 C.P.R. (4th) 189 (F.C.T.D.), (2004), 35 C.P.R. (4th) 1 (F.C.A.), (2006), 49 C.P.R. (4th) 401 (S.C.C.).
21. *Miss Universe Inc. v. Bohna* (1994), 58 C.P.R. (3d) 381 (F.C.A.).
22. *Beverly Bedding & Upholstery Co. v. Regal Bedding & Upholstering Ltd.* (1980), 47 C.P.R. (2d) 145 (F.C.T.D.); (1982), 60 C.P.R. (2d) 70 (F.C.A.); *Canadian Tire Corp. v. Accessoires D'Autos Nordiques Inc.* 2006 FC 1431 (F.C.) appeal dismissed (2007), 62 C.P.R. (4th) 436 (F.C.A.).
23. *Smithkline Beecham Corporation v. Pierre Fabre Medicament* (2001), 11 C.P.R. (4th) 1 (F.C.A.); *Pierre Fabre Medicament v. Smithkline Beecham Corporation*, 2004 FC 811 (F.C.).
24. *British Drug Houses Ltd. v. Battle Pharmaceuticals Ltd.* [1944] Ex. C.R. 239 (Ex. Ct.); affirmed [1946] S.C.R. 50 (S.C.C.); *Canadian Tire Corp. v. Accessoires D'Autos Nordiques Inc.* 2006 FC 1431 (F.C.) appeal dismissed (2007), 62 C.P.R. (4th) 436 (F.C.A.).
25. *Mattel, Inc. v 3894207 Canada Inc.* (2006), 49 C.P.R. (4th) 321 (S.C.C.).
26. See *Coca-Cola Co. v. Pepsi-Cola Co.*, [1938] Ex. C.R. 263 (Ex. Ct.); reversed [1940] S.C.R 17 (S.C.C.); affirmed [1942] 2 W.W.R. 257 (P.C.); *Benson & Hedges v. St. Regis* (1968), 57 C.P.R. 1 (S.C.C.).

The determination of whether trademarks or trade names are confusing depends on the facts of each case. However, previously decided cases can be helpful by illustrating the application of the statutory factors and principles established by the courts.[27]

## b) Inherent Distinctiveness

The first factor to be considered is the inherent distinctiveness of the trademarks or trade names in issue and the extent to which they have become known.

Distinctiveness is the essence and cardinal requirement of a trademark.[28] Invented, unique, or non-descriptive words tend to be more inherently distinctive than weak marks made up of common everyday words or which have a geographic or descriptive connation.

The extent of the inherent distinctiveness of a mark will strongly influence the ambit of protection available to the mark.[29] No person is entitled to fence in common words in the English or French language and such words cannot be protected over a wide area.[30] When a mark is inherently weak, in the absence of acquired distinctiveness, small differences will be sufficient to distinguish it from other marks.[31]

Where a trademark consists of words which are common and which are also contained in a number of other trademarks in use in the same market, it will be less distinctive and entitled to less protection than in the case of a strong mark.[32] Trademarks consisting of initials[33] or numbers[34] fall within this category and will be typically be entitled to a small ambit of protection.

Similarly, if competitors use trademarks which are similar to the trademark in issue, this will limit the degree of distinctiveness of the trademark[35]

---

27. *Cochrane Dunlop Hardware Ltd. v. Capital Diversified Industries* (1976), 30 C.P.R. (2d) 176 (Ont. C.A.).

28. *Mattel, Inc. v 3894207 Canada Inc.* (2006), 49 C.P.R. (4th) 321 (S.C.C.).

29. *General Motors v. Bellows*, [1947] Ex. C.R. 568 (Ex. Ct.); affirmed [1949] S.C.R. 678 (S.C.C.); *Mattel, Inc. v. 3894207 Canada Inc.* (2006), 49 C.P.R. (4th) 321 (S.C.C.).

30. *Mattel, Inc. v. 3894207 Canada Inc.* (2006), 49 C.P.R. (4th) 321 (S.C.C.).

31. *Max Mara Fashion Group S.R.L. v. Provigo Distribution Inc.*, (2005), 46 C.P.R. (4th) 112 (F.C.).

32. *Kellogg Salada Canada Inc. v. Maximum Nutrition Ltd.* (1992), 43 C.P.R. (3d) 349 (F.C.A.); *Molson Cos. Ltd. v. John Labatt Ltd.* (1994), 58 C.P.R. (3d) 527 (F.C.A.); *Tradition Fine Foods Ltd. v. Groupe Traditional'l Inc.* (2006), 51 C.P.R. (4th) 342 (F.C.); *Ratiopharm Inc. v. Laboratoiries Riva Inc.*, (2006), 51 C.P.R. (4th) 415 (F.C.).

33. *GSW Ltd. v. Great West Steel Industries Ltd.* (1975), 22 C.P.R. (2d) 154.(F.C.T.D.).

34. *Pizza Pizza Ltd. v. Registrar of Trade-marks* (1989), 26 C.P.R. ( 3d) 355 (F.C.A.).

35. *Foodcorp Ltd. v. Chalet Bar BQ (Can.) Inc.* (1981), 55 C.P.R. (2d) 46 (F.C.T.D.); additional reasons at 56 C.P.R. (2d) 14 (F.C.T.D.); *Sunshine Biscuits Inc. v. Corporate Foods Ltd.* (1982),

or may cause the mark to become non-distinctive and not entitled to protection.[36]

When it is asserted that the distinctiveness of a mark is limited due to common use, evidence of actual use of the marks must be presented before inferences about the marketplace can be made, unless there are a large number of existing registrations.[37]

If a trademark consists of a new combination of words or designs, even though some of the components are common to the trade, the combination, when looked at as a whole, may have some distinctiveness.[38]

Trademark owners must diligently protect their trademarks from piracy or risk having their marks lose their distinctiveness and potentially their legal protection.[39] Similarly, if the owner of a trademark allows it to be used as the name of the wares or services in question, it may lose its distinctiveness and become generic.[40]

The "extent to which they have become known" relates to the acquired distinctiveness of the mark.[41] A mark, which is not inherently distinctive, may acquire distinctiveness through extensive use in the marketplace which makes the mark known to purchasers of the wares or services in issue.[42]

If the trademark owner owns a family of trademarks derived from an existing mark, a mark which is a part of the family, may be entitled to a broader ambit of protection.[43]

61 C.P.R. (2d) 53 (F.C.T.D.); *Farside Clothing Ltd. v. Caricline Ventures Ltd.* (2001), 16 C.P.R. (4th) 482 (F.C.T.D.), affirmed (2002), 22 C.P.R. (4th) 321 (F.C.A.).

36. *CocaCola Co. v. PepsiCola Co. of Can. Ltd.* [1940] S.C.R. 17 (S.C.C.); affirmed [1942] 2 W.W.R. 257 (P.C.).
37. *CocaCola Co. v. PepsiCola Co. of Can. Ltd.* [1940] S.C.R. 17 (S.C.C.); affirmed [1942] 2 W.W.R. 257 (P.C.); *Astro Dairy Products Ltd. v. Compagnie Gervais Danone*, (1999), 87 C.P.R. (3d) 262 (F.C.T.D.). Typically 20 or more registrations must exist.
38. *CocaCola Co. of Can. Ltd. v. PepsiCola Co. of Can. Ltd.* [1938] Ex. C.R. 263 (Ex. Ct.); reversed [1940] S.C.R. 17 (S.C.C.); affirmed [1942] 2 W.W.R. 257 (P.C.).
39. *Mattel, Inc. v 3894207 Canada Inc.* (2006), 49 C.P.R. (4th) 321 (S.C.C.); *Veuve Clicquot Ponsardin Maison Foneée en 1772 v. Boutiques Cliquot Ltée* (2000), 7 C.P.R. (4th) 189 (F.C.T.D.), (2004), 35 C.P.R. (4th) 1 (F.C.A.), (2006), 49 C.P.R. (4th) 401 (S.C.C.); *Cochrane-Dunlop Hardware Ltd. v. Capital Diversified Industries Ltd.* (1976), 30 C.P.R. (2d) 176 (Ont. C.A.); *Mr. Submarine Ltd. v. Amandista Investment Ltd.* (1986), 11 C.P.R. (3d) 425 (F.C.T.D.); 19 C.P.R. (3d) 3 (F.C.A.).
40. *Cheerio Toys & Games Ltd. v. Dubiner* (1964), 44 C.P.R. 134 (Ex. Ct.); [1966] S.C.R. 206 (S.C.C.).
41. See Chapter 2, part 2(c).
42. *Mattel, Inc. v 3894207 Canada Inc.* (2006), 49 C.P.R. (4th) 321 (S.C.C.) and see Chapter 2, part 2(c).
43. *McDonald's Corp. v. Yogi Yorgurt Ltd* (1982), 66 C.P.R. (2d) 101 (F.C.T.D.), *McDonald's Corp. v. Silcorp. Ltd.* (1989), 24 C.P.R. (3d) 207 (F.C.T.D.), 41 C.P.R. (3d) 67 (F.C.A.); *McDonald's Corp. v. Coffee Hut Stores Ltd* (1994), 55 C.P.R. (3d) 463, (1996), 68 C.P.R. (3d) 168 (F.C.A.).

## c) Duration of Use

The second factor to be considered is the length of time the marks in issue have been in use.[44] The duration of use is important since distinctiveness may be acquired as result of extensive use.[45] But if the trademarks in issue have been used concurrently for a lengthy period of time and evidence of instances of confusion is not brought forward, an inference may be drawn that confusion is not likely.[46]

## d) The Nature of the Wares, Service, or Business

The third factor to be considered is the nature of the wares, services or business.[47] The general class of wares and services, while relevant, is not controlling.[48]

The fact that there is an overlap in the wares or services must be considered but is not sufficient by itself to establish a likelihood of confusion.[49] A statement of wares or services should be read with a view to determining the probable type of trade or business intended to be reached rather than all possible trades that might be covered.[50] However, when there are no restrictions as to trade or price in the respective statements of wares, the two statements must be compared as listed.[51]

Where a trademark is inherently weak and does not have acquired distinctiveness, differences in the wares, services or businesses of a junior mark may be sufficient to avoid the likelihood of confusion.[52]

If the wares or services are expensive and a mythical purchaser would carefully consider a purchase, relatively minor differences between marks

44. Subsection 6(5)(b).
45. *Mattel, Inc. v 3894207 Canada Inc.* (2006), 49 C.P.R. (4th) 321 (S.C.C.).
46. *Mattel, Inc. v 3894207 Canada Inc.* (2006), 49 C.P.R. (4th) 321 (S.C.C.).
47. Subsection 6(5)(c); *Oshawa Holdings Ltd. v. Fjord Pacific Marine Industries Ltd.* (1980), 47 C.P.R. (2d) 86 (F.C.T.D.); affirmed 36 N.R. 71 (F.C.A.); *Mr. Submarine v. Amandista Investments Ltd.* (1987), 19 C.P.R. (3d) 1 (F.C.A.); *United Artists Corp. v. Pink Panther Beauty Corp.* (1998), 80 C.P.R. (3d) 247 (F.C.A.).
48. *Mattel, Inc. v 3894207 Canada Inc.* (2006), 49 C.P.R. (4th) 321 (S.C.C.).
49. *Max Mara Fashion Group S.R.L. v. Provigo Distribution Inc.* (2005), 46 C.P.R. (4th) 112 (F.C.).
50. *Unisys Corp. v. Northwood Technologies Inc.* (2002), 29 C.P.R. (4th) 115 (T.M.O.B.).
51. *Mr Submarine Ltd. v. Amandista Investments Ltd.* (1987), 19 C.P.R. (3d) 3 (F.C.A.); *Maison Cousin (1980) Inc. v. Cousins Submarines Inc.*, 2006 FCA 409, 60 C.P.R (4th) 369 (F.C.A.).
52. *Clorox Co. v. Sears Canada Inc.* 33 C.P.R. (3d) 48 (T.M.O.B.), 41 C.P.R. (3d) 483 (F.C.T.D.) 49 C.P.R. (3d) 217 (F.C.A.).

may be sufficient to distinguish them.[53] Conversely, if the wares or services are inexpensive and purchased hurriedly, this must be considered as well.[54]

In an opposition, the applicant's statement of wares or services and the wares or services shown to be used by the opponent in association with its mark govern the determination.[55]

## e) Famous Trademarks

Where a trademark has become famous by virtue of the goodwill associated with it, this fame may be capable of carrying the protection available to the mark across product lines while lesser marks would be limited by the wares or services for which they are registered.[56]

The totality of the circumstances will dictate how each of the statutory factors should be treated. Fame is a "surrounding circumstance" of importance, and differences in the wares and services will not always be the dominant consideration. A difference in the wares or services or the fame of the mark do not supersede, or "trump," all other factors. Each situation must be judged in its full factual context.[57]

Not all famous marks will be able to make a jump across product lines and the difference between the respective wares and services will continue to be a significant obstacle to overcome. As observed by the Supreme Court of Canada, "luxury champagne and mid-priced women's wear are as different as chalk and cheese."[58] The fame of a mark may be quite specific because of a very specific association with a product. But a famous mark which is widely used may be able to transcend product line differences.[59]

In this context, a mistaken inference can only be drawn if a link or association is likely to arise in the consumer's mind between the source of the famous product and the source of the less well-known product. If there is no

---

53. *General Motors Corp. v. Bellows*, [1947] Ex. C.R. 568 (Ex. Ct.); affirmed [1949] S.C.R. 678 (S.C.C.).
54. *General Motors Corp. v. Bellows*, [1947] Ex. C.R. 568 (Ex. Ct.); affirmed [1949] S.C.R. 678 (S.C.C.).
55. *Mr. Submarine Ltd. v. Amandista Investments Ltd.*, (1987), 19 C.P.R (3d) (F.C.A.).
56. *Mattel, Inc. v 3894207 Canada Inc.* (2006), 49 C.P.R. (4th) 321 (S.C.C.).
57. *Mattel, Inc. v 3894207 Canada Inc.* (2006), 49 C.P.R. (4th) 321 (S.C.C.); *Veuve Clicquot Ponsardin Maison Foneée en 1772 v. Boutiques Cliquot Ltée* (2000), 7 C.P.R. (4th) 189 (F.C.T.D.), (2004), 35 C.P.R. (4th) 1 (F.C.A.), (2006), 49 C.P.R. (4th) 401 (S.C.C.).
58. *Veuve Clicquot Ponsardin Maison Foneée en 1772 v. Boutiques Cliquot Ltée* (2000), 7 C.P.R. (4th) 189 (F.C.T.D.), (2004), 35 C.P.R. (4th) 1 (F.C.A.), (2006), 49 C.P.R. (4th) 401 (S.C.C.).
59. *Veuve Clicquot Ponsardin Maison Foneée en 1772 v. Boutiques Cliquot Ltée* (2000), 7 C.P.R. (4th) 189 (F.C.T.D.), (2004), 35 C.P.R. (4th) 1 (F.C.A.), (2006), 49 C.P.R. (4th) 401 (S.C.C.).

likelihood of a link, there can be no likelihood of a mistaken inference, and therefore no confusion within the meaning of the *Act*.[60]

The consideration of future events and possibilities of diversification is restricted to the potential expansion of existing operations. It does not include speculation as to diversification into entirely new ventures.[61]

## f) Nature of the Trade

The fourth factor to be considered is the nature of the trade.[62] The nature and kind of customer likely to purchase the wares or services,[63] whether different niche markets are involved,[64] the channels of distribution,[65] and the way in which the trademarks are used[66] are relevant in considering this factor. Geographical proximity is also relevant and if the premises of the parties are located close together, this may increase the prospect of confusion.[67]

Evidence concerning the actual channels of distribution should be considered, not speculation about future activities.[68] The question in an opposition is not whether the parties in issue sell their products in the same channels but whether they are entitled to do so.[69]

If the potential purchasers of the wares or services in issue are professionals carrying on business, this may lessen the prospect of confusion.[70] Similar considerations may apply to the wholesale trade as opposed to the retail trade.

---

60. *Mattel, Inc. v. 3894207 Canada Inc.*, (2006), 49 C.P.R. (4th) 321 (S.C.C.).
61. *Mattel, Inc. v 3894207 Canada Inc.* (2006), 49 C.P.R. (4th) 321 (S.C.C.).
62. Subsection 6(5)(d).
63. *General Motors v. Bellows* [1947] Ex. C.R. 568 (Ex. Ct.); affirmed [1949] S.C.R. 678 (S.C.C.); *Mattel, Inc. v. 3894207 Canada Inc.* (2006), 49 C.P.R. (4th) 321 (S.C.C.).
64. *Mattel, Inc. v 3894207 Canada Inc.* (2006), 49 C.P.R. (4th) 321 (S.C.C.) and see *BMW Canada Inc. v. Nissan Canada Inc.* (2007), 57 C.P.R. (4th) 81 (F.C.) appeal allowed on other grounds 60 C.P.R. (4th) 181, 2007 FCA 255 (F.C.A.).
65. *McDonald's Corp. v. Coffee Hut Stores Ltd* (1994), 55 C.P.R. (3d) 463, (1996), 68 C.P.R. (3d) 168 (F.C.A.)
66. *Coca-Cola Co. v. Pepsi-Cola Co.*, [1938] Ex. C.R. 263 (Ex. Ct.); reversed on other grounds [1940] S.C.R.17 (S.C.C.); affirmed [1942] 2 W.W.R. 257 (P.C.); *British Drug Houses Ltd. v. Battle Pharmaceuticals*, [1944] Ex. C.R. 239 (Ex. Ct.) affirmed [1946] S.C.R. 50 (S.C.C.); *United Artists Corp. v. Pink Panther Beauty Corp.* (1998), 80 C.P.R. (3d) 247 (F.C.A.).
67. *Cartem Inc. v. Souhaits Renaissance Inc.* (1982), 60 C.P.R. (2d) 1 (F.C.T.D.).
68. *Alticor Inc. v. Nutravite Pharmaceuticals Inc.* (2005), 42 C.P.R. (4th) 107 (F.C.A.).
69. *Clorox Co. v. E.I. Dupont de Nemours and Co.* (1995), 64 C.P.R. (3d) 79 (F.C.T.D.); *United Artists Corp v. Pink Panther Beauty Corp.* (1998), 80 C.P.R. (3d) 247 (F.C.A.).
70. *United Artists Corp v. Pink Panther Beauty Corp.* (1998), 80 C.P.R. (3d) 247 (F.C.A.); *Ratiopharm Inc. v. Laboratoiries Riva Inc.* (2006), 51 C.P.R. (4th) 415 (F.C.).

## g) Degree of Resemblance

The fifth factor to be considered is the degree of resemblance between the trademarks or trade names in appearance or sound, or in the ideas suggested by them. As discussed above, this may be the dominant factor.

### (i) Appearance

When trademarks consist of a combination of elements, it is not a proper approach to break them up into their elements, concentrate attention upon the elements that are different and conclude that, because there are differences in such elements, the marks as a whole are different. Trademarks may be similar when looked at in their totality even if differences may appear in some of the elements when viewed separately. It is the combination of the elements that constitutes the trademark and gives distinctiveness to it, and it is the effect of the trademark as a whole, rather than of any part in it, that must be considered[71] as perceived by a mythical consumer and not viewed side by side or broken into components. That is not to say that in some cases it is still possible to focus on particular features of the marks which may have a important influence on purchasers.[72]

Although the first component of a mark is often considered more important, when a word is a common, descriptive, or suggestive word, the significance of the first component decreases.[73] However, if the first or main component of a word mark is more distinctive, it may be relatively unimportant that the two marks in issue have different suffixes.[74]

The addition of "get up" or the fact that the plaintiff's mark is used with other marks should not be relevant in an action for infringement.[75]

### (ii) Sound

The degree of resemblance of the marks as sounded must be considered.[76] The words may be quite different in appearance but if they are pronounced in

---

71. *Canadian Tire Corp. v. Accessoires D'Autos Nordiques Inc.* 2006 FC 1431 (F.C.) appeal dismissed (2007), 62 C.P.R. (4th) 436 (F.C.A); *British Drug Houses Ltd. v. Battle Pharmaceuticals*, [1944] Ex. C.R. 239 (Ex. Ct.); affirmed [1946] S.C.R. 50 (S.C.C.).
72. *United Artists Corp v. Pink Panther Beauty Corp.* (1998), 80 C.P.R. (3d) 247 (F.C.A.); *Vibe Ventures LLC v. 3681441 Canada Inc.* 2005 FC 1650, 45 C.P.R. (4th) 18 (F.C.).
73. *Park Avenue Furniture Corp. v. Wickes/ Simmons Bedding Ltd.*, (1991), 37 C.P.R. (3d) 413 (F.C.A.).
74. *Sealy Sleep Products Ltd. v. Simpson-Sears Ltd.* (1960), 33 C.P.R. 129 (Ex. Ct.); *Coca-Cola Co. v. Pepsi-Cola Co.* [1938] Ex. C.R. 263 (Ex. Ct.); reversed [1940] S.C.R. 17 (S.C.C.); affirmed [1942] 2 W.W.R. 257 (P.C.).
75. *United Artists Corp. v. Pink Panther Beauty Corp.* (1998), 80 C.P.R. (3d) 247 (F.C.A.); *Canadian Tire Corp. v. Automobility Distribution Inc.*, (2006), 51 C.P.R. (4th) 452 (T.M.O.B.).
76. Subsection 6(5)(e).

the same way, this may be an important factor.[77] Pronunciation will be important when the wares or services in issue are ordered by telephone.[78] Evidence of pronunciation, including the expert opinions of individuals skilled in linguistics, is admissible in French or English.[79]

### (iii) Idea

Similarity of idea is a factor if it would reasonably have an impact on the average purchaser.[80] The "same idea" may be important if a link or association is likely to arise in a consumer's mind between the source of the wares or services of the senior mark and the source of the wares or services of the junior mark.[81] But a link may work against the owner of the senior mark if the link evokes an extrinsic matter.[82] Survey evidence, presented through a qualified expert, can be used to demonstrate the idea that a mark suggests.[83]

## h) Other Circumstances

The decision of the Trade-mark Opposition Board that disallowed the applicant's application for a trademark on the basis of confusion with the opponent's mark will be accorded little weight in a subsequent action by the opponent for infringement relating to use of the same mark because the record and burden of proof are different. The legal system is not a stranger to different outcomes arising out of the same factual situation where different issues were considered and different evidence is introduced.[84]

The intention of the owner of the junior mark is of little relevance to the issue of confusion.[85]

---

77.  *British Drug Houses Ltd. v. Battle Pharmaceuticals*, [1944] Ex. C.R. 239 (Ex. Ct.); affirmed [1946] S.C.R. 50 (S.C.C.); *Ultravite Laboratories Ltd. v. Whitehall Laboratories Ltd.*, [1964] Ex. C.R. 913 (Ex. Ct.) reversed [1965] S.C.R. 734 (S.C.C.).
78.  *Mead Johnson & Co. v. G.D. Searle Co.* (1967), 65 D.L.R. (2d) 56 (Ex. Ct.).
79.  *Ethicon Inc. v. Cyanamid of Can. Ltd.* (1977), 35 C.P.R. (2d) 126 (F.C.T.D.); *Pierre Fabre Medicament v. Smithkline Beecham Corporation*, 2004 FC 811 (F.C.).
80.  *Kimberly-Clark of Can. Ltd. v. Molnlycke Aktiebolag* (1982), 61 C.P.R. (2d) 42 (F.C.T.D.); *Michelin & Cie v. Astro Tire & Rubber Co. of Can.* (1981), 67 C.P.R. (2d) 254 (T.M.O.B.); affirmed 69 C.P.R. (2d) 260 (F.C.T.D.).
81.  *Veuve Clicquot Ponsardin Maison Foneée en 1772 v. Boutiques Cliquot Ltée* (2000), 7 C.P.R. (4th) 189 (F.C.T.D.), (2004), 35 C.P.R. (4th) 1 (F.C.A.), (2006), 49 C.P.R. (4th) 401 (S.C.C.).
82.  *Canadian Tire Corp. v. Accessoires D'Autos Nordiques Inc.* 2006 FC 1431 (F.C.) appeal dismissed (2007), 62 C.P.R. (4th) 436 (F.C.A.).
83.  *Canadian Tire Corp. v. Accessoires D'Autos Nordiques Inc.* 2006 FC 1431 (F.C.) appeal dismissed (2007), 62 C.P.R. (4th) 436 (F.C.A.).
84.  *Alticor Inc. v. Nutravite Pharmaceuticals Inc.* (2005), 42 C.P.R. (4th) 107 (F.C.A.).
85.  *Mattel, Inc. v 3894207 Canada Inc.* (2006), 49 C.P.R. (4th) 321 (S.C.C.).

# CHAPTER
# 12

# Opposition Proceedings

# 1. Introduction

As the Supreme Court of Canada recently put it, a trademark owner is required by law to protect its marks from piracy or risk having those marks lose their distinctiveness.[1] In this regard, a trademark owner should review trademark applications as they are advertised in the Trade-marks Journal[2] as well as monitoring the marketplace.

Trademark oppositions can play an important role in maintaining the distinctiveness of a registered trademark. If consideration is being given to opposing an application, it is prudent to search for other marks owned or applied for by the applicant since they may be relevant to the decision.

# 2. Statement of Opposition

## a) Time for Filing and Extensions

The *Trade-marks Act* provides that within two months after the advertisement of an application for the registration of a trademark, any person may, on payment of the prescribed fee, file a statement of opposition with the Registrar.[3] Since the *Act* refers to "any person" an opponent is not required to show that they would be adversely affected by registration.[4]

An extension of the time to file the statement of opposition may be requested before the expiration of the two-month time limit. Care should be taken to ensure that the request specifies the date the application was advertised in the Trade-marks Journal and that the request was received and processed,[5] or the application may be allowed which may preclude any opposition.[6] When any extension of time is granted to any party, the Registrar may thereafter grant any reasonable extension of time to any other party in which to take any subsequent step.[7]

---

1. *Mattel, Inc. v. 3894207 Canada Inc.*, (2006), 49 C.P.R. (4th) 321 (S.C.C.).
2. http://napoleon.ic.gc.ca/cipo/tradejournal.nsf/$$ViewTemplate+for+TMJournal+English? OpenForm.
3. Subsection 38(1) and see Canadian Intellectual Property Office Practice Notice, Practice in Trade-marks Opposition Proceeding in effect March 31, 2009.
4. *Centennial Grocery Brokers Ltd. v. Reg. T.M.*, [1972] F.C. 257 (F.C.T.D.).
5. The status of the opposition should be reflected on the Canadian Intellectual Property Office trademark database currently located at http://www.ic.gc.ca/app/opic-cipo/trdmrks.
6. *Sadhu Singh Hamdard Trust v. Registrar of Trade-marks* 2006 FC 171, 47 C.P.R. (4th) 373 (F.C), affirmed on appeal 2007 FCA 355, 62 C.P.R (4th) 245 (F.C.A.).
7. *Trade- marks Regulations*, SOR/96-195 as amended, section 47.

An extension applied for after the expiration of the above-noted time limit or the time extended by the Registrar and before the application is allowed, will not be granted unless the Registrar is satisfied that the failure to do the act or apply for the extension within that time or the extended time was not reasonably avoidable.[8]

The Registrar cannot extend the time for filing a statement of opposition concerning an application that has been allowed.[9] An exception applies where an application has been allowed without considering a previously filed request for an extension of time to file a statement of opposition. In this case the Registrar may withdraw the application from allowance at any time before issuing a certificate of registration and extend the time for filing a statement of opposition.[10]

Once an opposition is commenced, the opposed application will not be allowed until the opposition is decided in favour of the applicant.[11]

## b) Grounds of Opposition

An opposition may be based on any of the following grounds:[12]

(i) The application does not conform to the requirements of section 30.[13]
    This includes grounds such as
    - The applicant did not describe the wares or services in ordinary commercial terms.[14]
    - The applicant did not use the mark from the date set out in the application.[15]
    - The applicant did not use the mark in its country of origin when the application is based on foreign registration and use.[16]

---

8. Subsection 47(2) and see *Fjord Pacific Marine Industries Ltd. v. Reg. T.M.*, [1975] F.C. 536 (F.C.T.D.).

9. Subsection 39(2).

10. Subsection 39(3).

11. Subsection 39(1).

12. Subsection 38(2).

13. Subsection 38(2)(a) and see Chapter 7.

14. *Burrough Wellcome Inc. v. Novopharm Ltd.* (1994), 58 C.P.R. (3d) 511 (F.C.T.D.)

15. *Canadian Schenley Distilleries Ltd. v. Can.'s Man. Distillery Ltd.* (1975), 25 C.P.R. (2d) 1 (F.C.T.D.); *Community Credit Union Ltd. v. Canada (Registrar of Trade-marks)*, 2006 FC 1119 (F.C.).

16. *Allergan Inc. v. Lancôme Parfums & Beauté & Cie* (2007), 64 C.P.R (4th) 147 (T.M.O.B.).

- The applicant could not have been satisfied it was entitled to use the mark.[17]
- The applicant used the mark prior to filing an application for the mark on the basis of proposed use.[18]
- The applicant failed to refer to a predecessor in title who used the mark[19] or a licensee.[20]

(ii)  The trademark is not registrable.[21]

(iii)  The applicant is not the person entitled to registration.[22]

(iv)  The trademark is not distinctive.[23]

The owner of a foreign trademark who cannot satisfy the difficult requirements of showing its mark has been made known in Canada[24] may oppose an application on the basis of non distinctiveness. But in order to succeed with such a ground of opposition, it must be shown that at the date of filing the statement of opposition, the mark is known to some extent in Canada and the reputation of the mark in Canada is substantial, significant or sufficiently known so as to negate the distinctiveness of the applied for mark.[25]

## c) The Material Dates

Under the *Act* or as a result of case law, each ground of opposition is determined as of a specific date depending on the ground. This will also require

17.  *Sapodilla Co. v. Bristol-Myers* (1974), 15 C.P.R. 152 (T.M.O.B.); *Jones v. Dragon Tales Productions Inc.* (2002), 27 C.P.R. (4th) 369 (T.M.O.B.); *Mougey v. Janzen,* (2007), 62 C.P.R. (4th) 230 (T.M.O.B.).
18.  *E. Remy Martin & Co. S.A. v. Magnet trading Corp. (HK) Ltd.,* (1988), 23 C.P.R (3d) 242 (T.M.O.B); *Institut National des Apellations d'Origine v. Brick Brewing Co., Ltd.,* (1995), 66 C.P.R. (3d) 351 (T.M.O.B.); *Lottery Corp. v. Western Gaming Systems Inc.* (2002), 25 C.P.R. (4th) 572 (T.M.O.B.); *R. Griggs Group v. 359603 Canada Inc* (2005), 47 C.P.R. (4th) 215 (T.M.O.B.); *Parmalat Canada Inc. v. Sysco Corporation* 2008 FC 1104, 69 C.P.R (4th) 349 (F.C.).
19.  *Nature's Path Foods Inc. v. Jiva Manufacturing & Distributing Inc.,* (2007), 63 C.P.R. (4th) 64 (T.M.O.B.).
20.  *Alltemp Products Co. v. Bit Holder Inc.* (2007), 63 C.P.R. (4th) 112 (T.M.O.B.).
21.  Subsection 38(2)(b) and see Chapter 3.
22.  Subsection 38(2)(c) and see Chapter 6.
23.  Subsection 38(2)(d) and see Chapter 2, part 2(c) and see *Muffin House Inc. v. Muffin House Bakery Ltd.* (1985), 2 C.P.R. (3d) 272 (T.M.O.B.).
24.  See Chapter 4 part 2.
25.  *Bojangles' International, LLC v. Bojangles Cafe Ltd.,* (2006), 48 C.P.R. (4th) 427 (F.C.) and see *Bousquet v. Barmish,* (1991), 37 C.P.R. (3d) 516 (F.C. T. D.), 46 C.P.R. (3d) 510 (F.C.A).

that evidence relating to the facts at the relevant material date be filed. The material dates are as follows:

i) The date for determining compliance with section 30 is the date of filing of the application.
ii) The date for determining grounds relating to registrability is the hearing date.[26]
iii) The dates for determining grounds relating to entitlement are set out in section 16 of the *Act*. If the application is based on registration and use abroad or proposed use, the relevant date is the filing date unless a convention priority claim has also been made.[27] If the application is based on use, the relevant date is the date of first use specified in the application.
iv) The date for determining distinctiveness is the date of filing the statement of opposition.[28]

## d) Content

A statement of opposition should be considered as similar to a statement of claim relating to an action in the Federal Court. It must set out the grounds of opposition in sufficient detail to enable the applicant to reply.[29] If a ground of opposition is not properly pleaded, the Board at the hearing may refuse to consider it.[30] But in making this determination at the hearing stage, regard must be had to the evidence filed as well as the statement of opposition.[31]

Before filing and serving a counter statement, an applicant may request an interlocutory ruling to strike all or any potion of the statement of opposition.[32]

---

26. *Park Avenue Furniture Corp. v. Wickes/Simmons Bedding Ltd* (1991), 37 C.P.R. (3d) 413 (F.C.A.); *Canadian Council of Professional Engineers v. Lubrication Engineers, Inc.* (1992), 41 C.P.R. (3d) 243 (F.C.A.).
27. See Chapter 6, part 3.
28. *Re Andres Wines Ltd. and E. & J. Gallo Winery*, [1976] 2 F.C. 3 (F.C.A.).
29. Subsection 38(3)(a). *Massino De Beradinis v. Decaria Hair Studio,* (1984), 2 C.P.R. (3d) 319 (T.M.O.B.).
30. *Massino De Beradinis v. Decaria Hair Studio,* (1984), 2 C.P.R. (3d) 319 (T.M.O.B.).
31. See *Novopharm Ltd v. Ciba-Geigy Canada Ltd* (2001), 15 C.P.R. (4th) 327 (F.C.A.); *Novopharm Ltd v. Astra AB* (2002), 21 C.P.R. (4th) 289 (F.C.A.); *Coastal Culture Inc. v. Wood Wheeler Inc.,* (2007), 57 C.P.R. (4th) 261 (F.C.).
32. See Notice in *The Trade-marks Journal* Vol. No. 2715, November 8, 2006 and see *Novopharm Ltd v. Ciba-Geigy Canada Ltd* (2001), 15 C.P.R. (4th) 327 (F.C.A.); *Novopharm Ltd v. Astra AB* (2002), 21 C.P.R. (4th) 289 (F.C.A.) which prompted the change in practice.

The statement of opposition must set out the address of the opponent in Canada or the address of its principal office or place of business abroad and the name and address in Canada of some person upon whom service may be made.[33]

If the Registrar considers that the opposition is frivolous and does not raise a substantial issue for decision, the statement of opposition will be rejected and notice of decision given to the opponent.[34] Only one valid ground of opposition is required to satisfy the subsection. The words "substantial issue" are not equivalent to the words "substantial likelihood that the opponent will succeed."[35]

The Registrar must simply direct his or her mind to the question as to whether the statement of opposition raises an arguable case and no evidence will be considered.[36] If the Registrar considers that the opposition raises a substantial issue for decision, a copy of the statement of opposition must be forwarded to the applicant.[37]

### e)  Counter Statement

Within two months after the statement of opposition has been forwarded to the applicant, the applicant must file a counter statement with the Registrar and serve a copy on the opponent setting out the grounds on which the applicant relies to support its application.[38] An applicant can claim the benefit of section 14 in its counterstatement.[39]

If the applicant does not file and serve a counter statement in a timely fashion, the applicant is deemed to have abandoned the application.[40]

Any statement or other material required to be served on a party in an opposition may be served by personal service, by registered mail, by courier or in any other manner with consent of the other party or their trademark agent.[41] The party effecting service must notify the Registrar of the manner of

---

33.  Subsection 38(3)(b).
34.  Subsection 38(4); and see *Can. Tampax Corp. v. Reg. T.M.* (1975), 24 C.P.R. (2d) 187 (F.C.T.D.); *Pepsico Inc. v. Reg. T.M.*, [1976] 1 F.C. 202 (F.C.T.D.).
35.  *Pepsico Inc. v. Reg. T.M.*, [1976] 1 F.C. 202 (F.C.T.D.).
36.  *Koffler Stores Ltd. v. Reg. T.M.*, (1976), 28 C.P.R. (2d) 113 (F.C.T.D.) .
37.  Subsection 38(5).
38.  *Trade-Marks Regulations*, SOR/96-195 as amended, section 41.
39.  *Canadian Council of Professional Engineers v. Tekla Oyj*, (2008), 68 C.P.R. (4th) 228 (T.M.O.B.) and see Chapter 4, part 3.
40.  Subsection 38(7.2).
41.  *Trade-Marks Regulations*, SOR/96-195 as amended, section 37(1) and see Practice In Trade-Mark Oppositions Proceedings, in effect March 31, 2009 currently at <http://www.cipo.ic.gc.ca/eic/site/cipointernet-internetopic.nsf/eng/wr01558.html>.

service and clearly indicate the method employed for service and the date of such action in order that an effective date of service may be determined.[42]

## f) Amendments

No amendment to a statement of opposition or counter statement shall be allowed except with leave of the Registrar upon such terms as he or she may think fit.[43] The request to amend must be served on the opposite party, who will be granted an opportunity to respond.

The practice of the Trade-marks Opposition Board is to only grant leave if it is in the interest of justice to do so having regard to all the surrounding circumstances including a) the stage the proceedings have reached; b) the reasons advanced as to why the ground was not initially raised; c) the importance of the amendment sought; and d) the prejudice to be suffered by the other party. A decision relating to leave cannot be appealed other than in the framework of the final decision relating to the opposition,[44] but an application for judicial review may be possible. [45]

## 3. Evidence

## a) The Framework

Both the opponent and the applicant are given an opportunity, in the manner prescribed, to submit evidence and to make representations to the Registrar.[46] Within four months after the service of the counter statement, the opponent must file with the Registrar the evidence, by way of affidavit or statutory declaration or certified copies of documents or entries relating to the register, the opponent is relying on to support the opposition or a statement that the opponent does not wish to submit evidence and serve the applicant with a copy of such evidence or statement.[47] The opposition will be deemed to have

---

42. *Trade-Marks Regulations*, SOR/96-195 as amended, section 37(6) and see Practice In Trade-Mark Oppositions Proceedings, in effect March 31, 2009 currently at <http://www.cipo.ic.gc.ca/eic/site/cipointernet-internetopic.nsf/eng/wr01558.html>.

43. Trade-Marks Regulations, SOR/96-195 as amended, section 40.

44. *Nabisco Brands Ltd./Nabisco Brands Ltee v. Perfection Foods Ltd.* (1985), 8 C.I.P.R. 133 (T.M.O.B.), 12 C.P.R. (3d) 456 (F.C.T.D.); *Lendingtree, LLC v. Lending Tree Corp.* 2006 FC 373 (F.C.).

45. *Pharmalat Canada Inc. v. Sysco Corporation* 2008 FC 1104 (F.C.).

46. Subsection 38(7).

47. *Trade-Marks Regulations*, SOR/96–195 as amended, section 41.

been withdrawn if the opponent does not submit either evidence or the statement.[48]

If evidence or the statement is filed and served by the opponent, the applicant has a similar time within which to file evidence in support of its application or a statement that it does not wish to submit evidence and must serve the opponent with a copy of such evidence or statement, as the case may be.[49] The application will be deemed to have been abandoned if the applicant does not submit either evidence or the statement.[50]

Within one month after service upon the opponent of the applicant's evidence, the opponent may file with the Registrar evidence strictly confined to matters in reply and serve the applicant with a copy of the evidence.[51]

Every exhibit to an affidavit or declaration must be filed with the affidavit or declaration.[52] Each exhibit should be properly identified and signed.

No further evidence may be adduced by any party except with leave of the Registrar upon such terms as the Registrar determines to be appropriate.[53] If circumstances have changed concerning the state of the register leave should be granted.[54]

All evidence filed in an opposition is open to the public to inspect at the Trademarks Office.[55]

## b)  The Onus of Proof

In opposition proceedings, there is an initial onus on the opponent to establish the facts to support the grounds of opposition on which it relies.[56] Once this occurs, the onus of proof is on the applicant to satisfy the Registrar that the trademark ought to be registered.[57] This is a constant onus and includes the onus, where appropriate, of showing that confusion is unlikely.

To allow an application, the Registrar must be reasonably satisfied that, on the balance of probabilities, the applied-for mark is unlikely to create

---

48. Subsection 38(7.1).
49. *Trade-Marks Regulations*, SOR/96–195 as amended, section 42.
50. Subsection 38(7.2).
51. *Trade-Marks Regulations*, SOR/96–195 as amended, section 43 and see *Trade-Marks Regulations*, section 44 and 45 concerning additional evidence, cross-examination on affidavits and filing and serving exhibits In *Minolta-QMS, Inc. v. Cheng-Lang Tsai*, 2006 FC 1249 the applicant over came the disallowance of improper reply evidence on appeal to the Federal Court.
52. *Trade-Marks Regulations*, SOR/96–195 as amended, subsection 45(1).
53. *Trade-Marks Regulations*, SOR/96–195 as amended, subsection 44(1).
54. *Realestate World Services v. Realcorp Inc.*, (1993), 48 C.P.R. (3d) 397 (T.M.O.B.).
55. *Trade-Marks Regulations*, SOR/96–195 as amended, subsection 45(2).
56. *Wool Bureau of Can. Ltd. v. Queenswear (Can.) Ltd.* (1980), 47 C.P.R. (2d) 11 (F.C.T.D.); *Max Mara Fashion Group S.R.L. v. Provigo Distribution Inc.* (2005), 46 C.P.R. (4th) 112 (F.C.).
57. *United Artists Corp. v. Pink Panther Beauty Corp.* (1998), 80 C.P.R. (3d) 247 (F.C.A.).

confusion; the Registrar need not be satisfied beyond doubt that confusion is unlikely.[58]

## c) The Nature of the Evidence

All evidence, with the exception of certified copies, must be presented by affidavit or statutory declaration. It is prudent to ensure that such material complies with the Federal Court Rules since they will apply to in the event of an appeal.[59] The affidavit or declaration must be sworn or affirmed before a commissioner for taking oaths or a notary public in the country of the person who provides the evidence.[60]

Evidence dealing with the state of the register or the marketplace is frequently filed. In addition, evidence of relevant web pages, if otherwise admissible, may be considered.[61] Evidence produced by the Way Back Machine (www.archive.org) showing the state of websites in the past is generally reliable but entitled to no weight in the absence of evidence to show that Canadian consumers visited the website in question. [62]

Evidence that the marks in issue co-exist on foreign registers is not relevant[63] but evidence of extensive contemporaneous of the marks in those countries will be relevant. [64]

Evidence of colleagues, students, and employees of the agent of the parties will not be accepted on controversial issues.[65] This evidence should be presented through independent witnesses.

If an applicant wishes to rely on evidence previously filed during prosecution of the application, such as evidence pursuant to section 32 or section 14, the opponent and the Board must be advised and the affidavits or declarations must be included as part of the applicant's evidence[66] which will be subject to cross-examination.

58. *Dion Neckwear Ltd. v. Christian Dior, S.A.* et al (1996), 71 C.P.R. (3d) 268 (T.M.O.B.); affirmed (2000), 5 C.P.R. (4th) 304 (F.C.T.D.); reversed (2003), 20 C.P.R. (4th) 155 (F.C.A.).
59. See *Federal Court Rules, 1998*, SOR/98-106 as amended.
60. See form 80 under the *Federal Court Rules, 1998*, SOR/98–106 as amended.
61. *Generation Nouveau Monde Inc. v. Teddy S.P.A.* (2006), 51 C.P.R. (4th) 385 (T.M.O.B.).
62. *Candrug Health Solutions Inc. Thorkelson* (2007), 60 C.P.R (4th) 35 (F.C.).
63. *Vivat Holdings Ltd. Levi Straus & Co.* (2005), 41 C.P.R. (4th) 8 (F.C.T.D.).
64. *Kellogg Co. v. Imperial Oil Ltd.* (1996), 67 C.P.R. (3d) 426 (Ont. Ct. (Gen. Div.)).
65. *Cross-Canada Auto Body Supply (Windsor) Ltd. v Hyundai Auto Canada*, (2005), 43 C.P.R. (4th) 21 (F.C.), affirmed 2006 FCA 133, *Pernod Ricard v. Molson Canada*, (2007), 60 C.P.R. (4th) 338 (T.M.O.B.).
66. *Canadian Generic Pharmaceutical Association v. Sanofi-Synthelabo Inc.*, (2006), 60 C.P.R. (4th) 74 (T.M.O.B.).

At any time before notice requiring filing of argument, the Registrar may, on the application of any party and on such terms as may be directed, order the cross-examination under oath of any affiant or declarant on their affidavit or declaration.[67] If an affiant or declarant fails to attend for cross-examination, the affidavit or declaration shall not be part of the evidence.[68]

## 4. The Hearing

Not less than 14 days after completion of the evidence, the Registrar shall give the parties written notice that they may within one month after the date of such notice file written argument.[69] No written argument shall be filed after the expiration of the one-month period except with leave of the Registrar.[70] A copy of any argument filed is forwarded by the Registrar to every other party together with a notice that a hearing may be requested.[71]

Any party who desires to present oral argument to the Registrar must give written notice and the Registrar must send the parties written notice setting out a hearing date.[72]

After considering the evidence and representations of the opponent and the applicant, the Registrar shall refuse the application or reject the opposition and notify the parties of the decision and the reasons for the decision.[73]

The Registrar has no jurisdiction to deal with an issue not pleaded in the statement of opposition[74] or to ignore or amend or strike out a registration on substantive grounds in the course of opposition proceedings.[75]

The Registrar also has no jurisdiction to disqualify agents and solicitors on the grounds of alleged conflict of interest[76] or to grant a stay of proceedings on the ground of pending litigation.[77] In order to obtain a stay, proceedings must be instituted in the Federal Court which may grant such relief.[78]

---

67. *Trade-Marks Regulations*, SOR/96–195 as amended, subsection 44(2).
68. *Trade-Marks Regulations*, SOR/96–195 as amended, subsection 44(5).
69. *Trade-Marks Regulations*, SOR/96–195 as amended, subsection 46(1).
70. *Trade-Marks Regulations*, SOR/96–195 as amended, subsection 46(2).
71. *Trade-Marks Regulations*, SOR/96–195 as amended, subsection 46(3).
72. *Trade-Marks Regulations*, SOR/96–195 as amended, subsection 46(4).
73. Subsection 38(8); *Hardee's Food Systems Inc. v. Hardee Farms International Ltd.* (1982), 63 C.P.R. (2d) 86 (F.C.T.D.).
74. *Imperial Developments Ltd. v. Imperial Oil Ltd.* (1984), 79 C.P.R. (2d) 12 (F.C.T.D.).
75. *Bacardi & Co. v. Havana Club Holdings S.A.*, (2004) FCA 220 (F.C.A.).
76. *J-Star Industries, Inc. v. Berg Equipement Co. (Canada) Ltd*, (1992), 45 C.P.R. (3d) 72 (F.C.T.D.).
77. *Anheuser-Busch Inc. v. Carling O'Keefe Breweries of Can. Ltd.* (1982), 45 N.R. 126 (F.C.A.).
78. *Figgie International Inc. v. Citywide Machine Wholesale Inc.* (1993), 50 C.P.R. (3d) 89 (F.C.T.D.); *Royal Bank of Canada v. Canadian Imperial Bank of Commerce* (1994), 57 C.P.R.

In the absence of special circumstances, an application for Judicial Review concerning matters which may be raised and considered by the Register will be refused.[79]

## 5. Appeal

An appeal lies from a decision of the Registrar to the Federal Court within two months from the date upon which notice of decision was dispatched by the registrar or such further time as the court may allow, either before or after the expiry of the two months.[80]

The appeal is made by way of notice of appeal filed with the Registrar and the Federal Court.[81] The notice of appeal must be filed with the court and the Registrar and sent by registered mail to the registered owner of any trademark that has been referred to by the Registrar in the decision complained of and to every other person who was entitled to notice of such decision.[82] Under the Federal Court Rules, the appeal is commenced by Notice of Application.[83]

On appeal evidence in addition to that adduced before the Registrar may be adduced.[84] The court may exercise any discretion vested in the Registrar.[85]

---

(3d) 483 (F.C.T.D.). A stay will not be granted as a matter of course and requires the exercise of judicial discretion in determining whether a stay should be ordered in the particular circumstances of the case.

79. *Novopharm Ltd. v. Aktiebolaget Astra* (1996), 68 C.P.R. (3d) 117 (F.C.T.D.) and see *Lending Tree, LLC v. Lending Tree Corp.*, (2005), 48 C.P.R. (4th) 355 (F.C.) affirmed 2007 FCA 70 (F.C.A.) concerning an amendment to the identity of the applicant but see *Pharmalat Canada Inc. v. Sysco Corporation* 2008 FC 1104 (F.C.).

80. *Trade-marks Act*, subsection 56(1). The procedure relating to an appeal is set out part 5 of the *Federal Court Rules, 1998*, SOR/98–106 as amended.

81. Subsection 56(2).

82. Subsection 56(3).

83. The procedure relating to an appeal is set out part 5 of the *Federal Court Rules, 1998*, SOR/98–106 as amended. See *Simpson Strong-Tie Company, Inc. v. Peak Innovations* 2008 FC 52 (F.C.) concerning the form of the notice of application.

84. Subsection 56(5). By virtue of section 60 of the *Act*, when an appeal has been made, the Registrar must, on the request of any of the parties, transmit all documents on file relating to the matters in question. See *Austin Nichols & Co. v. Cinnabon Inc.* (1997), 76 C.P.R. (3d) 45 (F.C.T.D.), 82 C.P.R. (3d) 513 (F.C.A.).

85. Subsection 56(5); see *Beverley Bedding & Upholstery Co. v. Regal Bedding & Upholstering Ltd.* (1982), 133 D.L.R. (3d) 255 (F.C.A.); affirming 110 D.L.R. (3d) 189 (F.C.T.D.).

Generally a new ground of opposition will not be added by amendment in the course of an appeal.[86]

The Registrar's expertise must be given deference. In the absence of additional evidence, decisions of the Registrar, whether of fact, law, or discretion, within the Registrar's area of expertise, are reviewed on the standard of reasonableness.[87] But if additional evidence is adduced that would have materially affected the Registrar's findings of fact or the exercise of discretion, the judge hearing the appeal must come to his or her own conclusion as to the correctness of the Registrar's decision.[88]

Generally, the additional evidence must be substantial and significant.[89] The more substantial the additional evidence, the closer the court may come to making the finding of fact for itself and not be obliged to give deference to the Registrar's decision.[90]

A further appeal lies to the Federal Court of Appeal as of right.[91] On such an appeal, the question whether the Federal Court applied the proper standard of review to the decision of the Registrar is reviewable by the Federal Court of Appeal on a correctness standard. [92]

86. *Sun World International Inc. v. Parmalat Dairy & Bakery Inc.* (2007), 60 C.P.R. (4th) 291, 2007 FC 641 (F.C.) (Prothonotary) affirmed (2007), 60 C.P.R. (4th) 300, 2007 FC 861 (F.C) but see *Labatt Brewing Co. v. Benson & Hedges (Canada)*, (1996), 67 C.P.R. (3d) 258 (F.C.) where new grounds on a pure question of law was added but only in reference to evidence which was before the Registrar.
87. *Mattel, Inc. v. 3894207 Canada Inc.* (2006), 49 C.P.R. (4th) 321 (S.C.C.) and see *Dunsmuir v. New Brunswick*, 2008 SCC 9 (S.C.C.).
88. *John Labatt Ltd. v. Molson Breweries, a Partnership* (2000), 5 C.P.R. (4th) 180, (F.C.A.); *Canadian Tire Corp. v. Accessoires D'Autos Nordiques Inc.* 2006 FC 1431 (F.C.) appeal dismissed (2007), 62 C.P.R. (4th) 436 (F.C.A.).
89. *Tradition Fine Foods Ltd. v. Groupe Traditional'l Inc.* (2006), 51 C.P.R. (4th) 342 (F.C.).
90. *Maison Cousin (1980) Inc. v. Cousins Submarines Inc.*, 2006 FCA 409, 60 C.P.R (4th) 369 (F.C.A)
91. *Re Andres Wines Ltd. and E. & J. Gallo Winery*, [1976] 2 F.C. 3 (F.C.A.).
92. *Canadian Tire Corp. v. Accessoires D'Autos Nordiques Inc.* 2006 FC 1431 (F.C.) appeal dismissed (2007), 62 C.P.R. (4th) 436 (F.C.A.) .

# CHAPTER

# 13

# Infringement

# 1. Infringement

## a) Statutory Framework

### i) Section 19

Section 19 of the *Trade-marks Act* provides that, subject to sections 21, 32, and 67, the registration of a trademark in respect of any wares or services, unless shown to be invalid, gives to the owner the exclusive right to the use throughout Canada of the trademark in respect of those wares or services. A breach of section 19 occurs when the infringer uses a trademark which is identical to the registered mark in association with wares or services which are identical to those for which the mark is registered.[1]

The exceptions mentioned in the section are limited. Section 21 relates the concurrent use of confusing trademarks;[2] section 32 relates to territorial restrictions applicable to registrations obtained under subsection 12(2) or section 13;[3] and section 67 relates to marks registered or pending in Newfoundland prior to April 1, 1949.

In order to succeed with a claim under the section, the following elements must be shown by a plaintiff:

a) the ownership of a registered trademark;
b) use of the identical trademark by the defendant;
c) in association with any of the wares or services that are included in the registration.

### ii) Section 20

Section 20 provides that a registered trademark owner's right to the exclusive use of a trademark is deemed to be infringed by a person not entitled to its use who sells, distributes, or advertises wares or services in association with a confusing trademark or trade name. Section 6 of the *Act* sets out the matters to be considered in making a determination as to whether trademarks or trade names are confusing.[4]

The owner of a registered trademark may bring proceedings for infringement with respect to any confusing trademark or trade name in relation to

---

1. *Tradition Fine Foods Ltd. v. The Oshawa Group Limited* (2005), 44 C.P.R. (4th) 81 (F.C.A.); *A & W Food Services of Canada Inc. v. McDonald's Restaurants of Canada Limited* (2005), 40 C.P.R. (4th) 126 (F.C.).
2. See Chapter 8, part 5.
3. See Chapter 3, part 4 and Chapter 2, part 2(d).
4. See Chapter 11.

any wares or services, unlike section 19, which is limited. The date for determining whether trademarks or trade names are confusing is the date the proceedings are heard.[5] Section 20 is sufficiently broad to apply to both forward and reverse confusion.[6]

Once a trademark owner is aware of infringing activities, proceedings should be brought promptly. Like gardens, trademark cases frequently get worse with neglect.[7]

Section 20 is also subject to exceptions. The section states that no registration of a trademark prevents a person from making:

(a) any *bona fide* use of his or her personal name[8] as a trade name; or
(b) any *bona fide* use, other than as a trademark:
  (i) of the geographical name of his or her place of business, or
  (ii) of any accurate description of the character or quality of his or her wares or services
  in such a manner as is not likely to have the effect of depreciating the value of the goodwill attaching to the registered trademark.[9]

A person seeking to take advantage of an exception must show that they were acting in good faith. In addition, they must show that their use did not likely have the effect of depreciating the value of the goodwill attached to the trademark in issue.

Depreciation of goodwill occurs when there is a reduction of the esteem in which the mark itself is held or through the direct persuasion and enticement of customers who would otherwise be expected to buy or continue to buy goods bearing the trademark.[10]

Since the definition of a trademark includes a distinguishing guise,[11] an action may be brought for the infringement of a distinguishing guise pursuant to sections 19 or 20. The appeal to the eye of the respective guises will be particularly important in determining whether infringement has occurred.

---

5. *Alticor Inc. v. Nutravite Pharmaceuticals Inc.* (2005), 42 C.P.R. (4th) 107 (F.C.A.)
6. *A & W Food Services of Canada Inc. v. McDonald's Restaurants of Canada Limited* (2005), 40 C.P.R. (4th) 126 (F.C.).
7. *Phones4U Ltd. v. Phone4u.co.uk Internet Ltd.,* [2006] EWCA Civ 244 (U.K.C.A.).
8. The subsection only applies to personal names not corporate names; *KayserRoth Can. (1969) Ltd. v. Fascination Lingerie Inc,* (1971), 3 C.P.R. (2d) 27 (Ex. Ct.); *Visa International Service Assn. v. Visa Motel Corp.* (1984), 1 C.P.R. (3d) 109 (B.C.C.A.).
9. *Bonus Foods Ltd. v. Essex Packers Ltd.* (1964), 43 C.P.R. 165 (Ex. Ct.); *National Hockey League v. Pepsi-Cola Canada* (1995), 59 C.P.R. (3d) 216 (B.C.C.A.).
10. *Clairol International Corporation v. Thomas Supply & Equipment Co.* [1968] 2 Ex. C.R. 552 (Ex. Ct.) and see part 3 of this chapter.
11. See Chapter 2, part 2(d).

In order to succeed with a claim under the section, the following elements must be shown by the plaintiff:

(a) the ownership of a registered trademark;
(b) the absence of entitlement to the use by the defendant of the registered trademark;
(c) the sale, distribution, or advertisement of any wares or services by the defendant;
(d) in association with a confusing trademark or trade name.

## b) The Requirement to Show Use

In order to succeed in action relying on section 19 or 20, the plaintiff must show that the defendant has used the impugned mark as a trademark. This requires that the plaintiff show that the defendant's use of the mark satisfies the requirements of the definition of a trademark or trade name set out in section 2[12] and the definition of use as required by section 4 in association with wares or services.[13]

Both the intention of the defendant and recognition by the public are relevant factors and either may be sufficient to show that the defendant has used the impugned mark as a trademark. It is not necessary to show both, but one or the other must be shown.[14]

## c) Invalidity

The owner of a registered trademark benefits from a presumption that its registration is valid and the onus remains on an attacking party to show that it is invalid and should be expunged.[15] If it is found that the plaintiff's

---

12. See Chapter, part 2(a).
13. See Chapter 5 and *Cie générale des éstablissements Michelin-Michelin & Cie v. CAW-Canada* (1996), 71 C.P.R. (3d) 348 (F.C.T.D.); *Pepper King Ltd. v. Sunfresh Ltd* (2000), 8 C.P.R. (4th) 485 (F.C.T.D.).
14. *Tommy Hilfiger Licensing Inc. v. International Clothiers Inc.* (2004), 32 C.P.R. (4th) 289 (F.C.A.); *Tommy Hilfiger Licensing Inc. v. Produits de Qualite I.M.D.* (2005), 37 C.P.R. (4th) (F.C.).
15. *Cross-Canada Auto Body Supply (Windsor) Limited v. Hyundai Auto Canada*, 2007 FC 580, 60 C.P.R. (4th) (F.C.), 2008 FCA 98, 65 C.P.R. (4th) 121 (F.C.A.) but see *Cheap Tickets and Travel Inc. v. Emall.ca Inc.* 2008 FCA 50 (F.C.A.) where this presumption was categorized as weakly worded adding little to the onus already resting, in the usual way, on the attacking party. See Chapter 10, part 2.

trademark registration is invalid, this is a complete defense to a claim for of infringement[16]

## d) Comparison with a Claim for Passing Off

An action for infringement is based on the rights associated with the ownership of a registered trademark available under section 19 or 20 of the *Act*. An action for common law passing off, or section 7 of the *Act*, is based on the existence of goodwill, a misrepresentation and resultant damage.[17] While related, the causes of action differ in a number of ways including the following:

(a)  Infringement under section 19 or 20 of the *Act* is concerned only with one method of passing off, restricted to the use of a registered trademark and a confusing trademark.

(b)  In an action for infringement, once the plaintiff has shown use of a registered trademark and a confusing trademark, the defendant cannot avoid infringement by showing added matter distinguishes its wares or services from those of the trademark owner.[18]

(c)  In an action for the infringement, the plaintiff is entitled to rely on its registration as evidence of ownership and its exclusive rights throughout Canada, while the plaintiff in an action for passing off must establish goodwill in the trading indicia it seeks to protect, which may be territorially limited.[19]

A plaintiff may be unsuccessful with an action for infringement on the basis that the registration was invalid, but might still succeed with a claim for passing off on the same evidence.[20] As a result, in most actions seeking infringement, an alternative claim for passing off is pleaded.

---

16.  *Parke, Davis & Co. v. Empire Laboratories Ltd.* (1963), 41 C.P.R. 121 (Ex. Ct.), affirmed 43 C.P.R. 1 (S.C.C.).

17.  See Chapter 45 for a discussion of what must be shown in an action seeking relief for passing off.

18.  *Meubles Domani's v. Guccio Gucci S.P.A.* (1992), 43 C.P.R. (3d) 372 (F.C.A.).

19.  *Ciba–Geigy Canada Ltd. v. Apotex Inc.,* (1992), 44 C.P.R. (3d) 289 ( S.C.C.).

20.  *Parke, Davis & Co. v. Empire Laboratories Ltd.,* (1963), 41 C.P.R. 121 (Ex. Ct.), affirmed 43 C.P.R. 1 (S.C.C.); *Tommy Hilfiger Licensing Inc. v. International Clothiers Inc.* (2003), 9 C.P.R. (4th) 39 (F.C.T.D.).

### e) Grey Market Goods

The expression "grey market" or "gray market" generally refers to goods that are imported contrary to the wishes of the trademark owner or an authorized importer in a specific territory. It refers to goods which, as a general rule, are legitimately marketed in the foreign market, but whose presence in the local market is clouded by allegations of infringement. [21]

Goods originally sold by the trademark owner or on its behalf are not infringing because they are sold in a geographical market where the trademark owner does not wish them to be sold when they are imported into Canada.[22] Similar reasoning has been applied in cases involving goods which are exported from Canada.[23]

If there are material differences between the "grey market" goods and the goods sold by the trademark owner in Canada, infringement may occur. For example, if the formulation of the grey product is different from the domestic product, the importation of the grey product may be infringing.[24] In addition, the existence of notice of the difference to consumers may avoid a finding of infringement.[25]

## 2. Defenses to an Action for Infringement

### a) Invalidity of the Plaintiff's Registered Trademark

If is found that the plaintiff's registration is invalid this is a complete defense. In an action in the Federal Court, a counterclaim for expungement may be asserted or a separate application seeking expungement may be brought.[26]

---

21. *Coca-Cola Ltd v. Pardhan* (1999), 85 C.P.R. (3d) 489 (F.C.A.) leave to appeal to S.C.C. refused; *Re Stewart House Publishing Inc* (2003), 24 C.P.R. (4th) 488 (Ont. Sup. Ct of Justice).
22. *Smith & Nephew Inc. v. Glen Oak Inc.* (1996), 68 C.P.R. (3d) 153 (F.C.A.) leave to appeal to S.C.C. refused [1996] S.C.C.A. No. 433 (S.C.C.).
23. *Coca-Cola Ltd v. Pardhan* (1999), 85 C.P.R. (3d) 489 (F.C.A.) leave to appeal to S.C.C. refused; *Re Stewart House Publishing Inc* (2003), 24 C.P.R. (4th) 488 (Ont. Sup. Ct of Justice).
24. *H J Heinz Co. of Canada Ltd v. Edan Sales Inc* (1991), 35 C.P.R. (3d) 213 (F. C.); *Seiko Time Can. Ltd. v. Consumers Distributing Co.* (1980), 50 C.P.R. (2d) 147 (Ont. H.C.), affirmed 1 C.P.R. (3d) 1 (S.C.C.).
25. *Seiko Time Can. Ltd. v. Consumers Distributing Co.* (1980), 50 C.P.R. (2d) 147 (Ont. H.C.), reversed 1 C.P.R. (3d) 1 (S.C.C.).
26. See for example *WCC Containers Sales Limited v. Haul-All Equipment Ltd.* (2003), 28 C.P.R. (4th) 175 (F.C.T.D.); *Remo Imports Ltd. v. Jaguar Cars Limited,* (2007), 60 C.P.R. (4th) 130, 2007 FCA 258, 47 C.P.R. (4th) 1 (F.C.A.).

## b)  Ownership

The defendant may attack the plaintiff's title to the exclusive use of the trademark registered.[27]

## c)  Consent or License

If the defendant is entitled to use the mark in issue by virtue of consent or license, this will establish a defense.

## d)  Denial of Infringement

A denial of infringement is a complete defense if successful, but the discontinuance of use is not a defense.[28]

## e)  Plaintiffs Own Goods

Infringement must be in respect of spurious wares or services. There can be no infringement if the trademark in question is used in association with the plaintiff's goods.[29]

## 3.  Depreciating the Value of the Goodwill Attached to a Trademark

## a)  Statutory Definitions

In addition to the right to claim infringement under section 19 or 20, section 22 makes an additional statutory right available to the owner of a registered trademark. The section provides that no person shall use a trademark registered by any person in a manner likely to have the effect of depreciating the

---

27.  See for example *Chalet Bar B-Q (Canada) Inc. et al. v. Foodcorp Ltd.* (1981), 66 C.P.R. (2d) 56, varied (1982), 55 C.P.R. (2d) 46 (F.C.A.).
28.  See for example *Tommy Hilfiger Licensing Inc. v. International Clothiers Inc.* (2004), 32 C.P.R. (4th) 289 (F.C.A.).
29.  See for example *Seiko Time Can. Ltd. v. Consumers Distributing Co.* (1980), 50 C.P.R. (2d) 147 (Ont. H.C.), reversed 1 C.P.R. (3d) 1 (S.C.C.).

value of the goodwill attaching thereto.[30] Since the section was added to the *Act* in 1954, relatively few cases have considered its application.

The cause of action set out in section 22 is subject to a discretionary power vested in the court to decline to order the recovery of damages or profits and permit the defendant to continue to sell wares marked with the trademark in issue that were in its possession or under its control at the time notice was given to it that the owner of the registered trademark complained of the use of the trademark.[31]

It has been established that for the purposes of section 22, goodwill consists of reputation and connection built up by years of work or gained through significant expenditure of money and which is identified with the goods distributed by the owner in association with the trademark.[32]

The value of the goodwill attaching to a registered mark may be depreciated if any of the following occur:

(a) the esteem in which the wares or services are held is reduced,
(b) direct persuasion and enticing of customers who would otherwise be expected to buy or continue to buy goods bearing the trademark,
(c) disparagement of the mark, or
(d) the dilution of the distinctiveness or unique characteristics of a mark.

These circumstances are not exhaustive, as the courts have not yet considered the limits of the application of the section.[33]

A mental association of the two marks does not necessarily give rise to a likelihood of depreciation. There must be evidence of a "likelihood" of depreciation. This is a matter of evidence, not speculation. If the parties carry on business in unrelated fields, there may be no depreciation of goodwill.[34]

It has been held that the verb "use" in section 22 is to be interpreted by reference to the definition of the noun "use" in section 2 and 4.[35] This means that the application of section 22 is limited to a use which any person may make, in association with goods or services within the meaning of section 4 of another's registered trademark, in such a manner as to depreciate the value of the goodwill attaching thereto.

---

30. *Syntex Inc. v. Apotex Inc.* (1984), 1 C.P.R. (3d) 145 (F.C.A.); reversing 69 C.P.R. (2d) 264 (F.C.T.D.).
31. Subsection 22(2) and see *Clairol International Corp. v. Thomas Supply & Equipment Co.* (1968), 55 C.P.R. 176 (Ex. Ct.).
32. *Veuve Clicquot Ponsardin v. Boutiques Cliquot* [2006] 1 S.C.R 824, 49 C.P.R. (4th) 401 (S.C.C.); *Clairol International Corp. v. Thomas Supply & Equipment* Co. (1968), 55 C.P.R. 176 (Ex. Ct).
33. *Veuve Clicquot Ponsardin v. Boutiques Cliquot* [2006] 1 S.C.R 824, 49 C.P.R. (4th) 401 (S.C.C.); *Clairol International Corp. v. Thomas Supply & Equipment* Co. (1968), 55 C.P.R. 176 (Ex. Ct.).
34. *Veuve Clicquot Ponsardin v. Boutiques Cliquot* [2006] 1 S.C.R 824, 49 C.P.R. (4th) 401 (S.C.C.).
35. See Chapter 5 for a discussion of trademark "use."

The difference between the requirements for use in association with wares and services can lead to surprising results. For example, in a leading case it was found that the reproduction of the plaintiff's trademark on the defendant's packages was use within the meaning of section 22 but that the reproduction on the defendant's brochures was not.[36]

Section 22 does not require a demonstration that use of both marks in the same geographic area would likely lead to confusion. However, it does require the plaintiff to show that the defendant has used a mark sufficiently similar to the plaintiff's mark to evoke in the relevant universe of consumers a mental association of the marks that is likely to depreciate the value of the goodwill attached to the plaintiff's mark.[37] The test is the likelihood of depreciating the value of the goodwill attached to a trademark.

## b) The Elements Required to Be Shown

A claim under section 22 is quite different from a claim for infringement. In order to succeed with a claim under the section, the following elements must be shown:

(a) The plaintiff's registered trademark or at least its distinguishing feature was used by the defendant in connection with wares or services, whether or not such wares or services are competitive with those of the claimant.

(b) The plaintiff's registered trademark is sufficiently well known to have significant goodwill attached to it. The mark does not need to be well known or famous but goodwill must exist.

(c) The plaintiff's mark was used in a manner likely to have an effect on that goodwill (this is referred to as linkage). Linkage requires a mental association in the mind a reasonable buyer between the two parties and the mark. The likelihood of such a linkage is a matter of evidence, not speculation.

(d) The likely effect would be to depreciate the value of the goodwill (damage). Depreciation includes lowering the value of the goodwill as well as disparagement or tarnishing the trademark.[38]

---

36. *Clairol International Corp. v. Thomas Supply & Equipment Co.* (1968), 55 C.P.R. 176 (Ex. Ct.) and see *Cie générale des éstablissements Michelin-Micheline&Cie v. CAW-Canada* (1996), 71 C.P.R. (3d) 348 (F.C.T.D.) and see Chapter 5 for additional discussion of "use."
37. *Veuve Clicquot Ponsardin v. Boutiques Cliquot* [2006] 1 S.C.R 824, 49 C.P.R. (4th) 401 (S.C.C.).
38. *Veuve Clicquot Ponsardin v. Boutiques Cliquot* [2006] 1 S.C.R 824, 49 C.P.R. (4th) 401 (S.C.C.).

CHAPTER

# 14

# Common Law Rights—Passing Off

## 1. Passing Off

### a) The Nature of the Tort

The tort has a long history. Originally passing off was similar to the tort of deceit and required a misrepresentation concerning the origin of the goods which was calculated to deceive purchasers and divert business from the plaintiff to the defendant.[1] This is no longer the case. The tort of passing off has evolved to take into account changing commercial realities and is concerned with the protection of the community from the consequential damage of unfair competition or unfair trading.[2] It has also sought to protect the interest of traders in their names and reputation.[3]

Canadian Courts require that three elements must be established in order for a plaintiff to succeed in an action for passing off.[4] First, the plaintiff must establish the existence of goodwill or reputation attached to goods or services supplied, in the mind of the purchasing public by association with identifying "get-up" under which the particular goods or services are offered to the public, so that the get-up is recognized by the public as distinctive of the plaintiff's goods or services. The "get-up" may include a common law trademark or a trade description or individual features of labeling or packaging in which the goods are offered to the public. It is the external appearance of the goods in the form in which they are likely to be seen prior to purchase.[5] This type of goodwill is territorial in nature. The goodwill must be significant as a claim for passing off should not be allowed to protect goodwill which any reasonable person would consider trivial.[6]

Second, the plaintiff must demonstrate a misrepresentation by the defendant to the public (whether or not intentional) leading or likely to lead the public to believe that the goods or services offered by the defendant are the goods and services of the plaintiff.[7]

---

1. *Oxford Pendaflex Can. Ltd. v. Korr Marketing Ltd.* (1982), 64 C.P.R. (2d) 1 (S.C.C.).
2. *Seiko Time Can. Ltd. v. Consumers Distributing Co.* (1980), 50 C.P.R. (2d) 147 (Ont. H.C.), reversed [1984] 1 S.C.R. 583, 1 C.P.R. (3d) 1 (S.C.C.).
3. *Kirkbi Ag et al v. Ritvik Holdings Inc.* (2005), 43 C.P.R. (4th) 385 (S.C.C.).
4. *Ciba-Geigy Can. Ltd. v. Apotex Inc.* (1992), 44 C.P.R. (3d) 289 (S.C.C.); *Kirkbi Ag et al v. Ritvik Holdings Inc,* (2005), 43 C.P.R. (4th) 385 (S.C.C.).
5. *Ciba-Geigy Can. Ltd. v. Apotex Inc.* (1992), 44 C.P.R. (3d) 289 (S.C.C.); *Kirkbi Ag et al v. Ritvik Holdings Inc,* (2002), 20 C.P.R. (4th) 224 (F.C.) appeal dismissed 2003 F.C.A. 297 (F.C.A.), appeal dismissed (2005) 43 C.P.R. (4th) 385 (S.C.C.).
6. *Sutherland v. V2 Music Ltd.* U.K., [2002] EMLR 568 (U.K.Ch. D.), *Knight v. Beyond Properties Pty Ltd.,* [2007] EWHC 1251 (Ch. D.).
7. *Ciba-Geigy Can. Ltd. v. Apotex Inc.* (1992), 44 C.P.R. (3d) 289 (S.C.C.) but see *Phones4U Ltd. v. Phone4u.co.uk Internet Ltd.,* [2006] EWCA Civ 244 (U.K.C.A.) for a discussion of cases involving "mere confusion" which may not be enough to establish a misrepresentation.

The final consumer of a product must be taken into account in determining whether the tort of passing-off has occurred. In the context of prescription drugs the final consumer of the product includes physicians, pharmacists, dentists, and patients.[8]

Third, the plaintiff must demonstrate that it has suffered or that it will likely suffer damage by reason of the erroneous belief engendered by the defendant's misrepresentation that the source of the defendant's goods or services is the same as the source of those offered by the plaintiff.[9]

An action for passing off is different than an action for infringement of a registered trademark.[10]

## b)  Reputation or Goodwill

The plaintiff in any action for passing off must satisfy the court of the existence of goodwill or reputation attached to the goods or services supplied in the mind of the purchasing public by association with identifying "get-up" under which the particular goods or services are offered to the public, so that the get-up is recognized by the public as distinctive of the plaintiff's goods or services.

The plaintiff does not have to show it is the sole source of the goods or services in question or that consumers know its name or trademark so long as it can establish the three elements of the tort.[11]

It is not necessary that the plaintiff carry on business in Canada in order to show goodwill or a reputation which may be protected by way of an action for passing off.[12]

## c)  Trade Dress or Get Up

The term "get-up" is normally used in the context of a claim for passing-off to mean the visible external appearance of goods in the form in which they are presented to the public for purchase. If the goods are sold in packages, then their get-up means the appearance of the package taken as a whole.

---

8.  *Ciba-Geigy Can. Ltd. v. Apotex Inc.* (1992), 44 C.P.R. (3d) 289 (S.C.C.).
9.  *CibaGeigy Can. Ltd. v. Apotex Inc.* (1992), 44 C.P.R. (3d) 289 (S.C.C.); *Remo Imports Ltd. v. Jaguar Cars Limited* (2007), 60 C.P.R. (4th) 130, 2007 FCA 258, 47 C.P.R. (4th) 1 (F.C.A.).
10.  See Chapter 13, part 1(d).
11.  *Oxford Pendaflex Can. Ltd. v. Korr Marketing Ltd.* (1982), 64 C.P.R. (2d) 1, 134 D.L.R. (3d) 271 (S.C.C).
12.  *Orkin Exterminating Company v. Pestco Co. of Can.* (1984), 47 O.R. (2d) 265 (Ont. H.C.); (1985), 50 O.R. (2d) 726 (Ont. C.A.); *Walt Disney Productions v. Triple Five Corp.* (1994), 53 C.P.R. (3d) 129 (Alta C.A.).

If they are sold or displayed unpackaged, then the get-up must relate to the goods themselves.[13]

The look, the appearance, and the get-up of a product plays a crucial role in the purchase process since they are the chief means at the plaintiff's disposal to attract customers. The importance of visual impact is well known: what appeals to the eye is crucial. The product's appearance or its packaging—shape, size or color—may be characteristic of a particular source and have the effect making it recognizable on its own. In the mind of the customer appearance is not always linked to a trademark, that is, the consumer may rely on the appearance rather than the trademark to identify the product.[14]

Color by itself, even when combined with size, may not be sufficient to establish an action for passing off since it is difficult to establish it is distinctive in the sense required by the tort.[15]

The plaintiff does not need to establish that the totality of its get-up was copied as the plaintiff only needs to show a misrepresentation leading or likely to lead the public to believe that the goods or services offered by the defendant are the goods and services of the plaintiff.[16]

The addition of distinctive matter may eliminate the probability of passing off if it is sufficient to avoid the making of any misrepresentation.[17] The use of a disclaimer may assist in establishing a defense if its use would likely bring the qualification home to all types of potential customers including those with imperfect or partial memory.[18]

## d) Misrepresentation

An action for passing off is not confined to any particular means of misrepresentation. Doing of anything which would lead customers to think that there is a connection between the plaintiff's wares, services or business and the

---

13. *Ciba-Geigy Can. Ltd. v. Apotex Inc.* (1992), 44 C.P.R (3d) 289 (S.C.C.). For example, plaintiffs have successfully asserted rights relating to a lemon-shaped lemon juice dispenser, *Reckitt & Colman Products Ltd. v. Borden Inc.* [1990] 1 E.R. LL 873 (H.L.) or the shape and color of a snow brush and ice scraper, *Ray Plastics Ltd. v. Dustbane Products Ltd.* (1990), 33 C.P.R. (3d) 219 (H.C.J.).
14. *Ciba-Geigy Can. Ltd. v. Apotex Inc.* (1992), 44 C.P.R. (3d) 289 (S.C.C.).
15. *Prairie Maid Cereals Ltd. v. Christie, Brown & Co.* (1965), 48 C.P.R. 289 (B.C.C.A); *Ciba-Geigy Can. Ltd. v. Novopharm Ltd.* (1986), 12 C.P.R. (3d) 76 (Ont. H.C.); *Smith Kline and French Can. Ltd. v. Apotex Inc.* (1986), 12 C.P.R. (3d) 479 (Ont. H.C.).
16. *Oxford Pendaflex Can. Ltd. v. Korr Marketing Ltd.* (1982), 64 C.P.R. (2d) 1 (S.C.C.).
17. *Parke, Davis & Co. v. Empire Laboratories Ltd.*,(1963), 41 C.P.R. 121 (Ex. Ct.), affirmed 43 C.P.R. 1 (S.C.C.); *Reckitt & Colman Products Ltd. v. Borden Inc.*, [1990] 1 All E.R. 873 (H.L.).
18. *I. N. Newman Limited v. Richard T Adlem* [2005] EWCA Civ. 741 (U.K.C.A).

wares, services or business of the defendant, where such a connection does not exist may be actionable.[19]

The use of a word or device or one of the essential particulars by which the plaintiff's products or business is characterized may not be actionable but the copying of this type or other accompanying indicia may, in an appropriate case, be considered as "badges of fraud."[20]

The plaintiff is not required to show an intention to deceive, but if intention is shown it is evidence which tends to show that a misrepresentation has been made.[21]

The facts must be weighed in relation to an "ordinary" member of the public and "average" customer. Such a customer would take ordinary care in purchasing the goods they need, and, if desiring a particular brand, would take ordinary precautions to see that they get it.[22]

The average customer will not be the same for all products and will not have the same attitude at the time of purchase. In addition the attention and care taken by the same person may vary depending on the product being purchased. A customer will probably not exercise the same care in selecting goods from a supermarket shelf as they would when choosing a luxury item.[23]

## e) Damage

The plaintiff must show that it has suffered or that it will likely suffer damage by reason of the erroneous belief engendered by the defendant's misrepresentation that the source of the defendant's goods or services is the same as the source of those offered by the plaintiff.[24] The plaintiff must present evidence concerning its claim for damages.

---

19. *2 For 1 Subs Ltd. v. Ventresca*, (2006), 48 C.P.R. (4th) 311 (Ont. S.C.of Justice), *British Sky Broadcasting Group Plc v. Sky Home Services Limited*, [2006] EWHC 3165 (U.K.Ch. D.) where the erroneous belief induced by the misrepresentations was that the defendants' activities were authorized by the plaintiff; *Irvine v. Talksport Ltd.* [2002] All E.R. 414 (Ch. Div.), affirmed [2003] All E.R. 881 (U.K.C.A.) relating to a false endorsement.

20. *British Telecom plc v. One In A Million* [1998] 4 All E.R. 476 (U.K.C.A.); *Hughes v. Sherrif*, [1950] O.R. 206 (Ont. S.C.); [1950] O.W.N. 483 (Ont. C.A.).

21. *Cadbury Schweppes Pty Ltd. v. Pub Squash Co.* [1981] 1 All E.R. 213 (P.C.).

22. *CibaGeigy Can. Ltd. v. Apotex Inc.* (1992), 44 C.P.R. (3d) 289 (S.C.C.).

23. *CibaGeigy Can. Ltd. v. Apotex Inc* (1992), 44 C.P.R. (3d) 289 (S.C.C.).

24. *CibaGeigy Can. Ltd. v. Apotex Inc.* (1992),44 C.P.R. (3d) 289 (S.C.C.); *BMW Canada Inc. v. Nissan Canada Inc*, (2007), 57 C.P.R. (4th) 81 (F.C.), 60 C.P.R. (4th) 181, 2007 FCA 255 (F.C.A); *Remo Imports Ltd. v. Jaguar Cars Limited*, (2007), 60 C.P.R. (4th) 130, 2007 FCA 258, 47 C.P.R. (4th) 1 (F.C.A.).

### f) The Relevant Date

In an action for passing off the date for deciding whether the conduct of the defendant is actionable is the date on which the conduct commenced.[25] This is consistent with the statutory codification of passing off contained in the *Trade-marks Act.*

## 2. Subsection 7(b) and (c) of the *Trade-marks Act*

These subsections round out the Federal regulatory scheme concerning trademarks and are constitutionally valid.[26] The *Act* provides that no person shall:

> (b) direct public attention to his wares, services or business in such a way as to cause or be likely to cause confusion in Canada, at the time he commenced so to direct attention to them, between his wares, services or business, and the wares, services or business of another;

> (c) pass off other wares or services as and for those ordered or requested.

An action brought under section 7 of the *Act* the misrepresentation must be in relation to a registered or unregistered trademark.[27]

The statutory cause of action under subsection 7(b) essentially codifies the common law tort of passing off.[28] The reference to the time at which public attention is directed is similar to common law date.

The previous version of the subsection only applied to competitors. But subsection 7(b) was revised to refer to "another" and there is no requirement that the plaintiff and defendant be competitors.[29]

While the provisions of section 6 of the *Act* specifying when trade marks or names are confusing are not strictly applicable, it is useful to consider the

---

25. *Edward Chapman Ladies 'Shop Limited v. Edward Chapman Limited,* (2007), 60 C.P.R (4th) 1 (B.C.C.A.); *Cadbury-Schweppes Pty. Ltd. v. Pub Squash Co. Pty. Ltd.,* [1981] 1 All E.R. 213 (P.C.); *Orkin Exterminating Co. In. v. Pestco of Canada Ltd.* (1985), 5 C.P.R. (3d) 433 (Ont. C.A.).
26. *Asbjorn Horgard A/S v. Gibbs/Nortac Industries Ltd.* (1987), 14 C.P.R. (3d) 314 (F.C.A.); *Kirkbi Ag et al v. Ritvik Holdings Inc.* (2005), 43 C.P.R. (4th) 385 (S.C.C.).
27. *Kirkbi Ag et al v. Ritvik Holdings Inc.* (2002), 20 C.P.R. (4th) 224 (F.C.T.D.) appeal dismissed 2003 F.C.A. 297 and (2005), 43 C.P.R. (4th) 385 (S.C.C.); *WIC TV Amalco Inc. v. ITV Technologies, Inc.* (2005), 38 C.P.R. (4th) 481 (F.C.A.) leave to appeal to the S.C.C. granted.
28. *Kirkbi Ag et al v. Ritvik Holdings Inc,* (2005) 43 C.P.R. (4th) 385 (S.C.C.).
29. *Building Products Ltd. v. BP Canada Ltd.* (1961), 36 C.P.R. 121 (Ex. Ct.).

matters set out in that section in applying section 7(b).[30] It has also been suggested that in order to obtain trademark rights for the purpose of the subsections a trademark must be "used" as required by the *Act* including compliance with section 4 of the *Act*.[31]

Under subsection 7(c) the substitution of a competitor's wares or services as and for those ordered or requested is actionable. In order to succeed with a claim of this nature the plaintiff must show that its wares or services are known and ordered or requested by a specific trade name or mark.

## 3. Defenses

### a) The Absence of Reputation or Goodwill

(i) Lack of Distinctiveness

If a plaintiff does not show that the "get-up" under which the particular goods or services are offered to the public is recognized by the public as distinctive of its goods or services, it will not succeed in an action for passing off.[32]

If a defendant uses the characteristic features of the get-up used in the trade in which it is engaged and this may be a defense to a claim for passing off.[33]

(ii) Concurrent Right

If a defendant has been using the same trade mark, get up or trade name as the plaintiff with equal claim to its independent use, it will be difficult for the plaintiff to succeed unless it can be shown that the defendant has extended its use to the plaintiff's area of business and beyond the area where the defendant has carried on business.

---

30. *Aluminum Company of Canada v. Tisco Home Building Products* (1977), 33 C.P.R. (2d) 145 (F. C.T.D.); *Asbjorn Horgard A/S v. Gibbs/Nortac Industries Ltd.* (1987), 14 C.P.R. (3d) 314 (F. C.A.).
31. *BMW Canada Inc. v. Nissan Canada Inc.* (2007), 57 C.P.R. (4th) 81 (F.C.), 60 C.P.R. (4th) 181, 2007 FCA 255 (F.C.A). While the imposition of such a requirement was reasonable in that case it may be too onerous as a general requirement.
32. *See Richfield Oil Corp. v. Richfield Oil Corp. of Can. Ltd.*, [1955] Ex. C.R. 17 (Ex. Ct.).
33. *Cheerio Toys & Games Ltd. v. Dubiner* (1965), 44 C.P.R. 134 (Ex. Ct.); affirmed [1966] S.C.R. 206, 48 C.P.R. 226 (S.C.C.); *Abbot Laboratories Ltd. v. Apotex* (1998), 81 C.P.R. (3d) 85 (Ont. Ct. Gen. Div.); *Kun Shoulder Rest Inc. v. Josepk Kun Violin* (1998), 83 C.P.R. (3d) 331 (F.C.T.D.)

### (iii)  Descriptive Words or Marks

The applicable principles are similar to those under the *Trade-marks Act.* A descriptive word or mark is not usually capable of being protected in an action for passing off unless it can be shown that the descriptive word or mark has acquired a secondary meaning and associated goodwill.[34]

The onus of proving the acquisition of secondary meaning, which is on the plaintiff, is a heavy one when the mark in question is a descriptive word. In order to satisfy the onus it is not sufficient to show that mark is distinctive in the channels of trade as, for example, to the manufacturer or wholesaler, but it must be distinctive to probable purchasers including the ultimate consumer.[35] If, the descriptive word or mark is also the name of the goods themselves, it will be extremely difficult for the word to acquire a secondary meaning.[36]

In addition, if a plaintiff is relying on the descriptive word or mark relatively small differences in the word or mark used by the defendant should be sufficient to avoid a misrepresentation.[37]

If the plaintiff's descriptive word or mark is not used as a trademark but as the name of the type of good in issue it may be generic[38] and extremely difficult to protect.[39] In cases where the question is whether a particular word or mark has been used for the purpose of distinguishing the wares of a particular manufacturer or whether it has been used principally as a description or a name of the wares themselves, the whole course of conduct of the plaintiff must be considered in order to find out whether it has lost its distinctiveness or not.[40]

---

34.  *Frank Reddaway & Co. Ltd. v. George Banham & Co. Ltd.,* [1896] A.C. 199 (H.L.); *Standard Industries Ltd. v. Rosen* (1954), 24 C.P.R. 41 (Ont. H.C.).

35.  *Parke, Davis & Co. v. Empire Laboratories Ltd.* (1963), 41 C.P.R. 121 (Ex. Ct.); affirmed 43 C.P.R. 1 (S.C.C.).

36.  *Can. Shredded Wheat Co. v. Kellogg Co. of Can. Ltd.,* [1936] O.R. 613 (Ont. C.A.); affirmed [1938] 1 All E.R. 618 (P.C.).

37.  *Office Cleaning Services v. Westminster Window and General Cleaners* (1946), 63 R.P.C. 39 (H.L.); *Westfair Foods Ltd. v. Jim Pattison Industries Ltd.* (1989), 26 C.P.R. (3d) (B.C.S.C.) affirmed 30 C.P.R. (3d) 174 (B.C.C.A.); and see *Phones4U Ltd. v. Phone4u.co.uk Internet Ltd.* [2006] EWCA Civ 244 (U.K.C.A.).

38.  *Burberrys v. J.C. Cording & Co.* (1909), 26 R.P.C. 693 (Ch. D.).

39.  *Linoleum Manufacturing Co. v. Nairn* (1878), 7 Ch. D. 834.

40.  *Cheerio Toys & Games Ltd. v. Dubiner* (1965), 44 C.P.R. 134 (Ex. Ct.); affirmed [1966] S.C.R. 206, 48 C.P.R. 226. (S.C.C.).

### (iv) Geographical Words or Marks

A trader is entitled to use the name of the locality where their wares are produced or business is carried on[41] unless a plaintiff can show that such word or mark has acquired a secondary meaning in that locality and satisfy the other requirements to show that passing off has occurred.[42]

### (v) Functionality

Like trade marks any combination of elements which are primarily designed to perform a function cannot be protected through a claim for passing off.[43] The fact that the party seeking protection obtained a patent relating to the article in question is evidence of functionality.[44]

## b) Other Defenses

### (i) Use of a Registered Trademark

If the alleged passing off relates to the defendant's use of a registered trademark in association with the wares or services of the registration, the existence of the registration will be a defense to a claim for passing off as a result of the rights granted under the *Trade-marks Act*.[45]

### (ii) Use of an Individual's Own Name

An individual defendant has a right to use his or her own name and the fact that confusion may occur does not constitute passing off by itself.[46]

---

41. *Grand Hotel of Caledonia Springs v. Wilson,* [1904] A.C. 103; *Hopton Wood Stone Firms Ltd. v. Gething* (1910), 27 R.P.C. 605; *General Motors of Canada v. Decarie Motors Inc.* (2000), 9 C.P.R. (4th) 368 (F.C.A.).
42. *Steinberg v. Belgium Glove & Hosiery Co. of Canada Ltd.* (1953), 19 C.P.R. 56 (Ex. Ct).
43. *Canadian Shredded Wheat Co., Ltd. v. Kellogg Co. of Canada, Limited,* [1938] 1 All. E.R. 618 (PC.), [1938] 2 D.L.R. 145; *Parke, Davis & Co. v. Empire Laboratories Ltd* (1963), 41 C.P.R. 121 (Ex. Ct), affirmed [1964] S.C.R. 351 (S.C.C.); *Thomas & Betts, Ltd. v. Panduit Corp.* (2000), 4 C.P.R. (4th) 498 (F.C.A); *Kirkbi Ag et al v. Ritvik Holdings Inc.* (2005), 43 C.P.R. (4th) 385 (S.C.C.).
44. *Parke, Davis & Co. v. Empire Laboratories Ltd* (1963), 41 C.P.R. 121 (Ex. Ct) affirmed [1964] S.C.R. 351 (S.C.C.).
45. *Molson Canada v. Oland Breweries Ltd.* (2002), 19 C.P.R. (4th (F.C)) 201 (Ont. C.A.); *Remo Imports Ltd. v. Jaguar Cars Limited,* (2007), 60 C.P.R. (4th) 130, 2007 FCA 258, 47 C.P.R. (4th) 1 (F.C.A.); *Veuve Clicquot Ponsardin v. Boutiques Cliquot* [2006] 1 S.C.R 824, 49 C.P.R. (4th) 401 (S.C.C.).
46. *Edward Chapman Ladies' Shop Ltd. v. Edward Chapman Ltd.* (2006) 45 C.P.R. (4th) 321 (B.C. S.Ct.) affirmed (2007), 60 C.P.R. (4th) 1, 2007 BCCA 370 (B.C. C.A.).

However, if confusion occurs, which is brought to the attention of that defendant, they are under an obligation to take reasonable care to qualify the representation implied in his or her conduct so as to avoid confusion.[47]

### (iii) Plaintiff's Own Goods

It is not passing off to use the plaintiff's name or mark in connection with wares that are the plaintiff's original wares.[48] But a trader cannot represent that wares, which are the plaintiff's wares, are of a particular class or quality if they are not. For example, it is actionable to offer wares of inferior or deteriorated quality as the plaintiff's original goods[49] or the plaintiff's wares in an materially altered form as the original.[50] The fact that notice of the difference is given to consumers at the time of sale may avoid a finding of passing off.[51]

---

47. *Hurlburt Co. Ltd. v. Hurlburt Shoe Co.,* [1925] S.C.R. 141 (S.C.C.); *Meubles Domani's v. Guccio Gucci S.P.A.* (1992), 43 C.P.R. (3d) 372 (F.C.A.).
48. *Seiko Time Canada v. Consumers Distributing,* [1984] 1 S.C.R. 583 (S.C.C.); *Spalding v. Gamage* (1915), 32 R.P.C. 273 (H.L.).
49. *Spalding v. Gamage* (1915) 32 R.P.C. 273 (H.L.).
50. *Westinghouse Brake & Saxby Signal Co. v. Varsity Eliminator Co.* (1935), 52 R.P.C. 295.
51. *Seiko Time Can. Ltd. v. Consumers Distributing Co.* (1980), 50 C.P.R. (2d) 147 (Ont. H.C.), reversed [1984] 1 S.C.R. 583, 1 C.P.R. (3d) 1 (S.C.C.).

# CHAPTER
# 15

# Actions for Infringement and Passing Off

The practice in actions for passing off is substantially similar to actions for infringement, and in this chapter the two actions are dealt with together, although they are separate and distinct causes of action.

## 1. Jurisdiction

Both the Federal Court[1] and any court of competent jurisdiction of a province have jurisdiction to hear and determine an action for the infringement of a trademark.[2] The rights associated with a registered trademark are territorial and a Canadian court does not have jurisdiction concerning infringement that takes place wholly abroad. [3]

A claim for passing off is also territorial in nature since it is restricted to the area in which the plaintiff can establish the existence of goodwill. Actions for passing off at common law may only be brought in courts of competent jurisdiction of the provinces. The Federal Court has no statutory jurisdiction to hear an action for passing off unless the claim is interconnected with a claim over which the court has jurisdiction.[4]

Actions claiming relief under subsection 7(a) or (b) of the *Trade-marks Act*, the statutory codification of passing off, may be brought in the Federal Court or in courts of competent jurisdiction in the provinces.

A Canadian court may decline jurisdiction under the doctrine known as *forum non conveniens*.[5] In addition, a Canadian Court may in its discretion stay an action on the ground that the claim is being proceeded with in another jurisdiction.[6]

---

1. *Trade- marks Act*, R.S.C. 1985, c. T-13, section. 55; *Federal Court Act*, R.S.C. 1985, c. F-7, section. 20.
2. *Shredded Wheat Co. v. Kellogg Co. of Can. Ltd.*, [1936] O.R. 613 (Ont. C.A.); affirmed [1938] 2 D.L.R. 145 (P.C.). See section 11 of *Courts of Justice Act*, R.S.O. 1990, c. C.43.
3. *Beloit Canada Ltée/Ltd. et al. v. Valmet-Dominion Inc. (now Valmet Montreal Inc.)* (1997), 73 C.P.R. (3d) 321. (F.C.A.); *Pro Swing Inc. v. Elta Golf Inc.*, [2006] 2 S.C.R 612 (S.C.C.).
4. *Kirkbi Ag et al v. Ritvik Holdings Inc.* (2002), 20 C.P.R. (4th) 224 (F.C.T.D.) appeal dismissed 2003 F.C.A. 297; appeal dismissed (2005) 43 C.P.R. (4th) 385 (S.C.C.).
5. *Folkes v. Greensleeves Publishing Ltd* (1997), 76 C.P.R. (3d) 360 (Ont. Ct. (Gen. Div.)) appeal dismissed 85 C.P.R. (3d) 144 (Ont. C. A.).
6. *Courts of Justice Act*, R.S.O. 1990, c. C.43, 106 and *Federal Court Act*, R.S.C. 1985, c. F-7, section. 50.

## 2. Interim Proceedings

### a) Proceedings for Interim Custody

Pursuant to section 53 of the *Trade-marks Act* where a court[7] is satisfied, on application of any interested person, that any registered trademark or any trade name has been applied to any wares that have been imported into Canada or are about to be distributed in Canada in such a manner that the distribution of the wares would be contrary to the *Act*, or that any indication of a place of origin has been unlawfully applied to any wares, the court may make an order for the interim custody of the wares, pending a final determination of the legality of their importation or distribution in an action commenced within such time as is prescribed by the order. An application for such an order may be made by any person interested, in an action or otherwise, and either on notice or *ex parte*.[8]

Before making an order under section 53, the court may require the applicant to furnish security, in an amount fixed by the court, to answer any damages that may by reason of the order be sustained by the owner, importer or consignee of the wares and for any amount that may become chargeable against the wares while they remain in custody under the order.[9]

An application for an interim order will be considered by a court as involving the exercise of extraordinary jurisdiction to preserve the applicant's rights pending a final determination. As a result, the court will likely apply the principles relating to the granting of interim and interlocutory injunctions.

Where in any action under section 53 the court finds that the importation is or the distribution would be contrary to the *Act*, it may make an order prohibiting the future importation of wares to which the trademark, trade name or indication of origin has been applied.[10] The importation of any goods in respect of which such an order has been made is prohibited by the Customs Tariff.[11] However, a consent or default judgment does not satisfy the requirement for a final determination required by this provision and custom officers have refused to enforce such judgments.[12]

---

7. Section 52 provides that "court" means the Federal Court or the superior court of a province in sections 53 to 53.3.
8. Subsection 53(5). "Person interested" is broadly defined in section 2.
9. Subsection.53(2).
10. Subsection 53(4).
11. *Customs Tariff*, R.S.C. 1985, c. C-54.01, section 114.
12. *Adidas Sportschuhfabriken Adi Dassler KG. v. Kinney Shoes of Can. Ltd.* (1971), 2 C.P.R. (2d) 227 (Ex. Ct.); *Montres Rolex S.A. v. M.N.R.* (1987), 17 C.P.R. (3d) 507 (F.C.T.D.); *Montres Rolex S.A. v.Balshin* (1992), 45 C.P.R. (3d) 174 (F.C.A.).

## b)  Proceedings for Detention by Minister

Where a court is satisfied, on application by the owner of a registered trade mark, that any wares to which the trade mark has been applied are about to be imported into Canada or have been imported into Canada but have not yet been released, and that the distribution of the wares in Canada would be contrary to the *Trade-marks Act,* the court may make an order

    (a)  directing the Minister of National Revenue to take reasonable measures, on the basis of information reasonably required by the Minister and provided by the applicant, to detain the wares;

    (b)  directing the Minister to notify the applicant and the owner or importer of the wares, forthwith after detaining them, of the detention and the reasons therefor; and

    (c)  providing for such other matters as the court considers appropriate.[13]

Such an application may be made in an action or otherwise, and either on notice or *ex parte,* except that it must always be made on notice to the Minister.[14] Before making an order the court may require the applicant to furnish security, in an amount fixed by the court, (a) to cover duties, storage, and handling charges, and any other amount that may become chargeable against the wares; and (b) to answer any damages that may by reason of the order be sustained by the owner, importer or consignee of the wares.[15]

An application for such an order will likely be considered by a court as involving the exercise of extraordinary jurisdiction to preserve the applicant's rights pending a final determination. As a result, the court will likely apply the principles relating to the granting of interim and interlocutory injunctions.

The sections only applies when wares to which the trademark has been applied are "about to be imported" or "have been imported into Canada but have not yet been released." It is difficult to obtain such information which significantly restricts the application of the section.

The Canada Customs and Revenue Agency (CCRA) has published memorandum D19-43, dated May 19, 2000, setting out its requirements relating to such applications. Representatives of the Minister have the right to make submissions when the application is heard and may apply to the court for directions in implementing an order that has been made.[16]

---

13.  Subsection 53.1(1).
14.  Subsection 53.1(2).
15.  Subsection 53.1(3).
16.  Subsection 53.1(4).

Unless an order made on the application provides otherwise, the Minister shall, subject to the *Customs Act* and to any other Act of Parliament that prohibits, controls or regulates the importation or exportation of goods, release the wares without further notice to the applicant if, two weeks after the applicant has been notified of the detention, the Minister has not been notified that an action has been commenced for a final determination by the court of the legality of the importation or distribution of the wares.[17]

Where, in an action commenced under the section, the court finds that the importation is or the distribution would be contrary to the *Act*, the court may make any order that it considers appropriate in the circumstances, including an order that the wares be destroyed or exported, or that they be delivered up to the plaintiff as the plaintiff's property absolutely.[18] Conversely, if the court finds that the importation was not contrary to the *Act*, the defendant(s) may seek costs and any damages suffered by reason of the order.

## 3. Parties

### a)  Plaintiff

The statutory provisions relating to infringement have been discussed in Chapter 13. The plaintiff in an action for infringement, with one exception relating to a licensee, must be the owner of the registered trademark in issue.[19] The assignee of a registered trademark may institute an action for infringement without registering the assignment as registration is not necessary to make an assignment of a trademark effective against a third party.[20] A plaintiff may sue for infringement of a trademark even though not a resident of Canada.[21]

The plaintiff in an action for passing off must be the owner of the goodwill in issue and have suffered or will likely suffer damage by reason of the defendant's misrepresentation.[22]

---

17. Subsection 53.1(6).
18. Subsection 53.1(7).
19. See sections 19 and 20 and *Can. Safeway Ltd. v. Man. Food & Commercial Workers, Loc. 832*, (1983), 73 C.P.R. (2d) 234 (Man. C.A.).
20. *Wilkinson Sword (Can.) Ltd. v. Juda* (1966), 51 C.P.R. 55 (Ex. Ct.); *McCurdy Enterprises Ltd. v. Shamrock Spring Water Inc.* (2005), 45 C.P.R. (4th) 55 (Nfld and Lab. Sup. Ct. T.D.) and see Chapter 9, part 1(b) .
21. *Creamette Co. v. Famous Foods Ltd.*, [1933] Ex. C.R. 200 (Ex. Ct.).
22. See Chapter 14 and *Glen Oak Inc. v. Smith & Nephew Inc.* (1996), 68 C.P.R. (3d) 153 (F.C.A.).

## b) Licensee

Subject to any agreement subsisting between an owner of a trademark and a licensee of the trademark, the licensee may call on the owner to take proceedings for infringement thereof, and, if the owner refuses or neglects to do so within two months after being so called on, the licensee may institute proceedings for infringement in the licensee's own name as if the licensee were the owner, making the owner a defendant.[23]

## c) Defendants

The primary defendant in an action for infringement will be the owner of the impugned mark which is being "used"[24] to the detriment of the plaintiff. In addition, section 20 refers to persons who sell, distribute or advertise wares or services in association with a confusing trademark which broadens the net particularly when combined with an allegation of inducement.

Similar considerations apply in an action for passing off although there is more flexibility since a person may be sued if they have authorized or enabled passing off[25] or aided and abetted someone else to pass off.[26]

## d) Directors and Officers

Generally speaking, the directors or officers of a corporation are not personally liable for the infringing activities of the corporation and accordingly should not be parties, unless they formed the corporation for the purpose of infringing or they have directly ordered or authorized the acts complained of. In order to find personal liability there must be circumstances from which it is reasonable to conclude that the purpose of the director or officer was not the direction of the manufacturing and selling activity of the company in the ordinary course of his or her relationship to it but the deliberate, willful, and knowing pursuit of a course of conduct that was likely to constitute infringement or reflected an indifference to the risk of it. A broad appreciation

---

23. Subsection 50(3).
24. See Chapter 5.
25. *Taft Broadcasting Co. v. Rogers Cable T. V. Ltd.* (1974), 18 C.P.R. (2d) 94 (F.C. T.D.); *Ray Plastics Ltd. v. Canadian Tire Corporation, Limited* (1995), 62 C.P.R. (3d) 247 (Ont. Gen. Div.), an appeal from this decision was settled. The decision is questionable since it resulted in a double recovery.
26. *Robert Simpson Co. Ltd. v. Simpson's-in-the-Strand Ltd.* (1980), 49 C.P.R. (2d) 16 (Ont. H.C.).

of the circumstances of each case must be made to determine whether as a matter of policy they call for personal liability.[27]

If an unfounded allegation is made against a director or an officer, a motion to strike the relevant portion of the statement of claim may be brought.

## 4. Pleadings

### a) Basic Requirements

Pleadings in an action for infringement or passing off are governed by the rules of practice of the court in which the action is brought. A concise statement of the material facts must be pleaded to establish an arguable cause of action assuming that the allegations in the statement of claim are true. If the *Trade-marks Act* or any other statute is pleaded the sections relied upon and the material facts giving rise to the cause of action must be pleaded.[28] It is not necessary to allege that a defendant intended to violate the plaintiff's rights in an action for infringement or passing off.

### b) Particulars

The function of particulars is to enable the party requesting them to know the nature of the case it has to meet, to prevent surprise and to limit the issues to be tried.[29] A request for particulars should not to be a fishing expedition and should not to be ordered concerning how the issues are to be proved.[30]

A demand for particulars should be made before a motion is brought.[31] As a general rule, particulars will not be ordered unless it is established that they are both necessary for pleading and are not within the knowledge of the party seeking them, unless the pleading is, on its face, inadequate or in violation of the rules.[32]

---

27. *Mentmore Manufacturing Company Limited et al v. National Merchandising Manufacturing Company Inc.* (1978), 89 D.L.R. (3d) 195 (F.C.A.).
28. *Schering Can. Inc. v. Pentagone Laboratories Ltd.* (1985), 6 C.P.R. (3d) 261 (F.C.T.D.).
29. *Gulf Canada Ltd. v. Tug "Mary Mackin,"* [1984] 1 F.C. 884 (F.C.A.).
30. *Embee Electronic Agencies v. Agence Sherwood Agencies, Inc., et al.* (1979), 43 C.P.R. (2d) 285 (F.C.T.D.).
31. *Rules of Civil Procedure*, R.R.O 1990, Regulation 194 as amended, Rule 25.10; *Federal Court Rules, 1998*, SOR/98–106, rule 181.
32. *Telemedia v. 624654 Ont. Ltd.* (1987), 17 C.P.R. (3d) 355 and 570 (F.C.T.D.); *Windsurfing Int'l Inc. v. Novaction Sports Inc.* (1988), 18 C.P.R. (3d) 230 (F.C.T.D.).

## 5. Interlocutory Injunctions

### a) Purpose

The purpose for granting an interlocutory injunction is to protect the plaintiff against injury as a result of the violation of a right for which the plaintiff could not be adequately compensated by an award of damages.[33] The interlocutory injunction preserves the status quo concerning the plaintiff's claim until trial in such a case.

A condition precedent to the grant of an interlocutory injunction is an undertaking from the plaintiff to assume responsibility for the damages sustained by the defendant in the event that the plaintiff is ultimately unsuccessful on the merits when the action is heard. The purpose of the undertaking is to counterbalance the harm the wrongly enjoined defendant would suffer as a consequence of the interlocutory injunction.[34] The court may order, in appropriate circumstances, that the plaintiff secure this undertaking by providing to the court suitable security.[35]

A plaintiff who successfully obtains an interlocutory injunction is under a duty to proceed with reasonable dispatch to bring the action to trial. If the plaintiff fails to do so, the defendant may move to dissolve the injunction.[36]

On the dissolution of an interlocutory injunction, the defendant is entitled to an enquiry as to the damages sustained by reason of the injunction.[37]

Refusing or neglecting to obey an interlocutory injunction may constitute contempt of court.[38] A person found to be in contempt of court is subject to fine or imprisonment.[39]

---

33. *American Cyanamid* v. *Ethicon* [1975] 1 All E.R. 504 (H.L.).
34. *Rules of Civil Procedure*, R.R.O 1990, Regulation 194 as amended Rule 40.03; *Federal Court Act*, R.S.C. 1985, c. F-7 as amended, section 44 and see *Mattel Canada Inc v GTS Acquisitions Ltd* (1998), 82 C.P.R. (3d) 57 (F.C.T.D.).
35. *Nelson Burns & Co. Ltd.* v. *Gratham Industries Ltd.* (1981), 59 C.P.R. (2d) 113 (Ont. H.C).
36. *Bourganis v. Glarentzos* (1978), 19 O.R. (2d) 328 (H.C.J.); *Ciba-Geigy Ltd. v. Novopharm Ltd.* (1997), 77 C.P.R. (3d) 428 (F.C.T.D.).
37. *Mattel Canada Inc v GTS Acquisitions Ltd* (1998), 82 C.P.R. (3d) 57 (F.C.T.D.);
38. *Cutter (Canada) Ltd. v. Baxter Travenol Laboratories of Canada Ltd,* (1987), 14 C.P.R. (3d) 449.
39. See Ontario *Rules of Civil Procedure*, R.R.O. 1990, Regulation 194, as amended, Rule 60.11 and *Federal Court Rules 1998*, SOR/98–106, Rules 466–472.

## b) The Test for Granting an Interlocutory Injunction

A three-stage test is applied in considering whether to grant an interlocutory injunction:[40]

i)   A preliminary assessment must be made of the merits of the case to ensure that there is a serious question to be tried.

ii)  It must be determined whether the applicant would suffer irreparable harm if the application were refused.

iii) An assessment must be made as to which of the parties would suffer greater harm from the granting or refusal of the remedy pending a decision on the merits.

An interlocutory injunction is a discretionary equitable remedy. The applicant must come to the court with "clean hands"[41] and equitable defenses may be raised.

Delay in commencing proceedings is an important consideration that may preclude the grant of an interlocutory injunction.[42]

## c) A Serious Question to Be Tried

To determine whether a serious question to be tried has been established, it is necessary to look at the pleadings and respective causes of action in light of the evidence presented.[43] It is not the function of the court at this stage to attempt to resolve conflicts of evidence based on affidavits or to decide difficult questions of law.[44] These issues should be dealt with at trial.

If the refusal to grant an injunction will, practically speaking, dispose of the action, a court should require that a strong *prima facie* case be established.[45]

---

40.  *RJR-Macdonald Inc. v. Canada (Attorney General)* [1994] 1 S.C.R. 311, 54 C.P.R. (3d) 114; *American Cyanamid v. Ethicon* [1975] 1 All E.R. 504 (H.L.).

41.  *Dableh v. Ontario Hydro* (1993), 50 C.P.R. (3d) 290 (F.C.T.D.), 68 C.P.R. (3d) 129 (F.C.A.).

42.  *Turbo Resources Ltd. v. Petro-Can Ltd.* (1989), 24 C.P.R. (3d) 1 (Fed. C.A.); *Irwin Toy Ltd. v. Marie-Anna Novelties Inc.* (1986), 12 C.P.R. (3d) 145 (Ont. H.C.).

43.  *Turbo Resources Ltd. v. Petro-Can Ltd.* (1989), 24 C.P.R. (3d) 1 (Fed. C.A.).

44.  *American Cyanamid v. Ethicon* [1975] 1 All E.R. 504 (H.L.).

45.  *RJR-Macdonald Inc. v. Canada (Attorney General)* [1994] 1 S.C.R. 311, 54 C.P.R. (3d) 114; *N.W.L. Ltd. v. Woods*, [1979] 1. W.L.R. 129 (H.L.); *Syntex Inc. v. Apotex Inc.* (1985), 1 C.P.R. (3d) 145 (Fed. C.A.).

## d) Irreparable Harm

Establishing irreparable harm is essential to obtain an interlocutory injunction. The moving party must convince the court that it will suffer irreparable harm if an interlocutory injunction is not granted.[46] "Irreparable" refers to the nature of the harm rather than its magnitude. It is harm which either cannot be quantified in monetary terms or which cannot be cured, frequently because one party cannot collect damages from the other.[47]

The Federal Court of Appeal has strictly required that the moving party present evidence of irreparable harm which is clear and not speculative.[48] Proof of irreparable harm cannot be inferred and it is not sufficient that such harm might likely be suffered; it must be shown that it would be suffered.[49]

## e) The Balance of Convenience

This test is in effect a determination of which of the two parties will suffer the greater harm from the granting or refusal of the interlocutory injunction pending trial.[50] The factors to be taken into account include the following:

(i) where a plaintiff's recoverable damages resulting in the continuance of the defendant's activities pending trial would be an adequate remedy that the defendant would be financially able to pay, an interlocutory injunction should not normally be granted;

(ii) where such damages would not provide the plaintiff an adequate remedy but damages (recoverable under the plaintiff's undertaking) would provide the defendant with such a remedy for the restriction on his activities, there would be no ground for refusing an interlocutory injunction;

(iii) where doubt exists as to the adequacy of these remedies in damages available to either party, regard should be had to where the balance of convenience lies;

---

46. *RJR-Macdonald Inc. v. Canada (Attorney General)* [1994] 1 S.C.R. 311, 54 C.P.R. (3d) 114. (S.C.C).

47. *Manitoba (A.G.) v Metropolitan Stores (MTS) Ltd.* (1987), 38 D.L.R (4th) 321 (S.C.C).

48. *Imperial Chemical Industries PLC v. Apotex* (1989), 27 C.P.R. (3d) 345, (F.C.A.); *Syntex Inc. v. Novopharm Limited,*(1991), 36 C.P.R (3d) 129 (F.C.A.), leave to appeal to the S.C.C. refused [1991] 3 S.C.R. xi; *Nature Co. v. Sci-Tech Educational Inc.* (1992), 41 C.P.R. (3d) 359, (F.C.A.); *Centre Ice Ltd. v. National Hockey League* (1994), 53 C.P.R. (3d) 34, (F.C.A.).

49. *Centre Ice* and *Syntex Inc.* v. *Novopharm Ltd.* (1991), 36 C.P.R. (3d) 129, (F.C.A.).

50. *Manitoba (A.G.) v Metropolitan Stores (MTS) Ltd.* (1987), 38 D.L.R (4th) 321 (S.C.C); *RJR-Macdonald Inc. v. Canada (Attorney General)* [1994] 1 S.C.R. 311, 54 C.P.R. (3d) 114. (S.C.C).

(iv) where other factors appear to be evenly balanced, it is prudent to take such measures as will preserve the status quo;

(v) where the evidence on the application is such as to show one party's case to be disproportionately stronger than the other's, this factor may be permitted to tip the balance of convenience in that party's favor provided the uncompensatable disadvantage to each party would not differ widely; and

(vi) other unspecified special factors may possibly be considered in the particular circumstances of individual cases.[51]

If an interlocutory injunction is not ordered the defendant is frequently ordered to keep an account of the allegedly infringing sales or may be subject to other terms.[52] A court may also order that the trial of the action be expedited.

## 6. *Anton Piller* Orders

### a) Purpose

The courts, on *ex parte* motion by the plaintiff, where a defendant may conceal or destroy evidence, may make a mandatory order requiring the defendant to permit the plaintiff and its representatives to enter the defendant's premises to inspect articles or documents relevant to the proceeding and to remove them or make copies in order that such evidence may be preserved. Orders of this type are referred to as *Anton Piller* orders after the order issued in the United Kingdom case of *Anton Piller KG v. Manufacturing Processes Ltd.*[53]

Unlike a search warrant, the order does not authorize forcible entry, but exposes the target to contempt proceedings unless permission to enter is given. To the ordinary citizen faced on his or her doorstep with an *Anton Piller* order this may be seen as a distinction without a meaningful difference.[54]

An *Anton Piller* order is an exceptional remedy which will be cautiously granted. In addition, the granting of such an order imposes very serious responsibilities on counsel and those who execute the order.

---

51. *Turbo Resources Ltd. v. Petro-Can Ltd.* (1989), 24 C.P.R. (3d) 1 (Fed. C.A.) summarizing what was said in *American Cyanamid v. Ethicon* [1975] 1 All E.R. 504 (H.L.).
52. *Beamscope Canada Inc. v. 2439-0692 Quebec Inc,* (1991), 36 C.P.R. (3d) 1 (F.C.T.D.); *Minnesota Educational Computing Corp. v. MECC (Software) Inc.* (1992), 41 C.P.R. (3d) 186 (F.C.T.D.).
53. [1976], 1 Ch.55 (Ch. Div.).
54. *Celanese Canada Inc. v. Murray Demolition Corp.,* (2006), 50 C.P.R. (4th) 241 (S.C.C.).

*Anton Piller* orders have been frequently issued in cases involving counterfeiters or "pirates" who are consciously flouting the rights of trademark owners. In this context, the orders are frequently combined with an interim injunction.

## b) Conditions for Granting an Order

Before granting an *Anton Piller* order, a court must be satisfied that:[55]

i) There must be an extremely strong *prima facie* case and the plaintiff's intellectual property right and its infringement must be clearly shown.[56]
ii) The damage to the plaintiff caused by the defendant's alleged misconduct, potential or actual, must be very serious.[57]
iii) There must be clear evidence that the defendants have in their possession incriminating documents or things and that there is a real possibility that they may destroy such material before any application *inter partes* can be made.[58]

Because of the significant negative impact on a defendant resulting from granting an *Anton Piller* order, a plaintiff seeking this type of order must make full and fair disclosure to the court of all relevant facts.[59] The affidavits filed in support of the order should err on the side of excessive disclosure.[60] If it subsequently appears that such disclosure was not made, the order is liable to be set aside and the plaintiff required to pay all of the defendant's costs and damages.

The plaintiff is usually required to post security for damages which may be suffered by the defendant as a result of the inappropriate grant of such an order.[61]

---

55. *Celanese Canada Inc. v. Murray Demolition Corp.*, (2006), 50 C.P.R. (4th) 241 (S.C.C.).
56. *Netboard Inc. v. Avery Holdings Inc.*, (2005), 48 C.P.R. (4th) 241 (F.C); *Castlemore Marketing Inc. v. Intercontinental Trade* (1995), 64 C.P.R. (3d) (F.C.T.D.).
57. *Celanese Canada Inc. v. Murray Demolition Corp.*, (2006), 50 C.P.R. (4th) 241 (S.C.C.).
58. The documents or things at risk must be vital not peripheral to the plaintiff's case *Nintendo of America Inc v. Coinex Video Games Inc.* (1982), 69 C.P.R. (2d) 122 (F.C.A.).
59. *Pulse Microsystems Ltd. v. SafeSoft Systems Inc.* (1996), 67 C.P.R. (3d) 202 (Man. C.A.); *MAI Systems Corp. v. Banwell Computer Services Inc.* (1992), 41 C.P.R. (3d) 57 (Ont. Ct. (Gen. Div.))
60. *Columbia Picture Industries Inc. v. Robinson* [1986] 3 All E.R. 338 (Ch. Div.).
61. *Nintendo of America Inc. v. Coinex Video Games Inc.* (1982), 69 C.P.R. (2d) 122 (F.C.A.).

## c) Safeguards in the Order

The Supreme Court of Canada[62] has said that safeguards for the respondents to such an order cannot be implicit and must be specified in the *Anton Piller* order. Unless and until model orders are developed by legislation or recommended by law societies pursuant to their responsibility for professional conduct, the following guidelines for preparation and execution of an *Anton Piller* order will apply depending on the circumstances:

### i) Basic Protection for the Rights of the Parties

(i) The order should appoint a supervising solicitor who is independent of the plaintiff or its solicitors and is to be present at the search to ensure its integrity. The key role of the independent supervising solicitor is to ensure that the execution of the *Anton Piller* order and everything that flows from it, is undertaken as carefully as possible and with due consideration for the rights and interests of all involved. He or she is an officer of the court charged with a very important responsibility regarding an extraordinary remedy.

(ii) Absent unusual circumstances the plaintiff should be required to provide an undertaking and/or security to pay damages in the event that the order turns out to be unwarranted or wrongfully executed.

(iii) The scope of the order should be no wider than necessary and no material shall be removed from the site unless clearly covered by the terms of the order.

(iv) A term setting out the procedure for dealing with solicitor-client privilege or other confidential material should be included with a view to enabling defendants to advance claims of confidentiality over documents before they come into the possession of the plaintiff or its counsel, or to deal with disputes that arise. Before permitting entry to the premises by any person other than the Supervising Solicitor, the defendant may, for a short time (not to exceed two hours, unless the Supervising Solicitor agrees to a longer period), (a) gather together any documents he or she believes may be privileged; and (b) hand them to the Supervising Solicitor for an assessment of whether they are privileged as claimed. If the Supervising Solicitor decides that any of the documents may be privileged or is in any doubt as to their status, he or she will exclude them from the search and retain them pending further order of the court if in doubt as to whether they are privileged, or return them to the defendant and retain a list of the

---

62. *Celanese Canada Inc. v. Murray Demolition Corp.* (2006), 50 C.P.R. (4th) 241 (S.C.C.).

documents if the documents are privileged. A Respondent wishing to take legal advice and gather documents as permitted must first inform the Supervising Solicitor and keep him or her informed of the steps being taken.

(v) The order should contain a limited use clause (i.e., items seized may only be used for the purposes of the pending litigation).

(vi) The order should state explicitly that the defendant is entitled to return to court on short notice to (a) discharge the order; or (b) vary the amount of security.

(vii) The order should provide that the materials seized be returned to the defendants or their counsel as soon as practicable.

## ii) The Conduct of the Search

(i) In general, the order should provide that the search should be commenced during normal business hours when counsel for the party about to be searched is more likely to be available for consultation.

(ii) The premises should not be searched or items removed except in the presence of the defendant or a person who appears to be a responsible employee of the defendant.

(iii) The persons who may conduct the search-and-seize evidence should be specified in the order or should specifically be limited in number.

(iv) On attending at the site of the authorized search, plaintiff's counsel (or the supervising solicitor), acting as officers of the court should serve a copy of the statement of claim and the order and supporting affidavits and explain to the defendant or responsible corporate officer or employee in plain language the nature and effect of the order.

(v) The defendant or its representatives should be given a reasonable time to consult with counsel prior to permitting entry to the premises.

(vi) A detailed list of all evidence seized should be made and the supervising solicitor should provide this list to the defendant for inspection and verification at the end of the search and before materials are removed from the site.

(vii) Where this is not practicable, documents seized should be placed in the custody of the independent supervising solicitor, and defendant's counsel should be given a reasonable opportunity to review them to advance solicitor-client privilege claims prior to release of the documents to the plaintiff.

(viii) Where ownership of material is disputed, it should be provided to the supervising solicitor or to the defendant's solicitors for safekeeping.

### iii) Procedure Following the Search

(i) The order should make it clear that the responsibilities of the supervising solicitor continue beyond the search itself to deal with matters arising out of the search, subject of course to any party wishing to take a matter back to the court for resolution.

(ii) The supervising solicitor should be required to file a report with the court within a set time limit describing the execution, who was present and what was seized.

(iii) The court may wish to require the plaintiff to file and serve a motion for review of the execution of the search returnable within a set time limit such as 14 days to ensure that the court automatically reviews the supervising solicitor's report and the implementation of its order even if the defendant does not request such a review.

### iv) Solicitor-Client Privilege

An *Anton Piller* order should set out the procedure for dealing with solicitor-client privilege or other confidential material as set out above. If the plaintiff's lawyers inadvertently obtain possession of the defendant's documents which are subject to solicitor-client privilege, they may be disqualified from continuing to act for the plaintiff in the action.

If the plaintiff's lawyers are shown to have received confidential information attributable to a solicitor relationship relevant to the matter in issue, they bear the onus of showing there is no real risk such confidences will be used to prejudice of the defendant. The court will infer that confidences will be shared and that there is a risk that such confidences will be used to the prejudice of the defendant, unless the plaintiff's lawyers can show that the public represented by a reasonably informed person would be satisfied that no use of the information would occur. Only where there is clear and convincing evidence to the contrary will the presumption be rebutted. The fact that the disclosure of the confidential information was inadvertent does not affect the presumption and the onus remains on the plaintiff's lawyers.[63]

Disqualification of the receiving solicitors is not automatic and if a remedy short of removal will cure the problem, it should be considered. The following factors are relevant: (i) how the documents came into the possession of the plaintiff and its counsel; (ii) what the plaintiff and its counsel did upon recognition that the documents were potentially subject to solicitor-client privilege; (iii) the extent of the review of the privileged material; (iv) the contents of the solicitor-client communications and the degree to which they are

---

63. *Macdonald Estate v. Martin* [1990] 3 S.C.R. 1235; *Celanese Canada Inc. v. Murray Demolition Corp.* (2006), 50 C.P.R. (4th) 241 (S.C.C.).

prejudicial; (v) the stage of the litigation; and (vi) the potential effectiveness of an ethical wall or other precautionary steps to avoid mischief.[64]

### v) Setting Aside the Order

A defendant may move to set aside an *Anton Piller* order pursuant to the terms of the order or the relevant provisions of the rules of practice of the court involved.[65] The motion may be based on an attack of any of the conditions relating to the grant of the order or the failure to make full and frank disclosure.

# 7. Discovery

Discovery of documents, examinations for discovery and inspection of property are available in infringement or passing off actions under the rules of the court in which the action is brought.[66]

# 8. Delay and Acquiescence

A plaintiff's delay, that is not for a longer time than prescribed by the applicable statutory limitation, is not a bar to an action.[67] Delay will be taken into consideration in determining the availability of equitable remedies such an injunction or an accounting of profits. In general it is the effect of delay not the fact of delay which must be considered.

If a person consents to the use of their trademark or leads the defendant to believe that use of the trademark is not an infringement or passing off, a defense based on estoppel by acquiescence may be successful.[68]

---

64. *Celanese Canada Inc. v. Murray Demolition Corp.* (2006), 50 C.P.R. (4th) 241 (S.C.C.).
65. Ontario *Rules of Civil Procedure*, R.R.O 1990, Regulation 194 as amended, Rule 39.01(6) and the *Federal Court Rules, 1998*, SOR/98–106 rule 399.
66. Ontario *Rules of Civil Procedure*, R.R.O 1990, Regulation 194 as amended; *Federal Court Rules, 1998*, SOR/98–106.
67. *Alticor Inc. v. Nutravite Pharmaceuticals Inc.* (2004), 31 C.P.R. (4th) 12 (F.C.), 42 C.P.R. (4th) 107 (F.C.A.).
68. *Anheuser-Busch Inc. v. Carling O'Keefe Breweries of Canada Inc.*(1986), 10 C.P.R. (3rd) 433 (F.C.A.); *1013579 Ontario Inc. v. Bedessee Imports Ltd.* (1997), 77 C.P.R. (3d) 163 (F.C.A.).

## 9. Limitation Period

The relevant provincial Limitations Act may provide a defense. Infringement and passing off are continuous torts and a cause of action arises with each repetition of the impugned activity. The assessment of damages will include all those acts of infringement within the relevant limitation period.[69]

As the *Trade-marks Act* does not contain any limitation period, the determination of the applicable limitation depends on where the infringement occurred and the court in which the proceedings are instituted. If an action is brought in a court in Ontario the Ontario *Limitations Act, 2002*[70] will apply. Under this *Act* unless otherwise provided, a proceeding shall not be commenced in respect of a claim after the second anniversary of the day on which the claim was discovered.[71]

If an action is brought in the Federal Court, section 39 of the *Federal Courts Act*[72] applies. If the cause of action arises in a specific province the limitation provisions of that province will apply. If the cause of action arises otherwise than in a province, an action must be brought within six years after the cause of action arose. The words "otherwise than in a province" have been interpreted to mean that in an action for passing off if the alleged confusion is not limited to a province than the six-year limitation of section 39 applies.[73]

## 10. Evidence at Trial

### a) Plaintiff's Ownership in an Action for Infringement

Evidence of the plaintiff's ownership and use of a registered trademark and the use of a confusing trademark is sufficient to establish a *prima facie* case.[74] Filing a certified copy of a trademark registration may be sufficient to show ownership.[75]

---

69. See, e.g., *Limitations Act, 2002*, S.O. 2002, Chapter 24, Schedule B as amended; section 4 and see, *Mastini v. Bell Telephone Co. of Can.* (1971), 18 D.L.R. (3d) 215 (Ex. Ct.).
70. S.O. 2002, Chapter 24, Schedule B as amended.
71. *Limitations Act, 2002*, S.O. 2002, Chapter 24, Schedule B as amended; sections 4 and 5.
72. *Federal Courts Act*, R.S.C. 1985, c. F-7.
73. *Kirkbi Ag et al v. Ritvik Holdings Inc.* (2002), 20 C.P.R. (4th) 224 (F.C.T.D.) appeal dismissed 2003 F.C.A. 297; appeal dismissed (2005), 43 C.P.R. (4th) 385 (S.C.C.). The limitation issue was not considered on appeal.
74. See Chapter 13.
75. Subsection 54.

## b) Infringement

In leading evidence of infringement, at a minimum all that need be shown is that the alleged infringing trademark has been used as a trademark and is identical to or confusing with the plaintiff's registered trade mark.[76]

Expert evidence may be led with respect to pronunciation of the trademark or how many persons would be aware of the mark.[77]

Evidence obtained by public surveys is acceptable so long as the survey is both reliable (in the sense that if the survey was repeated it would likely produce the same result) and valid (in the sense that the right questions have been put to the right pool of respondents in the right way, in the right circumstances to provide the information sought).[78]

Evidence may be presented concerning each of the statutory factors set out in subsection 6(5) of the *Act*.[79] Voluminous evidence to show the extent to which the plaintiff's trademark has become known is typically presented.

In order to show "confusion" for the purpose of the *Act* it is not necessary to show actual consumer confusion but evidence of such confusion is persuasive.[80] Conversely, an adverse inference may be drawn from the lack of evidence of instances of confusion in circumstances where it would readily be available if the allegation of likely confusion was justified.[81]

## c) Passing Off

The plaintiff in an action for passing off must establish

a)  the existence of goodwill or reputation attached to the goods or services supplied in the mind of the purchasing public by association with identifying "get-up" under which the particular goods or services are offered to the public, so that the get-up is recognized by the public as distinctive of the plaintiff's goods or services;

b)  a misrepresentation by the defendant to the public (whether or not intentional) leading or likely to lead the public to believe that the goods

---

76.  See Chapter 13.
77.  *Canadian Tire Corp. v. Accessoires D'Autos Nordiques Inc.* 2006 FC 1431 (F.C.) appeal dismissed (2007), 62 C.P.R. (4th) 436 (F.C.A.).
78.  *Mattel, Inc. v 3894207 Canada Inc.* (2006), 49 C.P.R. (4th) 321 (S.C.C.).
79.  See Chapter 11.
80.  *Mr Submarine Ltd. v. Amandista Investments Limited* (1986), 11 C.P.R. (3d) 425 (F.C.T.D.), reversed (1987), 19 C.P.R. (3d) 3 (F.C.A.) and see *Mattel, Inc. v 3894207 Canada Inc.* (2006), 49 C.P.R. (4th) 321 (S.C.C.).
81.  *Mattel, Inc. v 3894207 Canada Inc.* (2006), 49 C.P.R. (4th) 321 (S.C.C.).

or services offered by the defendant are the goods and services of the plaintiff; and

c)   that it has suffered or that it will likely suffer damage by reason of the erroneous belief engendered by the defendant's misrepresentation that the source of the defendant's goods or services is the same as the source as those offered by the plaintiff.[82]

In addition, evidence may be led to show that certain features are common to the trade, how articles or services are described by potential purchasers, and the characteristics and education of prospective purchasers.[83]

## 11. Remedies

### a) The *Trade-marks Act*

Where a court is satisfied, on application of any interested person, that any act has been done contrary to this *Act*, the court may make any order that it considers appropriate in the circumstances, including an order providing for relief by way of injunction and the recovery of damages or profits and for the destruction, exportation or other disposition of any offending wares, packages, labels, and advertising material and of any dies used in connection therewith.[84]

The relief granted to a successful plaintiff in a common law passing off action is similar to that granted in an action for infringement of trademark, namely, an injunction, damages or an account of the profits made by the defendant and destruction or delivery up for defacement of all falsely marked articles.

### b) Permanent Injunction

In an action for infringement or relying on subsection 7(b) or (c) of the *Act*, if a plaintiff establishes at trial that infringement has occurred, the plaintiff is *prima facie* entitled to an injunction subject to any applicable equitable defenses. Similar considerations apply to a claim for common law passing off.

---

82.  *Reckitt & Colman Products Ltd. v. Borden Inc.*, [1990] 1 All E.R. 873 (H.L.); *CibaGeigy Can. Ltd. v. Apotex Inc.* (1992), 44 C.P.R. (3d) 289 (S.C.C.); and see Chapter 14.

83.  *Smith Kline & French Can. Ltd. v. Novopharm Ltd.* (1982), 62 C.P.R. (2d) 36 (Ont. H.C.).

84.  Section 53.2.

For example, long and unexplained delay by the plaintiff when fully aware of its legal rights may deprive a plaintiff of a permanent injunction.[85]

A person who breaches an obligation contained in an injunction is guilty of contempt of court.[86] A person found to be in contempt is subject to imprisonment, fine, additional orders of the court, sequestration of assets, and further orders for costs.[87] Imprisonment for even a willful breach may be suspended in order to give the offending party a further opportunity of complying with terms of the injunction.

Contempt proceedings must be conducted in accordance with the principles of fundamental justice including the right to be presumed innocent until proven guilty beyond a reasonable doubt and to have a reasonable time to prepare a defense and to call witnesses.[88] A person alleged to have committed a contempt cannot be compelled to testify.[89]

## c) Profits or Damages

### (i) Alternative Remedies

A successful plaintiff in an action for infringement is entitled to the recovery of damages or profits made by the defendant.[90] The plaintiff must elect for one or the other before judgment or an order for a reference is made.[91] In an action *quia timet* nominal damages may be granted.[92]

### (ii) Assessment of Damages

The general rule in relation to "economic" torts is that the measure of damages is to be, so far as possible, that sum of money which will put the injured

---

85. *Institut National des appellations d'origine des vins & eaux-de-vie v. Andres Wines Ltd.* (1987), 60 O.R. (2d) 316, 16 C.P.R. (3d) 385 (Ont. H.C.), affirmed 30 C.P.R. (3d) 279 (Ont. C.A.).
86. *Federal Court Rules, 1998*, SOR/98-106 rule 466(b); *Rules of Civil Procedure*, R.R.O 1990, Regulation 194 as amended, rule 60.11(1).
87. *Federal Court Rules, 1998*, SOR/98-106 rule 472; *Rules of Civil Procedure*, R.R.O. 1990, Regulation 194 as amended, rule 60.11(5). See *Apotex Fermentation Inc. v. Novopharm Ltd* [1998] 2 W.W.R. 725 (Man Q.B.) for a general discussion of factors relevant to the imposition of a substantial fine.
88. *R. v. B.E.S.T. Plating Shoppe Ltd.* (1987), 59 O.R. (2d) 145 (Ont. C.A.).
89. *Federal Court Rules, 1998*, SOR/98-106 rule 470(2) and see *Vidéotron Ltée. v. Industries Microlec Produits Électroniques Inc.* (1992), 45 C.P.R. (3d) 1. (S.C.C.).
90. Section 53.2; *3925928 Manitoba Ltd. v. 101029530 Saskatchewan Ltd.* (2005), 44 C.P.R. (4th)161 (F.C.).
91. *Beloit Canada Lt6e v. Valmet Oy* (1987), 16 C.P.R. (3d) 92 (Fed. C.A.); *3925928 Manitoba Ltd. v. 101029530 Saskatchewan Ltd.* (2005), 44 C.P.R. (4th)161 (F.C.).
92. *Hughes v. Sherrif* [1950] O.R. 206 (Ont. S.C.); 12 C.P.R. 79 (Ont. C.A.).

party in the same position as he or she would have been in if they had not sustained the wrong.[93] The plaintiff can recover loss which is foreseeable, caused by the wrong and not excluded from recovery by public or social policy.[94]

There are two essential principles in determine the amount of damages to be awarded: first, that the plaintiff has the burden of proving its loss; and second, as the defendant is the wrongdoer, damages should be liberally assessed but with the object of compensating the plaintiff not punishing the defendant. Damages are typically not capable of being mathematically ascertained by an exact figure.[95]

Any injury to the plaintiff's reputation, goodwill, or trade is relevant and may be taken into consideration.[96] A reduction in sales may have a direct effect on the amount of damages to be awarded but it does not necessarily follow that the reduced sales were caused by the infringement.[97] Where the plaintiff would not have made the sales made by the defendant, the principle of royalty may be applied in assessing the quantum of damages.[98]

Damages may be presumed from interference and confusion.[99] If the amount of damages cannot be proved, nominal damages may be awarded.[100]

## (iii) Account of Profits

If the plaintiff elects for an account of profits the damages suffered are irrelevant.[101] The right to an account of profits or damages extends to the date of judgment or of the account.[102]

By analogy to cases involving patent infringement, the plaintiff is only entitled to that portion of the infringer's profit which is causally attributable to the infringement.[103] This is consistent with the general law that it is essential that the losses awarded are only those which, on a common sense view of causation, were caused by the breach.[104]

---

93. *Allied Signal Inc. v. Dupont Canada* (1998), 78 C.P.R. (3d) 129 (F.C.T.D.).
94. *Gerber Garment v. Lectra Systems Ltd.* [1997] R.P.C. 443 (U.K.C.A).
95. *Allied Signal Inc. v. Dupont Canada*, (1998), 78 C.P.R. (3d) 129 (F.C.T.D.).
96. *David Dixon & Son Ltd. v. Cornwall Pants & Clothing* Co. (1942), 2 C.P.R. 81 (Ont. S.C.).
97. *Allied Signal Inc. v. Dupont Canada*, (1998), 78 C.P.R. (3d) 129 (F.C.T.D.).
98. *Allied Signal Inc. v. Dupont Canada*, (1998), 78 C.P.R. (3d) 129 (F.C.T.D.); *Lightning Fastener Co. v. Colonial Fastener Co.,* [1936] Ex. C.R. 1 (Ex. Ct.); [1937] S.C.R. 36 (S.C.C.).
99. *Marc-Aurele v. Ducharme* (1976), 34 C.P.R. (2d) 155 (Fed. T.D.).
100. *Louis Vuitton Malletier S.A. v. 486353 B.C. Ltd.* 2008 BCSC 799 (B.C. S.C.)
101. *3925928 Manitoba Ltd. v. 101029530 Saskatchewan Ltd.* (2005), 44 C.P.R. (4th)161 (F.C.).
102. *Dubiner v. Cheerio Toys and Games Ltd.* [1966] Ex. C.R. 801 (Ex. Ct.).
103. *Schmeiser et al. v. Monsanto Canada Inc.,* (2004), 31 C.P.R. (4th) 161 (S.C.C); *Lubrizol Corp. v. Imperial Oil Ltd.* (1996), 71 C.P.R (3d) 26 (F.C.A.).
104. *Cadbury Schweppes Inc. v. FBI Foods Ltd.* [1999] 1 S.C.R. 142, 83 C.P.R. (3d) 289 (S.C.C)

The preferred means of calculating profits is what has been termed the value-based or "differential profit" approach, where profits are allocated according to the value contributed to the defendant's wares by the infringement. A comparison should be made between the defendant's profit attributable to the infringement and the profit if the best non-infringing option was used.[105]

An account of profits is an equitable remedy and subject to equitable defenses. The absence of clean hands[106] or delay[107] may be sufficient to deny the remedy.

In cases involving an account of profits, the courts have imposed a requirement to pay compound interest on profits to reflect the fact that the original profits retained or made would be used as the infringing activities progressed.[108]

Frequently, a court will order that an account of profits be determined on a reference. On a reference, the referee may order that the parties be examined for discovery and order the production for inspection and copying by a party of any document or other material relevant to the matters in issue. In addition, the attendance of witnesses to give evidence at a reference may be enforced by subpoena.[109]

## d) Destruction, Exportation or Other Disposition of Offending Wares

Under section 53.2 of the *Act*, a court may make any order that it considers appropriate in the circumstances, including an order for the destruction, exportation or other disposition of any offending wares, packages, labels, and advertising material and of any dies used in connection therewith.[110] Orders of this nature are discretionary and subject to equitable defenses. The breach of an order may be punished as a contempt of court.

---

105. *Schmeiser et al. v. Monsanto Canada Inc.*, (2004), 31 C.P.R. (4th) 161(S.C.C).
106. *Dableh v. Ontario Hydro* (1993), 50 C.P.R. (3d) 290 (F.C.T.D.), 68 (3d) 129 (F.C.A.).
107. *Invacare Corp. v. Everest & Jennings Canadian Ltd.* (1987), 14 C.P.R. (3d) 156 (F.C.T.D.).
108. *Teledyne Industries Inc. v. Lido Industrial Products Ltd.* (1982), 68 C.P.R. (2d) 204 (F.C.T.D.) and *Wellcome Foundation Ltd. v. Apotex Inc.*, (1997), 82 C.P.R. (3d) (F.C.T.D.).
109. *Federal Court Rules,1998*, SOR/98-106 rule 153 to 164 ; *Rules of Civil Procedure*, R.R.O 1990, Regulation 194 as amended, rule 54 and 55.
110. See *Cheerio Toys and Games Ltd. v. Dubiner* (1964), 48 C.P.R. 226 (Ex. Ct.); affirmed [1966] S.C.R. 206 (S.C.C.); *Cheerio Toys and Games Ltd. v. Cheerio Yo-Yo & Bo-Lo Co.* (1964), 43 C.P.R. 111 (Ex. Ct.); *Thurston Hayes (Hays) Developments Ltd. v. Horn Abbot Ltd.* (1985), 5 C.P.R. (3d) 124 (Fed. C.A.); reversing in part 4 C.P.R. (3d) 376 (Fed. T.D.) concerning similar orders made before the section was added to the *Act*.

There is little case law dealing with the making of orders requiring that infringing goods be exported but in some cases such an order may be in the interest of all of the parties to an action.

With the exception of orders for exportation, similar orders have been commonly made in actions for passing off.[111]

## e) Costs

The granting of costs is in the discretion of the court[112] but frequently costs follow the event and the successful party is entitled to an order in its favor. Reference should be made to the practice and procedure of the court involved concerning the awarding of costs[113] and the effect of offers to settle.[114]

111.  *Cheerio Toys & Games Ltd. v. Cheerio Yo-Yo & Bo-Lo Co.* (1964), 43 C.P.R. 111 (Ex. Ct.); *Noshery Ltd. v. Penthouse Motor Inn Ltd.* (1969), 61 C.P.R 207 (Ont. H.C.).

112.  Ontario *Rules of Civil Procedure*, O. Reg. 560/84, r. 57.01 and *Federal Court Rules, 1998*, C.R.C.1978, vol. VI, c. 663, r. 344.

113.  *Rules of Civil Procedure*, R.R.O 1990, Regulation 194 as amended, rule 57 and *Federal Court Rules, 1998*, SOR/98-106 rule 400–404.

114.  *Rules of Civil Procedure*, R.R.O 1990, Regulation 194 as amended, rule 49 and *Federal Court Rules, 1998*, SOR/98-106 rule 419–422.

# CHAPTER
# 16

# Domain Names

## 1. The Internet

To reach another person on the Internet you have to type an address into your computer—a name or a number. That address, which consists of an Internet Protocol (IP) number, has to be unique so computers know where to find each other. Alpha-numeric domain names were introduced as a mnemonic for IP numbers.

Domain names are the alpha-numeric text strings to the right of the "@" in an email address or immediately following the two slashes in a web address. The domain name designates an IP number consisting of a network address and a host ID on a TCP/IP network.

A domain name has three parts. For example, in the address www.oup. com, the ".com" is the Top Level Domain or (TLD) or root identifier, "oup" is the Second Level Domain (SLD) or host. Additional references can be added to specify a location on the host server. References of this sort are treated as a third or higher-level domain.

The host portion of a domain name may be generic or descriptive. It is unclear whether a domain is a form of intangible intellectual property although it is clear that in practice they are treated as if they were.[1]

The legacy root, the most widely used list of TLDs, is currently made up of 21 generic TLDs (gTLDs) and 250 two-letter country code TLDs (ccTLDs). Currently the TLDs are exclusively in Roman characters. The gTLDs include three-letter TLDs .com, .net, .org, .edu, .gov, .int, .mil., .biz, and. pro and four-letter TLDs including .arpa, .info, .name, .aero, and .coop as well as .museum. The ccTLDs are derived from the International Organization for Standards (IOS) Standard 3166 and include .ca for Canada and .us for the United States among others.

Some gTLDs are open and allow anyone to register as many available domain names as they wish without restrictions. Other gTLDs are restricted and a registrant must meet certain specifications. For example, .name is limited to individuals, and .pro is limited to accredited lawyers, doctors, and accountants. The ccTLDs follow a similar pattern; many ccTLDs are unrestricted although some are restricted and require a local presence or specific legal documentation. Canada's ccTLD, the .ca domain, is restricted.

The Internet Corporation for Assigned Names and Numbers (ICANN) is a non-profit corporation, created in 1998 to oversee a number of Internet-related tasks previously performed directly on behalf of the U.S. Government by other organizations. ICANN's tasks include responsibility for managing the assignment of domain names and IP addresses. ICANN coordinates these unique identifiers across the world.

---

1. George Vona, *Sex in the Courts: Kremen v. Cohen and the Emergence of Property Rights in Domain Names* (2006) 19 I.P.R. 393.

In 1999, it was decided that ICANN should add new gTLDs to the root and that there should be an initial rollout of new gTLDs, followed by an evaluation period. This was done throughout 2000 and .coop, .aero, and .biz. were introduced. After evaluation, further sponsored TLDs was introduced during 2003 and 2004 which included, among others, .mobi, and .travel.

ICANN has announced a new community developed policy that will enable potential applicants to self-select strings, consisting of any word or phrase of 3 to 63 characters in length, that are either the most appropriate for their customers or potentially the most marketable. The strings may use non-Roman characters such as Chinese, Arabic, or Cyrillic characters. It is expected that applicants will apply for targeted community strings as well as some generic strings. ICANN is engaged in finalizing the process to introduce these new gTLDs.[2] When introduced, this expansion of gTLD has the potential to widen the scope of the Internet. Trademark owners have expressed concerns that the policy may give rise to trademark abuse, consumer confusion, and a heavier enforcement burden. ICANN is attempting to address these concerns.

## 2. Domain Names

### a) First Come, First Served

In general terms the registration system is first come, first served and there is no assessment of registrability or entitlement or opposition proceedings. However, the practice has developed of allowing trademark owners the initial opportunity, at the launch of a new gTLDs, of obtaining domains which reflect their trademarks for a limited period of time. This is referred to as a Sunrise Period.

### b) gTLD Domain Names

Registrants who wish to register in the.com,.org, or.net domains or other gTLD domains must do so through a registrar who has been accredited by ICANN. Accredited registrars must enter into a written registration agreement with

---

2. Draft Applicant Guidebook: What You Told Us, 18 February 2009 at http://icann.org/en/ announcements/announcement-3-18feb09-en.htm.

an applicant for a domain name which includes provisions dealing with the following matters:

(a) The applicant shall provide to Registrar accurate and reliable contact details and promptly correct and update them during the term of the Registered Name registration;

(b) The applicant shall represent that, to the best of the applicant's knowledge and belief, neither the registration of the Registered Name nor the manner in which it is directly or indirectly used infringes the legal rights of any third party;

(c) An applicant's willful provision of inaccurate or unreliable information, its willful failure promptly to update information provided to Registrar, or its failure to respond for over fifteen (15) calendar days to inquiries by Registrar concerning the accuracy of contact details associated with the applicant's registration shall constitute a material breach of the Registered Name Holder-registrar contract and be a basis for cancellation of the Registered Name registration;

(d) The applicant shall agree that its registration of the Registered Name shall be subject to suspension, cancellation, or transfer pursuant to any ICANN-adopted specification or policy.[3]

ICANN's agreements with accredited registrars and with gTLD registry operators require compliance with various specifically stated procedures and also with "consensus policies." There are a number of consensus policies including the Uniform Domain Name Dispute Resolution Policy.[4]

Under the Expired Domain Deletion Policy all ICANN-accredited registrars must delete domain names by the conclusion of the 45-day automatic renewal period that follows expiration of a domain name, unless the registrant has consented to have the domain name renewed. Names deleted continue to be subject to a further 30-day hold period designed to allow registrars to restore names which were deleted accidentally or without the intent of the registrant.[5]

Under the Inter-Registrar Transfer Policy, gaining registrars must use a clear standardized form as well as obtaining reliable evidence of the identity of the registrant or administrative contact that has requested the transfer.[6]

3. This obligation is implemented through ICANN's Registrar Accreditation Agreements see Accreditation Agreement at http://www.icann.org/registrars/ra-agreement.
4. See http://www.icann.org/en/general/consensus-policies.htm and see part 4 of this chapter.
5. See complete policy at http://www.icann.org/en/registrars/eddp.htm.
6. See complete policy and related dispute resolution policy at http://www.icann.org/en/transfers/.

ICANN has indicated that if a registrar fails to adhere to any terms of the Registrar Accreditation Agreement, ICANN may pursue all remedies available to it under that Agreement including termination of accreditation.[7]

## c) .ca Domain Names

In order to obtain a registration in the.ca domain, applicants must satisfy the Canadian presence requirements.[8] An applicant must have a connection with Canada. The following individuals and entities, among others, are permitted to apply for the registration of, and to hold and maintain the registration of, a .ca domain name: a Canadian citizen, a permanent resident or a corporation incorporated under the laws of Canada or a province or the owner of a trademark registered in Canada, but in such case an application is limited to a .ca domain name consisting of or including to the exact word component of the registered mark.[9]

·The Canadian Internet Registration Authority (CIRA) is a not-for-profit Canadian corporation that is responsible for operating the .ca ccTLD. An applicant must use a CIRA certified registrar to effect the registration and agree to be subject to the CIRA domain name dispute resolution policy.

## d) Trademark Protection

A domain name that is registrable under the *Trade-marks Act*[10] and is used as a trademark[11] may be protected as a trademark.[12] Due to the requirements for use specified in the *Act*, this means that marks of this type must be registered in association with services.[13]

---

7.  See policy concerning enforcement at http://www.icann.org/compliance/.
8.  See registration rules at http://www.cira.ca.
9.  See registration rule 2.1 at http://www.cira.ca.
10. See Chapter 3, and see *Black v. Molson Canada* (2002), 21 C.P.R. (4th) 52 (Ont. S.C.J.); *Candrug Health Solutions Inc. v. Thorkelson*, (2007), 60 C.P.R (4th) 35 (F.C.), 2008 FCA 100 (F.C.A.) appeal allowed but on consent; and *Emall.ca Inc. v. Cheap Tickets and Travel Inc.*, 2007 FC 243, 56 C.P.R (4th) 82 (F. C.), appeal dismissed, 2008 FCA 50, 68 C.P.R. (4th) 381 (F.C.A.).
11. See Chapter 5.
12. *ITV Technologies Inc. v. WIC Television Ltd.* 2003 F.C. 1056, 40 C.P.R. (4th) 121 appeal dismissed 2005 FCA 96 (F.C.A.).
13. See *Pro-C Ltd. v. Computer City Inc.* (2001), 55 O.R. (3d) 577 (Ont. C.A.) and *Tesco Stores Limited v. Elogicom*, [2006] EWHC 403 (U.K. Ch. D.) where it was found that the defendant's use of a confusing domain name linked to the plaintiff's website was a service consisting of the provision of a pathway through the Internet.

## 3. Jurisdictional Issues

The operation of the Internet raises jurisdictional issues concerning which particular court should hear any applicable disputes. The courts of specific countries typically have specific rules for determining when jurisdiction will be exercised and rules or policies concerning when the jurisdiction of the courts of other countries will be respected.

The concept of jurisdiction was initially based on the royal prerogative. It was generally accepted that each ruler only had power within the territorial confines of their country. Generally jurisdiction remains territorial.

It has been difficult to apply the concept of jurisdiction to the Internet, since, as it is frequently said, the Internet knows no boundaries. When trademarks or copyright material are reproduced on a website, it must be determined which court has jurisdiction with respect to any disputes.

The Supreme Court of Canada has established that the applicability of national laws to communications that have international participants depends on whether there is a sufficient connection between Canada and the communication for Canada to apply its laws consistent with the principles of order and fairness that ensure security of cross-border transactions with justice.[14] The Court has said that the "real and substantial connection test" is the appropriate way to prevent overreaching and to control the exercise of jurisdiction over extra territorial and transnational transactions."[15] The test reflects the underlying reality of the territorial limits of law under the international legal order and respect for the legitimate actions of other states inherent in the principle of international comity.

For Internet related matters, relevant connecting factors include the situs of the content provider, the host server, the intermediaries, and the end user. The weight to be given to any particular factor will vary with the circumstances and the nature of the dispute.[16] The Court has recognized that where Canada is the country of transmission or the country of reception, this is a sufficient "connection" for taking jurisdiction.[17]

---

14. *Society of Composers, Authors and Music Publishers of Canada v. Canadian Association of Internet Providers*, 2004 SCC 45, 32 C.P.R. (4th) 1 (S.C.C.); *Morguard Investments Ltd. v. De Savoye* [1990] 3 S.C.R. 1077.
15. *Society of Composers, Authors and Music Publishers of Canada v. Canadian Association of Internet Providers*, 2004 SCC 45, 32 C.P.R. (4th) 1 (S.C.C.); *Tolofson v. Jensen* [1994] 3 S.C.R. 1022.
16. *Society of Composers, Authors and Music Publishers of Canada v. Canadian Association of Internet Providers*, 2004 SCC 45, 32 C.P.R. (4th) 1 (S.C.C.).
17. *Society of Composers, Authors and Music Publishers of Canada v. Canadian Association of Internet Providers*, 2004 SCC 45, 32 C.P.R. (4th) 1 (S.C.C.).

As a result, the real and substantial connection test is applied to disputes relating to e-commerce[18] although some Canadian courts before this decision applied the approach that has been developed in American jurisprudence.[19]

The courts have accepted a "click wrap" agreement which provides that all disputes were governed by the laws of a particular state and specifies the venue for any legal proceedings can be effective.[20]

## 4. The UDRP

### a) History

Since 1999, domain name registration agreements have required that an applicant submit to an administrative dispute resolution policy limited to cases of abusive registration of domain names. The policy is referred to as the Uniform Domain Name Dispute Resolution Policy[21] (UDRP).

The UDRP policy is included in domain name registration agreements entered into with applicants and sets out the terms and conditions applicable to a dispute between the registrant and a third party relating to the registration and use of a domain name.[22] The policy applies to the gTLDs (e.g., .biz, .com, .info, .mobi, .name, .net, .org), and to the ccTLDs that have adopted the UDRP Policy on a voluntary basis.

18. *UniNet Technologies Inc. v. Communication Services Inc.* (2005), 39 C.P.R. (4th) 1 (B.C.C.A.) *Disney Enterprises Inc. v. Click Enterprises Inc.* (2006), 49 C.P.R. (4th) 87 (Ont. Sup. Ct of Justice); *Desjean v. Intermix Media, Inc.*, 2006 FC 1395, 57 C.P.R (4th) 314 (F.C.), 2007 FCA 365 (F.C.A.).
19. *Braintech Inc. v. Kostich* (1999), 171 D.L.R. (4th) 46 (B.C.C.A.); *Pro-C Ltd. v. Computer City, Inc.* (2000), 7 C.P.R. (4th) 193 (Ont. Sup. Ct.), reversed on other grounds, 14 C.P.R. (4th) 441 (Ont. C.A.); *Easthaven, Ltd. v. Nutrisystems.com Inc.* (2001), 14 C.P.R. (4th) 22 (Ont. Sup. Ct.).
20. *Rudder v. Microsoft Corp* (1999), 2 C.P.R. (4th) 474 (Ont. Sup. Ct); *Kanitz v. Rogers Cable Inc.* (2002), 58 O.R. (3d) 299 (Ont. Sup. Ct.).
21. See http://www.icann.org/dndr/udrp/policy.htm.
22. WIPO publishes material relating to the UDRP which is very helpful See the Guide to the UDRP at http://arbiter.wipo.int/domains/guide/index.html., Model Complaint and Filing guidelines at http://arbiter.wipo.int/domains/complaint/index.html., and Index of WIPO Panel Decisions at http://arbiter.wipo.int/cgi-bin/domains/search/legalindex?lang=eng.

## b)  Applicable Disputes

A registrant is required to submit to a mandatory administrative proceeding
in the event that a complainant asserts that:

  (i)  the domain name is identical or confusingly similar to a trademark or
       service mark in which the complainant has rights;
 (ii)  the registrant has no rights or legitimate interest in the domain name;
       and
(iii)  the domain name has been registered and is being used in bad
       faith.[23]

The complainant must prove each of these elements are present[24] by filing
evidence to substantiate them. If a complainant owns a registered trademark,
this will satisfy the threshold requirement of having trademark rights.[25]
The place of registration of the trademark or the goods and/or services it is
registered for are irrelevant when finding rights in a mark.[26] Federal registration of a mark in Canada or the United States is *prima facie* evidence of the
complainant's rights in the mark but registration on the Supplemental
Register in the United States is not sufficient.[27]

A complainant may rely on a common-law trademark, but in such a case
it must be shown that the mark has become a distinctive identifier associated
with the complainant or its goods and services. Evidence of "secondary
meaning" must be presented including the duration and amount of sales in
association with the mark, the nature and extent of advertising, consumer
surveys, and media recognition. Generic terms that are not distinctive and
do not function as a trademark will not support a complaint under the
UDRP.[28]

The UDRP does not specifically protect personal names; however, where
an unregistered personal name is being used for trade or commerce, the

23.  UDRP Policy Paragraph 4(a).
24.  UDRP Policy Paragraph 4(a); *Nintendo of America, Inc. v. Pokemonplanet.net* WIPO case no.
     D2001-1020; *Shell International Petroleum Company Limited v. Alfred Donovan* WIPO case
     no. D2005-0538.
25.  WIPO Overview, Section 1.1 www.wipo.-int/amc/en/domains/search/overview. See *Uniroyal
     Engineered Products, Inc. v. Nauga Network Services*, WIPO case no. D2000-0503. See also
     *Consorzio del Formaggio Parmigiano Reggiano v. La casa del Latte di Bibulic Adriano*, WIPO
     case no. D2003-0661.
26.  WIPO Overview, Section 1.1. See *Thaigem Global Marketing Limited v. Sanchai Aree*, WIPO
     case no. D2002-0358.
27.  *Chiapetta v. Morales*, WIPO case no. D2002-1103; *Oil Changer, Inc. v. Name Administration,
     Inc.*, WIPO case no. D2005-0530.
28.  *Coming Attractions v.ComingAttractions.com*, NAF, case No. FA0003000094341; *The Car-
     phone Warehouse Limited v. Navigation Catalyst Systems Inc.* WIPO case no. D2008-0483.

complainant can establish common law trademark rights in the name. Personal names that are included in a registered trademark can be protected under the UDRP.[29]

The UDRP applies to the most direct and obvious forms of abusive registration, leaving all other cases to the courts.[30] The summary nature of the proceedings is not intended to resolve complicated factual issues or matters of credibility.

## c) Confusingly Similar

The complainant must establish that the impugned domain name is identical or confusingly similar to a trademark or service mark in which it has rights.

Generally, when a domain name is registered before trademark rights are established, the registration of a domain name will not be found to be in bad faith because the registrant could not have contemplated the complainant's non-existent right.[31]

In UDRP cases the panelists apply the policy criteria and it is not necessary to make out a case of trademark infringement. In these cases the addition of a non-distinctive prefix or suffix, such as "e" to designate "electronic," will receive little weight.[32]

Website content is irrelevant in determining whether the domain name is "confusingly similar."[33] The test for confusing similarity is directed at the trademark and the domain name. However, website content may be relevant when considering "bad faith."

## d) No Rights or Legitimate Interest

For the purpose of such proceedings any of the following circumstances, in particular but without limitation, if found by the Panel to be proved based on

---

29. WIPO Overview, Section 1.6.at www.wipo.-int/amc/en/domains/search/overview.
30. *Stephen Cleeve v. Domains by Proxy Inc./Consumer Protection*, WIPO case no. D2007-731, *Your Golf Travel Limited v. Hardelot Holidays Limited*, WIPO case no. D2007-1058.
31. *Stephen Cleeve v. Domains by Proxy Inc./Consumer Protection*, WIPO case no. D2007-073, and see WIPO Overview 1.4 at www.wipo.-int/amc/en/domains/search/overview.
32. *General Electric Co. v. Online Sales Inc.*, WIPO case no. D2000-0343, *Ticketmaster Corp. v. Brown*, WIPO case no. D2001-0716, *Sun Microsystems, Inc. v. Telmex Mgmt. Sers.* NAF case no. FA0206000114621 (Aug. 2002), *Canadian Tire Corporation, Limited v. Mike Rollo* WIPO case no. D2002-1069.
33. *AT&T Corp. v. Amjad Kausar,* WIPO case no. D2003-327, and see WIPO Overview 1.2 at www.wipo.-int/amc/en/domains/search/overview.

its evaluation of all evidence presented, shall demonstrate rights or legitimate interests to the domain name

   (i) before any notice of the dispute, use of, or demonstrable preparations to use, the domain name or a name corresponding to the domain name in connection with a *bona fide* offering of goods or services; or

   (ii) the respondent (as an individual, business, or other organization) has been commonly known by the domain name, even if no trademark or service mark rights have been acquired; or

   (iii) making a legitimate noncommercial or fair use of the domain name, without intent for commercial gain to misleadingly divert consumers or to tarnish the trademark or service mark at issue.[34]

Generally panelists require a complaint to make out an initial *prima facie* case that the respondent lacks rights or legitimate interest. Once this is done the burden shifts to the respondent to show rights or legitimate interest.[35]

Using a domain name that is a misspelling of the complainant's trademark to divert traffic to a competitive website is not a legitimate interest.[36] A pattern of other infringing activity tends to show a lack of legitimate interest as well as bad faith.[37] The defence of laches has no application under the UDRP policy[38] but delay may make it more difficult to show lack of legitimate interest and bad faith.[39]

## e) Bad Faith

For the purpose of such proceedings the following circumstances, in particular but without limitation, if found to be present, are evidence of registration and use of a domain name in bad faith:

   (i) circumstances indicating that the registrant has registered or acquired the domain name primarily for the purpose of selling, renting, or otherwise transferring the domain name registration to the complainant, who is the owner of the trademark or service mark or to a competitor

---

34. UDRP Policy Paragraph 4(c).
35. See WIPO Overview 2.1 at www.wipo.-int/amc/en/domains/search/overview.
36. *Ticketmaster Corp. v. Woofer Smith* WIPO case No. D2003-0346; *Canadian Tire Corporation, Limited v. C.C.C., Kevin Lyan,* WIPO case no. D2006-1049
37. *Budget Rent-a-Car Corp. v. John Zuccarini* WIPO case No. D2000-1020; *Sun Microsystems, Inc. v. Talmex Management Services* NAF case no. FA0206000114621.
38. *Those Characters From Cleveland Inc. v. User51235,* WIPO case no. D2006-0950
39. *WWF-World Wide Fund for Nature aka WWF International v. Moniker Online Services LLC,* WIPO case no. D2006-0975, *Geoffrey Inc. v. Not The Usual,* WIPO case no. D2006-0882.

of that complainant, for valuable consideration in excess of documented out-of-pocket costs directly related to the domain name;[40] or

(ii) the registrant has registered the domain name in order to prevent the owner of the trademark or service mark from reflecting the mark in a corresponding domain name, provided that the registrant has engaged in a pattern of such conduct; or

(iii) the registrant has registered the domain name primarily for the purpose of disrupting the business of a competitor; or

(iv) by using the domain name, the registrant has intentionally attempted to attract, for commercial gain, Internet users to its web site or other on-line location, by creating a likelihood of confusion with the complainant's mark as to the source, sponsorship, affiliation, or endorsement of the registrant's web site or location or of a product or service on the registrant's web site or location.[41]

UDRP decisions have expanded the definition of bad faith through precedent. The lack of active use of the domain name does not preclude a finding of bad faith and passive holding of a domain name may constitute bad faith use.[42] The panel will examine all the circumstances of the case to determine whether respondent is acting in bad faith. Examples of circumstances that tend to show bad faith include the fact that the complainant's trademark is well –known; no response to the complaint; concealment of identity including false or inaccurate contact information; and the impossibility of conceiving a good faith use of the domain name. Panels draw inferences concerning bad faith by considering all the circumstances relating to the registration.[43]

Finally, where a complainant owns a United States registered trademark and the respondent was located in the United States as well, some cases have found that the registration was constructive notice sufficient to constitute bad faith registration and use.[44]

The prevailing view is that good faith registration followed by bad faith use is not covered by the UDRP Policy.[45]

---

40. Panels have referred to "without prejudice " communications as evidence of bad faith, *McMullan Brothers v. Web Names Limited,* WIPO case no. D2004-0078; *Advance Magazine Publishers Inc. v. Marcellod Dusso*, WIPO case no. D2001-1049; and see WIPO Overview 3.6 at www.wipo.-int/amc/en/domains/search/overview.

41. *Nokia Corporation v. Phonestop,* WIPO case no. D2001-1237, *Canadain Tire Corporation, Limited v. Mike Rollo* WIPO case no. D2002-1069.

42. *Telstra v. Nuclear Marshmallows,* WIPO case no. D2000-0003.

43. See WIPO Overview 3.2 at www.wipo.-int/amc/en/domains/search/overview.

44. See WIPO Overview 3.4 at www.wipo.-int/amc/en/domains/search/overview.

45. *Elders Limited v. Private Company,* WIPO case no. D2007-1099.

## f) Procedure

The complainant selects an administrative dispute resolution service provider from a listed maintained by ICANN by submitting the complaint to that provider.[46] The selected provider will administer the proceeding, except in cases of consolidation, and select a single Administrative Panel to determine the dispute unless either of the parties elects to have a three-member panel. In the event of multiple disputes between the registrant and complainant, either may petition to consolidate the disputes before a single Administrative Panel. This petition shall be made to the first Administrative Panel appointed to hear a pending dispute between the parties. This Administrative Panel may consolidate before it any or all such disputes in its sole discretion, provided that the disputes being consolidated are governed by the UDRP Policy adopted by ICANN.[47]

All fees charged by the service provider are the responsibility of the complainant except if the registrant chooses to expand the number of arbitrators from one to three, the fees will be split evenly.[48]

The remedies available to a complainant pursuant to any proceeding before an Administrative Panel are limited to requiring the cancellation of the impugned domain name or the transfer of the domain name registration to the complainant.[49] If other relief such as damages or an injunction is required, an action must be brought in a court with jurisdiction.

The UDRP requirements do not prevent the respondent or the complainant from submitting the dispute to a court of competent jurisdiction for independent resolution before the UDRP proceeding is commenced or after such proceeding is concluded.[50]

If it is decided that the domain name should be canceled or transferred, the registrant is given 10 business days before the decision is implemented to commence legal proceedings against the complainant, if so advised.[51] Such proceedings must be instituted either in the jurisdiction in which the registrar is located, provided that the registrant contractually submitted to

---

46. UDRP Policy Paragraph 4(d).
47. UDRP Policy Paragraph 4(f) and see *Fulham Football Club (1987) Limited et al. v. Domains by Proxy Inc.* WIPO case no. D2009-0331.
48. UDRP Policy Paragraph 4(g).
49. UDRP Policy Paragraph 4(I) and see *Canadian Tire Corporation, Limited v. Digi Real Estate Foundation,* WIPO case no. D2006-117 concerning the transfer of a "co-branded" trademark but see *Toronto-Dominion Bank v. TM Watchdog,* (2005) 47 C.P.R. (4th) 171 (C.I.R.A.) where cancellation was ordered in similar circumstances.
50. UDRP Policy Paragraph 4(k).
51. UDRP Policy Paragraph 4(k).

jurisdiction there, or the location of the registrant as shown in the registrar's WHOIS database.[52]

While most arbitrations are not precedent-based, UDRP decisions typically cite other UDRP decisions. Panels consider it desirable that their decisions be consistent with prior panel decisions dealing with similar fact situations.[53] However, there are a multitude of decisions and no appeals.

## 5. The CDRP

### a) History

CIRA has developed and adopted its own domain name dispute resolution policy, the CIRA Domain Name Dispute Resolution Policy (CDRP).[54] While the CDRP appears to be have been modeled after the UDRP policy, there are differences between the two.

### b) Applicable Disputes

Paragraph 3.1 of the CDRP provides that a registrant must submit to a proceeding if a complainant asserts in a complaint submitted in compliance with the policy and the resolution rules that

(a) the registrant's dot-ca domain name is Confusingly Similar to a Mark in which the complainant had Rights prior to the date of registration of the domain name and continues to have such Rights;

(b) the registrant has no legitimate interest in the domain name as described in CDRP; and

(c) the registrant has registered the domain name in bad faith as described in the CDRP.

The complainant must establish elements a) and c) on a balance of probabilities and provide "some evidence" that the registrant has no legitimate interest

---

52. See *Black v. Molson Canada* (2002), 21 C.P.R. (4th) 52 (Ont. S.C.J.) where the UDRP decision was reviewed on the basis of correctness but compare with *Pankajkumar Patel v. Allos Therapeutics Inc.* an unreported decision of the UK High Court of Justice, Chancery Division, dated June 13, 2008 where the Court refused to intervene unless the complainant could show a cause of action relating to the domain name ordered to be transferred.

53. See WIPO Overview 4.1 at www.wipo.-int/amc/en/domains/search/overview.

54. Online at http://www.cira.ca/en/cat-dpr-policy.html.

in the domain name.[55] The complainant must also satisfy the Canadian presence requirements or the proceedings must relate to a trademark registered in Canada.[56]

If the trademark is registered before the domain name, the complainant need not demonstrate distinctiveness or use to establish "rights."[57] In all other cases, the mark or business name must have been used prior to registration of the impugned domain name and proof of such use must be submitted.[58]

The terms Confusingly Similar, Mark,[59] and Rights are defined in CDRP in a detailed fashion.

## c) Confusingly Similar

A domain name is "confusingly similar' to a "mark" if the domain name so nearly resembles the mark in appearance, sound, or the ideas suggested by the mark as to likely to be mistaken for the mark.[60] Like decisions decided under the UDRP, the addition of a non-distinctive prefix, suffix or generic term, such as "e" to designate "electronic," will receive little weight.[61] The suffix "ca" is not considered in the determination.[62]

By analogy an approach similar to that applied under section 9 of the *Trade-marks Act* has been adopted in the majority of cases.[63] Under this section, courts consider whether a person, on first impression having only an imperfect recollection of the official mark, would likely be confused by the impugned mark.[64]

---

55. See CDRP paragraph 4.1.
56. See CDRP paragraph 1.4. See *Six Continents Hotels, Inc. v. Virgin Enterprises Ltd.* (2005), 42 C.P.R. (4th) 364 (C.I.R.A.).
57. *911979 Alberta Inc. v. Morin* (2006), 51 C.P.R. (4th) 128 (C.I.R.A.).
58. See *Cheap Tickets & Travel Inc. v. Emall.ca Inc.* (2003), 25 C.P.R. (4th) 105 (C.I.R.A.); *Globe Media International Corp. v. Dawn Internet Telephony Systems Inc,* (2006), 53 C.P.R. (4th) 258 (C.I.R.A.); *Government of Canada v. Bedford* (2003), 27 C.P.R. (4th) S.C.C. (C.I.R.A.). An attack directed at the legitimacy of an assignment of a trademark was not considered since the resolution of the attack required consideration by a forum capable of receiving evidence and assessing issues of creditability. *Clover Gift. Inc. v. Morrison* (2005), 43 C.P.R. (4th) 380 (C.I.R.A.).
59. See *Wrigley Canada Inc. v. Brain Wave Holdings Inc.* (2006), 52 C.P.R. (4th) 124 (C.I.R.A.) licensee of an unregistered mark entitled to rely on the claim of a predecessor in title to the complainant's licensor.
60. See CDRP paragraph 3.4.
61. See *Canadian Broadcasting Corp. v. Quon* (2003), 25 C.P.R. (4th) 591 (C.I.R.A.).
62. See CDRP paragraph 1.2.
63. *Government of Canada v. Bedford* (2003), 27 C.P.R. (4th) 522 (C.I.R.A.); *Canadian Thermos Products Inc. v. Fagundes* (2006), 50 C.P.R. (4th) 296 (C.I.R.A.); *Choice Hotels International, Inc. v. Cox* (2006), 54 C.P.R. (4th) 222 (C.I.R.A.).
64. *Big Sisters Assn. v. Big Brothers of Canada* (1996), 75 C.P.R. (3rd) 177 (F.C.T.D.); *Canadian Olympic Association v. Technique Ltd.* (1999), 3 C.P.R. (4th) 298 (F.C.A.); *Glaxo Group*

Some panels have concluded that the registrant's domain was not confusingly similar when the claimant's trademark was made up of a word which was descriptive and generic in nature.[65]

### d) No Legitimate Interest

The complainant must provide some evidence that the registrant has no legitimate interest in the domain name as described in paragraph 3.6 of the CDRP.[66] The registrant's legitimate interest can trump the complaint's right to seek a transfer.[67]

Paragraph 3.6 sets out an exhaustive list of criteria for the determination. It is as follows

> The Registrant has a legitimate interest in a domain name if, and only if, before the receipt by the Registrant of notice from or on behalf of the Complainant, that a Complaint was submitted:
> (a) the domain name was a Mark, the Registrant used the Mark in good faith and the Registrant had Rights in the Mark;
> (b) the Registrant used the domain name in Canada in good faith in association with any wares, services, or business and the domain name was clearly descriptive in Canada in the English or French language of: (i) the character or quality of the wares, services, or business; (ii) the conditions of, or the persons employed in, production of the wares, performance of the services, or operation of the business; or (iii) the place of origin of the wares, services, or business;
> (c) the Registrant used the domain name in Canada in good faith in association with any wares, services, or business and the domain name was understood in Canada to be the generic name thereof in any language;
> (d) the Registrant used the domain name in Canada in good faith in association with a non-commercial activity including, without limitation, criticism, review, or news reporting;
> (e) the domain name comprised the legal name of the Registrant or was a name, surname, or other reference by which the Registrant was commonly identified; or
> (f) the domain name was the geographical name of the location of the Registrant's non-commercial activity or place of business.

---

*Limited v. Defining Presence Marketing Group (Manitoba)* (2004), 35 C.P.R. (4th) 528, BCICAC case no. 0020 (CIRA).

65. *Air Products Canada Ltd. v. Index Quebec Inc.* (2003), 30 C.P.R. (4th) 212 (C.I.R.A.); *Thrifty, Inc. v. Malaker* (2006), 50 C.P.R. (4th) 459 (C.I.R.A.).

66. See *Diners Club International Ltd. v. Planet Explorer Inc.* (2004), 32 C.P.R. (4th) 377 (C.I.R.A.).

67. See *Diners Club International Ltd. v. Planet Explorer Inc.* (2004), 32 C.P.R. (4th) 377 (C.I.R.A.).

> In paragraphs 3.6 (b), (c), and (d), "use" by the Registrants includes, but is
> not limited to, use to identify a web site.

As noted above, the paragraph expressly deals with good faith use of domains
names which are descriptive, generic, or a name or surname, or use with a
non-commercial activity including, without limitation, criticism, review, or
news reporting.

## e)  Bad Faith

"Bad Faith" is restrictively defined and is narrower than the enumerated factors of the UDRP. Paragraph 3.7 of the CDRP is as follows.

> For the purposes of paragraph 3.1(c), a Registrant will be considered to have
> registered a domain name in bad faith if, and only if:
> (a)  the Registrant registered the domain name, or acquired the Registration, pri-
>      marily for the purpose of selling, renting, licensing, or otherwise transferring
>      the Registration to the Complainant, or the Complainant's licensor or
>      licensee of the Mark, or to a competitor of the Complainant or the licensee
>      or licensor for valuable consideration in excess of the Registrant's actual costs
>      in registering the domain name, or acquiring the Registration;[68]
> (b)  the Registrant registered the domain name or acquired the Registration in
>      order to prevent the Complainant, or the Complainant's licensor or licensee
>      of the Mark, from registering the Mark as a domain name, provided that the
>      Registrant, alone or in concert with one or more additional persons, has
>      engaged in a pattern of registering domain names in order to prevent per-
>      sons who have Rights in Marks from registering the Marks as domain
>      names;[69] or
> (c)  the Registrant registered the domain name or acquired the Registration pri-
>      marily for the purpose of disrupting the business of the Complainant, or the
>      Complainant's licensor or licensee of the Mark, who is a competitor of the
>      Registrant.

Paragraph 3.7(c) requires a finding of bad faith if the registration of the
domain name was primarily for the purposes of disrupting the business of the
Complainant, who is a competitor of the Registrant. To date, panelists have

---

68. See for example *Canadian Broadcasting Corp. v. Quon* (2003), 25 C.P.R. (4th) 519
    (C.I.R.A.).
69. *Viacom International Inc. v. Harvey Ross Enterprises, Ltd.* (2003), 29 C.P.R (4th) 243 (C.I.R.A.);
    *Canadian Broadcasting Corp. v. Quon* (2003), 25 C.P.R. (4th) 519 (C.I.R.A.).

been unable to agree on the appropriate interpretation of the word "competitor".[70]

Showing actual bad faith by positive evidence can be quite difficult, particularly given the limited scope of the inquiry in CDRP proceedings. As a result, panels typically take into consideration all of the surrounding circumstances and draw inferences to determine whether bad faith has been shown.[71]

## f) Procedure

Three panelists must be appointed unless the respondent defaults in which case only one panelist is required. The procedures and remedies available are roughly similar to those under the UDRP.

## g) CDRP WHOIS Privacy Policy

Under this policy, the personal information of individual domain name registrants, including registrant name, home address, phone number, and e-mail address, is automatically protected as private. Full registration information for corporate domain name holders is accessible and individual registrants may choose to make their information accessible.

Under specific, limited circumstances certain registrant contact information may be disclosed in situations arising from child endangerment offenses, intellectual property disputes (e.g., cybersquatting), threats to the Internet, and identity theft.

In CDRP proceedings where the Registrant's identity is not published in the public WHOIS database, the Complainant has a right to make a further

---

70. See *Canadian Thermos Products Inc. v. Fagundes* (2006), 50 C.P.R. (4th) 296 (C.I.R.A.) but see *Microsoft Corp. v. Microscience Corp.* (2005), 41 C.P.R. (4th) 565 (C.I.R.A.), *Thrifty, Inc. v. Malaker* (2006), 50 C.P.R. (4th) 459 (C.I.R.A.) and *Choice Hotels International, Inc. v. Cox,* (2006), 54 C.P.R. (4th) 222 (C.I.R.A.) where a respondent who earned fees by directing Internet users to the websites of direct competitors of the complainant was found be a competitor as well, but see *Internet Movie Database, Inc. v. 384128 Canada Inc.*, (2005), 46 C.P.R. (4th) 223 (C.I.R.A.).
71. *Canadian Broadcasting Corp. v. Quon* (2003), 25 C.P.R. (4th) 519 (CIRA); *Google Inc. v. Fraser* (2005), 42 C.P.R. (4th) 560 (C.I.R.A.); *The Co-operators Group Ltd. v. Artbravo Inc,* (2006), 47 C.P.R. (4th) 460 (C.I.R.A.); *Caseware International Inc. v. Lee* (2006), 51 C.P.R. (4th) 231 (C.I.R.A.); *Honest Ed's Limited v. Imbrogno* (2006), 58 C.P.R. (4th) 168 (C.I.R.A.); *Abelsoft Corp. v. Fish* (2008), 65 C.P.R. (4th) 174 (C.I.R.A.), but not all cases see *Microsoft Corporation v. Microscience Corporation,* unreported decision dated July 19, 2005 (C.I.R.A.).

submission to the Panel, including adducing further evidence, limited to the issue of the Registrant's legitimate interest (or lack thereof) in a domain name.[72]

## 6. Actions in the Courts

Actions brought in the courts have been successful in enjoining activities that would be covered by the UDRP or CDRP. For example, where a defendant systematically registered domain names containing the brand names of well-known companies, presumably with the intention of selling them back to the brand owners, an action for passing off succeeded.[73]

But proceedings in the courts do not include all cases covered by the UDRP or CDRP. For example, to successfully assert a claim for trademark infringement, the plaintiff must show trademark "use" by the defendant.[74] Such "use" is frequently not present in a case involving cybersquatting. In addition, a claim for passing off is likely restricted to well known trademarks.

Finally, there is no Canadian equivalent of the U.S. *Anticybersquatting Consumer Protection Act.*

---

72. Paragraph 11.1 CIRA Domain Name Dispute Resolution Rules.
73. *British Telecom plc v. One In A Million* [1998] 4 All E.R. 476 (U.K.C.A.) and see *Saskatoon Star Phoenix Group Inc. v. Noton* (2001), 12 C.P.R. (4th) 4 (Sask. Q. B.); *Law Society of British Columbia v. Canadian Domain Name Exchange Corp.* (2002), 22 C.P.R. (4th) 88 (B.C. S.C.); *Rolls-Royce plc v. Fitzwilliam* (2002), 19 C.P.R. (4th) 1 (F.C.T.D.); *United Food and Commercial Workers International Union v. Sharyn Sigurdur* 2005 BCSC 1904 (B.C.S.C.); *D.& A.'s Pet Food'N More Ltd. v. Seiveright,* 2006, 48 C.P.R. (4th) 282 (F.C.); *Inform Cycle Ltd. v. Rebound Inc.,* 2006 ABQB 825 (Alberta Q.B, Master), appeal dismissed 2007 ABQB 319 (Alberta Q.B.) concerning vicarious liability in this context and 67 C.P.R. (4th) 151 (Alberta Q.B.) for assessment of damages.
74. See Chapter 13.

CHAPTER

# 17

# Copyright: Basic Concepts

## 1. Introduction

Under the *Copyright Act*[1] there are a number of basic concepts which apply to all types of protected works. For convenience of reference they will be discussed in this chapter.

### a) Acquisition

Copyright protection in Canada does not depend on registration or other formal steps[2] but subsists automatically without any act other than the creation of an original work that satisfies the points of attachment or conditions set out in the *Act*. Registration is permissive but helpful if it is likely an action will be brought for infringement.[3]

Copyright protection extends to authors of works who are Canadian nationals as well as to the nationals of other countries. As a party to the Berne Convention, the Agreement establishing the World Trade Organization (WTO) and the Agreement on Trade-Related Aspects of Intellectual Property Rights, including trade in Counterfeit Goods (TRIPS), which was annexed to the Agreement establishing the WTO, Canada is bound to give protection to the nationals of other countries.

Copyright subsists in Canada, in every original literary, dramatic, musical, and artistic work if any one of the following conditions is met:

  (a) in the case of any work, whether published or unpublished, including a cinematographic work, the author was, at the date of the making of the work, a citizen or subject of, or a person ordinarily resident in, a treaty country;[4]
  (b) in the case of a cinematographic work, whether published or unpublished, the maker, at the date of the making of the cinematographic work,
     (i) if a corporation, had its headquarters in a treaty country, or
     (ii) if a natural person, was a citizen or subject of, or a person ordinarily resident in, a treaty country; or
  (c) in the case of a published work, including a cinematographic work,
     (i) in relation to making copies available to the public, the first publication in such a quantity as to satisfy the reasonable demands of

---

1. See R.S.C. 1985, c. C-42 as amended; section 5.
2. *Gribble v. Manitoba Free Press Ltd.* [1932] 1 D.L.R. 169, [1931] 3 W.W.R. 570 (Man. C.A.).
3. See Chapter 26.
4. The definition of treaty country in section 2 of the *Copyright Act* includes countries which are a party to the Berne Convention or a WTO Member.

the public, having regard to the nature of the work, occurred in a treaty country, or

   (ii) in relation to the construction of an architectural work or the incorporation of an artistic work into an architectural work, the first publication occurred in a treaty country.[5]

The first publication described above is deemed to have occurred in a treaty country notwithstanding that it occurred previously elsewhere, if the interval between those two publications did not exceed 30 days.[6] Under the *Act* "publication" is defined to mean in relation to works, the making of copies of the work available to the public, among other things.[7]

## b) Originality

Copyright subsists only in original works. The originality required by the *Act* relates to the expression of thought in which the work is presented, however, a work does not have to be creative in the sense of being novel or unique. What is required to attract copyright protection in the expression of an idea is an exercise of skill and judgment. Skill in this context means the use of an individual's knowledge, developed aptitude, or practiced ability in producing the work. Judgment means the use of one's capacity for discernment or ability to form an opinion or an evaluation by comparing different possible options in producing the work. The exercise of skill and judgment will necessarily involve intellectual effort.[8]

Such an exercise must not be so trivial that it could be characterized as a purely mechanical exercise. The skill and judgment involved in simply changing the font of a work to produce another work would be too trivial to merit copyright protection as "original" work.[9] Similarly, a work which is a slavish copy of an earlier work will not be entitled to copyright as it is not original.[10] However, a work which is substantially derived from pre-existing material may be the proper subject-matter of copyright if sufficient skill and judgment have been exercised.[11]

---

5. Section 5. This subsection applies after September 1, 1997.
6. Subsection 5(1.1). This subsection applies after September 1, 1997.
7. Section 2.2.
8. *The Law Society of Upper Canada v. CCH Canadian Limited* (2004), 30 C.P.R. (4th) 1 (S.C.C.). This case changed the requirements for originality and previously decided cases must be read subject to it.
9. *The Law Society of Upper Canada v. CCH Canadian Limited* (2004), 30 C.P.R. (4th) 1 (S.C.C.).
10. *University of London Press v. University Tutorial Press,* [1916] 2 Ch. 601; *Ladbroke (Football) Ltd. v. William Hill (Football) Ltd.* [1964] 1 All E.R. 465 (H.L.).
11. *Interlego A.G. v. Tyco Industries Plc.* [1989] A.C. 217 (P.C.).

The amount of skill and judgment required cannot be defined in precise terms and each case must be decided on its own facts.[12] In addition, the type of work in issue may influence the determination; for example, a photograph is typically considered in different terms than other works.[13]

While the owner of copyright in the protected work is entitled to the specific rights set out in the *Act*, they are not entitled to a monopoly. Another person may produce the same work so long as they do so independently and their work is original in the sense in which that word is used in the *Act*.[14]

Copyright does not extend to schemes, systems, or methods,[15] since copyright is confined to the expression of ideas.[16] It is not an infringement of copyright to use the ideas of another or to publish information derived from another, as long as there is no copying of the expression in which the ideas or the information have previously been presented.[17] However, such actions may be in breach of another obligation such as a breach of confidence, etc.


## c)  Fixation

To be entitled to copyright, a work must be expressed in material form, capable of identification, and have a character of reasonable substance or permanence.[18] For example, a person's oral statements in an interview or conversation are not typically recognized in that form as literary creations and do not attract copyright protection.[19]

---

12. *Interlego A.G. v. Tyco Industries Plc.* [1989] A.C. 217 (P.C.).
13. *Viceroy Homes Ltd. v. Ventry Homes Inc.* (1991), 34 C.P.R. (3d) 385 (Ont.Ct.)(Gen. Div.), (1996), 69 C.P.R. (3d) 459 (Ont. C.A.).
14. *Ladbroke (Football) Ltd. v. William Hill (Football) Ltd.* [1964] 1 All. E.R. 465 (H.L.).
15. *Canadian Admiral Corporation Ltd. v. Rediffusion Inc. et al.* [1954] Ex. C.R. 382, 20 C.P.R. 75 (Ex. Ct.).
16. *Commercial Signs v. General Motors Products of Canada Ltd. et al.* [1937] O.W.N. 58 (H.C.J.), [1937] 2 D.L.R. 310, aff'd [1937] 2 D.L.R. 800 (Ont.C.A.); *Moreau v. St. Vincent*, [1950] Ex. C.R. 198, 12 C.P.R. 32, [1950] 3 D.L.R. 713; *Stevens v. Robert Simpson Co. Ltd. et al.* (1964), 41 C.P.R. 204 (Ont. C.A.).
17. *Deeks v. Wells* [1931] O.R. 818 (Ont. H.C.), [1931] 4 D.L.R. 533, [1933] 1 D.L.R. 353 (Ont.C.A.).
18. *Canadian Admiral Corporation Ltd. v. Rediffusion Inc. et al.* [1954] Ex. C.R. 382, 20 C.P.R. 75.
19. *Gould Estate et al. v. Stoddart Publishing Co. Ltd.* (1996), 74 C.P.R. (3d) 206 (Ont. Gen. Div.) affirmed (1998), 80 C.P.R. (3d) 161 (Ont. C.A.).

## d) Compilations

The *Act* provides that a "compilation" means

    a) a work resulting from the selection or arrangement of literary, dramatic, musical, or artistic works or parts thereof, or

    b) a work resulting from the selection or arrangement of data.[20]

A compilation containing two or more of the categories of literary, dramatic, musical, or artistic works is deemed to be a compilation of the category making up the most substantial part of the compilation.[21] The mere fact that a work is included in a compilation does not increase, decrease, or otherwise affect the protection conferred by the *Act* in respect of the copyright in the work or the moral rights in respect of the work.[22]

Copyright protects originality of form or expression. A compilation takes existing material and casts it in a different form. The arranger may not have copyright in the individual components. A part of the compilation by itself may be entitled to copyright while other parts of the work are not. However, the arranger may have copyright in the form represented by the compilation. It is not the several components that are the subject of the copyright, but the over-all arrangement of them, which the plaintiff through his industry has produced.[23]

## e) Derivative Works

The *Act* does not refer expressly to derivative works, but a work that is derived from pre-existing material may be protected by copyright if sufficient skill and judgment has been directed to its creation.[24]

The owner of copyright is entitled to the rights set out in the *Act* which include the right to make works derived from the owner's work. If another individual wishes to make a "derivative" work, they will require the consent of the owner to do so, unless the work is in the public domain. For example, the owner of copyright in a literary work is entitled to produce and publish a translation of the work. While a separate copyright may subsist in the translation, if sufficient skill and judgment has been exercised, in the absence of consent, the "derivative" translation will infringe the rights of the author of the original literary work.

---

20. Section 2.
21. Subsection 2.1(1).
22. Subsection 2.1(2).
23. *The Law Society of Upper Canada v. CCH Canadian Limited* (2004), 30 C.P.R. (4th) 1 (S.C.C.), *Slumber-Magic Adjustable Bed Co.* (1984), 3 C.P.R. (3d) 81 (B.C.S.C.).
24. *Interlego A.G. v. Tyco Industries Plc.*, [1989] A.C. 217 (P.C.).

# CHAPTER
# 18

## Literary, Dramatic, Musical, and Artistic Works

## 1. Introduction

Historically, copyright protection was made available to the authors of original literary, dramatic, musical, and artistic works and subsequently extended to other neighboring rights that border traditional copyright. This chapter deals with the works subject to traditional copyright protection.

## 2. Literary Works

### a) What Is Protected

The *Act* provides that a literary work includes "tables, computer programs, and compilations of literary works."[1] The use of the word "includes" and the categories of works which follow are illustrative and do not exclude the ordinary meaning of the term "literary work." The definition covers a wide field and includes all works that are expressed in print or writing irrespective of whether their quality or style is high.[2]

The sole distinguishing characteristic of a literary work is that it is in print or writing not its quality as literature or art.[3] The *Act* contains no requirements relating to the literary value or merit of a literary work.[4]

### b) Computer Programs

The *Act* provides that a computer program means "a set of instructions or statements, expressed, fixed, embodied, or stored in any manner, that is to be used directly or indirectly in a computer in order to bring about a specific result."[5] There are three distinct elements of the definition. First, there must be a "set of instructions or statements." Second, the "set of instructions or statements" must be: a) expressed; b) fixed; c) embodied; or d) stored in any manner. This portion of the definition ensures the protection of programs in a wide variety of media. Finally, the "set of instructions or statements" must be used, directly or indirectly, in a computer in order to bring about a specific result. Programs consisting of source or object code come within this element of the definition.

---

1. Section 2.
2. *University of London Press* v. *University Tutorial Press* [1916] 2 Ch. 601.
3. *Apple Computer Inc v. Mackintosh Computers Ltd.*, [1988] 1 F. C. 673 (F.C.A.).
4. *University of London Press* v. *University Tutorial Press*, [1916] 2 Ch. 601.
5. Section 2.

There are two specific exemptions from what would otherwise constitute infringement of the copyright in a computer program. First, the making by a person, who owns a copy of a computer program, which copy is authorized by the owner of the copyright, of a single reproduction of the copy by adapting, modifying, or converting the computer program or translating it into another computer language, if the person proves that the reproduced copy is:

(i)   essential for the compatibility of the computer program with a particular computer;
(ii)  solely for the person's own use; and
(iii) destroyed immediately after the person ceases to be the owner of the copy

does not constitute infringement.[6]

Second, the making by a person, who owns a copy of a computer program, which copy is authorized by the owner of the copyright, of a single reproduction of the copy or reproduction referred to above for backup purposes does not constitute infringement, if the person proves that the reproduction is destroyed immediately when the person ceases to be the owner of the copy of the computer program.[7]

## c)  The Rights Associated with a Literary Work

Copyright in a literary work means the sole right to:

a)  produce or reproduce the work or any substantial part in any material form whatever,
b)  to perform the work or any substantial part in public,
c)  if unpublished, to publish the work or any substantial part of it, and includes the sole right,
d)  to produce, reproduce, perform, or publish any translation of the work,
e)  in the case of a novel or other non-dramatic work to convert it into a dramatic work, by way of performance in public or otherwise,
f)  to make any sound recording, cinematograph film or other contrivance by means of which the work may be mechanically reproduced or performed,
g)  to reproduce, adapt, and publicly present the work as a cinematographic work,

---

6. Section 30.6(1).
7. Section 30.6(2).

h) to communicate the work to the public by telecommunication,

i) in the case of a computer program that can be reproduced in the ordinary course of its use, other than by a reproduction during its execution in conjunction with a machine, device or computer, to rent out the computer program

and to authorize such acts.[8]

## 3. Dramatic Works

### a) What Is Protected

The *Act* provides that a "dramatic work" includes:

(a) any piece for recitation, choreographic work, or mime, the scenic arrangement or acting form of which is fixed in writing or otherwise,

(b) any cinematographic work, and

(c) any compilation of dramatic works.[9]

A "choreographic work," is defined to include "any work of choreography, whether or not it has any storyline."[10]

The *Act* provides that "cinematographic work" includes any work expressed by any process analogous to cinematography, whether or not accompanied by a soundtrack. Section 11.1, which sets out the term of protection for cinematographic works, excludes cinematographic works in which the arrangement or acting form or the combination of incidents represented give the work a dramatic character.

Subparagraph a) of the definition set out above includes "piece for recitation" and "mime" as being included as "dramatic works" when their scenic arrangement or acting form is fixed in writing or otherwise. Apart from this inclusion the concept of "dramatic work" is undefined.

The playing of a sporting event such as a football game is not protected by a dramatic copyright because of the unpredictability of such events and the lack of certainty.[11] However, the television broadcast of the event would be a "cinematographic work" which is now included in the definition of "dramatic work."

---

8. Section 3.
9. Section 2.
10. Section 2.
11. *FWS Joint Sports Claimants v. Copyright Board* (1991), 36 C.P.R. (3d) 483 (F.C.A.).

Scenic or stage effects may be protected as part of a drama, but only in exceptional circumstances would they be protected on their own. The *Act* grants specific statutory rights and there should be certainty concerning those rights in order to avoid injustice to the rest of the world.[12]

The use of made up facial contortions, and comic "business" and gags consisting of variations introduced into a work by an actor and changed from time to time without being reduced to any permanent form, are not the subject of copyright.[13]

A character from a work may be entitled to copyright if the character is sufficiently clearly delineated in the work which is also subject to copyright and the character is distinctive[14] or perhaps widely known and recognized.[15]

While the idea of a dramatic work is not protected, the arrangement or acting form or the combination of incidents represented, if fixed in writing or some other method, may be protected apart from the language in which they are expressed.[16]

## b) Cinematographic Works

As noted above, cinematographic works are included in the definition of a dramatic work. One of the points of attachment or conditions set out in the *Act* relating to the subsistence of copyright in a cinematographic work relates to the status of the "maker."[17] "Maker" means in relation to cinematographic work, the person by whom the arrangements necessary for the making of the work are undertaken.[18] The maker may be a corporation.[19] The concept of a "maker" is different from the concept of an "author" and an assessment using traditional principles applicable to dramatic works must be made to determine who is the author of a cinematographic work.

The *Act* defines a "sound recording" as meaning a recording, fixed in any material form, consisting of sounds, whether or not of a performance of a

---

12. *Kantel* v. *Grant, Nisbet & Auld Ltd.* [1933] Ex. C.R. 84; *Green v. Broadcasting Corp. of N.Z.* [1989] 2 All E.R. 1056 (P.C.).

13. *Tate* v. *Fullbrook*, [1908] 1 K.B. 821; *Tate* v. *Thomas*, [1921] 1 Ch. 503 (C.A.).

14. *Ann of Green Gables Licensing Authority Inc. v. Avonlea Traditions Inc.* (2000), 4 C.P.R. (4th) 289 (Ont. S. C. J.).

15. *Preston v. 20th Century Fox Canada Ltd.* (1990), 33 C.P.R. (3d) 242 (F.C.T.D.) affirmed (1993), 53 C.P.R. (3d) 407 (F.C.A.).

16. *Corelli v. Grey* (1913) 29 T.L.R 570 (Ch. D.) aff'd 30 T.L.R. 116 (U.K.C.A.), and see *Kelly* v. *Cinema Houses Ltd.* [1932] Macg. Cop. Cas. 362 (U.K.C.A.).

17. Subsection 5(1) of the *Act*.

18. Section 2 and see *Re F.G.(Films) Ltd.* [1953] 1 W.L.R. 483 (Ch. D.); *Adventure Film Productions Ltd v. Tulley* (October 14, 1982), The Times.

19. Paragraph 5(1)(b) of the *Act*.

work, but excludes any soundtrack of a cinematographic work where it accompanies the cinematographic work.[20]

A cinematograph film may itself be an original work entitled to copyright. Frequently, a film will be a derivative work, in that it is derived from an existing literary or dramatic work, however it will still be entitled to copyright protection even if it infringes copyright in the work it is derived from.

There may be separate and independent copyrights in a dramatic work, the script for a film adapted from such work, and a cinematographic work produced from the script.

### c)  The Rights Associated with a Dramatic Work

Copyright in a dramatic work means the sole right to:

a) produce or reproduce the work or any substantial part in any material form whatever,
b) to perform the work or any substantial part in public,
c) if unpublished, to publish the work or any substantial part of it, and includes the sole right
d) to produce, reproduce, perform, or publish any translation of the work,
e) to convert the work into a novel or other non-dramatic work,
f) to make any sound recording, cinematograph film or other contrivance by means of which the work may be mechanically reproduced or performed,
g) to reproduce, adapt, and publicly present the work as a cinematographic work,
h) to communicate the work to the public by telecommunication,

and to authorize such acts.[21]

The cinematographic rights set out in item f) and g) above are separate from the other applicable rights in the work and may be separately dealt with and assigned.[22]

---

20. Section 2.
21. Section 3.
22. *Tate* v. *Thomas*, [1921] 1 Ch. 503.

## 4. Musical Works

### a) What Is Protected

The *Act* provides that a "musical work" means "any work of music or musical composition, with or without words, and includes any compilation thereof." Unlike the definitions of "literary work" or "dramatic work," the definition of a "musical work" is exhaustive.

A new arrangement or adaptation of an existing work may be protected by copyright so long as the new work is sufficiently original. The principles used to determine whether a compilation of unoriginal material is entitled to protection are applicable.[23]

The rights of an adapter or arranger may be subordinate to the rights of the original composer so long as the original composer's copyright is still subsisting.[24] This is because the original composer has the sole right to reproduce the work or any substantial part in any material form whatever, which is likely broad enough to include a new arrangement or adaptation.

### b) The Rights Associated with a Musical Work

Copyright in a musical work means the sole right to

a) produce or reproduce the work or any substantial part in any material form whatever,
b) to perform the work or any substantial part in public,
c) if unpublished, to publish the work or any substantial part of it, and includes the sole right,
d) to produce, reproduce, perform, or publish any translation of the work,
e) to make any sound recording, cinematograph film, or other contrivance by means of which the work may be mechanically reproduced or performed,[25]
g) to reproduce, adapt, and publicly present the work as a cinematographic work,

---

23. See Chapter 17, part (b) and *The Law Society of Upper Canada v. CCH Canadian Limited* (2004), 30 C.P.R. (4th) 1 (S.C.C.).
24. *ZYX Music GmbH v. King* [1995] 3 All E.R. 1 (Ch. D.) appeal dismissed [1997] 2 All E.R. 129 (U.K.C.A.).
25. See Chapter 19, part 3.

> h) to communicate the work by telecommunication, and
> i) to rent out a sound recording in which the work is embodied,[26]

and to authorize such acts.[27]

The right to perform a work or any substantial part in public, which is frequently referred to as the performing right, exists side by side with the traditional right to make copies of a work. The performing right is limited to performing the work *in public*. Anyone may perform a work in private.[28]

The *Act* provides that "performance" means "any acoustic or visual representation of the a work, . . . including a representation made by means of any mechanical instrument, radio receiving set, or television receiving set." The definition covers "any" acoustic representation and the fact that it goes on to add that it includes a representation made by means of any mechanical instrument, etc., does not limit the generality of the word "any."[29]

## 5. Artistic Works

### a) What Is Protected

The *Act* provides that "artistic work" includes paintings, drawings, maps, charts, plans, photographs, engravings, sculptures, and works of artistic craftsmanship, architectural works, and compilations of artistic works."[30]

The *Act*[31] also provides that

> "architectural work" means any building or structure or any model of a building or structure.
> "engravings" includes "etchings, lithographs, woodcuts, prints, and other similar works, not being photographs";
> "photograph" includes a "photo-lithograph and any work expressed by any process analogous to photography";[32] and
> "sculpture" includes casts and models.

---

26. See Chapter 19, part 3.
27. Section 3.
28. *Mellor* v. *Australian Broadcasting Commission*, [1940] 2 All E.R. 20 (Austr.—J.C.P.C.).
29. *Canadian Cable Television Assoc.* v. *Copyright Board* (1993), 46 C.P.R. (3d) 359 (F.C.A.), leave to appeal to the Supreme Court of Canada refused (1993), 51 C.P.R. (3d) v.
30. Section 2.
31. Section 2.
32. *Canadian Admiral Corporation Ltd.* v. *Rediffusion Inc. et al.*, [1954] Ex. C.R. 382, 20 C.P.R. 75.

It is a question of fact in any particular case whether the work which is being considered is a painting.[33] The term "drawing" is very broad and presumably would include any two-dimensional work in which shapes are depicted by lines.

The term "works of artistic craftsmanship" unlike other definitions makes specific reference to the intrinsic quality of the specific type of work. It has been difficult to give meaning to the words "artistic craftsmanship" and the case law is unsettled.[34]

The phrase "artistic work," with the exception "works of artistic craftsmanship," is used as a generic description of works which find expression in a visual medium as opposed to works of literary, musical, or dramatic expression. It is used in the same fashion as "literary" in the definition of "literary work." As a result, a work can be protected as an artistic work irrespective of its artistic merit or aesthetic value.[35]

Copyright in artistic works does not extend to ideas, conceptions or methods, but is confined to their expression in material form.[36]

### b) The Rights Associated with an Artistic Work

Copyright in an artistic work means the sole right to:

a) produce or reproduce the work or any substantial part of the work in any material form whatever;

b) if unpublished, to publish the work or any substantial part of it; and includes the sole right,

c) to convert the work into a dramatic work, by way of performance in public or otherwise;

d) to reproduce, adapt, and publicly present the work as a cinematographic work;

e) to communicate the work by telecommunication;

---

33. *Merchandising Corporation of America Inc. v. Harpbond Ltd.* [1983] F.S.R. 32 (U.K.C.A.); *Mansell v. Star Printing & Publishing Co. of Toronto Ltd.*, [1937] 3 All E.R. 912, [1937] A.C. 872, [1937] 4 D.L.R. 1. (Ont.- J.C.P.C.)

34. *DRG Inc. v. Datafile Ltd.*(1987), 18 C.P.R. (3d) 538 (F.C.T.D.), (1991), 35 C.P.R. (3d) 243 (F.C.A.); *Eldon Industries Inc. et al. v. Reliable Toy Co. Ltd. et al.* [1966] 1 O.R. 409, 54 D.L.R. (2d) 97 (Ont. H.C.J.).

35. *DRG Inc. v. Datafile Ltd.* (1987), 18 C.P.R. (3d) 538 (F.C.T.D.), (1991), 35 C.P.R. (3d) 243 (F.C.A.).

36. *Kenrick & Co. v. Lawrence & Co.* (1890), 5 Q.B. 99 (Q.B.D.); *Canadian Admiral Corporation Ltd. v. Rediffusion Inc.* [1954] Ex. C.R. 382, 20 C.P.R. 75.

f)  to present at a public exhibition, for a purpose other than sale or hire, a
    work created after June 7, 1988, other than a map, chart, or plan,

and to authorize such acts.[37]

## c)  Designs Applied to Useful Articles

The *Industrial Design Act* provides that "design" means features of shape,
configuration, pattern, or ornament and any combination of those features
that, in a finished article, appeal to and are judged solely by the eye.[38] It is well
established that to be entitled to registration, a "design" must be original and
there must be some substantial difference between the new design and pre-
existing designs. The protection available under the *Industrial Design Act* is
for a maximum of 10 years,[39] which is significantly shorter than that available
for copyright.

The boundary between copyright and industrial design protection has
been difficult to determine for "artistic works." Sections 64 and 64.1 of the
*Act* attempt to determine the boundary. Subsections 64(2) and 64(3) apply
only to designs created after June 8, 1988.[40]

### i)  Definitions

Subsection 64(1) of the *Act* contains the following definitions which apply to
sections 64 and 64.1:

"article" means anything that is made by hand, tool, or machine;
"design" means features of shape, configuration, pattern, or ornament and
    any combination of those features that, in a finished article, appeal to
    and are judged solely by the eye;
"useful article" means an article that has a utilitarian function and includes
    a model of any such article;
"utilitarian function," in respect of an article, means a function other than
    merely serving as a substrate or carrier for artistic or literary matter.[41]

---

37. Section 3.
38. *Industrial Design Act*, R.S.C. 1985, c. I-9, section.2 and see Chapter 33.
39. See Chapter 33.
40. Subsection 64(4) of the current *Act* provides that the *Copyright Act*, R.S.C. 1985, c. C-42 and
    the *Industrial Design Act*, R.S.C. 1985, c. I-9, as they read immediately before June 8, 1988,
    as well as the rules made under them, continue to apply in respect of designs created before
    that date.
41. Subsection 64(1).

Similar definitions are contained in the *Industrial Design Act*.[42]

Under section 64 the concept of a "design" is applicable only to finished articles which are useful, and the section does not apply to works such as sculptures. The words "in a finished article" in the definition of "design" contained in section 64 only mean in a physical embodiment, as opposed to a mere scheme or preliminary conception of an idea.[43]

Sections 64 and 64.1 only apply to useful articles which are defined to mean articles, including models, which have a utilitarian function, that is a function other than merely serving as a substrate or carrier for artistic or literary matter. An article such as a poster does not come within the sections.

## ii)  Non-Infringement Designs of Eye Appealing Features Applied to Useful Articles

Subsection 64(2) provides that where copyright subsists in a design applied to a useful article, or in an artistic work from which the design is derived and, by or under the authority of the person who owns the copyright in Canada or elsewhere:

a)  the article is reproduced in a quantity of more than fifty; or

b)  where the article is a plate,[44] engraving, or cast, the article is used for producing more than fifty useful articles,
    it is not an infringement of the copyright or the moral rights for anyone

c)  to reproduce the design of the article or a design not differing substantially from the design of the article by:
    (i)  making the article; or
    (ii)  making a drawing or other reproduction in any material form of the article; or

d)  to do with an article, drawing or reproduction that is made as described in paragraph (c) anything that the owner of the copyright has the sole right to do with the design or artistic work in which the copyright subsists.[45]

---

42.  S.C. 1988, c. 15, s. 18, 19.
43.  *Milliken & Company et al. v. Interface Flooring Systems (Canada) Inc.* (1998), 83 C.P.R. (3d) 470 (F.C.T.D.), affirmed (2000) 5 C.P.R. (4th) 209 (F.C.A.).
44.  Section 2 of the *Act* provides that "plate" includes (*a*) any stereotype or other plate, stone, block, mould, matrix, transfer, or negative used or intended to be used for printing or reproducing copies of any work, and (*b*) any matrix or other appliance used or intended to be used for making or reproducing sound recordings, performer's performances or communication signals.
45.  Subsection 64(2).

Subsection 64(2) restricts protection for eye-appealing features of useful articles since it provides that actions which would otherwise constitute infringement are not actionable.[46] The limitation applies only to useful articles which have a utilitarian function, that is a function other than merely serving as a substrate or carrier for artistic or literary matter.[47] The section does not preclude protection under the *Industrial Design Act.*

The section expressly applies to an artistic work from which the design is derived. If a drawing or plan portrays the design, the section will apply to a design derived from that work. Since a model of a useful article is included in the definition of "useful article," a similar result would apply to a design of a model.

If it is shown that the events set out in either paragraphs 64(2)(a) or 64(2)(b) have occurred, paragraphs 64(2)(c) and 64(2)(d) apply. A defendant may reproduce the design of the article or a design not differing substantially from the design of the article by making the article, or making a drawing or other reproduction in any material form of the article, or otherwise doing anything that the owner of the copyright has the sole right to do. If the events set out in paragraphs 64(2)(a) or 64(2)(b) have not occurred, the copyright in the work is unaffected. The burden of proof in an action pleading that the subsection applies will be on the defendant. The intentions of the owner of the copyright are not relevant in determining whether the above described paragraphs apply.

Subsection 64(2) does not apply in respect of copyright in an artistic work in so far as the work is used as and for:

a) a graphic or photographic representation that is applied to the face of an article;
b) a trademark or a representation thereof or a label;[48]
c) material that has a woven or knitted pattern or that is suitable for piece goods or surface coverings or for making wearing apparel;[49]
d) an architectural work that is a building or a model of a building;
e) a representation of a real or fictitious being, event, or place that is applied to an article as a feature of shape, configuration, pattern, or ornament;
f) articles that are sold as a set, unless more than fifty sets are made; or
g) such other work or article as may be prescribed by regulation.[50]

---

46. The subsection does not effect the subsistence of copyright, *Magasins Greenberg Ltée v. Imports-Export René Derby (Canada) Inc.* (1995), 61 C.P.R. (3d) 133 (F.C.T.D.).
47. *Pyrrha Design Inc. v. 623735 Saskatchewan Ltd* (2004), 30 C.P.R. (4th) 310 (F.C.), 2004 FCA 423 (F.C.A.).
48. *Specialty Sprts Ltd. v. Kimpex International Inc.* (1997) 72 C.P.R. (3d) 538 (F.C.T.D.).
49. *Crocs Canada Inc. v. Holey Sales Holdings Ltd.* 2008 FC 188 (F.C.).
50. Subsection 64(3).

### iii)  Non-Infringement—Useful Article Features

Section 64.1 provides that the following acts do not constitute infringement of the copyright or moral rights in a work:

a) applying to a useful article features that are dictated solely by a utilitarian function of the article;
b) by reference solely to a useful article, making a drawing or other reproduction in any material form of any features that are dictated solely by a utilitarian function of the article;
c) doing with a useful article having features described in paragraph (a), or with a drawing or reproduction made as described in paragraph (b), anything that the owner of the copyright has the sole right to do with the work; and
d) using any method or principle of manufacture or construction.[51]

Section 64.1 deals with the application to a useful article of features which are dictated solely by a utilitarian function of the article. The application to a useful article of features which are dictated solely by a utilitarian function of the article does not constitute infringement of the copyright or moral rights in the work from which they are copied.[52] The process of reverse engineering from a useful article to create a drawing or other reproduction, in any material form, of any features that are dictated solely by a utilitarian function of the article, does not constitute infringement.[53]

Section 64.1 does not affect copyright or moral rights in a record, perforated roll, cinematograph film, or other contrivance by means of which a work may be mechanically reproduced, performed, or delivered.[54]

---

51. Subsection 64.1(1).
52. Paragraph 64.1(1)(a).
53. Paragraph 64.1(1)(b).
54. Subsection 64.1(2).

# CHAPTER
# 19

# Neighboring Rights

# 1. Introduction

Before 1994, a performers' performance was not protected, presumably due to the ephemeral nature of a performance. With the use of sound recordings and broadcasting, performances could be fixed and reproduced for distribution to the public. As a result, it was agreed internationally that they should be protected. These rights are referred to as "neighboring rights" since the rights conferred are close to or "neighbor" traditional copyright.

Protection of neighboring rights goes side by side with the protection of authors. Neighboring rights are nearly always derivative because they are dependent upon a pre-existing work.

Canada's adoption of the Agreement on Trade-Related Aspects of Intellectual Property Rights ("TRIPS"), obligated Canada to legislate to provide standards of protection for performers, producers of sound recordings, and broadcasting organizations consistent with the Rome Convention, 1961. As a result, the *Copyright Act* was amended.

The rights granted to performers, producers of sound recordings, and broadcasting organizations, although different from those available to an author under section 3, are included in the definition of "copyright" in the *Act*. As a result, the general provisions of the *Act*, such as those dealing with infringement, are applicable to these rights.

# 2. Performers' Rights

## a) What Is Protected

The *Copyright Act* contains the following definitions of "performance" and "performers' performance"[1]

> "performance" means any acoustic or visual representation of a work, performer's performance, sound recording, or communication signal, including a representation made by means of any mechanical instrument, radio receiving set, or television receiving set.
>
> "performer's performance" means any of the following when done by a performer:
> (a) a performance of an artistic work, dramatic work or musical work, whether or not the work was previously fixed in any material form, and whether or not the work's term of copyright protection under this Act has expired,

---

1. Section 2.

    (b) a recitation or reading of a literary work, whether or not the work's term of copyright protection under this *Act* has expired, or

    (c) an improvisation of a dramatic work, musical work, or literary work, whether or not the improvised work is based on a pre-existing work.

The definition is restricted and is linked to artistic, dramatic, musical, or literary works and is limited to individuals who perform such works. As a result, the performers of variety and circus acts[2] or athletes participating in sporting events will not be protected.[3]

    The word "performer" is not defined in the *Act*, but presumably is the individual who gave the performance. If a performance is given by more than one performer, each individual involved in giving the performance is entitled to the rights provided under the relevant sections of the *Act*.[4]

## b) Canada and Rome Convention Countries

The *Act* provides that "Rome Convention country" means a country that is a party to the International Convention for the Protection of Performers, Producers of Phonograms, and Broadcasting Organisations, done at Rome on October 26, 1961.[5] The United States of America is not currently a member of the Rome Convention.

### (i) Rights Associated with a Performers' Performance

Section 15 of the *Act* provides that, subject to the existence of specific points of attachment or connecting factors, a performer has a copyright in a performer's performance consisting of the sole right to do the following in relation to the performer's performance or any substantial part thereof:

    (a) if it is not fixed,
        (i) to communicate it to the public by telecommunication,
        (ii) to perform it in public, where it is communicated to the public by telecommunication otherwise than by communication signal, and
      (iii) to fix it in any material form,

---

2. If the act was protected as a choreographic work the result would be different.
3. See *Guide to the Rome Convention* (Geneva: WIPO, 1981).
4. *Experience Hendrix LLC v. Purple Haze Records Ltd.* [2005] EWHC 249 (U.K.Ch.), appeal dismissed [2007] EWCA Civ 501 (U.K.C.A.).
5. Section 2.

(b) if it is fixed,

    (i) to reproduce any fixation that was made without the performer's authorization,

    (ii) where the performer authorized a fixation, to reproduce any reproduction of that fixation, if the reproduction being reproduced was made for a purpose other than that for which the performer's authorization was given, and

    (iii) where a fixation was permitted under one of the exceptions to infringement, or for private use, to reproduce any reproduction of that fixation, if the reproduction being reproduced was made for a purpose other than one permitted under the exceptions to infringement or for private use , and

(c) to rent out a sound recording of it,

and to authorize any such acts.[6]

The right to communicate the performers' performance to the public by telecommunication is not limited to communications taking place at the time of the performers' performance.[7]

The right to perform performers' performance in public only applies where it is communicated to the public by telecommunication[8] otherwise than by "communication signal."[9] Presumably this means the right is limited to transmission by wire or the like such as through a cable television system or the like.

The right to fix the performer's performance is not limited and the performance can be fixed in any material form.

A performer is not entitled to the sole right to reproduce the fixation of the performers' performance since the copyright owner in the underlying work is already entitled to the sole right to make a sound recording of the work pursuant to subsection 3(1)(d). However, the performer has rights with respect to sound recordings or other fixations which were not authorized by the performer, or which exceed the authorization given or go beyond the exceptions contained in the *Act*.

The right to rent out a sound recording of the performers' performance exists concurrently with the rental right available to the maker of a sound recording.[10]

---

6. Section 15 in force September 1, 1997
7. See sections 2.3 and 2.4 and subsection 3(1)(f) and (1.1).
8. Section 2 provides that "Telecommunication" means any transmission of signs, signals, writing, images, or sounds or intelligence of any nature by wire, radio, visual, optical, or other electromagnetic system.
9. Section 2 provides that "communication signal" means radio waves transmitted through space without any artificial guide for reception to the public.
10. See part 3 of this chapter.

### (ii)  Contracting Out

Nothing in section 15 prevents the performer from entering into a contract governing the use of the performer's performance for the purpose of broadcasting, fixation, or retransmission.[11]

Where a performer authorizes the embodiment of the performer's performance in a cinematographic work, the performer may no longer exercise, in relation to that performer's performance, the copyright referred to in subsection 15(1).[12]

### (iii)  Points of Attachment

The rights available relating to a performer's performance under section 15 subsist only if prescribed points of attachment are satisfied. The rights will only be available if the performers' performance:

(a)  takes place in Canada or in a Rome Convention country;
(b)  is fixed in
  (i)  a sound recording whose maker, at the time of the first fixation,
    (A)  if a natural person was a Canadian citizen or permanent resident of Canada within the meaning of the *Immigration and Refugee Protection Act*, or a citizen or permanent resident of a Rome Convention country, or
    (B)  if a corporation, had its headquarters in Canada or in a Rome Convention country, or
  (ii)  a sound recording whose first publication in such a quantity as to satisfy the reasonable demands of the public occurred in Canada or in a Rome Convention country; or
(c)  is transmitted at the time of the performer's performance by a communication signal broadcast from Canada or a Rome Convention country by a broadcaster that has its headquarters in the country of broadcast.[13]

First publication is deemed to have occurred in Canada or a Rome Convention country, as the case may be, notwithstanding that it in fact occurred previously elsewhere, if the interval between the two publications does not exceed 30 days.[14]

---

11.  Section 16.
12.  Subsection 17(1) and see subsection 17(2) concerning the enforcement of performers rights to collect residuals under Guild agreements between organizations such as ACTRA and producers.
13.  Subsection 15(2).
14.  Subsection 15(3).

## c)  Performers' Rights—WTO Countries

Pursuant to subsection 26(1) of the *Act*, where a performer's performance takes place on or after January 1, 1996 in a country that is a WTO Member, the performer has, as of the date of the performer's performance, a copyright in the performer's performance, consisting of the sole right to do the following in relation to the performer's performance or any substantial part thereof:

(a)  if it is not fixed, to communicate it to the public by telecommunication and to fix it in a sound recording, and

(b)  if it has been fixed in a sound recording without the performer's authorization, to reproduce the fixation or any substantial part thereof,

and to authorize any such acts.[15]

These rights are more limited to the rights available for Canada and Rome Convention countries under the *Act*.

The provisions of the *Act* relating to the assignment and licenses of copyright[16] apply to a performer's right under section 26.[17] However, notwithstanding an assignment of a performer's right under section 26, the performer, as well as the assignee, may

(a)  prevent the reproduction of any fixation of the performer's performance, or any substantial part of such a fixation, where the fixation was made without the performer's consent or the assignee's consent;

(b)  prevent the importation of any fixation of the performer's performance, or any reproduction of such a fixation, that the importer knows or ought to have known was made without the performer's consent or the assignee's consent.[18]

## d)  The Right to Equitable Remuneration

### (i)  Entitlement

Where a sound recording has been published, the performer and the maker are entitled, so long as prescribed points of attachment or connecting factors exist, to be paid equitable remuneration for its performance in public or its communication to the public by telecommunication, except for any retransmission.[19]

---

15. See subsections 26(2)–(4) concerning transitional provisions.
16. Subsections 13(4) to (7).
17. Subsection 26(6).
18. Subsection 26(7).
19. Section 19(1).

For the purpose of funding this entitlement, a person who performs a published sound recording in public or communicates it to the public by telecommunication is liable to pay royalties:

(a) in the case of a sound recording of a musical work to the collective society authorized to collect them,[20] or

(b) in the case of a sound recording of a literary work or dramatic work to either the maker of the sound recording or the performer.[21]

Performance in public or communication to the public by telecommunication of a sound recording triggers the right to be paid royalties. The person liable is the person who engages in these activities.[22]

The royalties to be paid are divided so that the performer or performers receives in aggregate 50 percent and the maker or makers receive in aggregate 50 percent.[23]

The right to remuneration conferred on performers under section 19 terminates 50 years after the end of the calendar year in which the performers' performance was first fixed in a sound recording or its performance occurred if it was not fixed in a sound recording.[24]

### (ii) The Points of Attachment

The right to remuneration applies only if:

(a) the maker was, at the date of the first fixation, a Canadian citizen or permanent resident of Canada within the meaning of the *Immigration and Refugee Protection Act*, or a citizen or permanent resident of a Rome Convention country, or, if a corporation, had its headquarters in one of the foregoing countries; or

(b) all the fixations done for the sound recording occurred in Canada or in a Rome Convention country.[25]

If the maker of a sound recording was a United States citizen or a corporation with headquarters in the United States, the right of remuneration will not be available since the United States is not a Rome Convention country. However, if all the fixations done for the sound recording occurred in Canada or a

---

20. See Chapter 32.
21. Subsection 19(2)
22. *NRCC Statement of Royalties, Tariff No. 3 Use and supply of Background Music (2003–2009)*, (2006), 52 C.P.R. (4th) 189 (Copyright Board).
23. Subsection 19(3).
24. Subsections 23(1) and (2) which subsections apply whether the fixation, performance or broadcast occurred before or after September 1, 1997, subsection 23(3).
25. Subsection 20(1) paragraphs (a) and (b).

Rome Convention country, remuneration will be available notwithstanding the domicile of the maker.

If so requested by a party to the North American Free Trade Agreement, the right to remuneration may be extended by the Minister of Industry to performers or makers from Mexico or the United States whose sound recordings embody dramatic or literary works.[26] In addition, the Minister may also extend reciprocity to countries other than Rome Convention countries through statements published in the Canada Gazette.[27]

Where Canadian nationals do not receive remuneration in a Rome Convention country similar to what they receive in Canada, the Minister may, by a statement published in the Canada Gazette, limit the scope and duration of the protection for the sound recordings of the nationals of that country.[28]

### (iii) The Amount of the Royalty

The amount of the royalty is determined by the submission of proposed tariffs to the Copyright Board.[29]

### (iv) Performer's Rights and Rights under Part I of the *Act*

Section 90 of the *Act* provides that no provision of the *Act* relating to

(a) copyright in performer's performances, sound recordings or communication signals, or
(b) the right of performers or makers to remuneration

shall be construed as prejudicing any rights conferred by Part I of the *Act* relating to traditional copyright and the author's moral rights or, in and of itself, as prejudicing the amount of royalties that the Board may fix in respect of those rights.

## 3. Sound Recordings

## a) What Is Protected

The *Act* provides that "sound recording" means a recording, fixed in any material form, consisting of sounds, whether or not of a performance of a

---

26. Subsection 20(3).
27. Section 22.
28. Subsection 20(2) and see regulation SOR/99–143 effective March 23, 1999.
29. See Chapter 32 part 4 concerning the process relating to the determination.

work, but excludes any soundtrack of a cinematographic work where it accompanies the cinematographic work.[30] The definition does not require that the sounds be musical or have any meaning.

The owner of the copyright in the musical or literary work is entitled to the sole right to make any sound recording by means of which the work may be mechanically reproduced or performed[31] and in the case of a musical work, to rent out a sound recording in which the work is embodied,[32] and to authorize any acts.[33] As a result, only the author of the original work may make or authorize the making of a sound recording by means of which the work may be mechanically reproduced or performed.

A sound recording is frequently a derivative work, in that it is derived from an existing musical or literary work. Sound recordings of this type are entitled to separate copyright protection, but the rights of the owner of the copyright in the sound recording are subordinate to the rights of the original copyright owner so long as those rights subsist.[34]

The first owner of the copyright in a sound recording is the maker.[35] The *Act* provides that "maker" means the person by whom the arrangements necessary for the first fixation of the sounds are undertaken.[36]

## b) The Rights Associated with a Sound Recording[37]

Section 18 sets out the rights associated with a sound recording which are as follows:

> (1) Subject to subsection (2), the maker of a sound recording has a copyright in the sound recording, consisting of the sole right to do the following in relation to the sound recording or any substantial part thereof:
> (a) to publish it for the first time;
> (b) to reproduce it in any material form; and
> (c) to rent it out,
> and to authorize any such acts.

---

30. Section 2. The soundtrack of a cinematographic work will be protected as part of the cinematographic work.
31. Section 3 (1) (d).
32. Section 3 (1) (i).
33. Section 3.
34. *Fly By Night Music v. Record Wherehouse* (1975), 20 C.P.R. (2d) 263 (F.C.T.D.); *ZYX Music GmbH v. King* [1995] 3 All E.R. 1 (Ch. D.).
35. Section 24.
36. Section 2.
37. These rights apply after September 1, 1997.

Subsection 18(2) of the *Act* sets out specific points of attachment or connecting factors which must be satisfied in order for the rights under subsection 18(1) to be available. The subsection is as follows:

> (2) Subsection (1) applies only if
>> (a) the maker of the sound recording was a Canadian citizen or permanent resident of Canada within the meaning of subsection 2(1) of the *Immigration and Refugee Protection Act*, or a citizen or permanent resident of a Berne Convention country, a Rome Convention country or a country that is a WTO Member, or, if a corporation, had its headquarters in one of the foregoing countries,
>>> (i) at the date of the first fixation, or
>>> (ii) if that first fixation was extended over a considerable period, during any substantial part of that period; or
>> (b) the first publication of the sound recording in such a quantity as to satisfy the reasonable demands of the public occurred in any country referred to in paragraph (a).

The first publication of a sound recording is deemed to have occurred in a country referred to in the above subsection notwithstanding that it in fact occurred previously elsewhere, if the interval between those two publications does not exceed thirty days.[38]

The right to rent out a sound recording is subject to section 2.5. Subsection 2.5(1) provides that an arrangement, whatever its form, constitutes a rental of a sound recording if, and only if,

> (a) it is in substance a rental, having regard to all the circumstances; and
> (b) it is entered into with motive of gain in relation to the overall operations of the person who rents out the sound recording.

A person who rents out a sound recording with the intention of recovering no more than the costs, including overhead, associated with the rental operations, does not by that act alone have a motive of gain in relation to the rental operations.[39]

The rights granted by the *Act* to the maker of a sound recording, do not include the right to perform the underlying work in public or the right to use, or authorize the use, of a sound recording for the purpose of performing the underlying work in public.[40]

---

38. Subsection 18(3).
39. Subsection 2.5(2).
40. *Télé Métropole Inc. v. Bishop* [1990] 2 S.C.R. 467.

### c)  The Right to Equitable Remuneration

Pursuant to subsection 19(1) where a sound recording has been published, the performer and maker are entitled, subject to satisfying specific points of attachment, to be paid equitable remuneration for its performance in public or its communication to the public by telecommunication, except for any retransmission.[41]

## 4.  Broadcaster's Communication Signal[42]

### a)  What Is Protected

The *Act* provides that "broadcaster" means a body that, in the course of operating a broadcasting undertaking, broadcasts a communication signal in accordance with the law of the country in which the broadcasting undertaking is carried on, but excludes a body whose primary activity in relation to communication signals is their retransmission.[43] "Communication signal" means radio waves transmitted through space without any artificial guide, for reception by the public.[44]

### b)  The Rights Associated with a Broadcaster's Communication Signal

Subsection 21(1) sets out the rights available to broadcasters. It provides that:

> Subject to subsection (2), a broadcaster has a copyright in the communication signals that it broadcasts, consisting of the sole right to do the following in relation to the communication signal or any substantial part thereof:
> (a)  to fix it,
> (b)  to reproduce any fixation of it that was made without the broadcaster's consent,
> (c)  to authorize another broadcaster to retransmit it to the public simultaneously with its broadcast, and

---

41.  Subsection 19(1) and see part 2(d) of this chapter.
42.  The rights available under the *Act* apply after September 1, 1997.
43.  Section 2.
44.  Section 2.

> (d) in the case of a television communication signal, to perform it in a place open to the public on payment of an entrance fee, and to authorize any act described in paragraph (a), (b) or (d).

Subsection 21(2) sets out the points of attachment which must be in existence in order for copyright to be available:

> (2) Subsection (1) applies only if the broadcaster
> (a) at the time of the broadcast, had its headquarters in Canada, in a country that is a WTO Member or in a Rome Convention country; and
> (b) broadcasts the communication signal from that country.

Where a Rome Convention country or a country that is a WTO Member does not grant the right mentioned in paragraph (1)(d), the Minister may, by a statement published in the Canada Gazette, declare that broadcasters that have their headquarters in that country are not entitled to that right in Canada.[45]

The term "communication signal" is limited to radio waves transmitted through space without any artificial guide. The right to communicate a work to the public by telecommunication is substantially broader [46] as "telecommunication" is defined to mean any transmission of signs, signals, writing, images, or sounds or intelligence of any nature by wire, radio, visual, optical, or other electromagnetic system.[47]

The *Act* further restricts rights available to broadcasters as a result of the compensation system with respect to retransmission of works by a cable retransmission system or similar system. The rights do not extend to cable retransmission or other systems which fall outside the definition of "communication signal."

Section 31 provides that it is not an infringement of copyright for a retransmitter[48] to communicate to the public by telecommunication any literary, dramatic, musical, or artistic work if:

> (a) the communication is a retransmission of a local or distant signal;
> (b) the retransmission is lawful under the *Broadcasting Act*;

---

45. Subsection 21 (3).
46. Subsection 3(1)(f).
47. Section 2.
48. Subsection 31(1) of the *Act* provides that "retransmitter" means a person who performs a function comparable to that of a cable retransmission system, but does not include a new media retransmitter; and "new media retransmitter" means a person whose retransmission is lawful under the *Broadcasting Act* only by reason of the *Exemption Order for New Media Broadcasting Undertakings* issued by the Canadian Radio-television and Telecommunications Commission as Appendix A to Public Notice CRTC 1999–197, as amended from time to time.

(c) the signal is retransmitted simultaneously and without alteration, except as otherwise required or permitted by or under the laws of Canada

(d) in the case of the retransmission of a distant signal, the retransmitter has paid any royalties, and complied with any terms and conditions, fixed under this *Act*; and

(e) the retransmitter complies with the applicable conditions, if any, referred to in paragraph 3(b).

For the purpose of this provision, "signal" is defined to mean a signal that carries a literary, dramatic, musical, or artistic work and is transmitted for free reception by the public by a terrestrial radio or terrestrial television station.

The subsistence of copyright in a communication signal does not effect any other copyright subsisting in the material which is broadcast, such as the copyright in a film or a sound recording. The owners of copyright in these works will have rights which are independent of the copyright in the communication signal. However, a broadcaster's communication signal relating to a live event, such as a football game or the like which may not be protected by copyright, will be protected by the broadcaster's copyright.

The first owner of the copyright in a communication signal is the broadcaster which broadcasts the signal.[49]

---

49. Section 24.

# CHAPTER
# 20

# Moral Rights

## 1. What Is Protected

"Moral rights" means the rights described in subsection 14.1(1)[1] of the *Copyright Act*. Subsection 14.1(1) states that the author of a work has, subject to section 28.2, the right to the integrity of the work and, in connection with an act mentioned in section 3, the right, where reasonable in the circumstances, to be associated with the work, as its author by name or under a pseudonym, and the right to remain anonymous. Since section 14.1 refers to "a work," moral rights are restricted to literary, dramatic, musical, or artistic works and do not apply to a performer's performance, a sound recording, or a communication signal.

Subsection 28.2(1) provides that the author's right to the integrity of a work is infringed only if the work is, to the prejudice of the honor or reputation of the author, distorted, mutilated, or otherwise modified or used in association with a product, service, cause, or institution.

Neither section 14.1 or section 28.2 contain any specific provisions with respect to works of joint authorship. Presumably moral rights are available to joint authors but the *Act* provides no clear direction.

The legislation bringing into force the sections dealing with moral rights provides that those rights subsist in respect of the work, even if the work was created before June 8, 1988 when the sections came into force.[2] However, remedies available for infringement of moral rights under the current sections may only be obtained where the infringement occurred after June 8, 1988.[3]

## 2. The Right to the Integrity of the Work

The right to control the use of a work "in association with a product, service, cause, or institution" does not require a change in the physical appearance of a work and the association of the work with a specific product, service, cause, or institution by itself may be sufficient.

The right of integrity is dominated by the requirement that an author alleging infringement of the right show prejudice to his or her honor or reputation. The *Act* does not state on what basis the determination of whether there is prejudice of the honor or reputation of the author is to be made. It has been suggested that the determination should be made on an objective basis,[4]

---

1. Section 2.
2. S.C. 1988, c. 10 (4th Supp.), s. 23.
3. S.C. 1988, c. 10 (4th Supp.), s. 23(2) and see s. 23(3) for further transitional limitations.
4. *Prise de parole Inc. v. Guérin Éditeur Ltée*, (1995), 66 C.P.R. (3d) 257, appeal dismissed 73 C.P.R. (3d) 557 (F.C.A.).

but there is some support for the view that the author's judgment, so long as it is reasonably exercised, should be considered.[5]

In the case of a painting, sculpture, or engraving, the prejudice is deemed to have occurred as a result of any distortion, mutilation, or other modification of the work.[6] The presumption only applies to an author of a painting, sculpture, or engraving, and the author of other types of work must show prejudice.

A change in the location of a work, the physical means by which a work is exposed or the physical structure containing a work, or steps taken in good faith to restore or preserve a work, do not by those acts alone constitute a distortion, mutilation, or other modification of the work.[7]

## 3. The Right to Be Associated with the Work or to Remain Anonymous

The author of a work has, in connection with an act mentioned in section 3 of the *Act*, the right, where reasonable in the circumstances, to be associated with the work as its author by name or under a pseudonym and the right to remain anonymous.[8]

The right is only available to the author and not to the copyright owner, and is specific to a work. In addition, the right only applies where it is reasonable in the circumstances. The onus of showing that it is reasonable to give effect to the right is on the author.

## 4. Waiver

Under the *Act*, moral rights may not be assigned, but may be waived in whole or in part.[9] An assignment of copyright in a work does not by that act alone constitute a waiver of any moral rights.[10]

The right to the integrity of the work or the right to be associated with the work or to remain anonymous can be waived in whole or in part. In addition,

---

5. *Snow v. The Eaton Centre* (1982), 70 C.P.R. (2d) 105 (Ont.H.C.J.).
6. Subsection 28.2(2).
7. Subsection 28.2(3).
8. Subsection 14.1(1).
9. Subsection 14.1(2).
10. Subsection 14.1(3).

different rights may be waived in favor of different persons and in association with different uses of the work.

The *Act* provides no direction concerning the form of the waiver and presumably, a waiver need not be in writing, but may be verbal and could presumably be implied.

Subsection 14.1(4) extends the benefit of a waiver. It provides that

> Where a waiver of any moral right is made in favor of an owner or a licensee of copyright, it may be invoked by any person authorized by the owner or licensee to use the work, unless there is an indication to the contrary in the waiver.[11]

The *Act* contains no limitations with respect to nature of the authorization and presumably this word will be broadly interpreted. Persons who are not authorized to use the work are not protected by the waiver.

## 5. Term of Protection and Succession

The moral rights in respect of a work subsist for the same term as the copyright in the work.[12] Subsection 14.2(2) provides that the moral rights in respect of a work pass, on the death of its author, to

(a) the person to whom those rights are specifically bequeathed;
(b) where there is no specific bequest of those moral rights and the author dies testate in respect of the copyright in the work, the person to whom that copyright is bequeathed; or
(c) where there is no person described in paragraph (a) or (b), the person entitled to any other property in respect of which the author dies intestate.[13]

Subsection 14.2(2) also applies with appropriate modifications on the death of any person who holds the moral rights.[14]

---

11. Subsection 14.1(3).
12. Subsection 14.2(1).
13. Subsection 14.2(2).
14. Subsection 14.2(3).

# CHAPTER
# 21

# Term of Protection

# 1. The General Term of Protection

Section 6 of the *Copyright Act* provides that the term for which copyright shall subsist, except as otherwise expressly provided in the *Act*, is the life of the author, the remainder of the calendar year in which the author dies, and a period of 50 years following the end of that calendar year.

The *Act* provides for a different term of protection for the following works:

a) anonymous and pseudonymous works;
b) posthumous works;
c) works of joint authorship;
d) photographs;
e) cinematographic works;
f) Crown copyright; and
g) performer's performances, sound recordings, and communication signals.

# 2. Anonymous and Pseudonymous Works

Section 6.1 of the *Act* provides that except as provided in section 6.2, where the identity of the author of a work is unknown, copyright in the work subsists for whichever of the following terms ends earlier:

(a) a term consisting of the remainder of the calendar year of the first publication of the work and a period of 50 years following the end of that calendar year, and
(b) a term consisting of the remainder of the calendar year of the making of the work and a period of 75 years following the end of that calendar year.

If during the applicable term, the author's identity becomes commonly known, the general term provided in section 6 applies.

Section 6.2 applies where the identity of all the authors of a work of joint authorship is unknown.[1] In such a case, copyright in the work subsists for whichever of the following terms ends earlier

(a) a term consisting of the remainder of the calendar year of the first publication of the work and a period of 50 years following the end of that calendar year, and

---

1. Sections 6.1 and 6.2 apply in respect of all works, whether made before or after January 1, 1994, but do not extend to or revive the term applicable to a work which expired before January 1, 1994, see S.C. 1993, c. 44, s. 75.

(b) a term consisting of the remainder of the calendar year of the making
   of the work and a period of 75 years following the end of that calendar
   year.

If during the applicable term, the identity of one or more of the authors
becomes commonly known, copyright shall subsist for the life of whichever
of those authors dies last, the remainder of the calendar year in which that
author dies, and a period of 50 years following the end of that calendar year.

## 3. Posthumous Works

Section 7(1) provides that subject to subsection (2), in the case of a literary,
dramatic, or musical work, or an engraving in which copyright subsists at the
date of the death of the author or, in the case of a work of joint authorship, at
or immediately before the date of the death of the author who dies last, but
which has not been published or, in the case of a lecture or a dramatic or
musical work, not been performed in public or communicated to the public
by telecommunication, before that date, copyright shall subsist until publication, or performance in public, or communication to the public by telecommunication, whichever may first happen, for the remainder of the calendar
year of the publication, or of the performance in public, or communication to
the public by telecommunication, as the case may be, and for a period of
50 years following the end of that calendar year.

   Subsection 7(1) provides for perpetual copyright in unpublished works.
Subsection 7(2) was added to the *Act* to limit the applicability of subsection 7(1)
by providing that it only applies where the work in question was published,
or performed in public, or communicated to the public by telecommunication, as the case may be, before December 31, 1998.

   In addition, subsections 7(3) and (4) add two additional transitional
provisions. Subsection 7(3) applies where the relevant death occurred during
the period of 50 years immediately before December 31, 1998. Where a work
was not published, or performed in public, or communicated to the public by
telecommunication before December 31, 1998, copyright shall subsist in the
work for a period of 50 years, whether or not the work is published, or performed in public, or communicated to the public by telecommunication after
December 31, 1998.

   Subsection 7(4) applies where the relevant death occurred more than 50
years before December 31, 1998. Where a work was not published, or performed in public, or communicated to the public by telecommunication
before December 31, 1998, copyright shall subsist in the work for a period of
five years, whether or not the work is published, or performed in public, or
communicated to the public by telecommunication after December 31,
1998.

## 4. **Works of Joint Authorship**

Section 9(1) provides that in the case of a work of joint authorship, except as provided in section 6.2, copyright shall subsist during the life of the author who dies last, for the remainder of the calendar year of that author's death, and for a period of 50 years following the end of that calendar year. References in the *Act* to the period after the expiration of any specified number of years from the end of the calendar year of the death of the author are construed as references to the period after the expiration of the like number of years from the end of the calendar year of the death of the author who dies last.

Section 7 applies to any literary, dramatic, or musical work, or an engraving of joint authorship, in which copyright subsists immediately before the date of death of the author who dies last, but which has not been published, or, in the case of a lecture, or a dramatic or musical work, not been performed in public, or communicated to the public by telecommunication before that date. The period during which copyright subsists under this section has been previously discussed above. If the work is published during the life of the joint authors, or after the death of the author who first dies, but before the death of the author who dies last, the term of copyright will be that provided by section 9.

Authors who are nationals of any country, other than a country that is a party to the North American Free Trade Agreement, that grants a term of protection shorter than that granted by section 9(1) of the *Act*, are not entitled to claim a longer term of protection in Canada.[2]

## 5. **Photographs**

Subsection 10(2) provides that the person who

(a) was the owner of the initial negative or other plate at the time when that negative or other plate was made, or
(b) was the owner of the initial photograph at the time when that photograph was made, where there was no negative or other plate,

is deemed to be the author of the photograph and, where that owner is a body corporate, the body corporate is deemed for the purposes of this *Act* to be ordinarily resident in a treaty country if it has established a place of business therein.

---

2. Subsection 9(2).

Where the owner is an individual, the term for which copyright subsists is that set out in section 6: the life of the author, the remainder of the calendar year in which the author dies, and a period of 50 years following the end of that calendar year. [3]

Where the owner is a corporation, the term for which copyright subsists in a photograph is the remainder of the year of the making of the initial negative or plate from which the photograph was derived or, if there is no negative or plate, of the initial photograph, plus a period of 50 years.[4] Where the owner is a corporation, the majority of the voting shares of which are owned by a natural person who would have qualified as the author of the photograph except for the above provisions the term of copyright is the term set out in section 6.[5]

## 6. Cinematographic Works

Prior to January 1, 1994, cinematographic works were protected as dramatic works if the arrangement or acting form or the combination of incidents represented, gave the work an original character, or if not so qualified, were protected as photographs.

After January 1, 1994, section 11.1 of the *Act* applies to cinematographic works where the arrangement or acting form or the combination of incidents represented do not give the work a dramatic character.[6] The section provides that copyright in such a cinematographic work or a compilation of cinematographic works shall subsist:

(a) for the remainder of the calendar year of the first publication of the cinematographic work or of the compilation, and for a period of 50 years following the end of that calendar year; or

(b) if the cinematographic work or compilation is not published before the expiration of 50 years following the end of the calendar year of its making, for the remainder of the calendar year and a period of 50 years following the end of that calendar year.

For cinematographic works in which the arrangement of the acting form or the combination of incidents represented give the work an dramatic character, the term of protection will be the general term of protection under section 6.

---

3. Section 6.
4. Subsection 10(1).
5. Subsection 10(1.1) S.C. 1997, c. 24. Section 54.1 of *An Act to Amend the Copyright Act*, S.C. 1997, c. 24 contains transitional provisions relating photographs in existence on January 1, 1999.
6. See transitional provisions of S.C. 1993, c. 44, s. 75(2), s. 76(1), and 76(2).

## 7. Crown Copyright

Section 12 provides that, without prejudice to any rights or privileges of the Crown, where any work is, or has been, prepared or published by or under the direction or control of Her Majesty or any government department, the copyright in the work, subject to any agreement with the author, belongs to Her Majesty and in that case shall continue for the remainder of the calendar year of the first publication of the work and for a period of 50 years following the end of that calendar year. Before January 1, 1994, the section referred to a term 50 years after the date of first publication.[7]

## 8. Performer's Performances, Sound Recordings and Communication Signals

The rights conferred relating to a performer's performance terminate 50 years after the end of the calendar year in which its first fixation in a sound recording, or its performance, if it is not fixed in a sound recording, occurred.[8] In the case of a sound recording, the rights terminate 50 years after the end of the calendar year in which the first fixation occurred.[9] In the case of a communication signal, the rights terminate 50 years after the end of the calendar year in which it was broadcast.[10]

The right to remuneration conferred on performers and makers by section 19 has the same term, respectively, as those provided for a performer's performance and sound recordings.[11]

These provisions apply whether the fixation, performance, or broadcast occurred before or after September 1, 1997.[12]

---

7. Section 12 as set out above applies in respect of all works, whether made before or after January 1, 1994, but does not extend to or revive the term applicable to a work which expired before January 1, 1994. S.C. 1993, c. 44, s. 75.
8. Subsection 23(1)(a).
9. Subsection 23(1)(b).
10. Subsection 23(1)(c).
11. Subsection 23(2).
12. Subsection 23(3). Transitional provisions are set out in the *Act* which apply to countries that become Berne Convention countries, Rome Convention countries or WTO Members, as the case may be, after the date of the fixation or performance of a performer's performance, see subsections 23(4) and (5).

## 9. Abandonment

Copyright may be expressly abandoned to the public if there is clear evidence of the copyright owner's intention to do so.[13] In addition, if the owner of copyright dedicates a work to the public and gives a public permission to reproduce it, the owner cannot successfully bring an action for infringement.[14]

Whether an author may abandon a work to the public by conduct or implied license is not clear. Most of the cases dealing with this issue have arisen in situations where the plaintiff has obtained a patent and asserted copyright in drawings similar to drawings which were included in the patent application.[15] The Canadian jurisprudence on this issue is unsettled.[16]

13. *Mellor v. Australian Broadcasting Commission* [1940] A.C. 491 (H.L.).
14. *British Leyland Motor Corporation v. Armstrong Patents Co.* [1982] F.S.R. 481 (Ch.D.).
15. See *Catnic Components Ltd. et al v. Hill & Smith Ltd.* [1982] 9 R.P.C. 183 at 206 (Ch. D.), the plaintiffs were deemed to have abandoned their copyright in drawings that were the equivalent of patent drawings. This conclusion was not considered in appeals to the Court of Appeal and the House of Lords [1982] F.S.R. 237 (H.L.).
16. See *Rucker Co. v. Gavel's Vulcanizing Ltd.* (1985), 7 C.P.R. (3d) 294 (F.C.T.D.); *Energy Absorption Systems, Inc. v. Y. Boissonneault & Fils Inc.* (1990), 30 C.P.R. (3d) 420 (F.C.T.D).

# CHAPTER
# 22

# Ownership of Copyright

# 1. Authorship

## a) The Author Is the Owner

Subsection 13(1) of the *Copyright Act* provides that, subject to the *Act*, the author of a work shall be the first owner of the copyright in the work. The owner of the copyright in a work is entitled to exercise the rights set out in section 3 of the *Act*, including the right to authorize others to exercise such rights.[1] The author is also entitled to exercise the moral rights associated with the work.[2]

The *Act* specifies exceptions to this general principle that relate to:

a)   engravings, photographs, or portraits;[3]
b)   works made in the course of employment;[4]
c)   works created by or for the Crown;[5] and
d)   performer's performances, sound recordings, and communication signals.[6]

## b) The "Author"

The *Act* does not contain a definition of the term "author," but the author of a work, subject to the exceptions discussed in this chapter, is the person who has expressed the idea in material form.[7] In most cases, it will be readily apparent who is the "author" of a work. In situations where it is not clear who is the author of a work, the facts must be carefully analyzed to ascertain who created the work by the exercise of the skill and judgment, that resulted in the expression of the work in material form.[8]

---

1. Section 3; and see *Underwriters' Survey Bureau Ltd. et al. v. Massie & Renwick Ltd.* [1938] Ex. C.R. 103, [1940] S.C.R. 218 (S.C.C.).
2. See Chapter 20.
3. Subsection 13(2).
4. Subsection 13(3).
5. Section 12.
6. Section 24.
7. *Donoghue* v. *Allied Newspapers Ltd.*, [1937] 3 All E.R. 503 (Ch. D.).
8. *John Maryon Int., Ltd. v. New Brunswick Telephone* (1982), 141 D.L.R. (3d) 193 (N.B.C.A.).

Copyright does not subsist in an idea but the form in which the idea is expressed.[9] A person who merely suggests the idea of a work to another is not the author or a joint author.[10]

When an individual is interviewed by a member of the media, the person who reduces the oral statements to a fixed form is the owner of the copyright in that aspect of the interview if sufficient skill and judgment is exercised.[11] Whether the subject of the interview is entitled to copyright in the oral discussion making up the interview depends on the nature of the discussion. If the interview is of a casual nature, it is unlikely that the conversation would be protected by copyright.[12]

An amanuensis who takes down the words of another verbatim will not be the author of the resulting written work,[13] but if sufficient skill and judgment is exercised copyright may subsist in the resulting work. For example, a reporter who took down in shorthand five speeches delivered by a government official and published a report in a newspaper was the author of the report since the report was not a verbatim rendition of what had been said and skill and judgment was exercised in preparing it.[14]

It is not clear who is the author of a computer-generated work. There are many situations where a computer is used to generate works which would otherwise be protected by copyright. No Canadian case has considered this issue. One approach is to treat the program as being similar to a pen used by an author to write a work.[15]

## 2. Engravings, Photographs, or Portraits

Subsection 13(2) provides that in the case of an engraving, photograph, or portrait, the plate or other original was ordered by some other person and was made for valuable consideration, and the consideration was paid in

---

9. *Moreau* v. *St. Vincent*, (1950), 12 C.P.R. 32, (Ex Ct); *Stevens* v. *Robert Simpson Co. Ltd. et al.* (1964), 41 C.P.R. 204 (Ont. C.A).

10. *Kantel* v. *Grant, Nisbet & Auld Ltd* [1933] Ex. C.R. 84; *Kenrick* v. *Lawrence* (1890), 25 Q.B.D. 99 (Q.B.D.), U.K.

11. *Walter* v. *Lane* [1900] A.C. 539 (H.L); *Express Newspapers plc. v. News (UK) ltd.* [1990] 3 All E.R. 376 (U.K.Ch.D.); *Gould Estate v. Stoddart Publishing Co.* (1996), 74 C.P.R. (3d) 205 (Ont. Ct. (Gen. Div.)), (1998), 80 C.P.R. (3d) 161 (Ont.C.A.); *Hager v. E.C.W. Press Ltd.* (1998), 85 C.P.R. (3d) 289 (F.C.T.D.).

12. *Gould Estate v. Stoddart Publishing Co.* (1996), 74 C.P.R. (3d) 205 (Ont. Ct. (Gen. Div.)), (1998) 80 C.P.R. (3d) 161 (Ont.C.A.).

13. *Housden* v. *Marshall*, [1958] 3 All E.R. 639 (Ch. D.).

14. *Walter* v. *Lane*, [1900] A.C. 539 (H.L); *Express Newspapers plc. v. News (UK) Ltd.* [1990] 3 All E.R. 376 (Ch.D.).

15. *Express Newspapers PLC v. Liverpool Daily Post & Echo PLC*, [1985] 3 All E.R. 680 (Ch.D).

pursuance of that order, in the absence of any agreement to the contrary, the person by whom the plate or other original was ordered shall be the first owner of the copyright. This is an exception to the general rule that the author of a work is the first owner of copyright in the work.

The subsection only applies to "an engraving, photograph, or portrait." It does not apply to other artistic works such as sketches and drawings for which no engraving was made.[16] Surprising results can occur in the absence of a written assignment of copyright.[17]

## a) Photographs

### i) The Author of a Photograph

Subsection 10(2) of the *Act* provides that the person who

(a) was the owner of the initial negative or other plate[18] at the time when that negative or other plate was made, or

(b) was the owner of the initial photograph[19] at the time when that photograph was made, where there was no negative or other plate,

is deemed to be the author of the photograph and, where that owner is a body corporate, the body corporate is deemed for the purposes of this *Act* to be ordinarily resident in a treaty country if it has established a place of business therein. The individual who takes a photograph is not necessarily the author and the owner of copyright in the photograph.

As a result of the deeming provision, a corporation may be the author of a photograph. "Treaty country" is defined by the *Act* to mean a Berne Convention country, UCC country or WTO Member.[20]

While the *Act* provides for the ownership of copyright in a photograph, it does not deal with the limitations on the right to publish or use a photograph arising from privacy rights, publicity rights, or claims for breach of confidence.

---

16. *Toronto Carton Co. Ltd.* v. *Manchester McGregor Ltd.*, [1935] O.R. 144, [1935] 2 D.L.R. 94. (Ont. H.C.)

17. *Cselko Associates Inc. v. Zellers Inc* (1992), 44 C.P.R. (3d) 56 (Ont. Ct. (Gen. Div.)) relating to drawings commissioned for advertising purposes.

18. Section 2 provides that "plate" includes any stereotype or other plate, stone, block, mould, matrix, transfer, or negative used or intended to be used for printing or reproducing copies of any work.

19. Section 2 provides that "photograph" includes photo-lithograph and any work expressed by any process analogous to photography.

20. Section 2.

## ii) Photographs Ordered for Valuable Consideration

Subsection 13(2) provides that in the case of a photograph, the plate or other original was ordered by some other person and was made for valuable consideration, and the consideration was paid, in pursuance of that order, in the absence of any agreement to the contrary, the person by whom the plate or other original was ordered shall be the first owner of the copyright.

Subsection 10(2) specifies who is the author of the photograph, subsection 13(2), when applicable, specifies who is the first owner of copyright.[21]

In order for subsection 13(2) to apply it must be shown that:

a) the plate or other original was ordered by some other person;
b) for valuable consideration;
c) the consideration was paid; and
d) the absence of an agreement to the contrary.

### A) Order

In order for the subsection to apply the plate or other original must be made in pursuance of the order.[22] The subsection does not require an express reference to a plate or other original.[23]

It is a question of fact in each case whether there is a contract to pay for a photograph. If the other person is obligated to pay for taking the photograph, whether copies of the photograph are purchased or not by the other person, the subsection applies.[24]

When photographs are taken on speculation, as for example, groups of college students, sporting teams, etc., free of charge, on the basis of potential sales to individuals, the photographer will be the owner of the copyright.[25]

### B) Valuable Consideration

The words "and the consideration was paid" were added to subsection 13(2) effective July 1, 1998,[26] and have not yet been considered by he courts. The requirement that consideration be paid may make it more difficult to conclude that a photograph was ordered for consideration when the consideration is not

21. *Christopher Bede Studios Ltd.* v. *United Portraits Ltd.*, [1958] N.Z.L.R. 250 (N.Z. Sup. Ct.).
22. *Toronto Carton Co. Ltd.* v. *Manchester McGregor Ltd.*, [1935] O.R. 144, [1935] 2 D.L.R. 94 (Ont. H.C.); *Pro Arts, Inc.* v. *Campus Crafts Holdings Ltd.* (1980), 50 C.P.R. (2d) 230 (Ont. H.C.).
23. *Desmarais v. Edimag Inc. et al.* (2003), 26 C.P.R. (4th) 295 (Quebec C.A.).
24. *Pro Arts, Inc.* v. *Campus Crafts Holdings Ltd.* (1980), 50 C.P.R. (2d) 230 (Ont. H.C.).
25. *Planet Earth Productions Inc.* v. *Rowlands* (1990), 30 C.P.R. (3d) 129 (Ont. Sup. Ct.).
26. *Act to Amend the Copyright Act* S.C. 1997, c. 24.

expressly referred to by the parties. In the past, courts have inferred in some cases that the photograph was taken for consideration.[27]

### C) Agreement to the Contrary

A photographer may use a standard form of contract to overcome the effect of the subsection.[28]

The *Act* does not require that such an agreement be in writing and it may be oral or inferred from the circumstances including the practice or custom in the trade.[29]

### D) Contracts of Service

Where a photograph was taken and the photographer was in the employment of some person under a contract of service or apprenticeship and the photograph was made in the course of such employment by that person, the person by whom the author was employed shall, in the absence of agreement to the contrary, be the first owner of the copyright. However, if the requirements of subsection 13(2) are satisfied the person who ordered the photograph will be the first owner of the copyright.[30]

## b) Engravings

"Engravings" are defined as including "etchings, lithographs, woodcuts, prints, and other similar works, not being photographs."[31] The provisions of subsection 13(2) apply to such works in the same fashion they apply to photographs.[32]

---

27. *Paul Couvette Photographs v. The Ottawa Citizen* (1985), 7 C.P.R. (3d) 552 (Ont. Prov. Ct.); *Dobran v. Bier*, (1958), 29 C.P.R. 150, (Que. Q.B.).
28. *Christopher Bede Studios Limited v. United Portraits Limited* [1958] N.Z.L.R. 250 (Sup. Ct) and see *Pro Arts, Inc. v. Campus Crafts Holdings Ltd* (1980), 50 C.P.R. (2d) 230 (Ont. H.C.).
29. *Allen v. Toronto Star Newspapers Ltd* (1995), 63 C.P.R. (3d) 517 (Ont. Ct. (Gen. Div.)) reversed on appeal on other grounds (1997), 36 O.R. (3d) 201 (Div. Ct.).
30. Subsection 13(3); *Global Upholstery Co. Ltd. v. Galaxy Office Furniture Ltd* (1976), 29 C.P.R. (2d) 145 (F.C.T.D.).
31. Section 2.
32. *Toronto Carton Co. Ltd. v. Manchester McGregor Ltd.*, [1935] O.R. 144, [1935] 2 D.L.R. 94 (Ont. H.C.).

## c) Portraits

The *Act* does not contain a definition of a "portrait." Presumably a portrait refers to a likeness of a person made by drawing, painting, photography, or the like. Subsection 13(2) applies to portrait.

## 3. Other Commissioned Works

Where a person commissions and pays for the preparation of a work by a non-employee, other than a photograph, engraving, or portrait, the person commissioning the work does not own the copyright in the work unless there is an assignment of the copyright to such person, which must be in writing and signed by the author of the work.[33] For example, a lawyer who prepares legal documents on behalf of a client owns any applicable copyright in documents produced since the lawyer is not employed under a contract of service by the client.[34]

Even if there is no written assignment of the copyright signed by the non-employed owner of copyright, the owner may be precluded from exercising their statutory rights against the person who commissioned the work.[35]

A Canadian court could not likely grant relief by way of an equitable assignment in such situations since subsection 13(4) provides that an assignment of copyright must be in writing and section 89 provides that no person is entitled to copyright or any similar right in any work otherwise than under and in accordance with the *Act*.

## 4. Contracts of Service

## a) Employment Under a Contract of Service or Apprenticeship

Subsection 13(3) of the *Act* provides that where the author of a work was in the employment of some other person under a contract of service or apprenticeship and the work was made in the course of employment by that person, the person by whom the author was employed shall, in the absence of any

---

33. *Massie & Renwick Ltd. v. Underwriters' Survey Bureau Ltd. et al.*, [1940] S.C.R. 218, [1940] 1 D.L.R. 625; *Downing v. General Synod, et al*, [1943] O.R. 652 (C.A.).
34. *Arcon Canada Inc. v. Arcobec Aluminium Inc.* (1984), 7 C.P.R. (3d) 382 (Que.S.C.)
35. *Cselko Associates Inc. v. Zellers Inc.* (1992), 44 C.P.R. (3d) 56 (Ont. Gen. Div.).

agreement to the contrary, be the first owner of the copyright. The subsection also provides that where the work is an article or other contribution to a newspaper, magazine, or similar periodical, there shall, in the absence of any agreement to the contrary, be deemed to be reserved to the author a right to restrain the publication of the work, otherwise than as part of a newspaper, magazine, or similar periodical.

Subsection 13(3), when applicable, overrides the provisions of subsection 13(1) concerning first ownership of copyright. It is an exception to the general rule that the author is the first owner of copyright.

In order for the subsection to apply, it must be established that:

a) the author of a work was in the employment of some other person under a contract of service or apprenticeship,
b) the work was made in the course of employment by that person, and
c) the absence of any agreement to the contrary.

If these conditions are satisfied, the author's employer will be the first owner of copyright in the work without any assignment being necessary.

As the section uses the term "work," it does not apply to performer's performances, sound recordings, or communication signals to which section 24 applies.

The contract must be a "contract of service or apprenticeship" and not a "contract for services." Typically, a contract of service or apprenticeship involves an employee while a contract for services relates to an independent contractor. Unfortunately, in some cases it can be difficult to determine into which category the contract falls. There is no universal test to be applied and each case must be decided on its own facts. The courts have enunciated a number of tests to help make the determination.[36]

### i) The Control Test

This test emphasizes the degree of control exercised by the employer over the individual involved. The existence of direct control by the employer, the degree of independence on the part of the person who renders services, and the place where the service is rendered, are considered in determining whether there is a contract of service.[37] A contract of service involves the existence of a servant and the implication that there is an obligation to obey the orders

---

36. *Marotta v. R.* [1986] 2 F.C. 221 (F.C.T.D.) and *Amusements Wiltron Inc. v. Mainville* (1991), 40 C.P.R. (3d) 521 (Quebec Sup. Ct.).
37. *Simmons v. Heath Laundry Co.* [1910] 1 K.B. 543 (U.K.C.A.); *Stevenson Jordan & Harrison Ltd. v. Macdonald & Evans,* [1952] 1 T.L.R. 101, 69 R.P.C. 10 (U.K.C.A.).

of the employer. A servant is a person who is subject to the commands of a master as to the manner in which the servant must do the work that is required.[38]

The more control the more likely a contract of service,[39] but, where professional or other highly skilled individuals are involved, the control test may be less appropriate.[40]

### ii)  The Organization or Integration Test

It is often easy to recognize a contract of service when you see it. A ship's master, a chauffeur, and a reporter on the staff of a newspaper are all employed under a contract of service: but a ship's pilot and a newspaper contributor are more likely employed under a contract for services.[41] A distinguishing feature in these situations is that under a contract of service, a person is employed as part of the business and his or her work is done as an integral part of the business. However, under a contract for services, the work, although done for the business, is not integrated into it but is only accessory to it.[42]

The Supreme Court of Canada has said that while there is no universal test to determine whether a person is an employee or an independent contractor, the integration test is a persuasive approach. The central question is whether the person who has been engaged to perform the services is performing them as a person in business on his/her own account. In making this determination, the level of control the employer has over the worker's activities will always be a factor. Other factors to consider include whether the worker provides his/her own equipment, whether the worker hires his/her own helpers, the degree of financial risk taken by the worker, the degree of responsibility for investment and management assumed by the worker, and the worker's opportunity to profit in the performance of his or her task. These factors constitute a non-exhaustive list and there is no set formula as to their application. The relative weight of each depends on the particular facts and circumstances of the case.[43]

---

38. *University of London Press Ltd.* v. *University Tutorial Press Ltd.* [1916] 2 Ch. 601. (U.K.C.A.)
39. *Simmons* v. *Heath Laundry Co.*, [1910] 1 K.B. 543 (U.K.C.A.).
40. *Belof* v. *Pressdram Ltd.* [1973] 1 All.E.R. 241 (Ch. D.).
41. *Stevenson Jordan & Harrison Ltd.* v. *MacDonald & Evans* (1952), 69 R.P.C. 10 (U.K.C.A.); and see also *Gould* v. *Minister of National Insurance et al.* [1951] 1 All E.R. 368 (U.K.K.B.).
42. *Stevenson Jordan & Harrison Ltd.* v. *MacDonald & Evans* (1952), 69 R.P.C. 10 (U.K.C.A.).
43. *671122 Ontario Ltd.* v. *Sagaz Industries Canada Inc.* [2001] 2 S.C.R. 983 (S.C.C.) and see *Wiebe Door Services Ltd.* v. *M.M.R.* [1986] 3 F.C. 553 (Fed. C.A.); *Royal Winnipeg Ballet v Minister of National Revenue*, 2006 FCA 87 (F.C.A.).

### iii) The Economic Reality Test

Under this test, the focus of the inquiry is a determination of whether the individual involved is carrying on the business alone or on his or her own behalf and not for a superior. The test is not limited to control and considers (i) control; (ii) ownership of the tools; (iii) chance of profit; and (iv) risk of loss. Control in itself is not always conclusive. All of the elements of the relationship between the parties are considered. Frequently, the crucial question is whether the individual is carrying on the business on their own behalf and not for a superior.[44]

## b)  In the Course of Employment

In order for subsection 13(3) to apply, the work must have been made by the author in the course of employment. An individual who is employed under a contract of service may sometimes perform services outside the contract.[45]

A director of a company, in the absence of a specific contract of service, may not come within the subsection.[46]

## c)  Absence of Agreement to the Contrary

In order for the subsection to apply, there must be an "absence of any agreement to the contrary." Parties may contract out of the subsection.[47] The Act does not require that the agreement be in writing to be enforceable[48] and an agreement may be implied.[49]

## d)  Articles or Other Contributions to a Newspaper, Magazine, or Similar Periodical

Subsection 13(3) provides that "where the work is an article or other contribution to a newspaper, magazine, or similar periodical, there shall, in the

---

44. *Montreal Locomotive Works, Ltd. v. Montreal* [1947] 1 D. L. R. 161 (H.L.).
45. *Byrne* v. *Statist Co.* [1914] 1 K.B. 622 and see *Stevenson Jordan & Harrison Ltd.* v. *MacDonald & Evans* (1952), 69 R.P.C. 10 (U.K.C.A.).
46. *Antocks Lairn Limited v. I. Bloohn Limited*, [1972] R.P.C. 219 (Ch. D.).
47. *Harold Drabble Ltd.* v. *Hycolite Mfg. Co.* (1928), 44 T.L.R. 264 (Ch. D.).
48. *Canavest House Ltd. v. Lett* (1984), 2 C.P.R. (3d) 386 (Ont. H.C.).
49. *Dolmage v Erskine* (2003), 23 C.P.R. (4th) 495 (Ont. S.C.J).

absence of any agreement to the contrary, be deemed to be reserved to the author a right to restrain the publication of the work otherwise than as part of a newspaper, magazine, or similar periodical."

The right available under the subsection is a personal right, which like a moral right cannot be assigned. It is not clear how useful this right is to the author since the article or other contribution may be published in any number of newspapers, magazines, or similar periodicals. [50]

## 5. Collective Works

Section 2 of the *Act* provides that "collective work" means:

(a) an encyclopedia, dictionary, year book, or similar work,
(b) a newspaper, review, magazine, or similar periodical, and
(c) any work written in distinct parts by different authors, or in which works or parts of works of different authors are incorporated.

Subparagraph (c) was added to the *Act* to include works which may have been overlooked. [51]

Copyright may subsist in a collective work as a whole as well as in works or parts of works of different authors that are incorporated into it. The individual who has exercised skill and judgment, resulting in the general conception and design in material form of the work as a whole, will be the author of the collective work. If the parts of the collective work can be segregated, the creator of each part may be the author of that part.

In a case involving alleged infringement relating to the electronic reproduction of articles submitted by freelance authors typically for use on a one time basis in a newspaper, the Supreme Court of Canada observed that the real question was whether the electronic databases that contain articles from the newspapers reproduce the newspapers (or a substantial part of the newspapers) or merely reproduce the original articles. [52] It is open to the publishers to reproduce a substantial part of the collective work but an infringement to reproduce, without consent, the individual articles.

50. *Robertson v. Thompson Corporation* 2006 SCC 42 (S.C.C.).
51. *Chappel & Co v. Redwood Music Ltd*, [1980] 2 All E.R. 817 (H.L.).
52. *Robertson v. Thompson Corporation* (2006), 52 C.P.R. (4th) 417 (S.C.C.).

# 6. Compilations

The *Act* provides that a "compilation" means

a) a work resulting from the selection or arrangement of literary, dramatic, musical, or artistic works or parts thereof, or
b) a work resulting from the selection or arrangement of data.[53]

A compilation containing two or more of the categories of literary, dramatic, musical, or artistic works is deemed to be a compilation of the category making up the most substantial part of the compilation.[54] The mere fact that a work is included in a compilation does not increase, decrease, or otherwise affect the protection conferred by the *Act* in respect of the copyright in the work or the moral rights in respect of the work.[55]

Generally "compilations" and "collective works" have been treated as essentially similar.[56] However, the definition of "compilation" is broader since it extends to works resulting from the selection or arrangement of data, which may not be protected by copyright on its own. As a result of the use of the disjunctive "or," originality is not required in both selection and arrangement to result in a work that is protected under the *Act*.[57]

In order to be protected by copyright there must be some evidence that the creation of the compilation required the exercise of skill and judgment in selecting or arranging the material which imparted some quality or character that the raw material did not possess.[58] It is not the components, which may be taken from the public domain, that are the subject of the copyright, but the over-all arrangement of them which the author through his or her industry has produced.

The author of a compilation is the individual who exercised skill and judgment in selecting or arranging the material making up the compilation.[59]

---

53. Section 2.
54. Subsection 2.1(1).
55. Subsection 2.1(2).
56. *Chappel & Co v. Redwood Music Ltd.*, [1980] 2 All E.R. 817 (H.L.) and *Slumber-Magic Adjustable Bed Co. v. Sleep-King Adjustable Bed Co.* (1984), 3 C.P.R. (3d) 81 (B.C.S.C.), *Robertson v. Thompson Corporation* (2006), 52 C.P.R. (4th) 417 (S.C.C.).
57. *Robertson v. Thompson Corporation* (2006), 52 C.P.R. (4th) 417 (S.C.C.).
58. *The Law Society of Upper Canada v. CCH Canadian Limited* (2004) SCC 13 (S.C.C.).
59. See *Waterlow Publishers Limited v. Rose et al.* (1995), 22 F.S.R. 207 (U.K.C.A.).

## 7. Works of Joint Authorship

### a) Statutory Definition

The *Act* provides that a "work of joint authorship" means a work produced by the collaboration of two or more authors in which the contribution of one author is not distinct from the contribution of the other author or authors.[60] The definition is exhaustive and the concept of a work of joint authorship is limited to the statutory definition.

In order to come within the definition, it must be shown that

a)   the work was produced by the collaboration of two or more authors, and
b)   the contribution of one author is not distinct from the contribution of the other author or authors.

### b) Collaboration of Two or More Authors

In order to come within the statutory definition, the work must be produced by the collaboration of two or more authors. The use of the word "collaboration" suggests working in combination to produce a work.

### c) The Nature of the Contribution

The contribution must be that of an "author." An individual asserting a claim of joint authorship in a work must establish that they have made a significant and original contribution to the creation of the work pursuant to a common design. It is not necessary that the contribution to the work be equal in terms of either quantity, quality, or originality to that of the other collaborators.[61]

Typically four elements must be shown in the context of a musical work:

(1) the claimant made a contribution in the nature of authorship;
(2) it was significant;

---

60. Section 2.
61. *Stuart v. Barrett* [1994] E.M.L.R. 448 (U.K. Ch. D); *Godfrey v. Lees* [1995] E.M.L.R. 307 (U.K. Ch. D); *Robin Ray v. Classic F.M. P.L.C.* [1998] F.S.R. 622 (U.K. Ch. D).

(3) it was original; and

(4) the contribution found its way into the finished work.[62]

In the case of *Neudorf v. Nettwerk Productions Limited*,[63] the trial judge observed that there was a dearth of Canadian law on the meaning of the word "collaboration" in the definition of a "work of joint authorship." As a result, reference was made to American authorities dealing with the concept of joint authorship under U.S. legislation. It was concluded that mutual intent was a prerequisite for a finding of collaboration. As a result, it was found that the test for joint authorship, which should be applied, was as follows:

(1) did the plaintiff contribute significant original expression to the songs? If yes,

(2) did each of the plaintiff and defendant intend that their contributions be merged into a unitary whole? If yes,

(3) did each of the plaintiff and defendant intend the other to be a joint author of the songs?

There are substantial differences between the wording of the Canadian *Act* and the U.S. legislation. Normally, the concept of collaboration contemplates working in combination without the necessity of making an inquiry into the intention of the parties. It remains to be seen whether the application of the test set out above is appropriate for use in Canada.[64]

## d) The Nature of Joint Authors' Interest

In the absence of an agreement to the contrary or the existence of special circumstances, joint authors own a work as tenants in common in equal shares and not joint tenants.[65] When a joint author dies their interest passes to their beneficiaries rather than to the surviving joint author.

A joint author cannot grant a license of any of the exclusive rights available under the *Act* relating to the work without the consent of the other

---

62. *Hadley and Others v. Kemp* (April 30,1999) (U.K.Ch. D) (unreported); *Caala Homes South v. Alfred McAlpine Homes East Ltd.* [1995] F.S.R. 818 (U.K.Ch. D).

63. *Neudorf v. Nettwerk Productions Limited* (1999), 3 C.P.R. (4th) 129 (B.C.S.C.) a notice of appeal was filed but it appears the defendant filed an assignment in bankruptcy.

64. *Re Editor's Assn. of Canada, New Certification Order* (2002), 22 C.P.R. (4th) 21 (Canadian Artists and Producers Tribunal) the Tribunal refused to follow the approach set out in the *Neudorf* case and see *Hodgens v. Beckingham* [2003] EWCA CIV 143 (U.K.C.A.) which also refused to follow the approach set out in *Neudorf*.

65. *Lauri v. Renad*, [1892] 3 Ch. 402 (U.K.C.A).

joint author(s).[66] While title to copyright is divisible the right to exercise the exclusive rights is not.

A joint author may institute proceedings against another joint author to restrain that person from exercising the exclusive rights relating to a joint work without consent.[67] Each joint author has the right to institute proceedings against third parties for infringement without joining the other joint author or authors as plaintiffs.[68]

## 8. Cinematographic Works

In order to determine who is the author or a joint author of a cinematographic work, a determination must be made to ascertain who has exercised the skill and judgment which resulted in the expression of the work in material form.

The *Act* uses the concept of "Maker" as one of the points of attachment or connecting factors for the subsistence of copyright in a cinematographic work. "Maker," in relation to a cinematographic work is defined as meaning the person by whom the arrangements necessary for the making of the work are undertaken. This concept is separate and distinct from the determination of who is an "author."

## 9. Performer's Performances, Sound Recordings, and Communication Signals

Section 24 of the *Act* provides that the first owner of the copyright in a performer's performance is the performer.[69]

Section 24 of the *Act* provides that the first owner of the copyright in a sound recording is the maker. "Maker" is defined, in relation to sound recordings as meaning the person by whom the arrangements necessary for the first fixation of the sounds is undertaken.[70]

---

66. *Powell v. Head* (1879), 12 Ch. D. 686 (U.K.Ch.D); *Cescinsky v. Routledge & Sons Ltd.*, [1916] 2 K.B. 325. (U.K.K.B.)
67. *Cescinsky v. Routledge & Sons Ltd.*, [1916] 2 K.B. 325. (U.K.K.B.)
68. *Cescinsky v. Routledge & Sons Ltd.*, [1916] 2 K.B. 325. (U.K.K.B.)
69. See Chapter 19, part 2 concerning the meaning of the term "performer."
70. Section 2.

Section 24 of the *Act* provides that the first owner of the copyright in a communication signal is the broadcaster that broadcasts it.[71]

## 10. Presumptions as to Ownership

In any proceedings for infringement of copyright, the following matters will be presumed to exist where the defendant puts in issue either the existence of the copyright or the title of the plaintiff thereto.[72]

If the defendant puts in issue the existence of copyright or the plaintiff's title thereto,

(a) copyright shall be presumed, unless the contrary is proved, to subsist in the work, performer's performance, sound recording or communication signal, as the case may be; and

(b) the author, performer, maker, or broadcaster, as the case may be, shall, unless the contrary is proved, be presumed to be the owner of the copyright.[73]

In the circumstances described above and where no assignment of the copyright, or license granting an interest in the copyright, has been registered under the *Act*,

a) if a name purporting to be that of the author of the work, the performer of the performer's performance, the maker of the sound recording, or the broadcaster of the communication signal is printed or otherwise indicated thereon in the usual manner, the person whose name is so printed or indicated shall, unless the contrary is proved, be presumed to be the author, performer, maker, or broadcaster;

b) if no name is so printed or indicated, or if the name so printed or indicated is not the true name of the author, performer, maker, or broadcaster or the name by which that person is commonly known, and a name purporting to be that of the publisher or owner of the work, performer's performance, sound recording, or communication signal is printed or otherwise indicated thereon in the usual manner, the person whose name is printed or indicated as described above shall, unless the

---

71. See Chapter 19, part 4 concerning the meaning of the term "broadcaster."
72. Section 34.1 and see *Massie & Renwick Ltd. v. Underwriters' Survey Bureau Ltd. et al.,* [1940] S.C.R. 218.
73. Paragraph 34.1 (1).

contrary is proved, be presumed to be the owner of the copyright in question; and

c) if, on a cinematographic work, a name purporting to be that of the maker of the cinematographic work appears in the usual manner, the person so named shall, unless the contrary is proved, be presumed to be the maker of the cinematographic work.[74]

These presumptions do not take precedence over the provisions of subsection 53(2) which provide that a certificate of registration of copyright in a work is evidence that copyright subsists in the work and that the person registered is the owner of the work.[75]

---

74. Paragraph 34.1 (2).
75. *Circle Film Enterprises Inc. v. Canadian Broadcasting Corporation*, [1959] S.C.R. 602, 31 C.P.R. 57 (S.C.C.).

# CHAPTER
# 23

# Crown Copyright

# 1. Crown Copyright

## a) The Crown

Section 12 of the *Copyright Act* provides that, without prejudice to any rights or privileges of the Crown, where any work is, or has been, prepared or published by or under the direction or control of Her Majesty or any government department, the copyright in the work shall, subject to any agreement with the author, belong to Her Majesty and, in that case, shall continue for the remainder of the calendar year of the first publication of the work and for a period of 50 years following the end of that calendar year. The section preserves any rights arising from Crown prerogative and Crown immunity and deals with Crown copyright under the *Act*.

The *Interpretation Act*[1] provides that in every Act of the Parliament of Canada, "Her Majesty" or "The Crown" means the Sovereign of the United Kingdom, Canada, and Her other Realms and Territories and Head of the Commonwealth. The government of Canada is carried on in the Queen's name[2] but the Queen herself does not govern.

The Crown is the executive branch of Canada's government as distinct from the legislative and judicial branches of the government. It is the branch of government responsible for carrying out the law and performing the routine administration of the country.

The ability to exercise the rights and privileges of the Crown is granted to each of the provinces and the Federal government according to their respective legislative jurisdiction under the *Constitution Act, 1867*.[3] As a result, the reference to the "Crown" in the *Copyright Act* refers to the Crown in the Right of Canada and the Crown in the Right of each of the provinces, depending on the circumstances.

## b) Government Departments

The term "any government department" in section 12 is not defined in the *Act*. The words likely include a branch or division of the executive branch of the government.[4]

---

1. R.S.C. (1985), c.I-21.
2. *Constitution Act,* 1876 (UK), s. 9, 30 & 31 Vict., c. 3.
3. *Liquidators of the Maritime Bank of Canada v. Receiver General of New Brunswick* (1892), A.C. 437 (P.C.).
4. Federally the *Financial Administration Act*, R.S.C. 1985, c. F-11, defines "department" as any of the departments listed in Schedule I of the *Act*, any of the divisions or branches of the public service of Canada, a commission under the *Inquiries Act* designated by order of the Governor

## c) The Rights Available to the Crown

The Crown or a government department may assert rights under section 12 without prejudicing its claim to assert Crown prerogative.[5] In addition, the Crown, to the extent it employs individuals, will have rights under subsection 13(3). The rights available to the "Crown" under section 12 are referred to as "Crown copyright."

Section 12 applies to works that are prepared or published. Where a work is prepared under the direction or control of the Crown or a government department, the copyright in the work belongs to the Crown for a term which continues until the end of the calendar year of first publication, whenever this may occur, and for a period of 50 years following the end of that calendar year. The section provides no limitation on the length of the period of protection prior to publication.

Where a work is independently prepared but is later published by or under the control of the Crown or a government department, the author's copyright automatically passes to the Crown for a term which continues until the end of the calendar year of first publication and for a period of 50 years following the end of that calendar year.

The defense of public interest is available in proper circumstances against the assertion of Crown copyright.[6] Defenses based on the exceptions to infringement normally available under the *Act* may be asserted against the Crown.[7]

As a result of section 12, independent contractors may be in a substantially different position in their dealings with the Crown than in their dealings with private enterprise. If the work is prepared or published by or under the direction or control of the Crown, copyright will belong to the Crown unless there is an agreement to the contrary.[8]

---

in Council as a department, the staffs of the Senate, the House of Commons, and the Library of Parliament, and any departmental corporations listed in Schedule II.

5. *Eros-Equipe de Recherche Operationnelle en Sante Inc. v. Conseillers en Gestion et Informatique C.G.I. Inc,* (2004), 35 C.P.R. (4th) 105 (F.C.).
6. *R. v. James Lorimer & Co. Ltd.* (1984), 77 C.P.R. (2d) 262 (F.C.A.).
7. *R. v. James Lorimer & Co. Ltd.* (1984), 77 C.P.R. (2d) 262 (F.C.A.).
8. See *Pfizer Canada Inc. v. Canada* (1986), 10 C.P.R. (3d) 268 (F.C.T.D.); *Glaxo Canada Inc. v. Apotex Inc.* (1995), 64 C.P.R. (3d) 191 (F.C.A.), rev'g (1994), 58 C.P.R. (3d) 1 (F.C.T.D.); and *Procter & Gamble Pharmaceuticals Canada, Inv. v. Novopharm Ltd.* (1996), 68 C.P.R. (3d) 461 (F.C.T.C.).

## d) Federal Policy Relating to Crown Copyright

The current Federal government policy relating to government publications is published in the Treasury Board Manual: Information and Administrative Management—Communications, Appendix C Publishing, No. 5.[9] This policy states that Canadian government publications, both free and priced, are automatically protected by copyright under Section 12 of the *Act*.

Unless otherwise permitted by law or specified in the publication in issue, Crown copyrighted works may be reproduced by those outside of the Federal government provided prior permission is secured in writing.[10]

The Federal Government has also published a policy relating to enactments and decisions and reasons for decision of federally constituted courts and administrative tribunals. The policy provides that anyone may, without charge or request for permission, reproduce enactments and consolidations of enactments of the Government of Canada, and decisions and reasons for decision of federally constituted courts and administrative tribunals, provided due diligence is exercised to ensure the accuracy of the materials reproduced and the reproduction is not represented as an official version.[11]

## e) Other Rights under the *Act*

In addition to its rights under section 12, the Crown may become entitled to copyright by virtue of assignment or in its capacity as an employer. The rights obtained in this fashion will be subject to the general provisions of the *Act* including those relating to the term of copyright.[12]

## 2. Crown Prerogative

Section 12 expressly provides that it is "without prejudice to any rights or privileges of the Crown" and does not apply to claims of Crown prerogative with respect to printing and publishing. There is uncertainty concerning the scope of the Crown prerogative.

---

9. The Manual also contains policies relating to: author's moral rights; the reproduction of private sector copyright works; and the reproduction of Crown copyrighted work.
10. Section 5.4 of Appendix C Publishing, No. 5.
11. *Canada Gazette*, Part II, Vol. 131, No. 1 published January 8, 1997. The province of Ontario has adopted a similar policy on Copyright on Legal Materials see http:// www.gov.on.ca.
12. See *Hawley v. Canada* (1990), 30 C.P.R. (3d) 534 (F.C.T.D.).

While there are different theories concerning the scope of the prerogative, it seems reasonable to accept that it is derived from the duty resting upon the King or Queen as first executive magistrate, to superintend the publication of acts of the legislature and the Acts of State carrying with it a corresponding prerogative.[13]

The prerogative right of the Crown to the exclusive printing of Acts of Parliament, Orders in Council, state papers, and other public documents is well established.[14]

The Crown prerogative, unlike rights under the *Act*, continues in perpetuity[15] and is not limited to the term specified in the *Act*.

The extent of an existing prerogative may be modified by statute[16] and is subject to the Canadian Charter of Rights and Freedoms.[17]

## 3. Crown Immunity

Crown immunity is a part of the Crown prerogative. It is presumed that the Crown is not bound by statutory law unless stated otherwise. This has been incorporated into the Federal *Interpretation Act*[18] which states that no enactment is binding on Her Majesty or affects Her Majesty or Her Majesty's rights or prerogatives in any manner, except as mentioned or referred to in the enactment.[19]

It has been held that the wording of the *Patent Act* is not specific enough to abrogate the traditional immunity of the provincial Crowns and their agencies from suits in the Federal Court.[20]

---

13. *Attorney-General for New South Wales* v. *Butterworth and Co. (Australia) Ltd.* (1938) S.R.N.S.W. 195 (New South Wales, C.J.) but see *R. v. Bellman* [1938] 3 D.L.R. 548 (N.B.C.A.) where it was stated that constitutional changes have limited the prerogative to the sole right of printing a miscellaneous collection of works, no catalogue of which appears to be exhaustive.
14. *Rex* v. *Bellman*, [1938] 3 D.L.R. 548, 13 M.P.R. 37, 70 C.C.C. 171; (N.B.C.A) *Attorney-General for New South Wales* v. *Butterworth & Co. (Australia) Ltd.* (1938) S.R.N.S.W. 195.
15. *Millar* v. *Taylor* (1769), 4 Burr. 2401, 5 Bac. Abr. 598; Chitty, *Prerogatives of the Crown*, at 241.
16. *Operation Dismantle Inc.* v. *Queen* [1983] 1 F.C. 745 (F.C.A.), [1985] 1 S.C.R. 441; *Attorney-General* v. *De Keyser's Royal Hotel Ltd.* [1920] A.C. 508 .
17. *Operation Dismantle Inc.* v. *Queen* [1983] 1 F.C. 745 (F.C.A.).
18. R.S.C. 1970, c. I-23 section 17. In the case of *Alta.Govt. Tel.* v. *C.R.T.C.* [1989] 2 S.C.R. 225 it was confirmed that this section applies to both the Crown in right of a province as well as the Crown in right of Canada.
19. R.S.C. 1970, c. I-23.
20. *Dableh* v. *Ontario Hydro* (1990), 33 C.P.R. (3d), 544 (F.C.T.D.).

A Crown agent or employee may seek to assert Crown immunity as long as they do not step outside the ambit of Crown purposes.[21]

The Supreme Court of Canada held that the Crown could not benefit from rights conferred by legislation without being subject to the resulting burdens. Even where there is no indication that legislation applies to the Crown, the latter may make itself subject to the *Act* through its own actions. The theory of waiver requires, however, that there be a close nexus between the benefit received by the Crown and the burden it is being made to assume.[22]

---

21.  R. v. Eldorado Nuclear Ltd.,[1983] 2 S.C.R .551; *Eros-Equipe de Recherche Operationnelle en Sante Inc. v. Conseillers en Gestion et Informatique C.G.I. Inc.,* (2004), 35 C.P.R. (4th) 105 (F.C.).
22.  *Sparling v. Quebec* [1988] 2 S.C.R. 1015 (S.C.C); *Eros-Equipe de Recherche Operationnelle en Sante Inc. v. Conseillers en Gestion et Informatique C.G.I. Inc.,* (2004), 35 C.P.R. (4th) 105 (F.C.).

# CHAPTER
# 24

# Assignment

# 1. Assignments

## a) The Extent of the Right

The *Copyright Act* contains a broad right of assignment. Subsection 13(4) of the *Act* provides that the owner of the copyright in any work may assign the right, either wholly or partially, and either generally or subject to limitations relating to territory, medium, or sector of the market or other limitations relating to the scope of the assignment, and either for the whole term of the copyright or for any other part thereof, and may grant any interest in the right by license. However, no assignment or grant is valid unless it is in writing signed by the owner of the right in respect of which the assignment or grant is made, or by the owner's duly authorized agent.[1]

A copyright owner must take care to ensure that an assignment only extends to the specific rights intended to be granted to the assignee. A simple reference to copyright will include all of the rights set out in section 3.

A right of action for infringement of copyright may also be included with an assignment of copyright[2] including the right to sue for infringements committed before the assignment if expressly agreed to.

A grant of an exclusive license constitutes the grant of an interest in the copyright by licence.[3]

The general provisions of the *Act* relating to assignments apply to the rights available to performers, makers of sound recordings and broadcasters with such modifications as the circumstances require.[4]

## b) Partial Assignments

Copyright consists of the sole right to exercise, which includes the right to restrain others from exercising, the rights set out in section 3 of the *Act* relating to original literary, dramatic, musical, and artistic works, performers' performances, sound recordings and communication signals.[5] The rights may be subdivided and the owner may assign some or all of them in predetermined territories or mediums or sectors of the market or subject to other limitations relating to the scope of the assignment and either for the whole term of the copyright or for any other part thereof.

---

1. For assignments prior to September 1, 1997 see R.S.C. 1985 subsection 13(4) and subsections 55(3) and 58.1 of an *Act to Amend the Copyright Act*, S.C. 1997, c. 24.
2. Subsection 13(6).
3. Subsection 13(7).
4. Section 25.
5. This includes the right to authorize the acts set out in section 3.

In addition, the owner may assign a right which is not specifically mentioned in the *Act* so long as it is part of one of the specific statutory rights. For example, the owner of the literary work could assign the right to reproduce the work in magazine form.

Because the rights may be subdivided, it is possible that there may be two or more owners of interests in the copyright in any work at the same time. In such cases, the *Act* recognizes both the assignee and the assignor as owners of their respective rights. The assignee is treated as the owner of the part assigned, and the assignor as the owner of the part not assigned for the purposes of the *Act*.[6]

## c) The Rights of the Assignor

Once the owner of the copyright in any work has assigned rights associated with the work under the *Act*, the owner may be prevented from exercising those rights in the same fashion as any other person who infringes those rights.

An assignment does not operate to prevent the assignor from creating a new and different work even if it portrays the same subject[7] or from expressing the same idea or concept in a different form. But an assignor may be subject to contractual restrictions connected with the assignment which preclude such activities, which may be express or implied.[8]

An assignment of copyright in a work does not by that act alone constitute a waiver of moral rights,[9] and the author will continue to be entitled to these rights. As set out previously, moral rights may not be assigned but may be waived in whole or in part.[10]

## d) Must Be In Writing

An assignment or grant of an interest must be in writing, signed by the owner of the right in respect of which the assignment or grant is made or by the owner's duly authorized agent.[11] This direction has been interpreted by the

---

6. Subsection 13(5).
7. *Preston* v. *Raphael Tuck*, [1926] 1 Ch. 668. (U.K.Ch. D.)
8. *Morang and Co. v. LeSueur* [1911] 45 S.C.R. 95 (S.C.C.); *Tedesco v. Bosa* (1992), 45 C.P.R. (3d) 82 (Ont. Ct. Gen. Div.).
9. Subsection 14.1(3).
10. Subsection 14.1(2).
11. See *Ritchie v. Sawmill Creek Golf & Country Club* (2003), 27 C.P.R. (4th) 220 (Ont. S.C. J.), 35 C.P.R. (4th) 163 (Ont. S.C. J., Div. Ct.). Evidence of the existence of a written assignment

courts in Canada as a substantive requirement.[12] An assignment which does not comply will not be enforceable. A mark or a facsimile of a signature is acceptable if there is evidence to prove that it is the customary method of identification used by the owner.[13]

It is unlikely that a Canadian court could grant relief under the *Act* to an equitable assignee pursuant to an assignment that is not in writing, in light of the statutory limitations. Subsection 13(4) provides that an assignment of copyright must be in writing and section 89 provides that no person is entitled to copyright or any similar right in any work otherwise than under, and in accordance with the *Act*.[14]

Although an assignment must be in writing to be effective, the owner of a work made pursuant to either an oral contract or one that can be implied from the conduct of the parties may be precluded from exercising their rights under the *Act* against the other party to the contract.[15] Such a result is possible since infringement of copyright depends on the absence of consent by the owner of copyright. Consent need not be in writing and may be presumed from the circumstances, but the inference must be clear before it will operate as a defense, and must come from the person holding the particular right alleged to be infringed.

## e) Construction

The *Act* does not specify that an assignment be in any proscribed form apart from the requirement set out above. For each document which it is suggested assigns copyright, an assessment must be made to determine its meaning and whether it shows an intention to assign copyright or a part thereof. The aim is to determine the meaning of the document in an objective contextual sense. The plain meaning is the starting point.

---

may be made by way of oral testimony and without producing the actual written assignment *Motel 6 Inc. v. No. 6 Motel Ltd. et al.* (1981), 56 C.P.R. (2d) 44 (F.C.T.D.).

12. *Motel 6, Inc. v. No. 6 Motel Ltd.* (1981), 56 C.P.R. (2d) 44 (F.C.T.D.); *Jeffrey Rogers Knitwear Productions Ltd. et al. v. R.D. International Style Collections Ltd.* (1986), 19 C.P.R. (3d) 217 (F.C.T.D.); *C.P. Koch Ltd. et. al. v. Continental Steel Ltd.* .(1984), 82 C.P.R. (2d) 156 (B.C.S.C.), aff'd (1985), 4 C.P.R. (3d) 395 (B.C.C.A.).

13. *Milliken & Co. v. Interface Flooring Systems* [1998], 3 F.C. 301, 83 C.P.R. (3d) 470 (F.C.T.D.) affirmed 5 C.P.R. (4th) 209 (F.C.A.).

14. *Downing v. General Synod, et al* [1943] O.R. 652 (Ont. C.A.).

15. *Cselko Associates Inc. v. Zellers Inc.* (1992), 44 C.P.R. (3d) 56 (Ont. Gen. Div.) and *Montykola Investments v. Robert D. Sutherland Architects* (1996), 150 N.S.R. (2d) 281 (N.S.C.A.).

## f) Transfer of Possession of Physical Things

The ownership of copyright is separate from the ownership or possession of the physical object which is the vehicle for the work subject to copyright. Copyright is a bundle of exclusive statutory rights which are independent of any material object such as a manuscript or a recording of a musical work.

A transfer of possession of a physical object does not transfer any interest in any copyright related to it unless there is a written assignment of copyright. For example, the ownership of a manuscript does not affect the ownership of copyright in it or the possession of a computer program does not affect the ownership of copyright in the program.[16]

## g) Limitation where the Author Is the First Owner of Copyright

Subsection 14(1) contains a limitation on the right of the author, if the author is the first owner of the copyright, to make an assignment or grant an interest in copyright. The subsection provides that an assignment, except in relation to collective works, if made after June 4, 1921, otherwise than by will does not operate to vest in the assignee any rights in the copyright for more than 25 years after the author's death and the reversionary interest, notwithstanding any agreement to the contrary, devolves on the author's legal representatives as part of the author's estate.

The author is not the first owner of the copyright where subsection 13(2) relating to engravings, photographs or portraits,[17] or subsection 13(3) relating to a work made in the course of employment,[18] or section 12 relating to Crown copyright[19] apply. Subsection 14(1) does not apply in these three situations.

In addition, the subsection does not apply "to the assignment of the copyright in a collective work or a license to publish a work or a part of a work as part of a collective work."[20]

The subsection was intended to benefit an author's family who could be prejudiced by the making of improvident agreements which disposed of copyright during the author's lifetime.[21] But the benefits to the author's family provided by the subsection are of questionable value in most cases.

---

16. *Dynabec Ltee v. La Societe D'Informtique R.D.G.* (1985), 6 C.P.R. (3d) 332 (Quebec C.A.).
17. See Chapter 22, part 2.
18. See Chapter 22, part 4.
19. See Chapter 23.
20. Collective work is defined in section 2. See Chapter 22.
21. *Peer International Corporation v. Termidor Music Publishers Ltd.* [2006] EWHC 2883 (U.K. Ch.).

## h) Registration of Assignments and Licenses

Subsection 57(1) of the *Act* provides that the Registrar of Copyrights shall register an assignment of copyright, or a license granting an interest in a copyright, on being furnished with

(a) the original instrument or a certified copy of it, or other evidence satisfactory to the Registrar of the assignment or license; and

(b) the fee prescribed by or determined under the regulations.

Subsection 57(3) provides that:

> Any assignment of copyright, or any license granting an interest in a copyright, shall be adjudged void against any subsequent assignee[22] or licensee for valuable consideration without actual notice, unless the prior assignment or license is registered in the manner prescribed by this *Act* before the registering of the instrument under which the subsequent assignee or licensee claims.

Under the subsection, a registration made after the registration of a prior assignment will have no effect.[23] As a result, the registration of an assignment is a prudent course of action, even though registration of an assignment is voluntary.

## 2. Devolution

On the death of the owner, copyright vests in the personal representatives of the owner like any other property, to be disposed of in accordance with the terms of the copyright owner's will,[24] or, if the copyright owner has died intestate, to be held on behalf of the next of kin. The same principles apply to copyright in a performer's performance.[25] This approach is consistent with subsection 14(1), which provides that on the death of the author the reversionary interest in copyright mentioned in that section devolves on the author's legal representatives as part of the estate of the author.

---

22. The assignor's trustee in bankruptcy is not a "subsequent assignee" for the purposes of the subsection *Re Kobblensky* (1969), 62 C.B.R. 20 (Ont. Reg. Bankruptcy).

23. *Downing (Anglo-Canadian Music Co.)* v. *The General Synod of the Church of England in Canada et al.* [1943] O.R. 99, 2 C.P.R. 171, (Ont. H.C.), [1943] O.R. 652, 3 C.P.R. 49 (Ont. C.A.) but see *Poolman v Eiffel Productions S.A.* (1991), 35 C.P.R. (3d) 384 (F.C.T.D.).

24. See *In re Dickens* [1935] Ch. 267 (U.K.Ch. D.)

25. *Rickless v. United Artists Corporation*, [1988] Q.B. 40 (U.K.C.A.).

Specific provisions have been enacted regarding the devolution of moral rights.[26] Subsection 14.2(2) provides that the moral rights in respect of a work pass, on the death of its author, to:

(a) the person to whom those rights are specifically bequeathed;
(b) where there is no specific bequest of those moral rights and the author dies testate in respect of the copyright in the work, the person to whom that copyright is bequeathed; or
(c) where there is no person described in paragraph (a) or (b), the person entitled to any other property in respect of which the author dies intestate.

These provisions apply, with such modifications as the circumstances require, on the death of any person who holds moral rights.[27]

## 3. Bankruptcy

### a) The Property of the Bankrupt

On a bankruptcy order being made or an assignment being filed with an official receiver, a bankrupt ceases to have any capacity to dispose of or otherwise deal with their property, which shall, subject to the *Bankruptcy and Insolvency Act*, and to the rights of secured creditors, immediately pass to and vest in the trustee named in the bankruptcy order or assignment, and in any case of change of trustee the property shall pass from trustee to trustee without any assignment or transfer.[28] Although title to all property vests in the trustee, a bankrupt author will continue to have moral rights relating to the works of which they are the author, unless they have been waived in whole or in part.[29]

### b) Licenses

In the absence of a specific contractual term to the contrary, on the bankruptcy of a licensee, the trustee assumes all rights under any license agreement

---

26. Subsection 14.2(2).
27. Subsection 14.2(3).
28. *Bankruptcy and Insolvency Act*, R.S.C. 1985, c. B-3. subsection 71.
29. See Chapter 20.

which the bankrupt may have entered into and is entitled to enforce the terms of the license.[30]

It is unclear whether a trustee in bankruptcy of a licensor may disclaim a license agreement.[31]

## c) Proposals

The *Bankruptcy and Insolvency Act* provides that, where a notice of intention to file a proposal or a proposal has been filed in respect of an insolvent person, no person may terminate or amend any agreement with the insolvent person, or claim any accelerated payment under any agreement with the insolvent person by reason only that:

(a) the insolvent person is insolvent;
(b) a notice of intention or a proposal has been filed in respect of the insolvent person; or[32]
(c) the insolvent person has not paid royalties under a licensing agreement in respect of a period preceding the filing of a notice of intention to file a proposal or a proposal.[33]

Any provision in an agreement that has the effect of providing for or permitting anything that, in substance, is contrary to these provisions of the *Bankruptcy and Insolvency Act* is of no force or effect.[34]

In circumstances set out above, the licensor will be precluded from terminating the license or claiming any accelerated payment, but may apply to the court for relief from the stay if it can be shown that the operation of the stay would likely cause significant financial hardship.[35]

Under an amendment to the *Bankruptcy and Insolvency Act* a debtor, other than an individual who is making a proposal or who has filed a notice of intention to make a proposal, is given a right to disclaim any agreement to which the debtor is a party. But if the debtor has granted a right to use intellectual property to a party to an agreement, the disclaimer does not affect the party's right to use the intellectual property—including the party's right to

---

30. *Potato Distributor v. Eastern Trust* (1955), 35 C.B.R. 161 (P.E.I. C.A.).
31. *Re Erin Features #1 Ltd* (1991), 8 C.B.R. (3d) 205 (B.C.S.C.); *Royal Bank of Canada v. Body Blue Inc.* (2008), 42 C.B.R (5th) 125 (Ont. S.C.J.).
32. *Bankruptcy and Insolvency Act*, R.S.C. (1985), c.B-3 subsection 65.1(1).
33. *Bankruptcy and Insolvency Act*, R.S.C. (1985), c. B-3 subsection. 65.1(2). An applicant under the *Companies' Creditors' Arrangement Act*, R.S.C. (1985), c. C-36 as amended,. may also seek relief in terms similar to that provided for under the *Bankruptcy and Insolvency Act*.
34. *Bankruptcy and Insolvency Act*, R.S.C. (1985), c. B-3 , subsection 65.1(5).
35. *Bankruptcy and Insolvency Act*, R.S.C. (1985), c. B-3 subsection. 65.1(6).

enforce an exclusive use—during the term of the agreement, including any period for which the party extends the agreement as of right, as long as the party continues to perform its obligations under the agreement in relation to the use of the intellectual property.[36]

## d) Reversion of Copyright

Under section 83 of the *Bankruptcy and Insolvency Act*,[37] the author's manuscripts and any copyright or any interest in a copyright in whole or in part assigned to a publisher, printer, firm, or person who has become bankrupt shall,

(a) if the work covered by such copyright has not been published and put on the market at the time of the bankruptcy and no expense has been incurred in connection therewith, revert and be delivered to the author or his heirs, and any contract or agreement between the author or his heirs and such bankrupt shall then terminate and be null and void;

(b) if the work covered by such copyright has in whole or in part been put into type and expenses have been incurred by the bankrupt, revert and be delivered to the author on payment of the expenses so incurred and the product of such expenses shall also be delivered to the author or his heirs and any contract or agreement between the author or his heirs and the bankrupt shall then terminate and be null and void; but if the author does not exercise his rights under this paragraph within six months of the date of the bankruptcy, the trustee may carry out the original contract;

(c) if the trustee at the expiration of six months from the date of the bankruptcy decides not to carry out the contract, revert without expense to the author and any contract or agreement between the author or his heirs and such bankrupt shall then terminate and be null and void.[38]

Where, at the time of the bankruptcy, the work was published and copies are available in the marketplace, the trustee is entitled to sell, or authorize the

---

36. S.C. 2005, c. 47 adding section 65.11 to the *Act* assented to November 25, 2005 proclaimed in force September 18, 2009. A right to disclaim subject to the same limitation has been added to the *Companies' Creditors Arrangement Act*, Section 131, S.C. 2005, c. 47 assented to November 25, 2005 proclaimed in force September 18, 2009, adding section 32.

37. R.S.C. 1985, c., B-3.

38. Subsection 83(1) R.S.C. 1985, c., B-3.

sale or reproduction of, any copies of the published work, or to perform or authorize the performance of the work, but

(a) there shall be paid to the author or his heirs such sums by way of royalties or share of the profits as would have been payable by the bankrupt;

(b) the trustee is not, without the written consent of the author or his heirs, entitled to assign the copyright or transfer the interest or to grant any interest therein by license or otherwise, except on terms that will guarantee to the author or his heirs payment by way of royalties or share of the profits at a rate not less than the rate the bankrupt was liable to pay; and

(c) any contract or agreement between the author or their heirs and the bankrupt shall then terminate and be void or, in the Province of Quebec, null, except with respect to the disposal, under the subsection, of copies of the work published and put on the market before the bankruptcy.[39]

The trustee shall offer in writing to the author or his heirs the right to purchase the manufactured or marketable copies of the copyright work comprised in the estate of the bankrupt at such price and upon such terms and conditions as the trustee may deem fair and proper before disposing of such manufactured and marketable copies in the manner prescribed in this section.[40]

Section 83 is not limited to manuscripts and other written works and applies to musical works which have been assigned. The section does not apply to a performer's performance, a sound recording, or a communication signal since they are not "works."[41]

---

39. Subsection 83(2) R.S.C. 1985, c., B-3.
40. Subsection 83(3) R.S.C. 1985, c., B-3.
41. See *Re Song Corp.* (2002), 19 C.P.R. (4th) 235 (Ont. Sup. Ct. of Justice) which found that sound recordings of which the bankrupt was the "maker" were outside the section.

# CHAPTER
## 25

# Licenses

The provisions of the *Copyright Act* relating to licenses of literary, dramatic, musical, and artistic works also apply to the rights conferred on performers, makers of sound recordings, and broadcasters with such modifications as the circumstances require.[1]

## 1. Proprietary Licenses

The case law relating to intellectual property rights has generally distinguished three types of licenses:

a) An ordinary "license" which is a permission to the licensee to do something which would otherwise be unlawful. It leaves the licensor at liberty to do the action and to also grant licenses to other persons;

b) A "sole license" which is a permission to the licensee to do it, but no one else, except that it leaves the licensor at liberty to do it; and

c) An "exclusive license" which is a permission which is exclusive to the licensee, so that the licensor is excluded as well as anyone else.[2]

Subsection 13(4) provides that the owner of the copyright in any work may assign the right, either wholly or partially, and either generally or subject to limitations relating to territory, medium, or sector of the market or other limitations relating to the scope of the assignment, and either for the whole term of the copyright or for any other part thereof, and may grant any interest in the right by license, but no assignment or grant is valid unless it is in writing, signed by the owner of the right in respect of which the assignment or grant is made, or by the owner's duly authorized agent.

In the context of licenses, the subsection applies to rights that may be granted in the form of a license. It does not refer to an ordinary license to do an act, which would otherwise be unlawful, as the reference to the grant of an interest must mean a proprietary interest in the particular right. It is difficult to identify a proprietary interest in a particular right which could be subject to a license except for an exclusive license.

In order to clarify that an exclusive license comes within the subsection, the *Act* provides that for greater certainty, it is deemed always to have been the law that the grant of an exclusive license in a copyright constitutes the grant of an interest in the copyright by license.[3]

---

1. Section 25.
2. *Murray v. Imperial Chemical Industries Ltd.* [1967] Ch. 1038. (U.K.Ch. D.)
3. Subsection 13(7). The provision applies retrospectively see *Euro-Excellence Inc. v. Kraft Canada Inc.* (2007), 59 C.P.R (4th) 353 (S.C.C.).

Section 2.7 of the *Act* states that for the purposes of the *Act*, an exclusive license is an authorization to do any act that is subject to copyright to the exclusion of all others including the copyright owner, whether the authorization is granted by the owner or by an exclusive licensee claiming under the owner. The section is primarily a codification of the common law position, save for the right to grant such an authorization by an exclusive license.

An exclusive license is different from an assignment. Under an assignment, the assignee owns all of the rights assigned subject to the author's moral rights. The rights of an exclusive licensee are determined by the terms set out in the license.

## 2. Ordinary Licenses

As previously discussed an ordinary "license" is a permission to the licensee to do something which would otherwise be unlawful. A license granting an interest in the right is different from a license operating as a permission to do a certain thing. A license granting permission does not grant an interest in copyright. As a result, it is not subject to subsection 13(4) and there is no requirement that it be in writing.[4]

An ordinary license will only extend to the right actually licensed to be done.[5] It is a matter of fact in any case whether license has been given and the onus of establishing permission is on the defendant.[6] In addition, to be effective, the license must be in effect at the time the otherwise infringing activity took place.

## 3. Implied Licenses

An ordinary license which does not grant an interest in copyright may be implied, since there is no requirement that such a license be in writing.[7] This question has arisen frequently in the context of cases involving architectural plans. In this context, courts have implied terms limiting the rights available under copyright in architectural plans to permit repair of the structure.[8]

---

4. *Robertson v. Thompson Corp.* (2006), 52 C.P.R. (4th) 417 (S.C.C.).
5. *Galerie d'art du petit Champlain Inc v. Théberge* (2002), 17 C.P.R. (4th) 161 (S.C.C).
6. *Warner Brothers-Seven Arts Inc. v. CESM-TV Ltd.* (1971), 65 C.P.R. 215 (Ex. Ct).
7. *Robertson v. Thompson Corp.* (2006), 52 C.P.R. (4th) 417 (S.C.C.).
8. *Netupsky, et al v. Dominion Bridge Co. Ltd* (1971), 24 D.L.R. (3d) 484 (S.C.C.).

The engagement for consideration of a person to produce material protected by copyright implies a permission, consent, or license in favor of the
person providing the consideration to use the material in the manner and for
the purpose contemplated by the parties that it would be used, including the
right to transfer that right.[9]

## 4. Assignment

A license may state that it can be assigned. In the absence of an express right,
whether the license may be assigned depends on the construction of the
license. If a license imposes obligations of a personal nature on the parties or
is given to a person selected for their personal skill or reputation, the license
will not likely be assignable.

## 5. Withdrawal of Consent

An ordinary license, where consideration has not been given, may be withdrawn at will, even though expenses have been incurred by the licensee as a
result of the license.[10] However, the copyright owner may be estopped from
asserting rights where licensee has relied on the license.[11] The licensor may
also be required to provide the licensee with reasonable notice prior to revok-
ing the license.[12]

Where a license has been given for consideration, it may only be revoked
in accordance with the contract under which it has been granted.[13]

## 6. Licenses by Operation of Law

Where, on application to the Copyright Board by a person who wishes
to obtain a license to use a published work, a fixation of a performer's

---

9. *Netupsky, et. al. v. Dominion Bridge Co. Ltd.* (1971), 24 D.L.R. (3d) 490 (S.C.C.); *Robert D. Sutherland Architectss Ltd. v. Montykola Investments Inc.* (1996), 73 C.P.R. (3d) 269 (N.S. C.A.).
10. *Katz v. Cytrynbaum* (1983), 76 C.P.R. (2d) 276 (B.C.C.A.).
11. *Ritchie v. Sawmilll Creek Golf & Country Club* (2003), 27 C.P.R. (4th) 220 (Ont. S.C.J.), 35 C.P.R. (4th) 163 (Div. Ct.).
12. *Winter Garden Theatre (London) Ltd.. v. Millennium Productions Ltd.,* [1948] A.C. 173 (H.L.).
13. *Winter Garden Theatre (London) Ltd.. v. Millennium Productions Ltd.,* [1948] A.C. 173 (H.L.).

performance, a published sound recording, or a fixation of a communication signal in which copyright subsists, the Board is satisfied that the applicant has made reasonable efforts to locate the owner of the copyright and that the owner cannot be located, the Board may issue to the applicant a license to do any of the acts mentioned in section 3, 15, 18 or 21 of the *Act*, as the case may be.[14]

---

14. Subsection 77(1) and see Chapter 32.

CHAPTER

# 26

# Registration and Marking

## 1. Registration Is Not Required

Copyright protection in Canada does not depend on registration or other formal act,[1] which is in compliance with the Berne Convention. Copyright subsists automatically without any act beyond the creation of an original work. Registration is permissive but helpful in the event that proceedings for infringement are instituted.[2]

There is no obligation or requirement to use a copyright notice on wares or other material protected by copyright but it is prudent to do so. The existence of a notice in the usual form, © in conjunction with the name of the owner and year of publication, will put third parties on notice of the existence of copyright and trigger a presumption of ownership.[3]

## 2. Applying for Registration

An application for the registration of a copyright in a work may be made by or on behalf of the author of the work, the owner of the copyright in the work, an assignee of the copyright, or a person to whom an interest in the copyright has been granted by license.[4]

An application must be filed with the Copyright Office, be accompanied by the fee prescribed by or determined under the regulations, and contain the following information:

(a) the name and address of the owner of the copyright in the work;
(b) a declaration that the applicant is the author of the work, the owner of the copyright in the work, an assignee of the copyright, or a person to whom an interest in the copyright has been granted by license;
(c) the category of the work;
(d) the title of the work;
(e) the name of the author and, if the author is dead, the date of the author's death, if known;
(f) in the case of a published work, the date and place of the first publication; and
(g) any additional information prescribed by regulation.[5]

---

1. *Zamacoïs v. Douville et al.* (1943), 2 C.P.R. 270 (Ex. Ct.).
2. *Circle Film Enterprises Inc. v. C.B.C.*, [1959] S.C.R. 602 (S.C.C.).
3. Section 34.1 of the *Copyright Act* and see subsection 38.1 (2) of the *Act* concerning a claim for statutory damages.
4. Section 55. The registration of assignments and licenses is dealt with in Chapter 24.
5. Subsection 55(2) and see the *Copyright Regulations* SOR/97-457 as amended by SOR/ 2003-211.

Section 56 contains similar provisions relating to applications for registration of copyright in performer's performances, sound recordings, or communication signals.

The Register of Copyrights is maintained at the Copyright Office. The following information may be entered on it:

(a) the names or titles of works and of other subject-matter in which copyright subsists;
(b) the names and addresses of authors, performers, makers of sound recordings, broadcasters, owners of copyright, assignees of copyright, and persons to whom an interest in copyright has been granted by license; and
(c) such other particulars as may be prescribed by regulation.[6]

The Register and indices established under section 55 must be at all reasonable times open to inspection, and any person is entitled to make copies of or take extracts from the Register.[7]

On the filing of the application and payment of the required fee, the certificate applied for will be issued. Unlike trademark applications, the Copyright Office does not make any search or examination and does not take any responsibility for the truth of the statements contained in the application.[8]

Where a person purports to have the authority to apply for the registration of a copyright under section 55 or 56 on behalf of another person, any damage caused by a fraudulent or erroneous assumption of such authority is recoverable in any court of competent jurisdiction.[9]

A security interest in copyright may be registered by filing the original security agreement or a certified copy of it or other evidence satisfactory to the Registrar.

In the case of an encyclopedia, newspaper, review, magazine, or other periodical work, or work published in a series of books or parts, a single entry for the whole work is to be made, without the necessity of making a separate entry for each number or part.[10]

Moral rights or waivers of moral rights cannot be registered.

---

6. Subsection 54(1).
7. Subsection 54(5). The information is also available on line at http://www.ic.gc.ca/app/opic-cipo/cpyrghts/dsplySrch.do?lang=eng.
8. *Circle Film Enterprises Inc.* v. *Canadian Broadcasting Corporation* (1957), 28 C.P.R. 5, [1956–1960] Ex. C.R. 166, (Ex. Ct.), [1959] S.C.R. 602, 31 C.P.R. 57, 20 D.L.R. (2d) 211 (S.C.C.).
9. Section 56.1.
10. Subsection 54(3).

## 3. Rectification of the Register of Copyrights

The Federal Court may, on application of the Registrar of Copyrights or of any interested person,[11] order the rectification of the Register of Copyrights by:

(a) the making of any entry wrongly omitted to be made in the Register,
(b) the expunging of any entry wrongly made in or remaining on the Register, or
(c) the correction of any error or defect in the Register. [12]

Any rectification of the Register ordered shall be retroactive from such date as the Court may specify.[13] Clerical errors may be corrected under section 61 of the *Act* without the necessity of an application.

The *Federal Court Act*[14] also gives to that court exclusive original jurisdiction, in all cases of conflicting applications for the registration of copyright and in which it is sought to have any entry in the Register of copyrights made, expunged, varied, or rectified.

## 4. Effect of Registration

The registration of copyright or an assignment of copyright or a license granting an interest in a copyright is advantageous to the copyright owner. The potential benefits are discussed below.

### a) Admissibility

Certified copies of entries on the Register of Copyrights, which are issued under section 53 of the *Copyright Act*, are admissible in all courts in Canada without further proof or production of originals.[15]

---

11. The term is not defined in the *Act* but the provisions of the *Trade-marks Act* may be analogous see Chapter 10, part 2(c).
12. Subsection 57(4). *Laurin v. Champagne* (1991), 38 C.P.R. (3d) (F.C.T.D.).
13. Subsection 57(4).
14. R.S.C. 1985, c. F-7 as amended, s. 20(1).
15. Subsection 53(1) and (3) and see *Blue Crest Music Inc. v. Canusa Records Inc.* (1974), 17 C.P.R. (2d) 149 (F.C.T.D.); rev'd on other grounds (1976), 30 C.P.R. (2d) 14 (F.C.A.); aff'd, [1980] 1 S.C.R. 357 (S.C.C.).

## b) Evidence

A certificate of registration of copyright in a work is evidence that copyright subsists in the work and that the person registered is the owner of the copyright.[16] A certificate of registration of an assignment of copyright is evidence that the right recorded on the certificate has been assigned and that the assignee registered is the owner of that right.[17] A certificate of registration of a license granting an interest in a copyright is evidence that the interest recorded on the certificate has been granted and that the licensee registered is the holder of that interest.[18]

The certificate of registration is *prima facie* evidence[19] but it is not conclusive. The matters set out in the certificate will be presumed to be accurate and the party seeking to dispute them bears the onus of leading evidence to the contrary.[20]

It is unclear what effect will be given to a registration which was obtained after the alleged infringement.[21]

In response to a statement of claim claiming infringement and including a certificate of registration, a defendant is not entitled to rely upon a simple denial but must allege material facts which could, if proven, bring into question the matters set out in the registration.[22]

## c) Notice of Assignment or License

Any grant of an interest in copyright either by assignment or license will be void against a subsequent assignee or licensee for valuable consideration, unless the prior assignment or license is registered.[23]

---

16. Subsection 53(2).
17. Subsection 53(2.1).
18. Subsection 53(2.2).
19. *Bishop v. Tele Metropole Inc.* (1985), 4 C.P.R. (3d) 349 (F.C.T.D.); aff'd in part on other grounds (1987), 18 C.P.R. (3d) 257 (F.C.A.); affirmed [1990] 2 S.C.R. 467, 31 C.P.R. (3d) 394 (S.C.C.).
20. *Circle Film Enterprises Inc. v. C.B.C.*, [1959] S.C.R. 602 (S.C.C.); *Blue Crest Music Inc. v. Canusa Records Inc.* (1974), 17 C.P.R. (2d) 149 (F.C.T.D.); rev'd on other grounds (1976), 30 C.P.R. (2d) 14 (Fed. C.A.); aff'd, [1980] 1 S.C.R. 357 (S.C.C.).
21. See *Grignon v. Roussel* (1991), 38 C.P.R (3d) 4 (F.C.T.D.) and *R v. Laurier Office Mart, Inc.* (1994), 58 C.P.R. (3d) 403 (Ont. Ct. Pro. Div.), affirmed (1995), 63 C.P.R. (3d) 229 (Ont. Ct. Gen. Div.) in a criminal context.
22. *Samsonite Canada Inc. v. Costco Wholesale Corporation* (1993), 48 C.P.R. (3d) 5 (F.C.T.D.); (1995) 61 C.P.R. (3d) 293; *Apotex Inc. v. Glaxo Canada Inc.* (1994), 58 C.P.R. (3d) 1 (F.C.T.D.) reversed on appeal (1995) 64 C.P.R. (3d) 191 (F.C.A.).
23. Subsection 57(3) and see Chapter 24.

## d) Varying Presumptions

If a registration is not obtained, the presumptions set in the *Act* relating to ownership of copyright will apply.[24] A certificate of registration will prevail over the presumption set out in subsection 34.1(1)(b) of the *Act*, that the author is the owner of copyright because the certificate, when filed, is evidence to the contrary.[25]

## e) Statutory Notice

Subsection 39(1) of the *Act* provides that a defendant who alleges that they were not aware and had no reasonable ground for suspecting that copyright existed in a work is not liable to any other remedy against them other than an injunction. But subsection 39(2) provides that, if at the date of the infringement, the copyright was duly registered under the *Act*, the subsection(1) does not apply.[26]

---

24. Subsection 34.1 and see Chapter 22, part 10.
25. *Circle Film Enterprises Inc.* v. *Canadian Broadcasting Corporation* (1959), 31 C.P.R. (2d) 57 (S.C.C); *Apotex Inc.* v. *Glaxo Canada Inc.* (1994), 58 C.P.R. (3d) 1 (F.C.T.D.), reversed on appeal (1995) 64 C.P.R. (3d) 191 (F.C.A.).
26. *MCA Canada Ltd* v. *Gillberry & Hawke Advertising Agency Ltd.* (1976), 28 C.P.R, (2d) 52 (F.C.T.D.) and see Chapter 30, part 5(c)(i).

# CHAPTER
# 27

# Direct Infringement

## 1. The Sole Right

### a) The Nature of the Right

Subsection 27(1) of the *Copyright Act* provides that it is an infringement of copyright for any person to do, without the consent of the owner of the copyright, anything that by the *Act* only the owner of the copyright has the right to do. This is referred to as direct infringement.

The *Act* provides that "copyright" means the rights described in

    (a) section 3, in the case of a work,
    (b) sections 15 and 26, in the case of a performer's performance,
    (c) section 18, in the case of a sound recording, or
    (d) section 21, in the case of a communication signal.[1]

As a result of this definition the approach to the direct infringement of a work, performer's performance, sound recording, or a communication signal are the same.

The rights available under sections 3, 15, and 26, 18, and 21 consist of "the sole right" to engage in the activities described in the sections. Copyright includes the right to prevent others from exercising the rights available to the copyright owner under the *Act*.[2] Because of this, it is useful to consider whether or not the act complained of would, if done by the owner of the copyright, been an exercise of the rights conferred solely on the owner by the *Act*.[3]

In order to show that infringement has occurred, copyright must subsist in the work, performer's performance, sound recording, or a communication signal which is in issue.[4] The protection given under the *Act* is territorial and generally there is no jurisdiction to prevent infringement outside Canada.[5]

The sole right to do each of the acts set out in the sections referred to above is a separate statutory right. Anyone who without the consent of the owner of the copyright does any of these acts infringes copyright. Because the rights are statutory in nature, it is not helpful in interpreting them to apply tort concepts.[6] Since each infringement of each right is a separate cause of action, infringement is typically a continuing cause of action.[7]

---

1. Section 2.
2. *Canadian Admiral Corporation Ltd. v. Rediffusion Inc. et al.* [1954] Ex. C.R. 382, 20 C.P.R. 75.
3. *Jennings v. Stephens* [1936] 1 All E.R. 409 (U.K.C.A.).
4. *Canadian Admiral Corporation Ltd. v. Rediffusion Inc. et al.* [1954] Ex. C.R. 382, 20 C.P.R. 75.
5. *Def Lepp Music v. Stuart-Brown* [1968] R.P.C. 273 (U.K. Ch. D.); *Tyburn Productions Ltd v. Conan Doyle* [1991] Ch. 75 (U.K. Ch. D.); *Pearce v. Ove Arup Partnership Ltd.* [1997] 2 W.L.R. 779 (U.K. Ch. D.).
6. *Compo Co. v Blue Crest Music* [1980] 1 S.C.R. 357.
7. *Compo Co. v Blue Crest Music* [1980] 1 S.C.R. 357; *Bishop v. Stevens,* [1990] 2 S.C.R 647, 31 C.P.R. (3d) 394 (S.C.C.).

The *Act* provides for additional rights relating to infringement which are secondary in nature and are typically directed toward the unauthorized dealing with infringing articles.[8]

The infringement of moral rights is dealt with in a different fashion. Under section 28.1 any act or omission that is contrary to any of the moral rights of the author of a work is, in the absence of consent by the author, an infringement of the moral rights. Section 28.2 specifies the acts which constitute infringement of the author's right to the integrity of a work.

The *Act* contains a number of provisions referred to as exceptions which describe activities which do not infringe copyright. [9]

## b) Intention to Infringe

In order to show direct infringement under section 27(1), it is not necessary for the plaintiff to prove an intention to infringe or knowledge that infringement has occurred on the part of the defendant.[10] An innocent intent or lack of knowledge that the actions in issue infringed copyright is not a defense.[11]

In any proceedings for infringement of copyright, the plaintiff is not entitled to any remedy other than an injunction in respect of the infringement if the defendant proves that, at the date of the infringement, the defendant was not aware and had no reasonable ground for suspecting that copyright subsisted in the work or other subject-matter in question.[12] However, the defendant cannot assert such a claim if at the date of the infringement, the copyright was duly registered under this *Act*.[13]

The absence of intention to infringe may be relevant in assessing damages for infringement.

## c) Consent or Licence

Since subsection 27(1) expressly refers to the absence of consent of the owner of the copyright, the absence of consent is an essential element of the cause of action for direct infringement. In order to succeed a plaintiff must show that the

---

8. See Chapter 28.
9. See Chapter 29.
10. *Compo Co. v Blue Crest Music* [1980] 1 S.C.R. 357.
11. *Francis Day & Hunter Ltd. et al. v. Bron* [1963] 2 All E.R. 16 (Ch. D.).
12. Subsection 39(1) and see Chapter 30, part 5 concerning this defense which is generally of limited application.
13. Subsection 39(2).

defendant's actions were done without its consent. From the defendant's point of view consent or license is a defense which may be express or implied.[14]

The extent of the consent or license must be considered as actions going beyond the terms of the consent or license may constitute infringement.

Consent may be inferred from the circumstances but the inference must be clear before it will provide a defense.[15] In addition, the "consent" must come from the person entitled to exercise the right alleged to be infringed.[16]

## 2. Authorizing Infringement

### a) The Sole Right to Authorize

The owner of copyright in a work or a performer's performance or a sound recording or a communication signal, as the case may be, is entitled to the sole right to authorize the exercise of all of the exclusive rights available under the *Act*.[17] Direct infringement under subsection 27(1) includes liability for authorizing, without the consent of the owner of the copyright, the exercise of any of those rights.

Authorizing infringement and direct infringement of the other exclusive rights available to the owner under the *Act* are separate and distinct causes of action.[18]

In order to establish liability for authorizing infringement, the action which it is alleged was authorized must be actionable by itself. If the act that is authorized was done by a person having a right to do that act, there is no liability for authorizing infringement.[19]

---

14. See Chapter 25 concerning non-proprietary licenses, implied licenses and withdrawal of consent.
15. *Kantel v. Grant*, [1933] Ex. C.R. 84 (Ex. Ct.); *Warner Bros.—Seven Arts Inc. v. CESM TV Ltd.* (1971), 65 C.P.R. 215 (Ex. Ct.); *Bishop v Stevens* (1984), 4 C.P.R. (3d) 349 (F.C.T.D.), (1987), 18 C.P.R. (3d) 257 (Fed. C.A.), affirmed [1990] 2 S.C.R 647, 31 C.P.R. (3d) 394 (S.C.C.).
16. *Bishop v Stevens* (1984), 4 C.P.R. (3d) 349 (F.C.T.D.), (1987), 18 C.P.R. (3d) 257 (Fed. C.A.), affirmed [1990] 2 S.C.R 647, 31 C.P.R. (3d) 394 (S.C.C.).
17. See sections 3, 15, 26, 18, and 21 of the *Act*.
18. *Blue Crest Music Inc. v. Compo Co. Ltd.* (1976), 30 C.P.R. (2d) 14 (F.C.A.); aff'd, [1980] 1 S.C.R. 357 (S.C.C.).
19. *Composers, Authors and Publishers Association of Canada Ltd. v. CTV Television Network Ltd.* (1966), 48 C.P.R. 246 (Ex. Ct.) affirmed [1968] S.C.R. 676 (S.C.C.).

## b) Authorization

The word "authorize" means to "sanction, approve, and countenance."[20] Countenance in the context of authorizing copyright infringement must be understood in its strongest dictionary meaning, namely, "give approval to, sanction, permit, favor, encourage."[21]

Authorization is a question of fact that depends on the circumstances of each particular case and can be inferred from acts that are less than direct and positive, including a sufficient degree of indifference.[22] However, a person does not authorize infringement by authorizing the mere use of equipment that could be used to infringe copyright. Courts presume that a person who authorizes an activity does so only so far as it is in accordance with the law.[23] This presumption may be rebutted if it is shown that a certain relationship or degree of control existed between the alleged authorizer and the persons who committed the copyright infringement.[24]

## c) Infringement by Agents and Employees

A defendant may be responsible for an infringement committed by an agent[25] or by an employee acting in the course of employment.[26] This liability arises by virtue of common law principles without the necessity of establishing liability under the *Act*.

Liability for infringement carried out by agents or employees of a defendant or liability for authorizing infringement is separate and distinct from the issue of the joint liability of defendants. Defendants in an action for infringement may be found to be jointly liable when two or more of them acted in concert with one another pursuant to a common design relating to the infringement.[27]

---

20. *Muzak Corp. v. Composers, Authors and Publishers Association of Canada Ltd.* [1953] 2 S.C.R. 182; *De Tervagne v. Beloeil (Town)* [1993] 3 F.C. 227, 50 C.P.R. (3d) 419 (F.C.T.D.); *CCH Canadian Ltd. v. Law Society of Upper Canada* (2004), 30 C.P.R. (4th) 1 (S.C.C.).
21. *CCH Canadian Ltd. v. Law Society of Upper Canada* (2004), 30 C.P.R. (4th) 1 (S.C.C.).
22. *CCH Canadian Ltd. v. Law Society of Upper Canada* (2004), 30 C.P.R. (4th) 1 (S.C.C.); *CBS Inc. v. Ames Records & Tapes Ltd.* [1981] 2 All E.R. 812 (U.K. Ch. D.).
23. *CCH Canadian Ltd. v. Law Society of Upper Canada* (2004), 30 C.P.R. (4th) 1 (S.C.C.); *Muzak Corp. v. Composers, Authors and Publishers Association of Canada Ltd.* [1953] 2 S.C.R. 182.
24. *CCH Canadian Ltd. v. Law Society of Upper Canada* (2004), 30 C.P.R. (4th) 1 (S.C.C.); *Muzak Corp. v. Composers, Authors and Publishers Association of Canada Ltd.* [1953] 2 S.C.R. 182; *De Tervagne v. Beloeil (Town,* [1993] 3 F.C. 227, 50 C.P.R. (3d) 419 (F.C.T.D.).
25. *Canadian Performing Right Society Ltd. v. Ming Yee* (1943), 3 C.P.R. 64 (Alberta Dist. Ct.).
26. *Canadian Performing Right Society Ltd. v. Canadian National Exhibition Association* [1934] O.R. 610, [1934] 4 D.L.R. 154 (Ont. H.C.).
27. *de Tervagnae v. Town of Beloeil* (1993), 50 C.P.R. (3d) 419 (F.C.T.D.).

# CHAPTER

# 28

# Secondary Infringement

# 1. Secondary Infringement

## a) The Nature of the Right

Under subsection 27(2) of the *Copyright Act* it is an infringement of copyright for any person to

   a) sell or rent out,[1]
   b) distribute to such an extent as to affect prejudicially the owner of the copyright,[2]
   c) by way of trade distribute, expose, or offer for sale or rental or exhibit in public,[3] or
   d) possess or import into Canada for the purpose of doing anything referred to in paragraphs (a) to (c)

a copy of a work, sound recording, or fixation of a performer's performance or of a communication signal that the person knows or should have known infringes copyright or would infringe copyright if it had been made in Canada by the person who made it.

In determining whether there is an infringement in the case of an activity referred to in subparagraphs 27(2)(a) through (c) or possession for the purpose of a such an activity, in relation to a copy that was imported for the purpose of doing such activity, it is irrelevant whether the importer knew or should have known that the importation of the copy infringed copyright.[4]

Secondary infringement is unlike direct infringement since it is directed at dealing with copies of a work, sound recording, or fixation of a performer's performance, or of a communication signal that the person knows or should have known infringes copyright or would infringe copyright if it had been made in Canada by the person who made it.[5]

Three elements which must be shown to establish secondary infringement: (1) a direct or hypothetical direct infringement of copyright has taken place; (2) the secondary infringer knew or should have known that he or she was dealing with a product of infringement unless the product was imported as described above; and (3) the secondary infringer did something listed in subsection 27(2)(a) to (e).[6] Absent direct infringement, there can be no

---

1. Subsection 27(2)(a).
2. Subsection 27(2)(b) and (c).
3. Subsection 27(2)(c).
4. Subsection 27(2).
5. The subsection was substantially amended pursuant to an *Act to Amend the Copyright Act* S.C. 1997, c. 24 and cases decided under previous versions of the *Act* must be read with care.
6. *Euro-Excellence Inc. v. Kraft Canada Inc.* 2007 SCC 37, 59 C.P.R. (4th) 353 (S.C.C.).

secondary infringement, except that direct infringement need not be shown in the case of a copy which has been imported in the circumstance described above.[7]

Section 45 of the *Act* contains exceptions to infringement relevant to the importation of copies of works which are for personal use, governmental use or for the use of a library, archive, museum, or educational institution.

## b) Knowledge of Infringement

In the case of a person who engages in a an activity referred to in subparagraphs 27(2)(a) through (c) or possession for the purpose of a such an activity relating to a copy of a work, sound recording, or fixation of a performer's performance, or of a communication signal, it must be shown that such person knows or should have known that the copy infringes copyright or would infringe copyright if it had been made in Canada by the person who made it.

Under the subsection it is not necessary to prove actual knowledge. A plaintiff need only establish facts that would suggest to a reasonable person that a breach of copyright was being committed. A person cannot close his or her eyes to the facts. In addition, the requirement to show knowledge can be satisfied if the conduct of the defendant amounted to willful blindness. In some cases, the defendant will be required to closely investigate the facts to ascertain if the goods purchased were counterfeit.[8]

To avoid uncertainty with respect to knowledge, a plaintiff should provide written notice to the alleged infringer setting out how copyright has been infringed prior to bringing an action. If the defendant is shown to have been provided with such notice, it will be difficult for the defendant to deny knowledge. The alleged infringer should be given a reasonable time to investigate the alleged infringement or they may be able to assert the absence of such an opportunity by way of defense to a claim under the subsection.[9]

## c) Importation of Infringing Works

Paragraph 27(2)(e) is an exception to the rule that secondary infringement requires proof of direct infringement because, unlike paragraphs 27(2)(a) to (d), it does not require actual direct infringement. Instead, it requires only *hypothetical* direct infringement. Under paragraph 27(2)(e), it is an infringement of

---

7. See paragraph 27(2)(e).
8. *Microsoft Corporation v. 9038-3746 Quebec Inc.* (2007), 57 C.P.R. (4th) 204 (F.C.).
9. *CCH Canadian Ltd.. v. Law Society of Upper Canada* (2004), 30 C.P.R. (4th) 1 (S.C.C.).

copyright for any person to . . . import into Canada for the purpose of doing anything referred to in paragraphs (a) to (c) . . . a copy of a work . . . that the person knows . . . would infringe copyright if it had been made in Canada by the person who made it. [10]

Paragraph 27(2)(e) substitutes hypothetical direct infringement for actual direct infringement. It is possible that the infringing imports may have been lawfully made outside of Canada. However, they are deemed to infringe copyright if the importer imported into Canada works that *would have infringed* copyright if those works had been made in Canada by the persons who made the works abroad.[11]

The purpose of paragraph 27(2)(e) is to give owners of Canadian copyright an added layer of protection where the Canadian copyright owner does not own copyright in that work in foreign jurisdictions. Paragraph 27(2)(e) protects Canadian copyright owners against "parallel importation" by deeming an infringement of copyright to have occurred even where the imported works did not infringe copyright laws in the country in which they were made. Without paragraph 27(2)(e), the foreign copyright owners who could manufacture the work more cheaply abroad could flood the Canadian market with the work, thereby rendering the Canadian copyright worthless. [12]

The *Act* does not provide a definition of the words "import into Canada." Presumably importation occurs when the goods are physically received in a country and subject to the jurisdiction of the courts of that country.

There is uncertainty with respect to the rights of a Canadian exclusive licensee under the subsection. In the case of *Euro-Excellence Inc. v. Kraft Canada Inc.*,[13] five Judges of the Supreme Court of Canada said that an exclusive licensee in Canada can claim protection against secondary infringement when the copyright work was produced by the owner-licensor.[14] This is the position of a majority of the Judges of the Supreme Court of Canada and presumably binding on lower courts in future cases.

Four other Judges said that the exclusive licensee's property interest in the copyright was limited. An exclusive licence is not a complete assignment of copyright. The owner-licensor retains a residual ownership interest in the copyright that precluded it from being liable for copyright infringement. An owner-licensor is liable to its exclusive licensee for breach of the licensing agreement but not for copyright infringement.[15]

---

10. *Euro-Excellence Inc. v. Kraft Canada Inc.* 2007 SCC 37, 59 C.P.R. (4th) 353 (S.C.C.).
11. *Euro-Excellence Inc. v. Kraft Canada Inc.* 2007 SCC 37, 59 C.P.R. (4th) 353 (S.C.C.).
12. *Euro-Excellence Inc. v. Kraft Canada Inc.* 2007 SCC 37, 59 C.P.R. (4th) 353 (S.C.C.).
13. (2007), 59 C.P.R. (4th) 353 (S.C.C.).
14. (2007), 59 C.P.R. (4th) 353 (S.C.C.) the reasons of Bastarache J, Lebel J., and Charron J. at paragraph 75 and the reasons of McLachlin J. and Abella J, at paragraphs 114–128.
15. 59 C.P.R. (4th) 353 (S.C.C) the reasons of Binnie J., Deschamps J., and Rothstein J. and Fish J.

The exclusive licensee was unsuccessful in this action as the three Judges, who concurred with the lead plurality of three Judges, found against it for other reasons.

## d) Sale or Rental of Infringing Works

It is an infringement of copyright for any person to sell or rent out[16] a copy of a work, sound recording, or a fixation of a performer's performance, or of a communication signal that the person knows or should have known infringes copyright or would infringe copyright if it had been made in Canada by the person who made it.

In order to determine whether a sale has taken place, an assessment must be made to ascertain whether a binding contract relating to sale of the work in issue has taken place. The presence of a profit is not a necessary element of a sale.[17]

No infringement under paragraph 27(2)(a) results from the selling a copy of a work unless at the time of the sale the seller knows or should have known the copy infringes copyright or would infringe copyright if it had been made in Canada by the person who made it.

An attempt to sell or rent may not constitute infringement under paragraph 27(2)(a) but exposing or offering for sale or rental or exhibiting in public come under paragraph 27(2)(c) if done "by way of trade."

## e) Distribution to the Prejudice of the Copyright Owner

It is an infringement of copyright for any person to distribute to such an extent as to affect prejudicially the owner of the copyright a copy of a work, sound recording, or a fixation of a performer's performance, or of a communication signal that the person knows or should have known infringes copyright or would infringe copyright if it had been made in Canada by the person who made it.

In order to constitute infringement in this way, the plaintiff must show specific prejudice to the owner of the copyright not the author.[18]

---

16. See section 2.5 but motive of gain is not relevant under paragraph 27(2)(a).
17. *CCH Canadian Ltd. v. Law Society of Upper Canada* (2004), 30 C.P.R. (4th) 1 (S.C.C.).
18. *Compagnie Generale des Etablissements Michelin v. National Automobile, Aerospace, Transportation and General Workers Union of Canada* (1996), 71 C.P.R. (3d), 348 (F.C.T.D.).

### f) By Way of Trade Distribute, Expose, or Offer for Sale or Rental, or Exhibit in Public

It is an infringement of copyright for any person to by way of trade distribute, expose, or offer for sale or rental, or exhibit in public a copy of a work, sound recording, or a fixation of a performer's performance, or of a communication signal that the person knows or should have known infringes copyright or would infringe copyright if it had been made in Canada by the person who made it. It must be shown that each of the listed activities is done "by way of trade."

### g) Possession of Infringing Works

It is an infringement of copyright for any person to possess for the purpose of doing the activities set out in paragraphs 27(2) (a), (b), and (c), which have been described above, a copy of a work, sound recording, or fixation of a performer's performance, or of a communication signal that the person knows or should have known infringes copyright or would infringe copyright if it had been made in Canada by the person who made it.

This paragraph broadens the rights available to an owner of copyright, particularly in cases involving businesses where possession is consistent with an intention to sell or distribute.

### h) Possession of Plates Specifically Designed for the Purpose of Making Infringing Copies

Subsection 27(4) of the *Act* provides that it is an infringement of copyright for any person to make or possess a plate that has been specifically designed or adapted for the purpose of making infringing copies of a work or other subject-matter. The term "plate" is defined as including (a) any stereotype or other plate, stone, block, mould, matrix, transfer, or negative used or intended to be used for printing or reproducing copies of any work, and (b) any matrix or other appliance used or intended to be used for making or reproducing sound recordings, performer's performances, or communication signals.[19] The application of the subsection is limited to "plates" that have been specifically designed or adapted for the purpose of making infringing copies.

The owner of copyright in a work or other subject-matter may recover possession of all plates used or intended to be used for the production of infringing copies, as if those copies or plates were the property of the copyright owner.[20]

---

19. Section 2.
20. Section 38 and see chapter 30, part 11(b).

## 2. Permitting Infringing Performances
## in Theatres

Under subsection 27(5) it is an infringement of copyright for any person, for profit, to permit a theatre or other place of entertainment to be used for the performance[21] in public of a work or other subject-matter without the consent of the owner of the copyright unless that person was not aware, and had no reasonable ground for suspecting, that the performance would be an infringement of copyright.[22]

To establish liability under the subsection it must be shown, among other things, that the defendant permitted a theatre or other place of entertainment to be used for the performance in public that is in issue. This means it will be necessary to show that the defendant had the ability to control the use of the place of the performance and specific knowledge of the material to be performed.[23]

Permission should not be inferred from a general authorization to use a theatre for the performance of musical works.[24] It must be shown that the defendant knew that the works in issue were going to be performed.

There will be no liability under the subsection if the permission to use of the place of entertainment was given gratuitously.

## 3. Parallel Importation of Books

Parallel importation refers to books which were legitimately published in their country of origin but have been imported into Canada without the consent of the Canadian rights owner. Publishers and distributors invest time and money to gain the exclusive right to import and distribute books in this country pursuant to distribution agreements. The agreements are circumvented when booksellers or institutional buyers order copies of books from companies other than the exclusive distributor in Canada.

---

21. "Performance" means any acoustic or visual representation of a work, performer's performance, sound recording, or communication signal, including a representation made by means of any mechanical instrument, radio receiving set, or television receiving set, section 2.
22. See *de tervagne et al v. Town (Beloeil)* (1993), 50 C.P. R. (3d) 419 (F.C.T.D.) secondary and direct infringement are concurrent.
23. *Canadian Performing Right Society Ltd. v. Canadian National Exhibition Association* [1934] O.R. 610, [1934] 4 D.L.R. 154 (Ont. H.C.); *Performing Right Organization of Canada v. Lion d'Or (1981) Ltee* (1987), 17 C.P.R. (3d) 542 (F.C.T.D.).
24. *Canadian Performing Right Society Ltd. v. Canadian National Exhibition Association* [1934] O.R. 610, [1934] 4 D.L.R. 154 (Ont. H.C.).

## a)  Exclusive Distributor

Section 2 of the *Act* provides that " exclusive distributor" means, in relation to a book, a person who has, been appointed in writing, by the owner or exclusive licensee of the copyright in the book in Canada, as

> (i)  the only distributor of the book in Canada or any part of Canada, or
> (ii)  the only distributor of the book in Canada or any part of Canada in respect of a particular sector of the market, and

meets the criteria established by regulations made under section 2.6.[25]

An "exclusive distributor" may initiate proceedings and seek remedies like any other person having an interest in copyright, so long as appropriate notice has been given.[26]

## b)  The Nature of the Exclusive Distributor's Rights

Section 27.1 of the *Act* contains two potential claims for infringement relating to the importation of books. The section only applies where there is an exclusive distributor of the book and the acts described in the section take place in the part of Canada or in respect of the particular sector of the market for which the person is the exclusive distributor. [27]

First, subsection 27.1 (1) provides that, subject to the regulations that it is an infringement of copyright in a book for any person to import the book where

> (a)  copies of the book were made with the consent of the owner of the copyright in the book in the country where the copies were made, but were imported without the consent of the owner of the copyright in the book in Canada; and
> (b)  the person knows or should have known that the book would infringe copyright if it was made in Canada by the importer.

Second, subsection 27.1(2) provides that, subject to the regulations where the circumstances described in paragraph 27.1(1)(a) exist, it is an infringement of copyright in an imported book for any person who knew or should have

---

25.  See the *Book Importation Regulations* brought into force September 1, 1999, SOR/99-324.
26.  An exclusive distributor is deemed, for the purposes of entitlement to any of the remedies under the *Act* in relation to an infringement under section 27.1 to derive an interest in the copyright in question by license, see subsection 27.1 (4).
27.  Subsection 27.1(3).

known that the book would infringe copyright if it was made in Canada by the importer to

(a) sell or rent out the book;
(b) by way of trade, distribute, expose, or offer for sale or rental, or exhibit in public, the book; or
(c) possess the book for the purpose of any of the activities referred to in paragraph (a) or (b).

"Book" is restrictively defined to mean a volume or a part or division of a volume, in printed form, and does not include (a) a pamphlet, (b) a newspaper, review, magazine, or other periodical, (c) a map, chart, plan, or sheet music where the map, chart, plan, or sheet music is separately published, and (d) an instruction or repair manual that accompanies a product or that is supplied as an accessory to a service.[28]

The exceptions to infringement set out in section 45 of the *Act* are applicable to proceedings under section 27.1. The importation of books for personal use, governmental use, or for the use of a library, archive, museum, or educational institution in the circumstances set out in the section is lawful. [29]

Section 27.1(5) provides that an "exclusive distributor," copyright owner or exclusive licensee is not entitled a remedy under the *Act* in relation to an infringement under section 27.1 unless, before the infringement occurred, notice has been given within the prescribed time and in the prescribed manner to the person alleged to have breached the section, that there is an "exclusive distributor" of the book.[30]

Exclusive licensees may apply to the Federal Court or a superior court of a province for an order directing the Minister of Public Safety and Emergency Preparedness;

(i) to take reasonable measures, on the basis of information reasonably required by the Minister and provided by the applicant, to detain the work, and
(ii) to notify the applicant and the importer, forthwith after detaining the work, of the detention and the reasons therefor; and

providing for such other matters as the court considers appropriate.[31]

Exclusive licensees may not seek statutory damages pursuant to section 38.1 of the *Act* where the copy in question was made with the consent of the copyright owner in the country where the copy was made.[32]

---

28. Section 2.
29. See chapter 30, part2(c).
30. See the *Book Importation Regulations* brought into force September 1, 1999, SOR/99-324.
31. Section 44.2 and see chapter 30, part 2.
32. Section 38.1(6)(c).

# CHAPTER
# 29

# Exceptions

# 1. Application

The *Copyright Act* contains detailed exceptions from infringement which are set out in sections 29 to 32.2. Because there are numerous exceptions which are set out in great detail, it is very unlikely that a court would give effect to an implied exception from infringement.[1]

The Supreme Court of Canada has clarified some general considerations about the fair dealing exceptions to copyright infringement which may apply to all exceptions by analogy. Procedurally, a defendant is required to prove that his or her dealing with a work has been fair; however, the fair dealing exception is perhaps more properly understood as an integral part of the *Act* than simply a defense. Any act falling within the fair dealing exception will not be an infringement of copyright. The fair dealing exception, like other exceptions in the *Act*, is a user's right. In order to maintain the proper balance between the rights of a copyright owner and users' interests, it must not be interpreted restrictively.[2]

# 2. Fair Dealing

## a) The Excepted Activities

Sections 29, 29.1 and 29.2 of the *Act* apply to "fair dealing." They are as follows:

> 29.  Fair dealing for the purpose of research or private study does not infringe copyright.
> 29.1 Fair dealing for the purpose of criticism or review does not infringe copyright if the following are mentioned:
> (a)  the source; and
> (b)  if given in the source, the name of the
>     (i)  author, in the case of a work,
>     (ii)  performer, in the case of a performer's performance,
>     (iii)  maker, in the case of a sound recording, or
>     (iv)  broadcaster, in the case of a communication signal.
> 29.2 Fair dealing for the purpose of news reporting does not infringe copyright if the following are mentioned:
> (a)  the source; and
> (b)  if given in the source, the name of the
>     (i)  author, in the case of a work,
>     (ii)  performer, in the case of a performer's performance,

1. *Bishop v. Stevens* [1990] 2 S.C.R 647, 31 C.P.R. (3d) 394 (S.C.C.).
2. *CCH Canadian Ltd. v. Law Society of Upper Canada* (2004), 30 C.P.R. (4th) 1 (S.C.C.).

(iii) maker, in the case of a sound recording, or

(iv) broadcaster, in the case of a communication signal.

The sections are only relevant if an infringing activity has taken place. For example, if the reproduction in issue consists of less than a substantial part of a work, is not an infringement and the exceptions do not apply.

In Canada, the purpose of the dealing will be fair if it is for one of the allowable purposes under the *Act*, namely research, private study, criticism, review or news reporting.[3]

The Supreme Court of Canada has made it clear that the fair dealing exception should not be restrictively interpreted. The fair dealing exception like other exceptions in the *Act*, is a user's right. In order to maintain the proper balance between the rights of a copyright owner and a user's interest, it should be given a fair and balanced reading applicable to remedial legislation.[4]

U.S. legislation dealing with "fair dealing" is quite different from the *Act*. The U.S. legislation leaves a broad equitable jurisdiction to the court to apply a defense to infringement as the presiding judge may see fit. The exceptions in the *Act* are more narrowly drafted and refer to fair dealing for specifically listed purposes. U.S. cases dealing with fair dealing are not helpful in determining whether the fair dealing exceptions of the *Act* apply.[5]

## b) The Meaning of "Fair Dealing"

To take advantage of the exceptions set out above, a defendant must show that its dealings have been fair. What will constitute fair dealing is not defined in the *Act* and depends on the facts of each case. The elements of fairness are malleable and can be tailored to each unique set of circumstances. Constitutional and *Charter* values such as the rule of law, equality, and access to justice may be implicitly considered in the context of determining whether a dealing is fair.[6]

The Supreme Court of Canada has stated that following matters provide a useful analytical framework to govern the determination of fairness:[7]

a) The purpose for which the defendant is using the plaintiff's work. The court should make an objective assessment of the defendant's real

3. See sections 29, 29.1 and 29.2 of the *Act*.
4. *CCH Canadian Ltd. v. Law Society of Upper Canada* (2004), 30 C.P.R. (4th) 1 (S.C.C.).
5. *Cie Générale Des Établissements Michelin-Michelin & Cie v. C.A.W.-Canada* (1996), 71 C.P.R. (3d) 348 (F.C.T.D.).
6. *CCH Canadian Ltd. v. Law Society of Upper Canada* (2002), 18 C.P.R. (4th) 161 (F.C.A), (2004), 30 C.P.R. (4th) 1 (S.C.C).
7. *CCH Canadian Ltd. v. Law Society of Upper Canada* (2004), 30 C.P.R. (4th) 1 (S.C.C.).

purpose or motive in using the plaintiff's work. Some dealings, even if for an allowable purpose, may be more or less fair than others; research done for commercial purposes may not be as fair as research done for charitable purposes.[8]

b) The character of the dealing.[9] In assessing the character of the dealing, courts must examine how the works were dealt with. If multiple copies of works are being widely distributed, this will tend to be unfair. If, however, a single copy of a work is used for a specific legitimate purpose, then it may be more appropriate to conclude that it was a fair dealing.[10]

c) The importance and the amount of the work taken. The amount taken may also be more or less fair depending on the purpose. For example, for the purpose of research or private study, it may be essential to copy an entire academic article or an entire judicial decision. However, if a work of literature is copied for the purpose of criticism, it will not likely be fair to include a full copy of the work in the critique.[11]

d) Alternatives to the alleged infringing activity. Alternatives to dealing with the infringed work may affect the determination of fairness. If there is a non-copyrighted equivalent of the work that could have been used instead of the copyrighted work, this should be considered by the court. A court should attempt to determine whether the dealing was reasonably necessary to achieve the ultimate purpose. For example, if a criticism would be equally effective if it did not actually reproduce the copyrighted work it was criticizing, this may weigh against a finding of fairness.[12]

e) The nature of the work. Although not determinative, if a work has not been published, the dealing may be more fair in that its reproduction with acknowledgement could lead to a wider public dissemination of the work. This will be another factor to be considered.[13] If the plaintiff's work is confidential and has been "leaked," this will be important.[14]

---

8. *CCH Canadian Ltd. v. Law Society of Upper Canada* (2004), 30 C.P.R. (4th) 1 (S.C.C.).
9. *CCH Canadian Ltd. v. Law Society of Upper Canada* (2004), 30 C.P.R. (4th) 1 (S.C.C.).
10. *CCH Canadian Ltd. v. Law Society of Upper Canada* (2004), 30 C.P.R. (4th) 1 (S.C.C.).
11. *CCH Canadian Ltd. v. Law Society of Upper Canada* (2004), 30 C.P.R. (4th) 1 (S.C.C.).
12. *CCH Canadian Ltd. v. Law Society of Upper Canada* (2004), 30 C.P.R. (4th) 1 (S.C.C).
13. *CCH Canadian Ltd. v. Law Society of Upper Canada* (2004), 30 C.P.R. (4th) 1 (S.C.C.) and see *Hubbard v. Vosper*, [1972]1 All E.R.1023 (U.K.C.A.); *Beloff v. Pressdram Ltd.* [1973] 1 All E.R. 241 (U.K.Ch. D.); *Breen v. Hancock House Publishers Ltd.* (1985), 6 C.P.R. (3d) 433 (F.C.T.D.).
14. *CCH Canadian Ltd. v. Law Society of Upper Canada* (2004), 30 C.P.R. (4th) 1 (S.C.C.); *Beloff v. Pressdram Ltd*, [1973] 1 All E.R. 241 (U.K.Ch. D.).

d) The effect of the dealing on the work.[15] If the reproduced work is likely to compete in the market of the original work, this may suggest that the dealing is not fair. Although the effect of the dealing on the market of the copyright owner is an important factor, it is neither the only factor nor the most important factor that a court must consider in deciding if the dealing is fair.

In summary, the purpose of the dealing, the character of the dealing, the amount of the dealing, available alternatives to the dealing, the nature of the work, and the effect of the dealing on the work are all factors that should be considered to determine whether or not a dealing is fair. These factors may be more or less relevant to assessing the fairness of a dealing depending on the factual context of the allegedly infringing dealing. In some contexts there may be other factors which should be considered to decide whether the dealing was fair.[16]

The fair dealing is restricted to the purposes listed in sections 29, 29.1, or 29.2. The fact that a work is a parody of another is not generally a defense to a claim of infringement.[17] Fair dealing will only apply to a parody when the purpose of the parody comes within one of the listed purposes.[18]

## c) Fair Dealing for the Purpose of Research or Private Study

Section 29 provides that fair dealing for the purpose of research or private study does not infringe copyright. The meaning of the word "research" is not restricted by the reference to "private study" and all fair research, whether in a private setting or not is included.[19] Research is not limited to non-commercial or private contexts. Research carried out for profit is not automatically excluded from the exemption.[20] A library, archive, or museum or a person acting under its authority may take advantage of the exception.[21]

---

15. *CCH Canadian Ltd. v. Law Society of Upper Canada* (2004), 30 C.P.R. (4th) 1 (S.C.C.).
16. *CCH Canadian Ltd. v. Law Society of Upper Canada* (2004), 30 C.P.R. (4th) 1 (S.C.C.).
17. *Cie Générale Des Établissements Michelin-Michelin & Cie v. C.A.W.-Canada* (1996), 71 C.P.R. (3d) 348 (F.C.T.D.).
18. *Productions Avanti CinéVidéo Inc. v. Favreau* (1999), 1 C.P.R. (4th) 129 (Quebec C.A.).
19. *CCH Canadian Ltd. v. Law Society of Upper Canada* (2004), 30 C.P.R. (4th) 1 (S.C.C.).
20. *CCH Canadian Ltd. v. Law Society of Upper Canada* (2004), 30 C.P.R. (4th) 1 (S.C.C.) and see *Hubbard v. Vosper* [1972] 1 All E.R.1023 (U.K.C.A.); *Beloff v. Pressdram Ltd.* [1973] 1 All E.R. 241 (U.K.Ch. D.).
21. Subsection 30.2(1).

To take advantage of the " private study" exception, the individual involved must have engaged in the otherwise infringing activity personally.[22] Educational institutions or their staff do not come within the section since it is limited to "private study."[23]

## d) Fair Dealing for the Purpose of Criticism or Review

Section 29.1 provides that fair dealing for the purpose of criticism or review does not infringe copyright if the source and if given in the source, the name of the

(i) author, in the case of a work,
(ii) performer, in the case of a performer's performance,
(iii) maker, in the case of a sound recording, or
(iv) broadcaster, in the case of a communication signal

are mentioned.

The scope of the words "criticism or review" has not been considered by a Canadian appellate court but presumably should be given a large and liberal interpretation in order to ensure that user's rights are not unduly constrained.[24]

In the United Kingdom, it has been held that a similar section extended to the literary style of the work and also to the doctrine or philosophy of the writer as expressed in the literary work in question.[25]

## e) Fair Dealing for the Purpose of News Reporting

Section 29.2 provides that fair dealing for the purpose of news reporting does not infringe copyright if the source and if given in the source, the name of the

(i) author, in the case of a work,
(ii) performer, in the case of a performer's performance,
(iii) maker, in the case of a sound recording, or
(iv) broadcaster, in the case of a communication signal are mentioned.[26]

---

22. *CCH Canadian Ltd. v. Law Society of Upper Canada* (2004), 30 C.P.R. (4th) 1 (S.C.C.).
23. *University of London Press Ltd. v. University Tutorial Press Ltd.*, [1916] 2 Ch. 601.
24. *CCH Canadian Ltd. v. Law Society of Upper Canada* (2004), 30 C.P.R. (4th) 1 (S.C.C.).
25. *Hubbard v. Vosper*, [1972] 1 All E.R. 1023 (U.K.C.A.).
26. See *British Broadcasting Corporation v. Satellite Broadcasting Ltd.* [1992] Ch. 141 (U.K. Ch. D.).

## 3. Educational Institutions

### a) Definition of Educational Institution

The *Act* provides that "educational institution" means

(a) a non-profit institution licensed or recognized by or under an Act of Parliament or the legislature of a province to provide pre-school, elementary, secondary, or post-secondary education,

(b) a non-profit institution that is directed or controlled by a board of education regulated by or under an Act of the legislature of a province and that provides continuing, professional, or vocational education or training,

(c) a department or agency of any order of government, or any non-profit body, that controls or supervises education or training referred to in paragraph (a) or (b), or

(d) any other non-profit institution prescribed by regulation.[27]

### b) The Excepted Activities

In general terms, the excepted activities must be carried out by an educational institution or a person acting under its authority:

a) for the purposes of education or training;

b) on the premises[28] of the educational institution; and

c) without motive of gain. [29]

The excepted activities, which are relatively narrow in scope, are as follows:

(a) making a manual reproduction of a work onto a dry-erase board, flip chart, or other similar surface intended for displaying handwritten material;[30]

---

27. Section 2. Section 30.4 provides that for greater certainty, the exceptions to infringement of copyright provided for under sections 29.4 to 30.3 and 45 also apply in respect of a library, archive, or museum that forms part of an educational institution.

28. Section 2 provides that "premises" means, in relation to an educational institution, a place where education or training referred to in the definition "educational institution" is provided, controlled, or supervised by the educational institution.

29. Section 29.3. Subsection 29.3(2) provides that an educational institution, library, archive, or museum, or person acting under its authority does not have a motive of gain where it or the person acting under its authority, does anything referred to in section 29.4, 29.5, 30.2, or 30.21 and recovers no more than the costs, including overhead costs, associated with doing that act.

30. Subsection 29.4(1)(a).

(b) making a copy of a work to be used to project an image of that copy using an overhead projector or similar device,[31] but only if the work is not commercially available in an appropriate medium;[32]

(c) (i) reproducing, translating, or performing, in public on the premises of the educational institution, or (ii) communicating by telecommunication to the public situated on the premises of the educational institution, a work or other subject-matter as required for a test or examination,[33] but only if the work or other subject-matter is not commercially available in an appropriate medium;[34]

(d) the live performance in public, primarily by students of the educational institution, of a work; the performance in public of a sound recording or of a work or performer's performance that is embodied in a sound recording; and the performance in public of a work or other subject-matter at the time of its communication to the public by telecommunication, before an audience consisting primarily of students of the educational institution, instructors acting under the authority of the educational institution, or any person who is directly responsible for setting a curriculum for the educational institution;[35]

(e) making, at the time of its communication to the public by telecommunication, a single copy of a news program or a news commentary program, excluding documentaries, for the purposes of performing the copy for the students of the educational institution for educational or training purposes;[36]

(f) performing the copy in public, at any time or times within one year after the making of a copy, before an audience consisting primarily of students of the educational institution on its premises for educational or training purposes;[37]

(g) making a single copy of a work or other subject-matter at the time that it is communicated to the public by telecommunication and keeping

---

31. Subsection 29.4(1)(b).
32. Subsection 29.4(3).
33. Subsection 29.4(2).
34. Subsection 29.4(3).
35. Subsection 29.5.
36. Subsection 29.6(1)(a) and see subsection 29.9 concerning record keeping and marking requirements.
37. Subsection 29.6(1)(b). Subsection 29.6(2) provides that the educational institution must (a) on the expiration of one year after making a copy under paragraph (1)(a), pay the royalties and comply with any terms and conditions fixed under the *Act* for the making of the copy or destroy the copy; and (b) where it has paid the royalties referred to in paragraph (a), pay the royalties and comply with any terms and conditions fixed under the *Act* for any performance in public of the copy after the expiration of that year.

the copy for up to 30 days to decide whether to perform the copy for educational or training purposes.[38]

The exceptions described in paragraphs d) through g) above do not apply where the communication to the public by telecommunication was received by unlawful means.[39]

## c) Literary Collections

The publication in a collection, mainly composed of non-copyright matter, intended for the use of educational institutions, and so described in the title and in any advertisements issued by the publisher, of short passages from published literary works in which copyright subsists and not themselves published for the use of educational institutions, does not infringe copyright in those published literary works if

a) not more than two passages from works by the same author are published by the same publisher within five years;
b) the source from which the passages are taken is acknowledged; and
c) the name of the author, if given in the source, is mentioned.[40]

## 4. Libraries, Archives, and Museums

## a) Definitions

The *Act* provides that "library, archive, or museum" means

(a) an institution, whether or not incorporated, that is not established or conducted for profit or that does not form a part of, or is not administered or directly or indirectly controlled by, a body that is established or conducted for profit, in which is held and maintained a collection

---

38. Section 29.7 and see subsection 29.9 concerning record keeping and marking requirements. Subsection 29.7(2) provides that an educational institution that has not destroyed the copy by the expiration of the 30 days infringes copyright in the work or other subject-matter unless it pays any royalties, and complies with any terms and conditions, fixed under the *Act* for the making of the copy.
39. Section 29.8.
40. Section 30.

of documents and other materials that is open to the public or to researchers, or

(b) any other non-profit institution prescribed by regulation.[41]

In order to come within the statutory definition of a library, an institution (1) must not be established or conducted for profit; (2) must not be administered or controlled by a body that is established or conducted for profit; and (3) must hold and maintain a collection of documents and other material that is open to the public or to researchers. Libraries in the for-profit sector may not take advantage of the exceptions.

The Supreme Court of Canada found that the Great Library administered and operated by the Law Society of Upper Canada for the bar and the public came within the definition. It was not established or conducted for profit. It was administered and controlled by the Benchers of the Law Society. Although some of the Benchers, when acting in other capacities, practice law for profit, when they are acting as administrators of the Great Library, the Benchers were not acting as a body established or conducted for profit.[42]

## b)  The Excepted Activities

Section 30.1 provides it is not an infringement of copyright for a library, archive, or a museum or a person acting under the authority a library, archive, or a museum to make, for the maintenance or management of its permanent collection or the permanent collection of another library, archive, or museum, a copy of a work or other subject-matter, whether published or unpublished, in its permanent collection in accordance with the regulations, in the following circumstances:

(a)  if the original is rare or unpublished and is deteriorating, damaged, or lost, or at risk of such a fate;

(b)  for the purposes of on-site consultation, if the original cannot be viewed, handled, or listened to because of its condition or because of the atmospheric conditions in which it must be kept;

(c)  in an alternative format if the original is currently in an obsolete format or the technology required to use the original is unavailable;

(d)  for the purposes of internal record-keeping and cataloguing;

(e)  for insurance purposes or police investigations; or

(f)  if necessary for restoration.

---

41.  Section 2.
42.  *CCH Canadian Ltd v. Law Society of Upper Canada* (2004), 30 C.P.R. (4th) 1 (S.C.C.).

The exception does not apply to the activities described in paragraphs a) to c) if an appropriate copy is "commercially available"[43] in a medium and of a quality that is appropriate for the purposes of maintenance or management. In addition, intermediate or temporary copies must be destroyed as soon as they are no longer needed.[44]

Subsection 30.2 (1) provides that it is not an infringement for a library, archive, or museum or a person acting under the authority a library, archive, or a museum to do anything on behalf of any person that the person may do personally under section 29 or 29.1. It extends to a library, archive, or museum the exceptions relating to fair dealing for the purpose of research, private study, criticism, or review. [45]

Subsection 30.2 (2) provides that it is not an infringement of copyright for a library, archive, or museum or a person acting under the authority a library, archive, or a museum to make, by reprographic reproduction, for a person requesting to use the copy for research or private study, a copy of a work that is, or that is contained in, an article published in (a) a scholarly, scientific, or technical periodical; or (b) a newspaper or periodical, other than a scholarly, scientific, or technical periodical, if the newspaper or periodical was published more than one year before the copy is made. Paragraph (b) does not apply in respect of a work of fiction or poetry or a dramatic or musical work.[46]

The library, archive, or museum may make a copy only on condition that

(a) the person for whom the copy will be made has satisfied the library, archive, or museum that the person will not use the copy for a purpose other than research or private study; and

(b) the person is provided with a single copy of the work.[47]

The regulations provide that the library, archive, or museum or the person acting under the authority of one of them, that makes the copy of the work must inform the person requesting the copy by means of text printed on the copy or a stamp applied to the copy, if the copy is in printed form, or by other appropriate means that the copy is to be used for the purpose of research or

---

43. See section 2 which provides that "commercially available" means, in relation to a work or other subject-matter, (a) available on the Canadian market within a reasonable time and for a reasonable price and may be located with reasonable effort, or (b) for which a licence to reproduce, perform in public or communicate to the public by telecommunication is available from a collective society within a reasonable time and for a reasonable price and may be located with reasonable effort.
44. Subsection 30.1(3).
45. The Supreme Court of Canada. arrived at the same result in *CCH Canadian Ltd v. Law Society of Upper Canada* (2004), 30 C.P.R. (4th) 1 (S.C.C.).
46. Subsection 30.2(3).
47. Section 30.2(4).

private study and that any use of the copy for a purpose other than research or private study may require the authorization of the copyright owner.[48]

The exceptions extend to "a person acting under the authority of a library, archive, or museum" and individuals authorized to carry out the activities described in sections 30.1 and 30.2 may take advantage of those sections.

A library, archive, or museum may do, on behalf of a person who is a patron of another library, archive, or museum, the excepted activities described above that it is authorized to do on behalf of its patrons, but the copy given to the patron must not be in digital form.[49]

Under section 30.21, it is not an infringement of copyright for an archive to make a copy of an unpublished work that is deposited in the archive. In order to apply, the archive must give the person who deposits a work in an archive notice at the time of deposit that it may copy the work in accordance with the section. The archive may only copy the work if

(a) the person who deposited the work, if a copyright owner, did not, at the time the work was deposited, prohibit its copying;

(b) copying has not been prohibited by any other owner of copyright in the work; and

(c) the archive is satisfied that the person for whom it is made will use the copy only for purposes of research or private study and makes only one copy for that person.[50]

## 5. Machines Installed in Educational Institutions, Libraries, Archives, and Museums

### a) The Excepted Activities

Section 30.3 provides that:

(1) An educational institution or a library, archive, or museum does not infringe copyright where

(a) a copy of a work is made using a machine for the making, by reprographic reproduction, of copies of works in printed form;

(b) the machine is installed by or with the approval of the educational institution, library, archive, or museum on its premises for use by

---

48. *Exceptions for Educational Institutions, Libraries, Archives, and Museum Regulations*, SOR/ 99–325 section 7.
49. Subsection 30.2(5).
50. Subsection 30.21(3).

students, instructors, or staff at the educational institution or by persons using the library, archive, or museum; and

    (c) here is affixed in the prescribed manner and location, a notice warning of infringement of copyright.

(2) Subsection (1) only applies if, in respect of a reprographic reproduction,

    (a) the educational institution, library, archive, or museum has entered into an agreement with a collective society that is authorized by copyright owners to grant licenses on their behalf;

    (b) the Copyright Board has, in accordance with section 70.2, fixed the royalties and related terms and conditions in respect of a license;

    (c) a tariff has been approved in accordance with section 70.15; or

    (d) a collective society has filed a proposed tariff in accordance with section 70.13.

(3) Where a collective society offers to negotiate or has begun to negotiate an agreement referred to in paragraph (2)(a), the Board may, at the request of either party, order that the educational institution, library, archive, or museum be treated as an institution to which subsection (1) applies, during the period specified in the order.

(4) Where an educational institution, library, archive, or museum has entered into an agreement with a copyright owner other than a collective society respecting reprographic reproduction, subsection (1) applies only in respect of the works of the copyright owner that are covered by the agreement.

(5) The Governor in Council may, for the purposes of paragraph 1(c), prescribe by regulation the manner of affixing and location of notices and the dimensions, form, and contents of notices.

Concern that educational institutions and libraries could be liable for authorizing infringement relating to the use photocopiers on their premises lead to implementation of this exception.[51]

The regulations provide that an educational institution, a library, an archive, or a museum shall ensure that a notice that contains at least the following information is affixed to, or within the immediate vicinity of, every photocopier in a place and manner that is readily visible and legible to persons using the photocopier.[52]

---

51. The Supreme Court of Canada. in the case of *CCH Canadian Ltd v. Law Society of Upper Canada* (2004), 30 C.P.R. (4th) 1 (S.C.C.) found that the evidence did not establish that the Law Society authorized copyright infringement by providing self-service photocopiers and copies of the respondent publishers' works for use by its patrons in the Great Library.

52. See *Exceptions for Educational Institutions, Libraries, Archives and Museum Regulations*, SOR/99–325 section 8.

WARNING!

Works protected by copyright may be copied on this photocopier only if authorized by

    *(a)* the *Copyright Act* for the purpose of fair dealing or under specific exceptions set out in that *Act*;

    *(b)* the copyright owner; or

    *(c)* a license agreement between this institution and a collective society or a tariff, if any.

*For details of authorized copying, please consult the license agreement or the applicable tariff, if any, and other relevant information available from a staff member. The Copyright Act provides for civil and criminal remedies for infringement of copyright."*

# 6. Computer Programs

## a) The Excepted Activities

Section 30.6 provides that:

It is not an infringement of copyright in a computer program for a person who owns a copy of the computer program that is authorized by the owner of the copyright to

(a) make a single reproduction of the copy by adapting, modifying, or converting the computer program or translating it into another computer language if the person proves that the reproduced copy is
    (i) essential for the compatibility of the computer program with a particular computer,
    (ii) solely for the person's own use, and
    (iii) destroyed immediately after the person ceases to be the owner of the copy; or
(b) make a single reproduction for backup purposes of the copy or of a reproduced copy referred to in paragraph (a) if the person proves that the reproduction for backup purposes is destroyed immediately when the person ceases to be the owner of the copy of the computer program.

The exceptions are only available to a person who owns a copy of the computer program that is authorized by the owner of the copyright. A licensee of a computer program only has a right to use the program and does not own the copy of the program and will not be able to take advantage of the exceptions.

## 7. The Incidental Inclusion of a Work in Another Work

### a) The Excepted Activities

Section 30.7 provides that it is not an infringement of copyright to incidentally and not deliberately[53]

(a) include a work or other subject-matter in another work or other subject-matter; or
(b) do any act in relation to a work or other subject-matter that is incidentally and not deliberately included in another work or other subject-matter.

## 8. Ephemeral Recordings

### a) The Excepted Activities

Section 30.8[54] provides that:

(1) It is not an infringement of copyright for a programming undertaking to fix or reproduce in accordance with this section a performer's performance or work, other than a cinematographic work, that is performed live or a sound recording that is performed at the same time as the performer's performance or work, if the undertaking
(a) is authorized to communicate the performer's performance, work, or sound recording to the public by telecommunication;
(b) makes the fixation or the reproduction itself, for its own broadcasts;
(c) does not synchronize the fixation or reproduction with all or part of another recording, performer's performance, or work; and

---

53. See *The Football Association Premier League Ltd. v. Panini UK Ltd.*, [2003] EWCA Civ 995 (U.K.C.A.) concerning the interpretation of these words under the UK legislation. There are no Canadian cases.
54. *Regulations Prescribing Networks (Copyright Act)*, SOR/99–348 provides a definition of "prescribed networks."

    (d) does not cause the fixation or reproduction to be used in an advertisement intended to sell or promote, as the case may be, a product, service, cause, or institution.

(2) The programming undertaking must record the dates of the making and destruction of all fixations and reproductions and any other prescribed information about the fixation or reproduction, and keep the record current.

(3) The programming undertaking must make the record referred to in subsection (2) available to owners of copyright in the works, sound recordings, or performer's performances, or their representatives, within 24 hours after receiving a request.

(4) The programming undertaking must destroy the fixation or reproduction within 30 days after making it, unless
    (a) the copyright owner authorizes its retention; or
    (b) it is deposited in an archive, in accordance with subsection (6).

(5) Where the copyright owner authorizes the fixation or reproduction to be retained after the 30 days, the programming undertaking must pay any applicable royalty.

(6) Where the programming undertaking considers a fixation or reproduction to be of an exceptional documentary character, the undertaking may, with the consent of an official archive, deposit it in the official archive and must notify the copyright owner, within 30 days, of the deposit of the fixation or reproduction.

(7) In subsection (6), "official archive" means the Library and Archives of Canada or any archive established under the law of a province for the preservation of the official archives of the province.

(8) This section does not apply where a license is available from a collective society to make the fixation or reproduction of the performer's performance, work, or sound recording.

(9) A broadcasting undertaking, as defined in the *Broadcasting Act*, may make a single reproduction of a fixation or reproduction made by a programming undertaking and communicate it to the public by telecommunication, within the period referred to in subsection (4), if the broadcasting undertaking meets the conditions set out in subsection (1) and is part of a prescribed network that includes the programming undertaking.

(10) The reproduction and communication to the public by telecommunication must be made
    (a) in accordance with subsections (2) to (6); and
    (b) within 30 days after the day on which the programming undertaking made the fixation or reproduction.

(11) In this section, "programming undertaking" means
    (a) a programming undertaking as defined in subsection 2(1) of the *Broadcasting Act*;

> (b) a programming undertaking described in paragraph (a) that originates programs within a network, as defined in subsection 2(1) of the *Broadcasting Act*; or
> (c) a distribution undertaking as defined in subsection 2(1) of the *Broadcasting Act,* in respect of the programs that it originates.

The undertaking must hold a broadcasting license issued by the Canadian Radio-television and Telecommunications Commission under the *Broadcasting Act.*

Prior to adding section 30.8 to the *Act* in 1999, it was held by the Supreme Court of Canada that the right to broadcast a performance under subsection 3(1) of the *Act* did not include the right to make "ephemeral" recordings for the purposes of facilitating the broadcast.[55]

The exception is of limited application. It only applies to a performer's performance or work, other than a cinematographic work, that is performed live or a sound recording that is performed at the same time as the performer's performance or work. There are a significant number of conditions which must be satisfied and the section does not apply where a license is available from a collective society.

## 9. Pre-Recorded Recordings

### a) The Excepted Activities

Section 30.9 provides that:

> (1) It is not an infringement of copyright for a broadcasting undertaking to reproduce in accordance with this section a sound recording, or a performer's performance or work that is embodied in a sound recording, solely for the purpose of transferring it to a format appropriate for broadcasting, if the undertaking
> (a) owns the copy of the sound recording, performer's performance or work and that copy is authorized by the owner of the copyright;
> (b) is authorized to communicate the sound recording, performer's performance, or work to the public by telecommunication;
> (c) makes the reproduction itself, for its own broadcasts;
> (d) does not synchronize the reproduction with all or part of another recording, performer's performance, or work; and

---

55. *Bishop v. Stevens,* [1990] 2 S.C.R 647, 31 C.P.R. (3d) 394 (S.C.C.).

    (e) does not cause the reproduction to be used in an advertisement intended to sell or promote, as the case may be, a product, service, cause, or institution.

(2) The broadcasting undertaking must record the dates of the making and destruction of all reproductions and any other prescribed information about the reproduction, and keep the record current.

(3) The broadcasting undertaking must make the record referred to in subsection (2) available to owners of copyright in the sound recordings, performer's performances or works, or their representatives, within 24 hours after receiving a request.

(4) The broadcasting undertaking must destroy the reproduction when it no longer possesses the sound recording or performer's performance or work embodied in the sound recording, or at the latest within 30 days after making the reproduction, unless the copyright owner authorizes the reproduction to be retained.

(5) If the copyright owner authorizes the reproduction to be retained, the broadcasting undertaking must pay any applicable royalty.

(6) This section does not apply if a license is available from a collective society to reproduce the sound recording, performer's performance, or work.

(7) In this section, "broadcasting undertaking" means a broadcasting undertaking as defined in subsection 2(1) of the *Broadcasting Act* that holds a broadcasting license issued by the Canadian Radio-television and Telecommunications Commission under that *Act*.

The exception relates to the reproduction of a sound recording, or a performer's performance, or work that is embodied in a sound recording, solely for the purpose of transferring it to a format appropriate for broadcasting.

Like the exception for ephemeral recordings, the exception is subject to a significant number of conditions and does not apply where a license is available from a collective society to reproduce the sound recording, performer's performance, or work.

## 10. Retransmission

### a) The Excepted Activities

Section 31(2) provides that it is not an infringement of copyright for a retransmitter to communicate to the public by telecommunication any literary, dramatic, musical, or artistic work if

    (a) the communication is a retransmission of a local or distant signal;

(b)  the retransmission is lawful under the *Broadcasting Act*;

(c)  the signal is retransmitted simultaneously and in its entirety, except as otherwise required or permitted by or under the laws of Canada;

(d)  in the case of the retransmission of a distant signal, the retransmitter has paid any royalties, and complied with any terms and conditions, fixed under this *Act*; and

(e)  the retransmitter complies with the applicable conditions, if any, referred to in paragraph (3)(*b*).

In the section "new media retransmitter" means a person whose retransmission is lawful under the *Broadcasting Act* only by reason of the *Exemption Order for New Media Broadcasting Undertakings* issued by the Canadian Radio-television and Telecommunications Commission as Appendix A to Public Notice CRTC 1999–197,[56] as amended from time to time; "retransmitter" means a person who performs a function comparable to that of a cable retransmission system, but does not include a new media retransmitter; and "signal" means a signal that carries a literary, dramatic, musical, or artistic work and is transmitted for free reception by the public by a terrestrial radio or terrestrial television station.

The *Copyright Act* distinguishes between the transmission and the retransmission by telecommunication. In broad terms, those who transmit a work by telecommunication are subject to the rights of the copyright owners pursuant to section 3(1)(f) and those who engage in retransmission come within the compensation scheme created by section 31.

The Canada-United States Free Trade Agreement required that copyright holders be provided with a right of equitable and non-discriminatory remuneration for any retransmission to the public of a copyright holders' program where the original transmission of the program was carried in distant signals intended for free, over-the-air reception by the general public.[57]

Section 31 creates a compulsory license and compensation scheme for copyright owners with respect to the retransmission of their works by cable retransmission. The rights of copyright owners to communicate their works by telecommunication is limited and reduced to receiving remuneration for retransmission. The amount of the remuneration is fixed by the

---

56.  The effect of the order is to exclude third party Internet retransmitters from the compulsory license scheme of section 31.

57.  Article 2006 Canada-United States Free Trade Agreement.

Copyright Board and retransmitters may take advantage of the statutory license.[58]

No remuneration is payable under section 31 with respect to the retransmission of a "local signal." The *Local Signal and Distant Signal Regulations*[59] specify what is meant by these terms.

## 11. Persons with Perceptual Disabilities

### a) The Excepted Activities

Section 32 provides that it is not an infringement of copyright for a person, at the request of a person with a perceptual disability,[60] or for a non-profit organization acting for his or her benefit, to

(a) make a copy or sound recording of a literary, musical, artistic, or dramatic work, other than a cinematographic work, in a format specially designed for persons with a perceptual disability;

(b) translate, adapt, or reproduce in sign language a literary or dramatic work, other than a cinematographic work, in a format specially designed for persons with a perceptual disability; or

(c) perform in public a literary or dramatic work, other than a cinematographic work, in sign language, either live or in a format specially designed for persons with a perceptual disability.

The exception does not authorize the making of a large print book[61] and does not apply where the work or sound recording is commercially available in a format specially designed to meet the needs of any person referred to in that

---

58. See Chapter 32, part 7.
59. SOR/89–254.
60. Section 2 provides that "perceptual disability" means a disability that prevents or inhibits a person from reading or hearing a literary, musical, dramatic, or artistic work in its original format, and includes such a disability resulting from
    (a) severe or total impairment of sight or hearing or the inability to focus or move one's eyes,
    (b) the inability to hold or manipulate a book, or
    (c) an impairment relating to comprehension.
61. Subsection 32(2).

subsection, within the meaning of paragraph (a) of the definition "commercially available."[62]

## 12. Statutory Obligations

### a) The Excepted Activities

Section 32.1(1) provides that it is not an infringement of copyright for any person

> (a) to disclose, pursuant to the *Access to Information Act*, a record within the meaning of that Act, or to disclose, pursuant to any like Act of the legislature of a province, like material;
>
> (b) to disclose, pursuant to the *Privacy Act*, personal information within the meaning of that Act, or to disclose, pursuant to any like Act of the legislature of a province, like information;
>
> (c) to make a copy of an object referred to in section 14 of the *Cultural Property Export and Import Act*, for deposit in an institution pursuant to a direction under that section; and
>
> (d) to make a fixation or copy of a work or other subject-matter in order to comply with the *Broadcasting Act* or any rule, regulation, or other instrument made under it.

(2) Nothing in paragraph (1)(a) or (b) authorizes a person to whom a record or information is disclosed to do anything that, by this *Act*, only the owner of the copyright in the record, personal information or like information, as the case may be, has a right to do.

(3) Unless the *Broadcasting Act* otherwise provides, a person who makes a fixation or copy under paragraph (1)(d) shall destroy it immediately on the expiration of the period for which it must be kept pursuant to that *Act*, rule, regulation or other instrument.

---

62. Subsection 32(3) and see section 2 which provides that "commercially available" means, in relation to a work or other subject-matter, (a) available on the Canadian market within a reasonable time and for a reasonable price and may be located with reasonable effort.

## 13. Miscellaneous Exceptions

### a) Artistic Works

Section 32.2 (1)(a) provides that it is not an infringement of copyright for an author of an artistic work who is not the owner of the copyright in the work to use any mould, cast, sketch, plan, model, or study made by the author for the purpose of the work, if the author does not thereby repeat or imitate the main design of the work.

### b) Architectural Works, and Sculptures or Works of Artistic Craftsmanship Situated in Public Places

Section 32.2 (1)(b) provides that it is not an infringement of copyright for any person to reproduce, in a painting, drawing, engraving, photograph, or cinematographic work

  (i) an architectural work,[63] provided the copy is not in the nature of an architectural drawing or plan, or
 (ii) a sculpture or work of artistic craftsmanship or a cast or model of a sculpture or work of artistic craftsmanship, that is permanently situated in a public place or building.[64]

### c) Newspaper Report of Public Lecture

Section 32.2 (1)(c) provides that it is not an infringement of copyright for any person to make or publish, for the purposes of news reporting or news summary, a report of a lecture[65] given in public, unless the report is prohibited by conspicuous written or printed notice affixed before and maintained during the lecture at or about the main entrance of the building in which the lecture is given, and, except while the building is being used for public worship, in a position near the lecturer.

---

63. Section 2 provides that "architectural work" means any building or structure or any model of a building or structure.
64. The exhibition of a sculpture or work of artistic craftsmanship in a gallery or at temporary public exhibitions does not come within the section; *Therrien v. Schola Inc.* [1982] 1 F.C. D-864 (F.C.T.D.).
65. Section 2 provides that "lecture" includes an address, speech, and sermon.

### d)  Public Recitation of Extracts

Section 32.2 (1)(d) provides that it is not an infringement of copyright for any person to read or recite in public a reasonable extract from a published work.

### e)  Report of an Address of a Political Nature Given at a Public Meeting

Section 32.2 (1)(e) provides that it is not an infringement of copyright for any person to make or publish, for the purposes of news reporting or news summary, a report of an address of a political nature given at a public meeting.

### f)  Performance at any Agricultural or Agricultural-Industrial Exhibition or Fair

Section 32.2 (2) provides that it is not an infringement of copyright for a person to do any of the following acts without motive of gain at any agricultural or agricultural-industrial exhibition or fair that receives a grant from or is held by its directors under federal, provincial, or municipal authority:

(a)  the live performance in public of a musical work;
(b)  the performance in public of a sound recording embodying a musical work or a performer's performance of a musical work; or
(c)  the performance in public of a communication signal carrying
  (i)  the live performance in public of a musical work, or
  (ii)  a sound recording embodying a musical work or a performer's performance of a musical work.

The performance must be "without motive of gain." The words "without motive of gain" are not restricted to circumstances where the motive of gain is the main or the only motive. If financial advantage was one of the objects of the exhibition, the exception should not apply.[66]

---

66. *Composers, Authors and Publishers Association of Canada Ltd.* v. *Western Fair Association* (1950), 13 C.P.R. 26 (Ont. C.A.), [1951] S.C.R. 596, 15 C.P.R. 45, (S.C.C.).

## g) Performance by Religious, Educational, Charitable, or Fraternal Bodies

Section 32.2 (3) provides that no religious organization or institution, educational institution[67] and no charitable or fraternal organization shall be held liable to pay any compensation for doing any of the following acts in furtherance of a religious, educational or charitable object:

(a) the live performance in public of a musical work;

(b) the performance in public of a sound recording embodying a musical work or a performer's performance of a musical work; or

(c) the performance in public of a communication signal carrying
  (i) the live performance in public of a musical work, or
  (ii) a sound recording embodying a musical work or a performer's performance of a musical work.

The performance must be in furtherance of a religious, educational or charitable object.[68]

## h) Equitable Remuneration

Section 32.3, provides that for the purposes of the exceptions set out in sections 29 to 32.2, an act that does not infringe copyright does not give rise to a right to remuneration conferred by section 19.

## i) Library and Archives of Canada

Section 30.5 provides that it is not an infringement of copyright for the Librarian and Archivist of Canada under the *Library and Archives of Canada Act*, to

(a) make a copy of a work or other subject-matter in taking a representative sample for the purpose of preservation under subsection 8(2) of that *Act*;

(b) effect the fixation of a copy of a publication, as defined in section 2 of that *Act*, that is provided by telecommunication in accordance with subsection 10(1) of that *Act*;

---

67. See part 3 of this chapter for the definition.
68. *Composers, Authors and Publishers Association of Canada Ltd.* v. *Kiwanis Club of West Toronto* [1953] 2 S.C.R. 111, 19 C.P.R. 20 (S.C.C).

(c) make a copy of a recording, as defined in subsection 11(2) of that *Act*, for the purposes of section 11 of that *Act*; or

(d) at the time that a broadcasting undertaking, as defined in subsection 2(1) of the *Broadcasting Act*, communicates a work or other subject-matter to the public by telecommunication, make a copy of the work or other subject-matter that is included in that communication.

# CHAPTER
# 30

# Actions for Infringement of Copyright

# 1. Jurisdiction

The Federal Court has concurrent jurisdiction with provincial superior courts to hear and determine all proceedings, other than the prosecution of offences under section 42 and 43, for the enforcement of a provision of the *Copyright Act* or of the civil remedies provided by the *Act*.[1]

Provincial superior courts have general and inherent jurisdiction.[2] They are presumed to have jurisdiction.[3] However, a judgment of a provincial court is only effective in its particular jurisdiction.

The Federal Court is without any inherent jurisdiction.[4] In order to have jurisdiction, the following matters must be established:

a) a statutory grant of jurisdiction by the Federal Parliament;
b) an existing body of federal law which is essential to the disposition of the case and which nourishes the statutory grant of jurisdiction; and
c) the law on which the case is based must be "a law of Canada" as the phrase is used in s. 101 of the *Constitution Act*, 1867.[5]

Once it is shown that the Federal Court has jurisdiction, the Court has territorial jurisdiction for all of Canada and its judgments are effective across the country.

The grant of jurisdiction under the *Copyright Act* does not give the Federal Court jurisdiction in an action for breach of contract or concerning the terms of a license relating to copyright. However, if the contractual disagreement is incidental and the primary subject matter of the action relates to the infringement of copyright, the court will have jurisdiction.[6]

Copyright is territorial in nature, notwithstanding the existence of the International Conventions or other treaties. Historically, the territorial limits relating to copyright have precluded extra territorial proceedings on the basis that a territorial right cannot be violated by an extraterritorial act.[7]

A Canadian court may decline jurisdiction under the doctrine known as *forum non conveniens*.[8] In addition, a Canadian Court may in its discretion

---

1. *Copyright Act*, section 37; *Federal Court Act*, R.S.C. 1985, c. F-7 as amended, section 20.
2. *R. v. Thomas Fuller Construction Co (1958) Ltd.* [1980] 1 S.C.R. 695 (S.C.C.).
3. *Board v. Board,* [1919] A.C. 956 (J.C.P.C.).
4. *Roberts v. Canada,* [1989] 1 S.C.R. 322 (S.C.C.).
5. *Ito-Int. Terminal Operators Ltd. v. Miida Electronics Inc.,* [1986] 1 S.C.R. 752 (S.C.C.).
6. *Titan Linkabit Corp. v. S.E.E. Electronic Engineering Inc.* (1992), 44 C.P.R. (3d) 469 (F.C.T.D.); *Possian v. Canadian Olympic Association* (1996), 74 C.P.R. (3d) 509 (F.C.T.D.).
7. *Def Lepp Music v. Stuart-Brown* [1986] R.P.C. 273 (U.K. Ch.); *Pearce v. Ove Arup Partnership Ltd.* [1997] 2 W.L.R. 779 (U.K. Ch.).
8. *Folkes v. Greensleeves Publishing Ltd* (1997), 76 C.P.R. (3d) 359 (Ont.Ct. (Gen. Div.)), appeal dismissed (1998), 85 C.P.R. (3d) 144 (Ont. C.A.).

stay an action on the ground that the claim is being proceeded with in another jurisdiction.[9]

## 2. Seizure of Imported Copies

### a) Section 44

Section 44 of the *Act* provides that copies made out of Canada of any work in which copyright subsists that if made in Canada would infringe copyright and as to which the owner gives notice in writing to the Canada Border Services Agency that the owner desires that the copies not be imported into Canada, shall not be so imported and are deemed to be included in tariff item No. 9897.00.000 in the list of Tariff Provisions set out in the schedule to the *Customs Tariff* and section 136 of that *Act* applies accordingly.[10]

Under the section, the Minister is required to make a determination of the copyright owner's rights on an *ex parte* basis without any notice to the aggrieved importer. The Federal Court has refused applications for an order of mandamus to compel action under the section on the basis that there is no clear duty on the part of the Minister owed to the applicant to perform any specific act.[11]

### b) Sections 44.1–44.3

#### i) Works

Section 44.1, which deals with works, was added to the *Act* in 1993 to give effect to Canada's obligations under the North American Free Trade Agreement.[12] The section allows the making of a an order in proscribed form when the court is satisfied that

> (a) copies of the work are about to be imported into Canada, or have been imported into Canada but have not yet been released

---

9. *Federal Court Act*, R.S.C. 1985, c. F-7, section 50.
10. Section 44.
11. *Dennison Manufacturing Co. v. Min. of Nat. Revenue*, [1988] 1 F.C. 492 (F.C.T.D.); *Takara Co. Ltd. v. Gamex International Inc.* (1989), 28 C.P.R. (3d) 575 (F.C.T.D.).
12. *North American Free Trade Agreement Implementation Act*, S.C. 1993, c. 44, section 66 proclaimed into force January 1, 1994.

(b) either

    (i) copies of the work were made without the consent of the person who then owned the copyright in the country where the copies were made, or

    (ii) the copies were made elsewhere than in a country to which this *Act* extends; and

(c) the copies would infringe copyright if they were made in Canada by the importer and the importer knows or should have known this.

An application under the section may be made by the owner or the exclusive licensee of copyright in a work in Canada.[13]

## ii) Importation of Books

Section 44.2 allows the making of a an order when the court is satisfied that in relation to a book

(a) copies of the book are about to be imported into Canada, or have been imported into Canada but have not yet been released;

(b) copies of the book were made with the consent of the owner of the copyright in the book in the country where the copies were made, but were imported without the consent of the owner in Canada of the copyright in the book;

(c) the copies would infringe copyright if they were made in Canada by the importer and the importer knows or should have known this; and

(d) there is an exclusive distributor of the book and the acts objected to take place in the part of Canada or in respect of the particular sector of the market for which the person is the exclusive distributor.

An application may be made by the owner of the copyright in the book in Canada, the exclusive licensee of the copyright in the book in Canada, or the exclusive distributor of the book.[14]

An exclusive licensee of the copyright in a book in Canada and an exclusive distributor of a book may not obtain an order under section 44.2 against another exclusive licensee of the copyright in that book in Canada or against another exclusive distributor of that book.[15]

---

13. Subsection 44.1(2.1).
14. Subsection 44.2(2).
15. Section 44.3.

### iii) Other Subject Matter

Section 44.4 allows the making of a an order when the court is satisfied that in respect of a sound recording, performer's performance, or communication signal, where a fixation or a reproduction of a fixation of it

(a) is about to be imported into Canada, or has been imported into Canada but has not yet been released;
(b) either
    (i) was made without the consent of the person who then owned the copyright in the sound recording, performer's performance, or communication signal, as the case may be, in the country where the fixation or reproduction was made, or
    (ii) was made elsewhere than in a country to which Part II of the *Act* extends; and
(c) would infringe the right of the owner of copyright in the sound recording, performer's performance, or communication signal if it was made in Canada by the importer and the importer knows or should have known this.

### iv) Procedure

The same procedure applies whether an application is brought pursuant to sections 44.1, 44.2 or 44.4.

The sections only apply when copies of a work, book, or other subject-matter, as the case may be, is "about to be imported" or "has been imported into Canada but has not yet been released." It is difficult to obtain such information which significantly restricts the application of the sections.

An application must be heard by the Federal Court or the superior court of a province.[16] An application for an order may be made in an action or otherwise, and either on notice or *ex parte*, except that it must always be made on notice to the Minister of Public Safety and Emergency Preparedness.[17]

The court may make an order

(a) directing the Minister;
    ( i) to take reasonable measures, on the basis of information reasonably required by the Minister and provided by the applicant, to detain the work, and
    (ii) to notify the applicant and the importer, forthwith after detaining the work, of the detention and the reasons therefor; and
(b) providing for such other matters as the court considers appropriate.[18]

---

16. Subsection 44.1(1).
17. Subsection 44.1(4).
18. Subsection 44.1(3).

Before making an order the court may require the applicant to furnish security, in an amount fixed by the court, to cover duties, storage, and handling charges, and any other amount that may become chargeable against the work and to answer any damages that may, by reason of the order, be incurred by the owner, importer, or consignee of the work.[19]

The Minister of Revenue is given the right to apply to the court for directions in implementing an order made under the sections.[20]

The Minister may give the applicant or the importer an opportunity to inspect the detained work for the purpose of substantiating or refuting, as the case may be, the applicant's claim.[21]

Unless an order provides otherwise, the Minister shall, subject to the *Customs Act* and to any other Act of Parliament that prohibits, controls, or regulates the importation or exportation of goods, release the copies of the work without further notice to the applicant if, two weeks after the applicant has been notified by the Minister of the detention of the goods, the applicant has not notified the Minister that the applicant has commenced a proceeding for a final determination by the court of the matters in issue.[22]

Where, in a proceeding commenced under the section, the court finds that the circumstances required for the application of the section exist, the court may make any order that it considers appropriate in the circumstances, including an order that the copies of the work be destroyed, or that they be delivered up to the plaintiff as the plaintiff's property absolutely.[23]

The *Act* provides that for greater certainty, nothing in section 44.1 affects any remedy available under any other provision of the *Act* or any other Act of Parliament.[24]

## c) Exceptions

Section 45 of the *Act* contains exceptions relevant to the importation of copies of works. The section provides that notwithstanding anything in the *Act*, it is lawful for a person

(a) to import for their own use not more than two copies of a work or other subject-matter made with the consent of the owner of the copyright in the country where it was made;

---

19. Subsection 44.1(5).
20. Subsection 44.1(6).
21. Subsection 44.1(7).
22. Subsection 44.1(8).
23. Subsection 44.1(9).
24. Subsection 44.1(10).

(b) to import for use by a department of the Government of Canada or a province copies of a work or other subject-matter made with the consent of the owner of the copyright in the country where it was made;

(c) at any time before copies of a work or other subject-matter are made in Canada, to import any copies, except copies of a book, made with the consent of the owner of the copyright in the country where the copies were made, that are required for the use of a library, archive, museum, or educational institution;

(d) to import, for the use of a library, archive, museum, or educational institution, not more than one copy of a book that is made with the consent of the owner of the copyright in the country where the book was made; and

(e) to import copies, made with the consent of the owner of the copyright in the country where they were made, of any used books, except text-books of a scientific, technical, or scholarly nature for use within an educational institution in a course of instruction.

An officer of customs may, in the officer's discretion, require a person seeking to import a copy of a work or other subject-matter under these exceptions to produce satisfactory evidence of the facts necessary to establish the person's right to import the copy.[25]

## 3. Parties to Actions in the Courts

### a) The Owner of Copyright

The owner of the copyright in a work is entitled to exercise the rights set out in section 3 of the *Act*, including the right to authorize others to exercise such rights.[26] The right to sue for infringement is not available to agents who simply represent the interests of the copyright owner.[27]

---

25. Subsection 45(2).
26. Section 3 and section 34(1) and see Chapter 22, part 7 concerning a claim by a joint author.
27. *Bishop v. Stevens*, [1990] 2 S.C.R. 467 (S.C.C.).

A class action under the Ontario *Class Proceedings Act, 1992*[28] consisting of creators and/or owners of copyright is possible if the requirements of that *Act* are satisfied.[29]

## b) The Author

An author of a work is entitled to exercise the moral rights associated with the work.[30]

## c) Persons Deriving Rights from the Owner

Subsection 36(1) provides that any person or persons deriving any right, title, or interest by assignment or grant in writing from the owner, may individually for himself or herself, as a party to the proceedings in his or her own name, protect and enforce any right that he or she holds, and, to the extent of that right, title, and interest, is entitled to the remedies provided by this *Act*.[31]

In order that separate rights may be protected under the subsection, the right, title, or interest must be assigned or granted "in writing" and it must be a grant of a "right, title, or interest" in the copyright itself.[32]

The right available under the subsection is asserted "as a party to the proceedings in his or her own name." The subsection does not authorize the bringing of an action to which the copyright owner is not a party except

a) in respect of proceedings taken under section 44.1, 44.2, or 44.4;

b) in respect of interlocutory proceedings unless the court is of the opinion that the interests of justice require the copyright owner to be a party; and

c) in any other case, if the court is of the opinion that the interests of justice do not require the copyright owner to be a party.[33]

---

28. S.O. 1992.
29. *Robertson v. The Thompson Corporation* (1999), 43 O.R 161 (Ont Ct. (Gen. Div.): (2001) 15 C.P.R. (4th) 147 (Ont. Sup. Ct. of Justice); (2004) 34 C.P.R. (4th) 161 (Ont. C.A.); (2006) 52 C.P.R. (4th) 417 (S.C.C).
30. See Chapter 20 and see subsection 34(2).
31. *Ateliers Tango Argentin Inc. et al v. Festival d'Espagne et d'Amerique Latine Inc.* (1997), 84 C.P.R. (3d) 56 (Quebec Sup. Ct.).
32. See Chapter 24.
33. Subsection 36(2).

### i)  Proprietary Licenses

Typically, an exclusive license would come within subsection 36(1)[34] but the copyright owner must be made a party to those proceedings unless the exceptions set out in subsection 36(2) apply.[35]

A right of action for infringement of copyright may be assigned in association with the assignment of the copyright or the grant of an interest in the copyright by license.[36]

Subsection 27.1(4) of the *Act* provides that an exclusive distributor of a book[37] is deemed, for the purposes of entitlement to any of the remedies under Part IV of the *Act* in relation to an infringement under Section 27.1, to derive an interest in the copyright in question by license.

### ii)  Assignees

An assignee pursuant to an assignment or grant of an interest in writing, signed by the owner of the right in respect of which the assignment or grant is made or by the owner's duly authorized agent will come within subsection 36(1).[38] An assignment which does not comply with these requirements will not be enforceable.[39]

## f)  Defendants

The persons who have directly infringed,[40] engaged in secondary infringement,[41] or infringed an author's moral rights[42] are potential defendants.

In addition, under section 38 of the *Act*, the owner of the copyright in a work or other subject-matter may institute proceedings to recover possession of all infringing copies and plates used or intended to be used for the production of infringing copies, and for seizure of those copies or plates before judgment as if those copies or plates were the property of the copyright owner.[43]

---

34.  See subsection 13(7) and Chapter 25, part 1.
35.  See Chapter 28, part 1(c) for a discussion of *Euro-Excellence Inc. v. Kraft Canada Inc.* (2007), 59 C.P.R. (4th) 353 (S.C.C.) concerning exclusive licensees.
36.  Subsection 13(6).
37.  See Chapter 28, part 3.
38.  Subsection 13(4).
39.  See Chapter 24.
40.  See Chapter 27.
41.  See Chapter 28.
42.  See Chapter 20.
43.  See part 11(b) of this chapter.

It is not clear whether a person may be liable for aiding and abetting infringement.[44]

### i) Directors and Officers

Generally speaking, the directors or officers of a corporation are not personally liable for the infringing activity of the corporation and accordingly should not be parties, unless they formed the corporation for the purpose of infringing or they have directly ordered or authorized the acts complained of. In order to find personal liability, there must be circumstances from which it is reasonable to conclude that the purpose of the director or officer was not the direction of the manufacturing and selling activity of the corporation in the ordinary course of his relationship to it, but the deliberate, willful, and knowing pursuit of a course of conduct that was likely to constitute infringement or reflected an indifference to the risk of it.[45] The precise formulation of the appropriate test is obviously a difficult one. A broad appreciation of the circumstances of each case must be made to determine whether as a matter of policy they call for personal liability.[46]

The question is whether the director or officer truly acted for the corporation in the ordinary course of business (rather than acting in such a way as to make the act or conduct his own as distinct from that of the corporation) and would reasonably be perceived as doing so.[47]

A statement of claim alleging personal liability of a director or officer must be carefully drafted. If an allegation is made against a director or an officer which does not set out the appropriate material facts, a motion to strike the relevant portion of the statement of claim may be brought.

## 4. Pleadings

### a) Notice of Claim

In cases alleging direct infringement, it is not necessary that notice be given before serving the statement of claim. However, practical considerations typ-

44. *Apple Computer Inc. v. Mackintosh Computers Ltd.* (1986), 10 C.P.R. (3d) 1 (F.C.T.D.). referring to *Procter & Gamble v. Bristol-Myers Canada Ltd.* (1978), 39 C.P.R. (2d) 145 (F.C.T.D.).
45. *Apple Computer Inc. et al. v. Mackintosh Computer Ltd. et al* (1986), 10 C.P.R. (3d) 1 (F.C.T.D.).
46. *Mentmore Manufacturing Company Limited et al v. National Merchandising Manufacturing Company Inc.* (1978), 40 C.P.R. (2d) 164 (F.C.A.).
47. *Montreal Trust Co. of Canada et al. v. Scotia McLeod Inc. et al.* (1994), 15 B.L.R. (2d.) 160 (Ont. Ct., (Gen. Div.)), (1995). 26 O.R. (3d) 481 (Ont. C.A.).

ically require that notice be given if at all possible. In cases alleging secondary infringement, notice may be required.[48]

## b) Statement of Claim

Generally speaking, a plaintiff should set out the following matters in a statement of claim:

a) The work or other subject matter protected by copyright must be clearly identified;
b) the name of the author and the fulfillment of the relevant conditions for the subsistence of copyright;[49]
c) the material facts relating to the infringing activities of the defendant;[50]
d) that the infringing activities were done without the plaintiff's consent;[51]
f) the relief claimed.

## c) Statement of Defense

A statement of defense denying the existence of or title to copyright must be specifically pleaded.[52] A general denial is not sufficient and the material facts relating to the specific defense relied on must be set out.[53]

A defendant may claim the benefit of the exceptions set out in sections 29 to 32.2. Such defenses must include the material facts necessary to establish that the relevant exception is applicable.

### i) Lack of Awareness

Section 39 provides that in any proceeding for infringement of copyright, the plaintiff is not entitled to any remedy other than an injunction in respect of the infringement if the defendant proves that, at the date of the infringement, the defendant was not aware and had no reasonable ground for suspecting that copyright subsisted in the work or other subject-matter in question.

---

48. See Chapter 28.
49. See Chapter 17, part a) and Chapter 19.
50. *Eldon Industries Inc. v. Reliable Toy Co. Ltd.* (1966), 48 C.P.R. 109 (Ont. C.A.).
51. Subsection 27(1).
52. Section 34.1 and 53 (2) *Warner Bros.-Seven Arts Inc. v. CESM TV Ltd* (1969), 58 C.P.R. (2d) 97 (Ex Ct.); *Bally Midway MFG Co. v. Coinex Video Games Inc.* (1983), 72 C.P.R. (2d) 22 (F.C.T.D.).
53. *Modern Houseware Imports Inc v. International Sources Ltd.* (2000), 4 C.P.R (4th) 155 (F.C.T.D.).

However, the section does not apply if, at the date of the infringement, the copyright was duly registered under this *Act*.

The section is of limited application. Ignorance of the existence of copyright is not sufficient as the defendant must also prove there was no reasonable ground for suspecting that copyright subsisted in the work.[54]

In applying the section, courts have taken the approach that a defendant should assume that copyright subsists in a work about to be copied, unless there is evidence to the contrary.[55] Evidence to the contrary would include a reasonable belief that (a) that the period of copyright protection had expired; or (b) the work is of such character that it is not protected by copyright.[56]

## d) Particulars[57]

The material facts relating to a claim for infringement are the existence of the work, the ownership of copyright in the work, the existence of the infringing work and the absence of the owner's consent to the production or reproduction of the work. Nothing further is required to allow the defendant to respond to the claim. The means by which the plaintiff has become aware of these facts is not material.[58]

## 5. Interlocutory Injunctions[59]

## 6. *Anton Piller* Orders[60]

## 7. Summary Applications

Subsection 34(4) of the *Act* provides that proceedings for infringement of copyright or moral rights, to detain imported infringing copies pursuant to

---

54. *Gribble* v. *Manitoba Free Press Co.*, [1931] 3 W.W.R. 570, [1932] 1 D.L.R. 169 (Man. C.A.).
55. *Gribble* v. *Manitoba Free Press Co.*, [1931] 3 W.W.R. 570, [1932] 1 D.L.R. 169 (Man. C.A.); *Slumber Magic Adjustable Bed Co. Ltd.* v. *Sleep-King Adjustable Bed Co. Ltd.* (1984), 3 C.P.R. (3d) 81 (B.C.S.C.); *U&R Tax Services Ltd* v. *H&R Block Canada Inc* (1995), 62 C.P.R. (3d) 257 (F.C.T.D.); *Bulman Group Ltd.* v. *"One Write"Accounting Systems Ltd.* (1982), 62 C.P.R. (2d) (F. C. T.D.).
56. *Gribble* v. *Manitoba Free Press Co.*, [1931] 3 W.W.R. 570, [1932] 1 D.L.R. 169 (Man. C.A.).
57. See Chapter 15, part 4(b).
58. *Adacel Technologies Ltd.* v. *Nav Canada*, 2006 FCA 227 (F.C.A.); *Canadian Olympic Association* v. *National Gym Clothing* (1985), 2 C.P.R. (3d) 145 (F.C.T.D.).
59. See Chapter 15, part 5.
60. See Chapter 15, part 6.

section 44.1, 44.2, or 44.4, or in respect of a tariff certified under the *Act*, may be commenced or proceeded with by way of application[61] or action. In the case of an application, the proceedings are to be heard and determined without delay and in a summary way.[62]

Subsection 34(5) provides that the rules of practice and procedure in civil matters of the court in which proceedings are commenced by way of application, apply to those proceedings. If those rules do not provide for the proceedings to be heard and determined without delay and in a summary way, the court may give such directions as it considers necessary in order to so provide. The court in which proceedings are instituted by way of application may, where it considers it appropriate, direct that the proceeding be proceeded with as an action.[63]

## 8. Discovery

Discovery of documents, examinations for discovery and inspection of property are available under the procedural rules of the court in which an action for infringement is brought.[64]

An equitable bill of discovery is also potentially available. In essence, this is a form of pre-action discovery. This remedy permits a court, acting through its equitable jurisdiction, to order discovery of a person against whom the applicant for the bill of discovery has no cause of action and who is not a party to contemplated litigation. While it appears that an independent action for discovery cannot be brought against a person who is in the position of a "mere witness" or bystander to the cause of action, the case law suggests that a bill of discovery may be issued against an individual who is in some way connected to or involved in the misconduct.[65]

In order to obtain equitable discovery the plaintiff must show a *bona fide* claim and not a *prima facie* case. The plaintiff must also show that the information sought cannot be obtained from another source and consideration must be given to the costs incurred by the respondent in assembling the

---

61. Subsection 34(7) provides that in the section, "application" means a proceeding that is commenced other than by way of a writ or statement of claim.
62. See *Kraft Canada Inc. v. Euro Excellence Inc.* (2007), 59 C.P.R. (4th)353 (S.C.C.) where injunctive relief, damages and related relief was granted in an application.
63. Subsection 34(6).
64. *Rules of Civil Procedure*, R.R.O 1990, Regulation 194 as amended, Rules 30, 31, and 32. *Federal Court Rules, 1998*, SOR/98–106, Rules 222 to 249.
65. *Glaxo Wellcome Plc. v. M.N.R.* (1998), 81 C.P.R. (3d) 372 (F.C.A.), leave to appeal to the Supreme Court of Canada dismissed 82 C.P.R. (3d) vi; *BMG Canada Inc. v. John Doe* (2005), 39 C.P.R. (4th) 97 (F.C.A.).

information. The public interest in favor of disclosure must outweigh the legitimate privacy concerns of a person sought to be identified. Caution must be exercised in ordering disclosure of identity to ensure that privacy rights are invaded in the most minimal way. If an order is granted, directions should be given as to the type of information to be disclosed and the manner in which it can be used.[66]

## 9. Limitation Period for Civil Remedies

Section 41 of the *Act* provides that a court may not award a remedy in relation to an infringement unless

(a) in the case where the plaintiff knew, or could reasonably have been expected to know, of the infringement at the time it occurred, the proceedings for infringement are commenced within three years after the infringement occurred; or

(b) in the case where the plaintiff did not know, and could not reasonably have been expected to know, of the infringement at the time it occurred, the proceedings for infringement are commenced within three years after the time when the plaintiff first knew, or could reasonably have been expected to know, of the infringement.

The section also provides that a court shall apply the limitation periods described above only in respect of a party who pleads a limitation period.

Section 41 applies to all of the civil remedies available under the *Act*, including a claim for injunctive relief.

As infringement is frequently a continuing cause of action each individual act of infringement is actionable. For each infringement, a separate inquiry must be made concerning the applicable limitation period.[67]

## 10. Evidence at Trial

The onus is on the plaintiff to prove the allegations set out in the statement of claim on the balance of probabilities. Consideration should be given to the following matters.

---

66. *BMG Canada Inc. v. John Doe* (2005), 39 C.P.R (4th) 97 (F.C.A.).
67. *Wall v. Horn Abbot Ltd.* 2007 NSSC 197(N.S.S.C.).

## a) Presumptions

The parties must determine the effect of the application of the presumptions set out in the *Act* concerning the subsistence of copyright, ownership of copyright and the maker.[68]

## b) Certificate of Registration as Evidence

A certificate of registration of copyright or an assignment of copyright or a license granting an interest in a copyright is evidence in its own right of the matters set out in the registration. A plaintiff should take advantage of the benefits of filing such evidence.[69] If a certificate is filed, any presumption which would otherwise apply no longer applies.[70]

## c) Circumstantial Evidence

In many cases it is essential that the plaintiff establish that copying or reproduction has occurred. A plaintiff may be able to prove that copying took place by circumstantial evidence when direct evidence of copying is not available. Evidence of similarity and access to the plaintiff's work can support an inference of copying.[71]

Unexplained similarities or repetition of common errors may be circumstantial evidence of copying.[72] The weight to be given to such evidence depends on the strength of the inference which can be drawn from it.[73]

The deliberate introduction of errors into a compilation for the purpose of detecting infringement is a common practice. The existence of the same errors in the defendant's work is circumstantial evidence of access and copying.

## d) Expert Evidence

The evidence of expert witness can play an important role in cases involving copyright infringement. Expert evidence may be presented at trial concerning originality, to point out coincidences, similarities, or other evidence of

---

68. See Chapter 22, part 10.
69. See Chapter 26, part 4.
70. See Chapter 22, part 10.
71. *Francis, Day & Hunter Ltd. v. Bron*, [1963] 2 All E.R. 16 (U.K.C.A.); *Gondos v. Hardy* (1982), 64 C.P.R. (2d) 145 (Ont. H.C.).
72. *Deeks v. Wells*, [1933] 1 D.L.R. 353 (Ont. P.C.).
73. See Sophinka, Lederman, and Bryant, *The Law of Evidence in Canada* at p 40.

copying,[74] or in relation to claims for damages or profits.[75] The weight to be given such evidence will be determined by the court.[76]

## 11. Remedies

### a) Permanent Injunction

i) Grant

Subsection 34.(1) of the *Act* states that where copyright has been infringed, the owner of the copyright is, subject to the *Act*, entitled to all remedies by way of injunction, damages, accounts, delivery up, and otherwise that are or may be conferred by law for the infringement of a right. Subsection 34.(2) provides for similar jurisdiction in any proceedings for an infringement of a moral right of an author.

The applicable principles are much the same as in an action for trademark infringement as previously described.[77] A successful plaintiff is *prima facie* entitled to a permanent injunction and the onus is on the defendant to show that the existence of any applicable equitable defenses should preclude the grant of such an injunction.[78]

The jurisdiction to grant injunctions includes the power to restrain threatened infringement as distinguished from infringement which has already occurred. However, such jurisdiction is exercised sparingly and with caution and there must be a high degree of probability that the infringement will occur.[79]

Where the infringing parts of the work can be separated from the balance, a court may order that the defendant's product be rendered non-infringing.[80]

Subsection 40(1) of the *Act* provides that where the construction of a building or other structure that infringes or that, if completed, would infringe the copyright in some other work has been commenced, the owner of the

---

74. *Deeks* v. *Wells*, [1933] 1 D.L.R. 353 (Ont. P.C.).
75. *Gondos* v. *Hardy* (1982), 64 C.P.R. (2d) 145 (Ont. H.C.); *Hutton v. Canadian Broadcasting Corporation* (1990), 29 C.P.R. (3d) 398 (Alberta. Q.B.); *Prestone v. 20th Century Fox Canada Ltd.* (1991), 33 C.P.R. (3d) 242 (F.C.T.D.); *Lifestyle Homes v. Randall Homes* (1990), 30 C.P.R. (3d) 76 (Man. Q.B.); affirmed 33 C.P.R. (3d) 505 (Man. C.A.).
76. *Deeks v. Wells*, [1931] O.R. 818 (S.C.C.), aff'd [1933] 1 D.L.R. 353 (Ont. P.C.); *Collins v. Rosenthal*, (1974), 14 C.P.R. (2d) 143 (F.C.T.D.); *Geac Canada Ltd. v. Prologic Computer Corp.* (1989), 25 C.P.R. (3d) 565 (B.C.S.C.).
77. See Chapter 15, part 11.
78. *Queen v. James Lorimer* (1984), 77 C.P.R. (2d) 262 (F.C.A.).
79. *Operation Dismantle Inc. v. Canada*, [1985] 1 S.C.R. 441 (S.C.C.).
80. *Kraft Canada Inc. v. Euro Excellence Inc.* (2004), 33 C.P.R. (4th) 246 (F.C.).

copyright is not entitled to obtain an injunction in respect of the construction of that building or structure or to order its demolition.[81] Sections 38, relating to the recovery of possession of infringing copies, and 42, relating to criminal offences, do not apply in any case where subsection 40(1) applies.

### ii)  Wide Injunction

Section 39.1 of the *Act* provides that when granting an injunction in respect of an infringement of copyright in a work or other subject-matter, the court may further enjoin the defendant from infringing the copyright in any other work or subject-matter if

  (a)  the plaintiff is the owner of the copyright or the person to whom an interest in the copyright has been granted by license; and
  (b)  the plaintiff satisfies the court that the defendant will likely infringe the copyright in those other works or subject-matter unless enjoined by the court from doing so.

Subsection 39(2) further provides that a "wide injunction" may extend to works or other subject-matter

  (a)  in respect of which the plaintiff was not, at the time the proceedings were commenced, the owner of the copyright or the person to whom an interest in the copyright has been granted by licence; or
  (b)  that did not exist at the time the proceedings were commenced.

The section has not yet been judicially considered in detail. But this jurisdiction should be cautiously exercised.

### iii)  Breach of Injunction[82]

## b)  Possession of Infringing Copies

Under subsection 38(1)(a) of the *Act*, the owner of the copyright in a work or other subject-matter may recover possession of all infringing copies of that work or other subject-matter, and of all plates[83] used or intended to be used

---

81.  *Randall Homes Ltd. v. Harwood Homes Ltd.* (1987), 17 C.P.R. (3d) 372 (Man. Q.B.) the section only applies where the construction of a building or other structure has commenced.
82.  See Chapter 15, part 11(b).
83.  Section 2 provides that "plate" includes (a) any stereotype or other plate, stone, block, mould, matrix, transfer, or negative used or intended to be used for printing or reproducing copies of any work, and (b) any matrix or other appliance used or intended to be used for making or reproducing sound recordings, performer's performances, or communication signals.

for the production of infringing[84] copies, as if those copies or plates were the property of the copyright owner. The deemed ownership is not effective for all purposes and the copyright owner cannot seek damages in respect of the possession or conversion of the infringing copies or plates.[85]

Under subsection 38(1)(b) the owner of the copyright in a work or other subject-matter may take proceedings for seizure of those copies or plates before judgment if, under the law of Canada or of the province in which those proceedings are taken, a person is entitled to take such proceedings.

On application by the person from whom possession has been recovered or any person who has an interest in the copies or plates, a court may order that the copies or plates be destroyed, or may make any other order that it considers appropriate in the circumstances.[86] Before making such an order, the court must direct that notice be given to any person who has an interest in the copies or plates in question, unless the court is of the opinion that the interests of justice do not require such notice to be given.[87]

In making an order the court must have regard to all the circumstances, including

    (a) the proportion, importance, and value of the infringing copy or plate, as compared to the substrate or carrier embodying it; and

    (b) the extent to which the infringing copy or plate is severable from, or a distinct part of, the substrate or carrier embodying it.[88]

Where the construction of a building or other structure that infringes or that, if completed, would infringe the copyright in some other work has been commenced, the owner of the copyright is not entitled to relief under section 38.[89]

---

84. Section 2 provides that "infringing" means (a) in relation to a work in which copyright subsists, any copy, including any colorable imitation, made or dealt with in contravention of this *Act*, (b) in relation to a performer's performance in respect of which copyright subsists, any fixation or copy of a fixation of it made or dealt with in contravention of this *Act*, (c) in relation to a sound recording in respect of which copyright subsists, any copy of it made or dealt with in contravention of this *Act*, or (d) in relation to a communication signal in respect of which copyright subsists, any fixation or copy of a fixation of it made or dealt with in contravention of this *Act*. The definition includes a copy that is imported in the circumstances set out in paragraph 27(2)(e) and section 27.1 but does not otherwise include a copy made with the consent of the owner of the copyright in the country where the copy was made.
85. Subsection 38(5). Prior to September 1, 1997 such a claim could be asserted.
86. Subsection 38(2).
87. Subsection 38(3).
88. Subsection 38(4).
89. Subsection 40(2).

## c) Declaratory Relief

The Provincial superior courts of record and the Federal Court have jurisdiction to grant declaratory relief.[90] The *Act* prescribes a comprehensive regime of property rights concerning copyright and it is open to a court to declare the entitlement of certain persons to certain rights in accordance with that regime.[91] It is possible to bring an action for a declaration of non-infringement in a Provincial superior court of record [92] but it is unclear if the Federal Court has such jurisdiction.[93]

## d) Damages

### i) Assessment of Damages

Section 35 of the *Act* provides that

(1) Where a person infringes copyright, the person is liable to pay such damages to the owner of the copyright as the owner has suffered due to the infringement and, in addition to those damages, such part of the profits that the infringer has made from the infringement and that were not taken into account in calculating the damages as the court considers just.

(2) In proving profits,

    (a) the plaintiff shall be required to prove only receipts or revenues derived from the infringement; and

    (b) the defendant shall be required to prove every element of cost that the defendant claims.

Damages are assessed on the basis of the injury done to the plaintiff. The plaintiff should be restored to the position he or she was in before the infringement occurred. The general principle of assessment of damages is that the damages must flow directly from the acts complained of and they must not be too remote.[94]

---

90. Federal Court Rules 1998, SOR/98–106, Rule 64 and the *Courts of Justice Act* R.S.O. 1990, c .C. 43 section 97.
91. *Operation Dismantle Inc. v. Canada*, [1985] 1 S.C.R. 441; *Royal Doulton v. Cassidy's* [1986] F.C. 357 (F.C.T.D.).
92. *Research in Motion Ltd v. Atari Inc*, (2007), 51 C.P.R. (4th) 193 (Ont. S.C.J.).
93. *Peak Innovations Inc. v. Meadowland Flowers Ltd.* 2009 FC 661 (F.C.T.D.).
94. *Underwriters' Survey Bureau Ltd. v. Massie & Renwick Ltd.*, [1942] Ex. C.R. 1 (Ex. Ct); *Dictionnaires Robert Canada SCC v. Libraire du Nomande Inc.* (1987), 16 C.P.R. (3d) 319 (F.C.T.D.).

An infringer cannot avoid liability because damages are difficult to prove.[95] A court must do the best it can to achieve an equitable result.[96] Mathematical precision is not required. Damages are assessed at large[97] without the necessity to allege or prove special damage.[98]

The method of assessment varies depending on the facts of the case. In many cases the plaintiff will be entitled to receive the profit it would have made had it made the sales that the defendant made.[99] Where licenses are granted of similar rights, damages may be awarded on the basis of what would have been charged for license fees.[100]

Aggravated damages may be awarded. Aggravated damages are intended to compensate a person for intangible injuries such as mental distress, hurt feelings, and the motives and conduct of the defendant where they aggravate the injury done to the plaintiff.[101] Since a corporation cannot suffer mental distress or hurt feelings, it is questionable whether aggravated damages may be awarded to a corporation.[102] Aggravated damages are compensatory in nature and may only be awarded for this purpose.[103]

## ii) Nominal Damages

Where loss or damages cannot be clearly proved by the plaintiff as the direct result of the infringement, the plaintiff is entitled to nominal damages.[104]

## iii) Punitive or Exemplary Damages

Punitive or exemplary damages have been awarded in cases of copyright infringement.[105] Punitive damages are awarded against a defendant in exceptional cases for "malicious, oppressive, and high-handed" misconduct that "offends

95. *Hay and Hay Construction Co. Ltd. v. Sloan et al.* [1957] O.W.N. 445. (Ont.H.C.)
96. *U&R Tax Services Ltd. v. H&R Block Canada Inc.* (1995), 62 C.P.R. (3d) 257 (F.C.T.D.); *Prism Hospital Software Inc. v. H.M.R.I..* (1994), 57 C.P.R. (3d) 129 (B.C.S.C.).
97. *Standard Industries Ltd. v. Rosen* [1955] 4 D.L.R. 363 (Ont. H.C.J.).
98. *C.P. Koch Ltd. v. Continental Steel Ltd.* (1984), 82 C.P.R. (2d) 156 (B.C.S.C.); aff'd (1985), 4 C.P.R. (3d) 395 (B.C.C.A.); *Slumber-Magic, Adjustable Bed Co. v. Sleep-King Adjustable Bed Co.* (1985), 3 C.P.R. (3d) 81 (B.C.S.C.).
99. *Dictionnaires Robert Canada SCC v. Libraire du Nomande Inc.* (1987), 16 C.P.R. (3d) 319 (F.C.T.D.); *Prise de Parole Inc. v. Guerin, Editeur Ltee* (1995), 66 C.P.R. (3d) 17 (F.C.T.D.).
100. *Hager v. ECW Press Ltd.* (1998), 85 C.P.R. (3d) 289 (F.C.T.D.).
101. *Rookes v. Bernard,* [1964] 1 All E.R. 367 (H.L.).
102. *Thomas Management Ltd. v. Alberta (Minister of Environmental Protection)* (2006), 397 A.R. 339, 2006 ABCA 303 (Alberta C.A.).
103. *Vorvis v. Insurance Corporation of British Columbia* (1989), 58 D.L.R. (4th) 193 (S.C.C.).
104. *Underwriters' Survey Bureau Ltd. et al. v. Massie & Renwick Ltd.* [1938] Ex. C.R. 103; [1940] S.C.R. 218, [1940] 1 D.L.R. 625.
105. *Profekta International Inc. v. Lee* (1997), 75 C.P.R. (3d) 369 (F.C.).

the Court's sense of decency."[106] The test thus limits the award to misconduct that represents a marked departure from ordinary standards of decent behavior. Because their objective is to punish the defendant rather than compensate a plaintiff (whose just compensation will already have been assessed), punitive damages straddle the frontier between civil law (compensation) and criminal law (punishment).

## e) Account of Profits

In cases for infringement of a patent or a trademark, a plaintiff's claim for an account of the profits made by the defendant is an alternative to damages. The plaintiff must elect which remedy it will have and cannot have both.

In actions for infringement of copyright the situation is different. Section 35 of the *Act* provides that where a person infringes copyright, the person is liable to pay such damages to the owner of the copyright as the owner has suffered due to the infringement and, in addition to those damages, such part of the profits that the infringer has made from the infringement and that were not taken into account in calculating the damages as the court considers just.[107]

In proving profits, the plaintiff is required to prove only receipts or revenues derived from the infringement and the defendant must prove every element of cost that the defendant claims.[108]

At common law, an accounting of profits is an equitable remedy and subject to equitable defenses.[109] Presumably, reference can be made to case law decided in this context when considering a claim for profits under the *Copyright Act*.

## f) Statutory Damages

Section 38.1 of the *Copyright Act* provides for statutory damages. The section is as follows

(1) Subject to this section, a copyright owner may elect, at any time before final judgment is rendered, to recover, instead of damages and profits

---

106. *Hill v. Church of Scientology of Toronto* [1995] 2 S.C.R. 1130 (S.C.C).
107. Previously the section provided the plaintiff was entitled not only to damages but, in addition, if the court decided that such an award is just and proper, to the profits which the infringer made from such infringement.
108. Subsection 35(2).
109. See Chapter 15, part 11(c).

referred to in subsection 35(1), an award of statutory damages for all infringements involved in the proceedings, with respect to any one work or other subject-matter, for which any one infringer is liable individually, or for which any two or more infringers are liable, jointly and severally, in a sum of not less than $500 or more than $20,000 as the court considers just.

(2) Where a copyright owner has made an election under subsection (1) and the defendant satisfies the court that the defendant was not aware and had no reasonable grounds to believe that the defendant had infringed copyright, the court may reduce the amount of the award to less than $500, but not less than $200.

(3) Where
  (a) there is more than one work or other subject-matter in a single medium, and
  (b) the awarding of even the minimum amount referred to in subsection (1) or (2) would result in a total award that, in the court's opinion, is grossly out of proportion to the infringement,
  the court may award, with respect to each work or other subject-matter, such lower amount than $500 or $200, as the case may be, as the court considers just.

(4) Where the defendant has not paid applicable royalties, a collective society referred to in section 67 may only make an election under this section to recover, in lieu of any other remedy of a monetary nature provided by this *Act*, an award of statutory damages in a sum of not less than 3 and not more than 10 times the amount of the applicable royalties, as the court considers just.

(5) In exercising its discretion under subsections (1) to (4), the court shall consider all relevant factors, including
  (a) the good faith or bad faith of the defendant;
  (b) the conduct of the parties before and during the proceedings; and
  (c) the need to deter other infringements of the copyright in question.

(6) No statutory damages may be awarded against
  (a) an educational institution or a person acting under its authority that has committed an act referred to in section 29.6 or 29.7 and has not paid any royalties or complied with any terms and conditions fixed under this *Act* in relation to the commission of the act;
  (b) an educational institution, library, archive, or museum that is sued in the circumstances referred to in section 38.2; or
  (c) a person who infringes copyright under paragraph 27(2)(e) or section 27.1, where the copy in question was made with the consent of the copyright owner in the country where the copy was made.

(7) An election under subsection (1) does not affect any right that the copyright owner may have to exemplary or punitive damages.

### i) Availability

As set out above, in order to seek statutory damages, a copyright owner must elect, before final judgment is rendered, to seek such a recovery instead of damages and profits referred to in subsection 35(1). Any award of statutory damages is for all infringements involved in the proceeding with respect to "one work or other subject matter." The section applies to "works" and to a performer's performance, sound recording, and a communication signal.[110]

### ii) Assessment

The mandate of a judge assessing statutory damages under section 38.1 is to arrive at a reasonable assessment which considers the statutory provisions and all of the circumstances of the case, in order to yield a just result.[111]

The assessment of statutory damages is subject to a number of statutory directions, which are as follows:

a) the court may award a sum not less that $500 or more than $22,000 as it considers just;[112]
b) the court shall consider all relevant factors including (i) the good or bad faith of the defendant; (ii) the conduct of the parties before and during the proceeding; and (iii) the need to deter other infringements of the copyright in question;[113]
c) where the defendant satisfies the court that it was not aware and had no reasonable grounds to believe that it had infringed copyright, the court may reduce the amount of the award to less than $500, but not less than $200;[114]
d) the court may, as it considers just, award statutory damages in an amount lower than $500 or $200 where:
   (i) there is more than one work or other subject matter in a single medium, and

---

110. See *U&R Tax Services Ltd v. H&R Block Canada Inc* (1995), 62 C.P.R. (3d) 257 (F.C.T.D.) and the definition of "copyright" in section 2.
111. *Telewizja Polska Canada Inc. v. Radiopol Inc.* 2006 FC 584, 52 C.P.R. (4th) 445 (F.C.).
112. Subsection 38.1(1).
113. *Telewizja Polska Canada Inc. v. Radiopol Inc.* 2006 FC 584, 52 C.P.R. (4th) 445 (F.C.).
114. Subsection 38.1(2).

(ii)   the awarding of even the minimum amount referred to in subsections 38.1(1) or (2), would result in a total award that, in the Court's opinion, is grossly out of proportion to the infringement;

e)  where the defendant has not paid applicable royalties, a collective society may only make an election under subsection 38.1(1) to recover statutory damages in a sum not less than 3 and not more than 10 times the amount of the applicable royalties, as the court considers just.[115]

Unlike subsection 39(2),[116] a defendant's right to assert that it was not aware and had no reasonable grounds to believe that it had infringed copyright is not affected by the registration of the copyright under the *Act*. However, it may be difficult to take advantage of the subsection since its wording of the subsection is quite similar to that of subsection 39(1) which has been restrictively applied by the courts. This issue has yet to be considered by the courts.

A plaintiff who elects to recover statutory damages may still seek exemplary or punitive damages [117]

There are statutory limitations concerning potential awards against educational institutions, libraries, and museums which are set out in section 38.2.

## g)  Delivery Up

Section 34 provides that where copyright has been infringed, the owner of the copyright is, subject to the *Act*, entitled to the remedy known as delivery up. The grant of an order for delivery up of the infringing copies is a discretionary remedy.

Where the infringing portion of a work can be severed, the plaintiff may only be entitled to an order for delivery up of that portion of the work.[118]

Where the construction of a building or other structure that infringes or that, if completed, would infringe the copyright in some other work has been commenced, the owner of the copyright is not entitled to deliver up.[119]

## h)  Costs[120]

---

115. Subsection 38.1(4).
116. See part 4(c)(i) of this chapter.
117. Subsection 38.1(7).
118. *Apple Computer v. Mackintosh Computers Ltd.* [1987] F.C. 173 (F.C.T.D.); *Kraft Canada Inc. v. Euro Excellence Inc.* (2004), 33 C.P.R. (4th) 246 (F.C.).
119. Subsection 40(2).
120. See Chapter 15, part 11(d).

# CHAPTER
# 31

# Criminal Remedies

# 1. Criminal Proceedings

The *Copyright Act* provides for criminal remedies in appropriate cases. The prosecution of criminal proceedings does not preclude a copyright owner from subsequently bringing a civil action for the infringement of copyright. However, instituting civil proceedings will likely preclude subsequent criminal proceedings relating to the same facts. A previous criminal conviction may be relevant in civil proceedings relating to subsequent related infringement and support a claim for exemplary damages.[1]

In Canada there are three categories of criminal offences:

1. Offences in which *mens rea*, consisting of some positive state of mind such as intent, knowledge, or recklessness, must be proved by the prosecution either as an inference from the nature of the act committed or by additional evidence.
2. Offences in which there is no necessity for the prosecution to prove the existence of *mens rea*; the doing of the prohibited act *prima facie* imports the offence, leaving it open to the accused to avoid liability by proving that he or she took all reasonable care. This involves consideration of what a reasonable man would have done in the circumstances. The defense will be available if the accused reasonably believed in a mistaken set of facts which, if true, would render the act or omission innocent, or if the accused took all reasonable steps to avoid the particular event. These offences may properly be called offences of strict liability.
3. Offences of absolute liability where it is not open to the accused to avoid conviction by showing that he or she was free of fault.[2]

The doctrine of the guilty mind expressed in terms of intention or recklessness, but not negligence, is the foundation of the law of crimes and applies to the first category of offences. In such cases there is a presumption that a person should not be held liable for the wrongfulness of his or her act if that act is without *mens rea*:[3] *Mens rea* may be proved by showing recklessness or willful blindness[4] but showing negligence is typically not sufficient.[5]

---

1. *Profekta International Inc. v. Lee* (1997) 75 C.P.R. (3d) 369 (F.C.A.).
2. *R. v. Sault Ste. Marie* [1978] 2 S.C.R 1299, 85 D.L.R. (3d) 161.
3. *R. v. Sault Ste. Marie* [1978] 2 S.C.R 1299, 85 D.L.R. (3d) 161.
4. *R. v. Sansregret* [1985], 1 S.C.R. 570; *R. v. Théroux* [1993], 2 S.C.R. 5.
5. *R. v. Sault Ste. Marie* [1978] 2 S.C.R 1299.

## 2. Section 42 Offences

### a) Section 42(1)

Section 42(1) is as follows:

> 42 (1) Every person who knowingly
>  (a) makes for sale or rental an infringing copy of a work or other subject-matter in which copyright subsists,
>  (b) sells or rents out, or by way of trade, exposes or offers for sale or rental,[6] an infringing copy of a work or other subject-matter in which copyright subsists,
>  (c) distributes infringing copies of a work or other subject-matter in which copyright subsists, either for the purpose of trade or to such an extent as to affect prejudicially the owner of the copyright,[7]
>  (d) by way of trade exhibits in public an infringing copy of a work or other subject-matter in which copyright subsists, or
>  (e) imports for sale or rental into Canada any infringing copy of a work or other subject-matter in which copyright subsists
> is guilty of an offence and liable
>  (f) on summary conviction, to a fine not exceeding 25,000 dollars or to imprisonment for a term not exceeding six months or to both, or
>  (g) on conviction on indictment, to a fine not exceeding one million dollars or to imprisonment for a term not exceeding five years or to both.
> (3) The court before which any proceedings under this section are taken may, on conviction, order that all copies of the work or other subject-matter that appear to it to be infringing copies, or all plates in the possession of the offender predominantly used for making infringing copies, be destroyed or delivered up to the owner of the copyright or otherwise dealt with as the court may think fit.
> (4) Proceedings by summary conviction in respect of an offence under this section may be instituted at any time within, but not later than, two years after the time when the offence was committed.
> (5) No person may be prosecuted under this section for importing a book or dealing with an imported book in the manner described in section 27.1.

The offences set out in subsections 42(1) relate to making, selling, distributing, exhibiting, importing, and otherwise dealing with infringing copies of

---

6. A mere invitation to treat is an offer to sell, see *R. v. Laurier Office Mart Inc.* (1994), 58 C.P.R. (3d) 403 (Ont. Ct. (Prov. Div.)), affirmed (1995) 63 C.P.R. (3d) 229 (Ont. Ct. (Gen. Div.)).
7. *R. v. J.P.M.* (1996), 67 C.P.R. (3d) 152 (N.S.C.A.).

any work or other subject-matter in which copyright subsists. The *Act* provides that "infringing" means

    (a)  in relation to a work in which copyright subsists, any copy, including any colorable imitation, made or dealt with in contravention of the *Act*,

    (b)  in relation to a performer's performance in respect of which copyright subsists, any fixation or copy of a fixation of it made or dealt with in contravention of the *Act*,

    (c)  in relation to a sound recording in respect of which copyright subsists, any copy of it made or dealt with in contravention of the *Act*, or

    (d)  in relation to a communication signal in respect of which copyright subsists, any fixation or copy of a fixation of it made or dealt with in contravention of the *Act*.

The definition includes a copy that is imported in the circumstances set out in paragraph 27(2)(e) and section 27.1 but does not otherwise include a copy made with the consent of the owner of the copyright in the country where the copy was made.[8]

Subsection 42(1) uses the word "knowingly" in describing the specific offences. As a result, the offences under paragraphs a) through e) are full *mens rea* offences.[9]

Subsection 53(2) which provides that a certificate of registration of copyright in a work is evidence that copyright subsists in the work, and that the person registered is the owner of the copyright, is applicable in criminal proceedings. However, certificates of registration registered subsequent to the date of the alleged offence by themselves may not be sufficient evidence.[10]

## b)  Subsection 42(2)

Subsection 42(2) is as follows:

    (2) Every person who knowingly

        (a)  makes or possesses any plate that is specifically designed or adapted for the purpose of making infringing copies of any work or other subject-matter in which copyright subsists, or

---

8.  Section 2.

9.  *R. v. Ghnaim* (1988), 28 C.P.R. (3d) 463 (Alberta Prov. Ct.), affirmed in part (1989), 32 C.P.R. (3d) 487 (Alberta C.A.); *R. v. Laurier Office Mart Inc.* (1994), 58 C.P.R. (3d) 403 (Ont. Ct. (Prov. Div.)), affirmed (1995), 63 C.P.R. (3d) 229 (Ont. Ct. (Gen. Div.)).

10.  *R. v. Laurier Office Mart Inc.* (1994), 58 C.P.R. (3d) (Ont. Ct. (Prov. Div.)) affirmed on appeal (1995), 63 C.P.R. (3d) 229 (Ont. Ct. (Gen. Div.)).

(b) for private profit causes to be performed in public, without the consent of the owner of the copyright, any work or other subject-matter in which copyright subsists
is guilty of an offence and liable

(c) on summary conviction, to a fine not exceeding 25,000 dollars or to imprisonment for a term not exceeding six months or to both, or

(d) on conviction on indictment, to a fine not exceeding one million dollars or to imprisonment for a term not exceeding five years or to both.

Subsection 42(2)(a) refers to the making or possession of any plate. Section 2 of the *Act* provides that "plate" includes

(a) any stereotype or other plate, stone, block, mould, matrix, transfer, or negative used or intended to be used for printing or reproducing copies of any work, and

(b) any matrix or other appliance used or intended to be used for making or reproducing sound recordings, performer's performances, or communication signals.

Subsection 42(2) uses the word "knowingly" in describing the specific offences. As a result, the offences under paragraphs a) through b) are full *mens rea* offences.[11]

## c) Penalties

The court is given a wide discretion as to the amount of the fine and the disposition of the plates and infringing copies. Regard must be had not only to the nature of the material but also to the purposes for which the infringing copies were made, including the fact that copies are made for commercial profit.[12]

## 3. Section 43 Offences

## a) Performance of a Dramatic or Operatic Work or Musical Work

Subsection 43(1) of the *Act* provides that any person who, without the written consent of the owner of the copyright or of the legal representative of the

---

11. *R. v. Ghnaim* (1988), 28 C.P.R. (3d) 463 (Alberta Prov. Ct.), affirmed in part (1989) 32 C.P.R. (3d) 487 (Alberta C.A.); *R. v. Laurier Office Mart Inc.* (1994), 58 C.P.R. (3d) 403 (Ont. Ct. (Prov. Div.)), affirmed (1995) 63 C.P.R. (3d) 229 (Ont. Ct. (Gen. Div.)).

12. *R. v. Ghnaim* (1988), 28 C.P.R. (3d) 463 (Alberta Prov. Ct.), affirmed in part 32 C.P.R. (3d) 487 (Alberta C.A.).

owner, knowingly performs or causes to be performed in public and for private profit the whole or any part, constituting an infringement, of any dramatic or operatic work or musical composition in which copyright subsists in Canada is guilty of an offence and liable on summary conviction to a fine not exceeding 250 dollars.[13] In the case of a second or subsequent offence, the accused is subject to either that fine or to imprisonment for a term not exceeding two months or to both. As the subsection uses the word "knowingly" in describing the offence it is necessary to show *mens rea*.

### b) Change or Suppression of Title or Author's Name

Subsection 43(2) of the *Act* provides that any person who makes or causes to be made any change in or suppression of the title, or the name of the author, of any dramatic or operatic work or musical composition in which copyright subsists in Canada, or who makes or causes to be made any change in the work or composition itself without the written consent of the author or of his legal representative, in order that the work or composition may be performed in whole or in part in public for private profit, is guilty of an offence and liable on summary conviction to a fine not exceeding 500 dollars and, in the case of a second or subsequent offence, either to that fine or to imprisonment for a term not exceeding four months or to both.

The subsection does not use the word "knowingly" and is a strict liability offence where *mens rea* does not have to be proved.[14]

### 4. Criminal Code

Section 380 of the *Criminal Code*[15] provides that everyone who, by deceit, falsehood, or other fraudulent means, defrauds the public or any person of any property, money or valuable security is guilty of an indictable offence or an offence punishable on summary conviction where the value of the subject matter of the offence does not exceed $1,000.00. If the conduct of an accused relating to copyright is contrary to the provisions of the Criminal Code they may be prosecuted under the Code.[16]

---

13. *National Breweries v. Paradis*, [1925] S.C.R. 566, [1925] 3 D.L.R. 875 (S.C.C.).
14. *R. v. Sault Ste. Marie* [1978] 2 S.C.R 1299 (S.C.C.).
15. R.S.C. 1985. c. C-46.
16. *R. v. Adelphi Book Store Limited* (1972), 7 C.P.R. (2d) 166 (Sask. C.A.).

# CHAPTER
# 32

# Copyright Board and Collective Administration of Rights

# 1. The Copyright Board

The Copyright Board consists of not more than five members, including a chairman and a vice-chairman, who are appointed by the Governor in Council. The chairman must be a judge, either sitting or retired, of a superior, county, or district court. Each member of the Board holds office for a term not exceeding five years. A member of the Board is eligible to be re-appointed once only.[1]

# 2. Jurisdiction

The Copyright Board is an economic regulatory body empowered to establish, either mandatorily or at the request of an interested party, the royalties to be paid for the use of copyrighted works, when the administration of such copyright is entrusted to a collective-administration society. The Board also has the right to supervise agreements between users and licensing bodies and issues licences when the copyright owner cannot be located.

The specific responsibilities of the Copyright Board under the *Copyright Act* are to

a) oversee the collective administration of performing rights and the communication to the public by telecommunication of musical works, dramatico-musical works, performers performances of such works, or sound recordings embodying such works;[2]
b) oversee the collective administration of copyright under sections 3, 15, 18, and 21 of the *Act*;
c) oversee the collective administration of royalties to be paid by retransmitters[3] or educational institutions;[4]
d) set levies for the private copying of recorded musical works;[5]
e) rule on applications by persons who wish to obtain a licence to use a published work, a fixation of a performer's performance, a published sound recording, or a fixation of a communication signal where the owner of the copyright in the work cannot be found;[6]

---

1. Section 66.
2. Sections 67 to 68.2.
3. Paragraph 31(2)(d).
4. Subsection 29.6(2), 29.7(2) or (3).
5. Sections 79–88.
6. Section 77.

f) examine, at the request of the Commissioner of Competition, an agreement between a Collective Society[7] and a user that has been filed with the Board, where the Commissioner considers that an agreement is contrary to the public interest;[8]

g) determine the amount of the compensation for acts done with respect to such rights, the *Act* extends retrospective protection to for works which may not have been protected previously, when a country becomes a Berne Convention country or a WTO member.[9]

## 3. The Powers of the Copyright Board

The Copyright Board may engage on a temporary basis the services of persons having technical or specialized knowledge to advise and assist in the performance of its duties.[10]

The Copyright Board has, with respect to the attendance, swearing, and examination of witnesses, the production and inspection of documents, the enforcement of its decisions and other matters necessary or proper for the due exercise of its jurisdiction, all the powers, rights, and privileges as are vested in a superior court of record.[11]

The Copyright Board may, on application, make an interim decision[12] including the power to revise the period during which interim decision is in force.[13]

The Board can make an initial determination of the facts and law applicable as to whether a proposed statement of royalties is within the terms of the *Act*.[14]

A decision of the Copyright Board respecting royalties or their related terms and conditions that is made under subsection 68(3), sections 68.1 or 70.15, or subsections 70.2(2), 70.6(1), 73(1), or 83(8) of the *Act* may, on

---

7. Section 2.
8. Subsection 70.5 and 70.6.
9. Section 78.
10. Subsection 66.4(3).
11. Subsection 66.7(1).
12. Section 66.51.
13. *Performing Rights Organization of Canada Ltd. v. Canadian Broadcasting Corporation* (1986), 7 C.P.R.. (3d) 433 (F.C.A.).
14. *Canadian Cable Television Assn. v. Canada (Copyright Board)* (1991), 34 C.P.R. (3d) 521 (F.C.A.); *CTV Television Network Ltd. v. Canada (Copyright Appeal Board)* (1993), 46 C.P.R. (3d) 343 (F.C.A.), leave to Appeal to the S.C.C. refused (1993), 51 C.P.R. (3d), v. (note) (S.C.C.).

application, be varied by the Board if, in its opinion, there has been a material change in circumstances since the decision was made.[15]

Any decision of the Copyright Board may, for the purposes of its enforcement, be made an order of the Federal Court or of any superior court and is enforceable in the same manner as an order thereof.[16] To make a decision of the Board an order of a court, the usual practice and procedure of the court in such matters may be followed or a certified copy of the decision may be filed with the registrar of the court and thereafter the decision becomes an order of the court.[17]

Independently of any other provision of the *Act* relating to the distribution or publication of information or documents by the Copyright Board, the Board may at any time cause to be distributed or published, in any manner and on any terms and conditions that it sees fit, any notice that it sees fit to be distributed or published.[18]

The Copyright Board shall conduct such studies concerning its powers as are requested by the Minister.[19] In addition, the Board must, not later than August 31 in each year, submit to the Governor in Council through the Minister an annual report describing briefly the applications made to the Board, the Board's decisions, and any other matter that the Board considers relevant.[20]

The Copyright Board, with the approval of the Governor in Council, may make regulations governing:

a) the practice and procedure in respect of the Board's hearings, including the number of members that constitutes a quorum;
b) the time and manner in which applications and notices must be made or given;
c) the establishment of forms for the making or giving of applications and notices; and
d) the carrying out of the work of the Board, the management of its internal affairs and the duties of its officers and employees.[21]

To date the Copyright Board has yet to implement any formal rules of procedure pursuant to its power to make regulations.

---

15. Section 66.52.
16. Subsection 66.7(2).
17. Subsection 66.7(3).
18. Section 66.71.
19. Section 66.8.
20. Section. 66.9.
21. Section 66.6. Board also has power to make regulations under subsections 29.9(2), 68.1(3), and 68.1(3) of the *Act*.

The Governor in Council may make regulations issuing policy directions to the Copyright Board and establishing general criteria to be applied by the Board or to which the Board must have regard

(a) in establishing fair and equitable royalties to be paid pursuant to the *Act*; and

(b) in rendering its decisions in any matter within its jurisdiction.[22]

To date the Governor in Council has not passed regulations under this section. Under former subsection 70.63(3) regulations were passed establishing the criteria to be applied in establishing the manner of determining royalties for retransmission rights.[23]

## 4. Collective Administration of Performing Rights and Communication Rights

### a) Background

Performing Right Societies have licensed the right to perform copyrighted works publicly for many years. Performing Right Society in England, the American Society of Composers, Authors, and Publishers (known as ASCAP) in the United States and the Canadian Performing Right Society engaged in such licensing.

The Society of Composers, Authors, and Music Publishers of Canada (SOCAN) is the successor of the Canadian Performing Right Society. SOCAN is a not-for-profit corporation which is part of a worldwide network of similar societies administrating similar repertoires. SOCAN has filed and continues to file numerous tariffs.

In 1993,[24] the *Act* was amended to reflect the existence of specific collectives granting licenses for the communication of works to the public by telecommunication.[25] The communication of works to the public by telecommunication was added to the rights collectively administered by performing rights societies.

In 1997, the *Act* was amended to expand the rights subject to collective administration to include performer's performances of works and sound

---

22. Section 66.91.
23. *Retransmission Royalties Criteria Regulations*, SOR/91–690.
24. S. C. 1993, c. 23, referred to as the Socan Amendment.
25. S. C. 1993, c. 23, s. 3.

recordings embodying such works.[26] Specific collectives were established to administer the performers' and sound recording makers' right to equitable remuneration for the performance in public or the communication to the public by telecommunication of sound recordings.[27]

## b)  Performing Rights and Communication Rights Societies

In order to take part in the collective administration of performing rights and of communication rights, a society must satisfy the criteria set out in the *Act*. First, they must come within the definition of "collective society" which is as follows:

> "collective society" means a society, association or corporation that carries on the business of collective administration of copyright or of the remuneration right conferred by section 19 or 81 for the benefit of those who, by assignment, grant of licence, appointment of it as their agent or otherwise, authorize it to act on their behalf in relation to that collective administration, and
>
> (a) operates a licensing scheme, applicable in relation to a repertoire of works, performer's performances, sound recordings or communication signals of more than one author, performer, sound recording maker, or broadcaster, pursuant to which the society, association, or corporation sets out classes of uses that it agrees to authorize under this *Act*, and the royalties and terms and conditions on which it agrees to authorize those classes of uses, or
>
> (b) carries on the business of collecting and distributing royalties or levies payable pursuant to this *Act*.

Second, the collective society must carry on:

(a) the business of granting licenses or collecting royalties for the performance in public of musical works, dramatico-musical works, performer's performances of such works, or sound recordings embodying such works, or

(b) the business of granting licenses or collecting royalties for the communication to the public by telecommunication of musical works, dramatico-musical works, performer's performances of such works, or sound recordings embodying such works, other than the communication of

---

26.  *An Act to amend the Copyright Act* S.C. 1997, c.24.
27.  Section 19.

musical works or dramatico-musical works in the manner described in subsection 31(2).[28]

A collective society must also answer within a reasonable time all reasonable requests from the public for information about its repertoire of works, performer's performances, or sound recordings that are in current use.[29]

### i) Filing of Proposed Tariffs

A collective society must, on or before the March 31 immediately before the date when its last tariff approved expires, file with the Copyright Board a proposed tariff, in both official languages, of all royalties to be collected by the collective society.[30] A proposed tariff must provide that the royalties are to be effective for periods of one or more calendar years.[31]

As soon as practicable after the receipt of a proposed tariff, the Copyright Board must publish it in the Canada Gazette and give notice that, within 60 days after the publication of the tariff, prospective users or their representatives may file written objections to the tariff with the Board.[32]

Where a proposed tariff is not filed with respect to the work, performer's performance or sound recording in question, no action may be commenced by a collective society for infringement of the applicable rights or the recovery of royalties referred to in section 19 without the written consent of the Minister.[33]

Where a collective society files a proposed tariff any person entitled to perform in public or communicate to the public by telecommunication those works, performer's performances or sound recordings pursuant to the previous tariff may do so, even though the royalties set out in the tariff have ceased to be in effect. In addition, the collective society may collect the royalties in accordance with the previous tariff until the proposed tariff is approved.[34]

### ii) Overseeing the Proposed Tariffs

After a proposed tariff has been filed and published in the Canada Gazette, the Copyright Board must, as soon as practicable, consider the tariff and

---

28. Section 29.7 .
29. Section 67.
30. Subsection 67.1(1).
31. Subsection 67.1 (3).
32. Subsection 67.1 (5).
33. Subsection 67.1 (4) and see *Composers, Authors and Publishers Association of Canada Ltd.* v. *Maple Leaf Broadcasting Co. Ltd.*, [1953] Ex. C.R. 130, [1954] S.C.R. 624.
34. Subsection 68.2 (3).

any objections filed by prospective users or their representatives or raised by the Board. The Board then sends to the collective society who filed the tariff a copy of the objections to allow it to reply and sends to the persons who filed the objections a copy of any reply thereto.[35]

The Copyright Board must certify the tariffs as approved, with such alterations to the royalties and to the terms and conditions related thereto as the Board considers necessary, having regard to any objections to the tariffs which have been filed.[36]

The Board regulates the balance of market power between copyright owners and users.[37] The mandate of the Board is to set tariffs for the use of the rights in issue which have a reasonable and suitable or rational basis.

The Board may change or alter a formula previously used for fixing royalties as this is incidental to exercising its statutory discretion.[38] However, the Board must not act on the basis of irrelevant considerations or pursue consistency at the expense of the merits of an individual case.[39]

It is reasonable and necessary for the Board to base the rates for annual licenses on the income or a percentage thereof of the licensees, which income reflects to a greater or lesser degree the use by the licensee of the works in issue and the number of persons who would hear the performances of the licensees' works. In the case of broadcasting stations, the rates for annual licences may be fixed as a percentage of their gross revenue.[40]

The Board must publish the approved tariffs in the Canada Gazette as soon as practicable and send a copy of each approved tariff, together with the reasons for the Board's decision, to each collective society that filed a proposed tariff and to any person who filed an objection.[41]

---

35. Subsection 68(1).
36. Subsection 68(3).
37. *Performing Rights Organization of Can. Ltd. v. C.B.C.* (1986), 7 C.P.R. (3d) 433 (F.C.A.), *Canadian Association of Broadcasters v. SOCAN* (1994), 58 C.P.R. (3d) 190 (F.C.A.).
38. *Performing Rights Organization of Can. Ltd. v. C.B.C.* (1986), 7 C.P.R. (3d) 433 (F.C.A.); *Composers, Authors and Publishers Association of Canada Ltd. v. Maple Leaf Broadcasting Co. Ltd.,* [1953] Ex. C.R. 130, [1954] S.C.R. 624.
39. *Canadian Broadcasting Corporation v. Copyright Appeal Board* (1990), 30 C.P.R. (3d) 270 (F.C.A.).
40. *Maple Leaf Broadcasting Co. Ltd. v. Composers, Authors and Publishers Association of Canada Ltd.* (1953), 18 C.P.R. 1 (Ex. Ct.), [1954] S.C.R. 624, 21 C.P.R. 45 (S.C.C). This includes approving or prescribing the manner in which the amount of gross revenue is to be ascertained or verified including an examination of the licensee's books and accounts by the representatives of the performing rights society.
41. Subsection 68(4).

## c) Equitable Remuneration for Performers and Makers of Sound Recordings

Tariffs relating to equitable remuneration[42] are different from the tariffs relating to performing or communication rights in that they are not based on a licence. The right to receive equitable remuneration is a right of remuneration which must be exercised collectively.

In examining a proposed tariff relating to equitable remuneration the Copyright Board must ensure that

   (i) the tariff applies only in respect of performer's performances and sound recordings for which the points of attachment or connecting factors prescribed by subsections 20(1) and (2) of the *Act* are satisfied,[43]
  (ii) the tariff does not, because of linguistic and content requirements of Canada's broadcasting policy set out in section 3 of the *Broadcasting Act*, place some users that are subject to that *Act* at a greater financial disadvantage than others, and
 (iii) the payment of royalties by users pursuant to section 19 will be made in a single payment.[44]

The Copyright Board is also authorized to take into account any factor that it considers appropriate.[45]

Notwithstanding any tariffs approved by the Copyright Board relating to equitable remuneration, section 68.1 of the *Act* proscribes the royalties payable by certain systems as follows:

   (a) wireless transmission systems,[46] except community systems and public transmission systems, shall pay royalties for each year of $100 on the first 1.25 million dollars of annual advertising revenues[47] and 100 per cent of the royalties set out in the approved tariff on any portion of annual revenues exceeding 1.25 million dollars for that year;

---

42. See Chapter 19.
43. See Chapter 19 and see the limitations set out in regulation *Limitation of the Right to Equitable Remuneration of Certain Rome Convention Countries Statement*, SOR/99–143.
44. Subsection 68(2)(a).
45. Subsection 68(2)(b). See Chapter 19, the right of remuneration is not available for American recordings.
46. See *Definition of "Wireless Transmission System"* Regulations, SOR/98–307 which defines "wireless transmission systems."
47. See *Regulations Defining "Advertising Revenues,"* SOR/98–447.

(b) community systems shall pay royalties of $100 in respect of each year.[48]

The Copyright Board shall, in certifying a tariff as approved, ensure that there is a preferential royalty rate for small cable transmission systems.[49]

## d) The Effect of Fixing Royalties

Without prejudice to any other remedies available to it, a collective society may, for the period specified in its approved tariff, collect the royalties specified in the tariff.[50] If the royalties are not paid, the collective society may recover them in a court of competent jurisdiction,[51] including the Federal Court.[52]

No proceedings may be brought for the infringement of the right to perform in public or the right to communicate to the public by telecommunication, referred to in section 3 of the *Act*, or the recovery of royalties referred to in section 19 of the *Act* against a person who has paid or offered to pay the royalties specified in an approved tariff.[53]

## e) Radio Performances in Places Other Than Theatres

Subsection 69(2) provides that in respect of public performances by means of any radio receiving set in any place other than a theatre that is ordinarily and regularly used for entertainments to which an admission charge is made, no royalties shall be collectable from the owner or user of the radio receiving set, but the Copyright Board shall, in so far as possible, provide for the collection in advance from radio broadcasting stations of royalties appropriate to the conditions produced by the provisions of the subsection and shall fix the amount of the same.[54]

---

48. Subsection 68.1 (1). See *Re Socan/NRCC Statement of Royalties (Commercial Radio) 2003 to 2007* (2005), 44 C.P.R. (4th) 40 (Copyright Board).
49. Subsection 68.1 (4) and see *Definition of "Small Cable Transmission System" Regulations*, SOR/94–755 which defines "small cable transmission systems."
50. Once a tariff is approved it is no longer open to a defendant to dispute its validity, *Society of Composers, Authors and Music Publishers of Canada v. Maple Leaf Sports & Entertainment Ltd* (2005), 40 C.P.R. (4th) 28 (F.C.).
51. Subsection 68.2 (1).
52. Section 29.7 .
53. Subsection 68.2 (2).
54. See *Vigneux et al. v. Canadian Performing Right Society Ltd.* [1942] Ex. C.R. 129, [1943] S.C.R. 348, 2 C.P.R. 251 (S.C.C), (1943), 4 C.P.R. 65 (P.C.).

The royalty is determined by the Board on its own initiative not on the basis of a proposed tariff. In fixing royalties, the Board must take into account all expenses of collection and other outlays, if any, saved or savable by, for or on behalf of the owner of the copyright or performing right concerned or his agents, in consequence of subsection 69(2).[55]

## 5. The General Regime-Collective Administration in Relation to Rights under Sections 3, 15, 18, and 21

### a) Background

In 1988, the *Act* was amended to allow collectives to operate licensing schemes relating to any of the acts mentioned in section 3 of the *Act*.[56] In 1997, new collective societies were authorized to collectively administer the new rights relating to performer's performances under section 15, sound recordings under section 18, and communication signals under section 21.[57]

The Copyright Board refers to the regime applicable to these collective societies as the general regime. The general regime applies to all of the collective societies that are not subject to the specific regimes set out in the *Act*.

### b) General Regime Collective Societies

The *Act* contains two definitions relating to general regime collective societies.

> "collective society" means a society, association or corporation that carries on the business of collective administration of copyright or of the remuneration right conferred by section 19 or 81 for the benefit of those who, by assignment, grant of licence, appointment of it as their agent or otherwise, authorize it to act on their behalf in relation to that collective administration, and
>
> (a) operates a licensing scheme, applicable in relation to a repertoire of works, performer's performances, sound recordings, or communication signals of more than one author, performer, sound recording maker, or broadcaster, pursuant to which the society, association, or corporation sets out classes of uses that it agrees to authorize under this *Act*, and the royalties and terms and conditions on which it agrees to authorize those classes of uses, or

---

55. Subsection 69(3).

56. *An Act to amend the Copyright Act and other Acts in consequence thereof,* S.C. 1988, c. 15.

57. *An Act to amend the Copyright Act*, S.C. 1997, c.24 , section 46.

(b) carries on the business of collecting and distributing royalties or levies payable pursuant to this *Act*.[58]

The general regime applies to a collective society that operates

(a) a licensing scheme, applicable in relation to a repertoire of works of more than one author, pursuant to which the society sets out the classes of uses for which and the royalties and terms and conditions on which it agrees to authorize the doing of an act mentioned in section 3 in respect of those works;

(a.1) a licensing scheme, applicable in relation to a repertoire of performer's performances of more than one performer, pursuant to which the society sets out the classes of uses for which and the royalties and terms and conditions on which it agrees to authorize the doing of an act mentioned in section 15 in respect of those performer's performances;

(b) a licensing scheme, applicable in relation to a repertoire of sound recordings of more than one maker, pursuant to which the society sets out the classes of uses for which and the royalties and terms and conditions on which it agrees to authorize the doing of an act mentioned in section 18 in respect of those sound recordings; or

(c) a licensing scheme, applicable in relation to a repertoire of communication signals of more than one broadcaster, pursuant to which the society sets out the classes of uses for which and the royalties and terms and conditions on which it agrees to authorize the doing of an act mentioned in section 21 in respect of those communication signals.[59]

A collective society subject to the general regime must answer within a reasonable time all reasonable requests from the public for information about its repertoire of works, performer's performances, sound recordings, or communication signals.[60]

## c) Tariff or Agreement

A collective society may, for the purpose of setting out by license, the royalties and terms and conditions relating to classes of uses, either file a proposed tariff with the Copyright Board or enter into agreements with users.[61]

---

58. Section 2.
59. Section 70.1.
60. Section 70.11.
61. Section 70.12.

Where a collective society and users are unable to agree on the royalties or on their related terms and conditions, either of them or a representative of either may, after giving notice to the other, apply to the Board to fix the royalties and their related terms and conditions.[62] The Board will then commence the process of fixing the royalties but the Board will not proceed with the application where a notice is filed with the Board that an agreement touching the matters in issue has been reached.[63]

Where any royalties are fixed for a specific period by the Board, the person concerned may, during that period, subject to the related terms and conditions fixed by the Board and to the terms and conditions set out in the scheme and on paying or offering to pay the royalties, do the act with respect to which the royalties and their related terms and conditions are fixed. The collective society may, without prejudice to any other remedies available to it, collect the royalties or, in default of their payment, recover them in a court of competent jurisdiction.[64]

### d) Filing of Proposed Tariffs

Each collective society subject to the general regime shall, on or before the March 31 immediately before the date when its last tariff approved pursuant to subsection 70.15(1) expires, file with the Board a proposed tariff, in both official languages, of royalties to be collected by the collective society.[65] A proposed tariff must provide that the royalties are to be effective for periods of one or more calendar years.[66]

The procedures for the approval and the consideration of the proposed tariff are similar to those applied to the tariffs for performing and communication rights[67] subject to two exceptions. First, section 70.16 provides that independently of any other provision of the *Act*, the Board must notify persons affected by the proposed tariff by distributing or publishing a specific notice. Second, an agreement between a collective society and a person authorized to do an act mentioned in section 3, 15, 18, or 21, as the case may be, takes precedence over an approved tariff, if the agreement is in effect during the period covered by the approved tariff.[68]

Subject to the provisions of any agreement entered into with a collective society, no proceedings may be brought for the infringement of a right

---

62. Section 70.2.
63. Section 70.3.
64. Section 70.4.
65. Subsection 70.13 (1).
66. Subsection 70.14 and subsection 67.1 (3).
67. Subsection 70.14 and see part 4 of this chapter.
68. Section 70.191.

referred to in section 3, 15, 18, or 21 against a person who has paid or offered to pay the royalties specified in an approved tariff.[69]

Subject to the provisions of any agreement entered into with a collective society, where a collective society files a proposed tariff in accordance with section 70.13 of the *Act*, any person authorized by the collective society to do an act referred to in section 3, 15, 18, or 21, as the case may be, pursuant to the previous tariff may do so, even though the royalties set out therein have ceased to be in effect, and the collective society may collect the royalties in accordance with the previous tariff, until the proposed tariff is approved.[70]

## 6. Examination of Agreements

An agreement between a collective society and a person authorized to do an act mentioned in section 3, 15, 18, or 21 may be potentially contrary to the provisions of section 45 of the *Competition Act*,[71] which deals with agreements or arrangements which restrain or injure competition unduly. A collective society or the user may file a copy of an agreement with the Board within fifteen days after it is concluded[72] and section 45 of the *Competition Act* does not apply in respect of any royalties or related terms and conditions arising under the filed agreement.[73]

The Commissioner of Competition may have access to the copy of the agreement which has been filed.[74] Where the Commissioner considers that an agreement is contrary to the public interest, the Commissioner may, after advising the parties concerned, request the Board to examine the agreement.[75]

The Board must, as soon as practicable, consider the request to examine the agreement and may, after giving the Commissioner and the parties concerned an opportunity to present their arguments, alter the royalties and any related terms and conditions arising under the agreement.[76] As soon as practicable after rendering its decision, the Board shall send a copy of the decision together with any reasons to the parties concerned and to the Commissioner.[77]

---

69. Subsection 70.17.
70. Subsection 70.18.
71. R.S.C. 1985, c. C-34 as amended.
72. Subsection 70.5(2).
73. Subsection 70.5(3).
74. Subsection 70.5(4).
75. Subsection 70.5(5).
76. Subsection 70.6(1).
77. Subsection 70.6(2).

# 7. The Retransmission Regime[78]

## a) Background

Before 1988, the retransmissions of works through the use of co-axial cables was not subject to the *Act*.[79] Pursuant to the Canada-United States Free Trade Agreement, Canada agreed to amend the *Act* to provide to a copyright holder a right of equitable and non-discriminatory remuneration for any retransmission to the public of the copyright holder's program where the original transmission of the program was carried in distant signals intended for free, over-the-air reception by the general public.[80]

As a result, the *Act* was amended and all transmission of signs, signals, writing, images, sounds, or intelligence of any nature by wire, radio, visual, optical, or other electro-magnetic system are subject to the control of the copyright owner.[81] The Board was given jurisdiction to oversee the collective administration of royalties to be paid by retransmitters pursuant to a universal, statutory license scheme, which is referred to as the Retransmission regime.

## b) Retransmission Collective Societies

A collective society subject to the retransmission regime must come within the definition of "collective society" as discussed above in relation to the general regime.

The retransmission regime only applies to collective societies which carry on the business of collecting royalties for:

a) the retransmission of a distant signal,[82]

b) at the expiration of one year after their making, the making, at the time of its communication to the public by telecommunication, a single copy of a news program, or a news commentary program, excluding documentaries, for the purposes of performing the copy for the students of the educational institution for educational or training purposes;[83]

c) performing the copy in public, at any time or times after one year of the making of a copy, before an audience consisting primarily of students

---

78. See Chapter 29, part 10.
79. *Canadian Admiral Corporation Ltd.* v. *Rediffusion Inc. et al.* [1954] Ex. C.R. 382, 20 C.P.R. 75.
80. Sections 2005 and 2006.
81. See the section 2 definition of "telecommunication" and section 2.4.
82. Subsection 31(2)(d).
83. Subsection 29.6(1)(a), subsection 29.6 (2).

of the educational institution on its premises for educational or training purposes;[84]

d) making a single copy of a work or other subject-matter at the time that
it is communicated to the public by telecommunication and keeping
the copy for more than 30 days to decide whether to perform the copy
for educational or training purposes or to perform it before an audience consisting primarily of students of the educational institution on
its premises for educational or training purposes.[85]

Each collective society that carries on the business of collecting royalties
referred to in subsection 29.6(2), 29.7(2), or (3) or paragraph 31(2)(d) shall
file with the Board a proposed tariff, but no other person may file any such
tariff.[86]

Section 31 of the *Act* sets out the scheme by which royalties are paid by
retransmitters to copyright owners with respect to the retransmission of their
works by cable retransmission. The amount of the royalties is fixed by the
Board. No remuneration is payable with respect to the retransmission of a
"local signal."[87]

The regime has been described by the Board as a universal, statutory
license scheme. Any retransmitter who meets the conditions set out in subsection 31(2) of the *Act* acquires the retransmission right for all works embedded in the signals he or she retransmits. The license is free with respect to
local signals; distant signals command the payment of royalties set by the
Board. The amount of royalties is set at a level sufficient to compensate all
works carried on distant signals. Conversely, all copyright owners in all
works carried on a distant signal are entitled to a share of the remuneration
as long as they comply with the *Act*. They can get paid in one of two ways.
The vast majority have formed collective societies that filed proposed statements of royalties, thereby becoming entitled to collect from retransmitters a
share of the royalties, which the societies then distribute to their members.
Rights owners who have not joined a collective (sometimes referred to as
"orphans") can avail themselves of subsection 76(1) of the *Act* and claim their
share from one of the societies targeted in the tariffs.[88]

Sections 29.6, 29.7, and 29.9 of the *Act* deal specifically with the right of
educational institutions to make copies of and perform radio and television
programs in the circumstances described in those sections. The regime as it

---

84. Subsection 29.6(1)(b), subsection 29.6 (2).
85. Section 29.7 .
86. Section 29.7 .
87. Section 29.7 .
88. *Re Societe des Auteurs, Recherchistes, Documentalistes et Compositeurs designation application*
(1999), 86 C.P.R. (3d) 481 (Copyright Board); *FWS Joint Sports Claimants Inc. v. Border
Broadcasters Inc.* (2001), 16 C.P.R. (4th) 61 (F.C.A.).

applies to these rights is a universal, statutory license scheme. Anyone owning rights in the program that is copied and performed, including those who have not joined a collective society, is entitled to a share of the remuneration.[89]

## c) Filing of Proposed Tariffs

A collective society subject to retransmission regime must, on or before the March 31 immediately before the date when its last approved tariff ceases to be effective, file with the Board a proposed tariff.[90] The tariff must provide that the royalties are to be effective for periods of one or more calendar years.[91]

The procedures for the approval and the consideration of proposed tariffs are similar to those applied to the tariffs for performing and communication rights. However, the Board, in establishing a manner of determining royalties or in apportioning them, must not discriminate between owners of copyright on the ground of their nationality or residence[92] and must ensure that there is a preferential rate for small retransmission systems.[93]

Without prejudice to any other remedies available to it, a collective society may, for the period specified in its approved tariff, collect the royalties specified in the tariff and, in default of their payment, recover them in a court of competent jurisdiction.[94]

## d) Claims by Non-Members

Royalty claimants who are not members of a collective society are entitled to applicable royalties. Section 76 provides that an owner of copyright who does not authorize a collective society to collect, for that person's benefit, royalties during a period when an approved tariff that is applicable to that kind of work is effective, is entitled to be paid those royalties by the collective society that is designated by the Board, of its own motion or on application, subject to the same conditions as those to which a person who has so authorized that collective society is subject.[95] The right to make a claim under section 76 is

---

89. *Re ERCC Statement of Royalties, 1999-2002.* (2002), 23 C.P.R. (4th) 352 (Copyright Board) and see Chapter 29, part 3.
90. Subsection 71(2). See subsection 71 (3) relating to the filing of a first proposed tariff.
91. Subsection 71(4).
92. Subsection 73(2).
93. Section 74 and see Regulation SOR/94–755, which defines a "small retransmission system."
94. Section 75.
95. See *Re Societe des Auteurs, Recherchistes, Documentalistes et Compositeurs designation application* (1999), 86 C.P.R. (3d) 481 (Copyright Board).

the only remedy for the payment of royalties to which the owner of the copyright is entitled.[96]

The Copyright Board has by regulation determined that claims to entitlement under section 76 must be exercised within two years after the end of the calendar year in which the retransmission occurred.[97]

## 8. Private Copying

Part VIII to the *Act* which deals with private copying addresses the practical inability of rights-holders to enforce their reproduction rights in the context of mass infringement resulting from the accelerating access to blank media.[98]

Part VIII was enacted: (1) to legalize private copying (but not pirating, which would be copying for resale); (2) to provide a system for the payment of royalties to those with copyrights to be imposed by way of levies on importers and manufacturers of blank tapes when sold by them; (3) to delegate to the Copyright Board the power to certify tariffs setting the levies on the sale of the blank tapes by importers and manufacturers.[99]

The "eligible performer" and "eligible maker" are entitled to remuneration. "Eligible performer" means the performer of a performer's performance of a musical work, if the performer's performance is embodied in a sound recording and

   (a)  both the following two conditions are met:
      (i)  the performer was, at the date of the first fixation of the sound recording, a Canadian citizen or permanent resident within the meaning of subsection 2(1) of the *Immigration and Refugee Protection Act*, and
      (ii)  copyright subsists in Canada in the performer's performance, or
   (b)  the performer was, at the date of the first fixation of the sound recording, a citizen, subject or permanent resident of a country referred to in a statement published under section 85.

96. Subsection 76(3).
97. Subsection 76(4); and see *Regulations Establishing the Period Within Which Owners of Copyright not Represented by Collective Societies Can Claim Retransmission Royalties*, SOR/97–164.
98. *Canadian Private Copying Collective v. Canadian Storage Media Alliance*, 2004 FCA 424, 36 C.P.R. (4th) 289 (F.C.A.).
99. *The Evangelical Fellowship of Canada v. Canadian Music Rights Agency* (1999), 1 C.P.R. (4th) 497 (F.C.A.).

An "eligible maker" means a maker of a sound recording that embodies a musical work, if

 (a) both the following two conditions are met:
  (i) the maker, at the date of that first fixation, if a corporation had its headquarters in Canada or, if a natural person was a Canadian citizen or permanent resident within the meaning of subsection 2(1) of the *Immigration and Refugee Protection Act*, and
  (ii) copyright subsists in Canada in the sound recording, or
 (b) the maker, at the date of that first fixation, if a corporation, had its headquarters in a country referred to in a statement published under section 85 or, if a natural person was a citizen, subject, or permanent resident of such a country.

Section 85 provides that only non-Canadian performers and makers entitled to remuneration under the Private Copying scheme are those from countries that grant Canadian citizens or corporations similar reciprocal rights under their national copyright legislation.[100]

Section 80 provides that the act of reproducing all or any substantial part of a musical work embodied in a sound recording, a performer's performance of a musical work embodied in a sound recording, or a sound recording in which a musical work or a performer's performance of a musical work is embodied unto an audio recording medium for the private use of the person who makes the copy, does not constitute an infringement of copyright.

"Audio recording medium" means a recording medium, regardless of its material form, onto which a sound recording may be reproduced and that is of a kind ordinarily used by individual consumers for that purpose, excluding any prescribed kind of recording medium. "Blank audio recording medium" means (a) an audio recording medium onto which no sounds have ever been fixed, and (b) any other prescribed audio recording medium.[101]

Section 81 provides that eligible authors, performers, and makers have a right to receive remuneration from the manufacturers and importers of blank audio recording media in respect of such reproduction. Section 83 provides that collective societies may file with the Copyright Board a proposed tariff for the benefit of eligible authors, performers, and makers authorizing it to act on their behalf.

Section 82 provides that every person who, for the purpose of trade, manufactures a blank audio recording medium in Canada or imports such a medium into Canada, is liable, subject to prescribed exceptions, to pay a levy to the collecting body on selling or otherwise disposing of the medium in

---

100. Section 85.
101. Section 79.

Canada and must keep statements of account of such activities. No levy is payable on a blank audio recording medium which is exported from Canada[102] or where the manufacturer or importer sells the medium to a society, association or corporation that represents persons with a perceptual disability.[103] The collecting body may, for the period specified in an approved tariff, collect the levies due under the tariff and, in default of payment, recover them in a court of competent jurisdiction.[104]

The Board must consider such proposed tariffs and objections thereto and establish the manner of determining the levies and such terms and conditions related to those levies as the Board considers appropriate.[105] In exercising its power, the Board must satisfy itself that the levies are fair and equitable, having regard to any prescribed criteria.[106]

Tariffs have been in place since 1999 although there have been many objections and challenges. A collective called the Canadian Private Copying Collective/Société Canadienne des Perception de la Copie Privée serves as a collecting body to receive revenues from the levy.

It is clear that that the Board has no legal authority to certify a tariff on digital audio recorders or on the memory permanently embedded in digital audio recorders.[107]

## 9. Owners of Copyright Who Cannot Be Found

An application may be made to the Board by a person who wishes to obtain a license to use a published work, a fixation of a performer's performance, a published sound recording, or a fixation of a communication signal where the owner of the copyright in the work cannot be found.[108] Where the Board is satisfied that the applicant has made reasonable efforts to locate the owner of the copyright and that the owner cannot be located, the Board may issue to the applicant a license to do an act mentioned in section 3, 15, 18, or 21, as the case may be.[109] Any license issued is non-exclusive and is subject to such

---

102. Subsection 82(2).
103. Section 86.
104. Section 88 and see *Canadian Private Copying Collective v. Amico Imaging Services Inc.* 2004 F.C. 469 affirmed 2004 FCA 412 (F.C.A.).
105. Subsection 82(8).
106. Section 29.7 .
107. Section 29.7 .
108. Section 77.
109. Section 77(1).

terms and conditions as the Board may establish.[110] In an appropriate case the Board can exercise its discretion to issue a retroactive license.[111]

## 10. Compensation for Acts Done Before Recognition of Copyright

The Copyright Board determines the amount of the compensation, under certain circumstances, for formerly unprotected acts in countries that later become a WTO member, a Rome Convention country or a treaty country.[112] The *Act* extends retrospective protection to works which may not have been protected previously, when a country becomes a Berne Convention country or a WTO member.[113] The *Act* contains procedures for protecting the rights of parties who relied on the absence of such rights and allows the copyright owner to terminate such rights on payment of compensation as is agreed to between the parties or, failing agreement, as is determined by the Board.[114]

---

110. Section 77(2).
111. *Re Breakthrough Films and Television* (2006), 53 C.P.R. (4th) 240 (Copyright Bd.).
112. Section 78 and section 2 definitions of these terms.
113. See subsection 5(1.01).
114. See sections 32.4, 32.5, 33, and 78.

CHAPTER

# 33

# Industrial Designs

# 1. Definition of a Design

The *Industrial Design Act* provides that "design" means features of shape, configuration, pattern, or ornament and any combination of those features that, in a finished article, appeal to and are judged solely by the eye.[1] The reference in the definition to "any combination of those features" makes it clear that a design may be made up of one or more of the features of shape, configuration, pattern, or ornament.

The definition is limited by section 5.1 of the *Act* which provides that no protection afforded by the *Act* extends to:

(a) features applied to a useful article[2] that are dictated solely by a utilitarian function of the article, or

(b) any method or principal of manufacture or construction.

As a result of section 5.1, protection cannot be obtained for a feature applied to an article that is dictated solely by a utilitarian function of the article. The limitation does not apply to ornamental non-functional features. In considering an application, the Commissioner of Patents considers the whole shape or configuration of the design as registrable (assuming that it has eye appeal) unless every feature is dictated solely by functional considerations, in which case the exclusion applies even though the article might also have eye appeal. If any feature goes beyond being dictated solely by function, this may entitle the shape as a whole to protection.[3]

## a) Shape and Configuration

The word "shape" suggests the external form of the article. "Configuration" suggests the arrangement by which the shape of a composite article is arrived at including the physical relationship of the components of the design to each other. Each word suggests something in three dimensions.

---

1. *Industrial Design Act* R.S.C. 1985 c.I-9 as amended section 2.
2. Section 2 of the *Industrial Design Act* provides that "useful article" means an article that has a utilitarian function and includes a model of any such article. "Article" means any thing that is made by hand, tool or machine; "utilitarian function" in respect of an article, means a function other than merely serving as a substrate or carrier for artistic or literary matter. These definitions are similar to those set out in the *Copyright Act*.
3. *Re LTI Corp. Industrial Design Application 1998-2446* (2003), 25 C.P.R. (4th) 256 (Patent Appeal Board and Commissioner of Patents) following *Amp Inc. v. Utilux Proprietary Limited* [1972] R.P.C. 103 (U.K.H.L.) and *Interlego AG v Tyco Industries Inc.* [1988] 3 W.L.R. 678 (P.C.).

## b) Pattern or Ornament

The use of the term "pattern" suggests the article is made up of repetitive elements which are all the same. To come within the definition, the ornamentation must only distinguish the appearance of the article, there is no requirement that it beautify the article.[4]

Color by itself is not the subject-matter of a design and is typically regarded as a "trade variant" which does not alter the identity of the design. In exceptional cases it is possible that the colors and their arrangement may form part of the design.[5]

## c) Finished Article

The words "in a finished article" in the definition of "design" refer to a physical embodiment divorcing the design from a mere scheme or preliminary conception of an idea.[6]

## d) Appeal to and Judged Solely by the Eye

To be protected under the *Act*, the design must appeal to and be judged solely by the eye. The definition requires that the design be reviewed from the standpoint of the informed consumer.[7] Normally unmagnified vision will be the appropriate reference.[8]

## e) Sets

Frequently, articles which feature the same design are sold as a set.[9] Cutlery or glassware are common examples. Protection under the *Act* can be obtained by filing a single application if:

> (a) all of the pieces are of the same general character;

---

4. *D.R.G. Inc. v. Datafile Limited* (1987), 18 C.P.R. (3d) 538 (F.C.T.D.), 35 C.P.R. (3d) 243 (F.C.A.).
5. *D.R.G. Inc. v. Datafile Limited* (1987) 18 C.P.R. (3d) 538 (F.C.T.D.), 35 C.P.R. (3d) 243 (F.C.A.).
6. *Milliken & Company et al. v. Interface Flooring Systems (Canada) Inc.* [1998] 3 F.C. 103, 83 C.P.R (3rd) 470 (F.C.T.D.), affirmed (2000), 5 C.P.R (4th) 209(F.C.A.).
7. *Gandy v. Canada (Commissioner of Patents)* (1980), 47 C.P.R. (2d) 109 (F.C.T.D.); *Rothbury International Inc. v. Canada (Minister of Industry)* (2004), 36 C.P.R. (4th) 203 (F.C.).
8. *Amp Incorporated v. Utilux Proprietary Limited* [1970] R.P.C. 397 (U.K.C.A.), [1972] R.P.C. 103 (U.K.H.L.).
9. Section 2 provides that "set" means a number of articles of the same general character ordinarily on sale together or intended to be used together, to each of which the same design or variants thereof are applied.

(b) the same design or variants[10] thereof is applied to each piece of the set;

(c) all of the articles in the set must normally be on sale together or intended to be used together.[11]

## f) Kits

A design which is applied to a finished article assembled from a kit[12] may be protected if the following conditions are met:

(a) all, or substantially all of the parts required to construct the article are sold together as a unit;

(b) the parts must assemble to create a finished article;

(c) the description in the application must refer to features in the completely assembled view; and

(d) the completely assembled view must be illustrated in the drawings or photographs.

## 2. Industrial Designs and Other Intellectual Property Rights

## a) Copyright

Sections 64 and 64.1 of the *Copyright Act*,[13] set out the rules for determining the extent of copyright protection available to designs applied to a useful article, potentially subject to protection under the *Industrial Designs Act*.

## b) Patents

A patent grants a monopoly during its term and gives to the patentee, for the term of the patent, the exclusive right, privilege, and liberty of making, constructing, and using the invention and selling it to others to be used.[14]

---

10. Section 2 provides that "variants" means designs applied to the same article or set and not differing substantially from one another.

11. Section 2.

12. Section 2 provides that "kit" means a complete or substantially complete number of parts that can be assembled to construct a finished article.

13. S.C.1988, c.15, s. 11 and see Chapter 18.

14. *Patent Act*, R.S.C. 1985, c. P-4, s. 42.

If an article is patentable, it may be concurrently protected by a patent registration and industrial design registration so long as the respective requirements of *The Patent Act* and *Industrial Design Act* are satisfied.[15]

## c) Trademarks

A distinguishing guise may be registered under the *Trade-marks Act*.[16] A "distinguishing guise" means a shaping of wares or their containers or mode of wrapping or packaging wares, the appearance of which is used for the purposes of distinguishing such wares or services from those of others. [17]

Registration as a design will not preclude the subsequent registration of the design as a distinguishing guise under the *Trade-marks Act* if it is otherwise registrable.[18]

## 3. Originality

It is well established that to be entitled to registration, a "design' must be original.[19] The *Act* does not state expressly what is required to be shown to establish originality but some direction is provided. First, in order to register a design, the applicant must deposit a declaration that the design was not, to the proprietor's knowledge, in use by any person other than the first proprietor at the time the design was adopted by the first proprietor.[20] Second, it is provided that the Minister shall register the design if the Minister finds that it is not identical with, or does not so closely resemble any other design already registered so as to be confounded therewith.[21] Finally, a certificate signed by the Minister, or the Commissioner of Patents or an officer, clerk, or employee of the Commissioner's office, is, in the absence of proof to the contrary, sufficient evidence of the originality of the design.[22]

---

15. *Werner Motors Co.* v. *Gamage Ltd* (1904), 21 R.P.C. 137, 621 (U.K.C.A.).
16. R.S.C. 1985, c.T-13, as amended, section 13.
17. See Chapter 2, part 2(d).
18. *WCC Containers Sales Ltd. et al.* v. *Haul-All Equipment Ltd.* (2003), 28 C.P.R. (4th) 175 (F.C.T.D.).
19. *Clatworthy & Son Ltd.* v. *Dale Display Fixtures Ltd.* [1929] S.C.R. 429 (S.C.C.).
20. Subsection 4(1) (b).
21. Subsection 6(1). The practice of the Industrial Design Office is set out in the *Industrial Design Office Practices*, Canadian Intellectual Property Office (Industrial Design Office) (Ottawa: Industry Canada, 2004) at section 6.6.
22. Subsection 7 (3); *Angelstone Ltd.* v. *Artistic Stone Ltd.* [1960] Ex. C.R. 286, 33 C.P.R. 155.

In order for a design to be original there must be some substantial difference between the new design and pre-existing designs.[23] The introduction or substitution of ordinary trade variants in a design, or a change in the mode of construction, is not sufficient to make a design original.[24]

Originality involves at least a spark of inspiration on the part of the designer either in creating an entirely new design or hitting upon a new use for an old one.[25] There must be an exercise of intellectual activity so as to originate or suggest for the first time, something which had not occurred to anyone before as to applying by some manual, mechanical, or chemical means some pattern, shape, or ornament to some special subject-matter to which it had not been applied before.[26]

In order to determine if a design is original, a purely visual assessment of the features of the design must be made. This is consistent with the definition of a "design" contained in the *Act*.[27] Whether a design is original is a question of fact that must be assessed in accordance with the nature and character of the article to which the design refers.[28]

Originality must also be judged in the context of the article to which the design is applied.[29] If there is little scope for adding design features, a small difference in additional features may be important.[30]

If the design is well –known, its application for a purpose analogous to that for which it was originally applied will not likely be sufficiently original for the purpose of the *Act*.[31] However, the new application of a well-known design to a different material, for a different purpose may be sufficiently original.[32]

It is not necessary that every part of a design be original. A combination of well-known designs or configurations may produce an original design.[33]

---

23. *Clatworthy & Son Ltd.* v. *Dale Display Fixtures Ltd.* [1929] S.C.R. 429 (S.C.C.); *Re Industrial Design Application No. 1996—0991* (2000), 5 C.P.R. (4th) 317 (Patent Appeal Bd); *Re Industrial Design Application No. 1997—0381* (2002), 21 C.P.R. (4th) 339 (Patent Appeal Bd.).

24. *Renwal Mfg. Co. Ltd.* v. *Reliable Toy Co. Ltd. et al.* [1949] Ex. C.R. 188, 9 C.P.R. 67 (Ex. Ct.); *Angelstone Ltd.* v. *Artistic Stone Ltd.* [1960] Ex. C.R. 286, 33 C.P.R. 155 (Ex. Ct.).

25. *Bata Industries Ltd.* v. *Warrington Inc* (1985), 5 C.P.R. (3d) 339 (F.C.T.D.).

26. *Rothbury International Inc.* v. *Canada (Minister of Industry)* (2004), 36 C.P.R. (4th) 203 (F.C.).

27. *Rothbury International Inc.* v. *Canada (Minister of Industry)* (2004), 36 C.P.R. (4th) 203 (F.C.).

28. *Clatworthy & Son Ltd.* v. *Dale Display Fixtures Ltd.*, [1929] S.C.R. 429 (S.C.C.).

29. *Dover, Ltd.* v. *Nürnberger Celluloidwaren Fabrik Gebrüder Wolff* [1910] 2 Ch. 25 (U.K.C.A.); *Bata Industries Ltd.* v. *Warrington Inc.* (1985), 5 C.P.R. (3d) 339 (F.C.T.D.); *Re Industrial Design Application No. 1997—0381* (2002), 21 C.P.R. (4th) 339 (Patent Appeal Bd.).

30. *Re Industrial Design Application No. 1997—0381* (2002), 21 C.P.R. (4th) 339 (Patent Appeal Bd.).

31. *Dover Ltd.* v. *Nürnberger Celluloidwaren Fabrik Gebrüder Wolff* [1910] 2 Ch. 25 (U.K.C.A.); *Industrial Design Application No. 2001—1238* (2004), 30 C.P.R. (4th) 571 (Pat. App. Bd.).

32. *Industrial Design Application No. 1999-0058* (2003), 29 C.P.R. (4th) 93 (Pat. App. Bd.).

33. *Clatworthy & Son Ltd.* v. *Dale Display Fixtures Ltd.*, [1929] S.C.R. 429 (S.C.C.).

Originality of a design is assessed as of the date of the creation of the design, not the date of its registration.[34]

## 4. Publication

The *Act* provides that the registration of a design shall be refused if the application for registration is filed in Canada more than one year after the publication of the design in Canada or elsewhere.[35] Publication anywhere in the world must be considered.

Publication means offering or making an article available to the public. In this context the definition includes those who are, in fact, or are considered by the design owner as apt to be, interested in purchasing the article to which the design is applied or taking advantage of its availability. Disclosure of the design, for the purpose of obtaining orders for an article to be made according to the design, is a publication of the design.[36] Publication must generally be of a commercial nature. Publication to service providers by the design owner to develop a commercial version of the design does not constitute publication.[37]

All disclosures for the purpose of soliciting orders typically constitute publication.[38] The sale of the article to which the design is applied will be publication.

## 5. The Proprietor

### a) Author

The author of a design is the first proprietor of the design unless the author of a design has executed it for another person for consideration, in which case the person providing the consideration is the first proprietor of the design.[39]

---

34. *Bata Industries Ltd. v. Warrington* (1985), 5 C.P.R. (3d) 339 (F.C.T.D.).
35. Subsection 6(3)(a). Prior to January 1, 1994, the registration of a design was refused if the application for registration was filed in Canada more than one year after the publication of the design in Canada; *Durable Electric Appliance Co. Ltd. v. Renfrew Electric Products Ltd. et al.* [1926] 4 D.L.R. 1004, [1928] S.C.R. 8.
36. *Algonquin Mercantile Corp. v. Dart Industries Canada* (1984), 1 C.P.R. (3d) 75 (F.C.A.); *Ribbons (Montreal) Ltd. v. Belding Corticelli Ltd.* [1961] Ex. C.R. 388, 36 C.P.R. 65.
37. *Ribbons (Montreal) Ltd. v. Belding Corticelli Ltd.* [1961] Ex. C.R. 388, 36 C.P.R. 65; *Global Upholstery Co. Ltd. v. Galaxy Office Furniture Ltd.* (1976), 29 C.P.R. (2d) 145 (F.C.T.D.).
38. *Algonquin Mercantile Corp. v. Dart Industries Canada* (1984), 1 C.P.R. (3d) 75 (F.C.A.).
39. Subsection 12(1).

The *Act* does not contain a definition of the word "author" but generally speaking, the author of a design is the person who has developed the shape, configuration, pattern, or ornament or combination of those features which give rise to the design.[40] The personal responsibility of the "author" for the development of the design must be considered. Individuals who have merely carried out instructions provided by another will not likely be considered to be an "author."[41]

## b)  Designs Executed for Consideration

The *Act* provides that if the author of a design has executed it for another person for consideration, the person providing the consideration is the first proprietor of the design.[42] This provision applies to an independent contractor who is paid to produce a design and designs produced by individuals in the course of their employment.[43]

If an employee, who created a design in the course of employment, registers it in his or her personal name, the registration is invalid.[44]

## 6.  Application

## a)  The Requirements

The proprietor of a design may apply to register it by paying the prescribed fees and filing an application, in the form set out in the *Industrial Design Regulations*, with the Industrial Design section of the Office of Commissioner of Patents.[45] The application must include:

(a) a drawing or photograph of the design and a description of the design;

---

40. *Ribbons (Montreal) Ltd. v. Belding Corticelli Ltd.*, [1961] Ex. C.R. 388, 36 C.P.R. 65 (Ex. Ct.); *Uniformes Town & Country Inc. v. Labrie* (1992), 44 C.P.R. (3d) 514 (F.C.A.).
41. *Renwal Mfg. Co. Inc. v. Reliable Toy Co. Ltd. et al.*, [1949] Ex. C.R. 188 (Ex. Ct.); *Comstock Canada v. Electec Ltd.*, (1991), 38 C.P.R. (3d) 29 (F.C.T.D.).
42. Subsection 12(1).
43. *Renwal Mfg. Co. Inc. v. Reliable Toy Co. Ltd. et al.* [1949] Ex. C.R. 188, 9 C.P.R. 67 (Ex. Ct.); *Angelstone Ltd. v. Artistic Stone Ltd.* [1960] Ex. C.R. 286, 33 C.P.R. 155 (Ex. Ct.).
44. *Angelstone Ltd. v. Artistic Stone Ltd.*, [1960] Ex. C.R. 286, 33 C.P.R. 155 (Ex. Ct.); *Hassenfeld Bros. Inc. et al. v. Parkdale Novelty Co. Ltd.*, [1967] 1 Ex. C.R. 277 (Ex. Ct.).
45. See section 9, *Industrial Design Regulations*, SOR/2003-210; SOR/2007-92.

(b) a declaration that the design was not, to the proprietor's knowledge, in use by any other person than the first proprietor at the time the design was adopted by the first proprietor; and

(c) any prescribed information.[46]

There must be a written description of the design.[47]

On receipt of an application, the application is classified,[48] searched,[49] and examined by an examiner to ensure that the application meets all of the requirements of the *Act* and the *Industrial Design Regulations.*[50]

An application must relate to one design applied to a single article[51] or set, or to variants.[52] Where the Office of Commissioner of Patents determines that the application relates to more than one design, the applicant must limit the application to one design only. Any other design disclosed may be made the subject of a separate application.[53]

The application must include a title identifying the finished article or set in respect of which the registration of the design is requested.[54]

Each application is examined to ascertain whether the design meets the requirements of the *Act* for registration. The Examiner must give consideration to the drawing in conjunction with the description of the design as provided by the applicant.[55] If a design does not meet the requirements, a report is sent to the applicant setting out the objections and specifying a period for reply.[56]

---

46. Subsection 4(1) and see *Industrial Design Regulations*. The practice of the Industrial Design Office concerning drawings and photographs is set out in the *Industrial Design Office Practices*, Canadian Intellectual Property Office (Industrial Design Office) (Ottawa: Industry Canada, 2004) at section 6. See *Re Industrial Design Application No. 1998-2348* (2001), 14 C.P.R. (4th) 63 (Patent Appeal Bd) concerning the use of break lines in drawings.

47. Subsection 4(1)(a) and see *Industrial Design Office Practices*, section 6.4.5, 6.4. In *Re Industrial Design Application No. 1997-1768* (1999), 3 C.P.R (4th) 254 (Patent Appeal Bd.) a description defining the features of the design in the alternative was found to be unacceptable.

48. *Industrial Design Office Practices*, section 5.1.

49. *Industrial Design Office Practices*, section 5.2.

50. *Industrial Design Office Practices*, section 6.

51. See *Industrial Design Application No. 2000-2268/95949* (2006), 56 C.P.R. (4th) 154 (Patent Appeal Bd. and Commissioner of Patents) which found that an application for a faucet, which included both a spout and handles, was directed to a single article of manufacture.

52. *Industrial Design Regulations*, Section 10 and see *Industrial Design Application No. 2000-2268/95949* (2006), 56 C.P.R. (4th) 154 (Patent Appeal Bd. and Commissioner of Patents.

53. *Industrial Design Regulations*, Section 10 and see *Re Industrial Design Application No. 1998–0950* (2001), 14 C.P.R. (4th) 213 (Patent Appeal Bd.).

54. *Industrial Design Regulations*, subsection 9(2)(b).

55. *Re LTI Corp. Industrial Design Application No. 1998–2446,* (2003), 25 C.P.R. (4th) 256 (Patent Appeal Board and Commissioner of Patents).

56. Subsection 5.

If it is decided that a design is not registrable, the applicant may appeal to the Federal Court to review the decision.[57] The proper procedure is to bring an action in the Federal Court.[58]

## b) Identifying the Features that Constitute the Design

The description must indicate whether the design relates to the appearance of the entirety of the article or to an appearance of a portion of the article. Where the design is limited to the appearance of a portion of the article, that portion must be clearly identified.[59] The description must make clear which of the visual features shown in the drawings comprise the design.[60]

The description is important since it and the drawing or photograph of the design determine the extent of the exclusive right to which the proprietor is entitled. However, it is not appropriate to treat the description in the same fashion as a patent claim.[61]

## c) Priority Based on an Application Filed in Another Country

A six-month grace period for an application which has been filed in specified foreign countries is available. If the proprietor files an application for the same design in Canada within the grace period, the Canadian application will obtain the benefit of the foreign priority filing date.[62]

More specifically, an application for the registration of an industrial design filed in Canada by any person who has, or whose predecessor in title has, previously filed an application for the registration of the same industrial design in a foreign country has the same force and effect as the same application would have if filed in Canada on the date on which the application for the registration of the same industrial design was first filed in that foreign country, if

(a) the application in Canada is filed within six months from the earliest date on which the foreign application was filed; and

---

57. Section 22.
58. *Gandy v. Canada (Commissioner of Patents)*, (1980), 47 C.P.R. (2d) 109 (F.C.T.D.), *Rothbury International Inc. v. Canada (Minister of Industry)* (2004), 36 C.P.R. (4th) 203 (F.C.).
59. *Industrial Design Office Practices,* Sections 6.4.5.a).
60. *Industrial Design Office Practices,* Sections 6.4.5.b).
61. *Alkot Industries Ltd. v. Consumers Distributing Co. Ltd.* (1986), 11 C.P.R. (3d) 276 (F.C.T.D.).
62. *Industrial Design Office Practices,* Sections 3.4.1–3.4.4.

(b) the person requests priority in respect of the application filed in Canada in accordance with the regulations. [63]

The term "foreign country" means a country that by treaty, convention or law affords a similar privilege to citizens of Canada with respect to the effective date of an application for the registration of an industrial design, and includes a Member of the World Trade Organization.[64]

For the purposes of determining whether an application was filed more than one year after publication,[65] the foreign priority date does not apply in determining the filing date. [66]

## 7. Registration

An exclusive right for an industrial design is acquired by registration of the design under the *Act*.[67] During the existence of an exclusive right, no person shall, without the license of the proprietor of the design,

(a) make, import for the purpose of trade or business, or sell, rent, or offer or expose for sale or rent, any article in respect of which the design is registered and to which the design or a design not differing substantially therefrom has been applied; or

(b) do, in relation to a kit, anything specified in paragraph (a) that would constitute an infringement if done in relation to an article assembled from the kit.[68]

---

63. Section 29(1). Section 20 of the *Industrial Design Regulations* provides that a request for priority must be made in writing and indicate the date the application for registration of the design was first filed in or for the foreign country, the name of the country and the number assigned by that country to the application. If, at any time before the registration of the design for which priority is sought, an application is made for a design that is identical to or so closely resembles the design as to be confounded with it, the Commissioner must advise the applicant in writing and request that the applicant provide the following documents

   (a) a certified copy of the foreign application on which the request is based; and

   (b) a certificate from the office in which the application referred to in paragraph (a) was filed showing the date of its filing therein.

   The request for priority is suspended until the certified copy and the certificate have been filed.

64. Section 29(2).

65. Section 6(3).

66. Section 6(4).

67. Section 9.

68. Subsection 11(1).

After an application has been allowed, a certificate shall be signed by the Minister, the Commissioner of Patents, or an officer, clerk or employee of the Commissioner's office stating that the design has been registered in accordance with the *Act*.[69]

In the absence of proof to the contrary, the certificate is sufficient evidence of the design, the originality of the design, the name of the proprietor, the person named as proprietor being proprietor, the commencement and term of registration, and compliance with the *Act*.[70]

A certificate appearing to be issued under section 7 of the *Act* is admissible in evidence in all courts without proof of the signature or official character of the person appearing to have signed it.[71]

## 8. Marking

While the *Act* previously required that articles be marked with an indication that they were protected by an industrial design registration,[72] it no longer contains such a requirement. However, it is prudent that articles be marked with the capital letter "D" in a circle and the name, or the usual abbreviation of the name of the proprietor of the design.

The *Act* provides that in any proceedings brought for infringement of a design, a court must not award a remedy, other than an injunction, if the defendant establishes that, at the time of the act that is the subject of the proceedings, the defendant was not aware, and had no reasonable grounds to suspect, that the design was registered.[73] This defense is not available if the plaintiff establishes that the capital letter "D" in a circle and the name, or the usual abbreviation of the name of the proprietor of the design were marked on

(a) all, or substantially all, of the articles to which the registration pertains and that were distributed in Canada by or with the consent of the proprietor before the act complained of; or

(b) the labels or packaging associated with those articles. [74]

---

69. Subsection 7(1).
70. Subsection 7(3).
71. Subsection 7(4).
72. *Industrial Design Act* R.S.C. 1985, c.I-8 and see subsection 29.1(2) for the relevant transitional rule for applications filled before June 9, 1993 and see *L.M. Lipski Ltd. v. Dorel Industries Inc. et al.* [1988] 3 F.C. 594 (F.C.T.D.) concerning the effect of non-compliance.
73. Section 17 (1).
74. Section 17 (3).

## 9. Term

Subject to payment of prescribed fees, the duration of the right granted is ten years beginning on the date of registration of the design.[75] In order to maintain the exclusive right the proprietor must pay to the Commissioner of Patents an additional fee before the fifth anniversary of the registration. The proprietor has a grace period of six months from the expiry of the fifth anniversary of the registration to maintain the registration for which a further fee must be paid. If the design is not renewed within five years and six months, the term expires at the end of that time.[76]

## 10. Assignment and License

The *Act* provides that every design, whether registered or unregistered, is assignable in law, either as to the whole interest or any undivided part, by an instrument in writing, which shall be recorded in the office of the Commissioner of Patents on payment of the prescribed fees.[77] If the proprietor assigns its rights prior to filing an application, the assignee is entitled to apply to register the design.[78] After an assignment is made, the name of proprietor at the time the article, labels, or packaging were marked should be shown for the purposes of subsection 17(2) of the *Act*.[79]

Subsection 13(2) relates to the right to use a design. It provides that every proprietor of a design may grant and convey an exclusive right to make, use, and vend and to grant to others the right to make, use, and vend the design, within and throughout Canada or any part thereof, for the unexpired term of its duration or any part thereof. [80] Such a grant and conveyance shall be called a license and must be recorded in the same manner as an assignment.[81] The use of the word "exclusive" refers to the rights available to the proprietor under the *Act*, not the nature of the license. Both exclusive licenses and non-exclusive licenses may be granted.

---

75. Section 10.
76. Section 10(3) of the *Act* and *Industrial Design Regulations*, section 18.
77. Subsection 13(1).
78. Subsection 13(1) and see *Milliken & Company et al. v. Interface Flooring Systems (Canada) Inc* (1994), 55 C.P.R. (3d) 30 (F.C.T.D.).
79. Subsection 17(3).
80. Subsection 13(2).
81. Subsection 13(3).

## 11. Expungement and Alteration

Section 22 of the *Act* provides that the Federal Court may, on the information of the Attorney General or at the suit of any person aggrieved by any omission without sufficient cause to make any entry in the Register of Industrial Designs, or by any entry made without sufficient cause in the Register, make such order for making, expunging or varying any entry in the Register as the Court thinks fit, or the Court may refuse the application. The Federal Court has exclusive jurisdiction to hear and determine proceedings under the section.[82]

Section 22 is concerned with an omission without sufficient cause to make an entry in the Register or by any entry made without sufficient cause in the Register. In either case, the Federal Court may make such order with respect to the costs of the proceedings as it thinks fit and decide any question that may be necessary or expedient to decide for the rectification of the Register.[83]

The term "person aggrieved" has been given a wide interpretation.[84] A person is "aggrieved" if, as one of the public, an impugned design registration prevents them from using it.[85]

## 12. Infringement

### a) The Exclusive Right

Section 9 of the *Act* provides that an exclusive right for an industrial design may be acquired by registration of the design under the *Act*. A registration is required and there is no protection for activities which occur before registration.[86] The exclusive right is limited to Canada and infringing activities must occur within Canada to be actionable.

Subsection 11(1) of the *Act*[87] provides that during the existence of an exclusive right, no person shall, without the license of the proprietor of the design,

    (a)  make, import for the purpose of trade or business, or sell, rent, or offer or expose for sale or rent, any article in respect of which the design is

---

82. Subsection. 22(4); *Epstein v. O-Pee-Chee Co. Ltd.* [1927] Ex. C.R. 156, [1927] 3 D.L.R. 160.
83. Subsection 22(2) and (3).
84. *DeKuyper v. Van Dulken* (1894), 24 S.C.R. 114; *In Re Vulcan Trade Mark* (1915), 51 S.C.R. 411, 24 D.L.R. 621.
85. *Epstein v. O-Pee-Chee Co. Ltd.*, [1927] Ex. C.R. 156, [1927] 3 D.L.R. 160.
86. *Ulextra Inc. v. Pronto Luce Inc.* 2004 FC 590 (F.C.).
87. Section 11 was brought into force January 1, 1994 and is significantly different from the section that preceded it.

registered and to which the design or a design not differing substantially therefrom has been applied; or

(b) do, in relation to a kit, anything specified in paragraph (a) that would constitute an infringement if done in relation to an article assembled from the kit.

As previously set out, designs are registered in association with specifically identified articles. Infringement will occur when the design or a design not differing substantially therefrom has been applied to the article for which the design was registered.

For the purposes of subsection 11(1), in considering whether differences are substantial, the extent to which the registered design differs from any previously published design may be taken into account.[88]

In order to determine whether infringement has occurred, the following matters must be considered:

(a) were the activities of the defendant without the license of the proprietor of the design;

(b) did the defendant engage in one of the activities prescribed in section 11;

(c) was the allegedly infringing article an article in respect of which the design has been registered; and

(d) was the design or a design not differing substantially from the design applied to the allegedly infringing article.

## b) License

Since subsection 11(1) expressly refers to the absence of license of the proprietor of the exclusive right, the absence of license is an essential element of the cause of action for infringement. In order to succeed, a plaintiff must show that the defendant's actions were done without its license. Conversely, from the defendant's point of view license is a defense.

## c) The Activities

The activities described in subsection 11(1)(a) consist of:

(a) making;

(b) importing for the purposes of trade or business; [89]

---

88. Subsection 11(2).
89. See *Hansen International Inc. v. Whirley Industries Inc.* (2002), 22 C.P.R. (4th) 57 (F.C.T.D.).

(c)  selling or renting; or

(d)  offering or exposing for sale or rent

any article in respect of which the design is registered and to which the design or a design not differing substantially therefrom has been applied.

Section 11 has not been widely considered by the courts in Canada but the section is similar to section 7 of the United Kingdom *Registered Designs Act, 1949*[90] which has been considered by the courts of that country.

The activities must also take place during the term of the exclusive right in order to be actionable.[91]

## d)  The Article in Respect of which the Design Is Registered

In order to show that infringement has occurred, the plaintiff must show that the defendant has engaged in at least one of the activities described in the section in relation to an article in respect of which the plaintiff's design has been registered.

## e)  Whether a Design Not Differing Substantially from the Design Has Been Applied

If the design itself has been applied to an article in respect of which the plaintiff's design has been registered, the application of the section is clear. Frequently, there will be differences which must be considered to ascertain whether the designs differ substantially.

Since a "design" refers to "features . . . . that, in a finished article, appeal to and are judged solely by the eye," infringement must be determined on an ocular basis. The emphasis is on the visual image conveyed by the article.[92]

The appearance of the allegedly infringing article must be compared to the appearance of the registered design. Reference must be made to the drawings or photographs of the design and the description of it. It is appropriate to view articles which embody the registered design although care must be taken to avoid giving consideration to features not disclosed in the design.[93]

The *Act* provides that in considering whether differences are substantial, the extent to which the registered design differs from any previously published design may be taken into account.

---

90.  12, 13 & 14 Geo. 6, c. 88.

91.  Section 10.

92.  *Interlego AG v Tyco Industries Inc.* [1988] 3 W.L.R. 678 (P.C.).

93.  *Benchairs Limited v. Chair Centre Limited* [1974] R.P.C. 429 (U.K.C.A.).

A design which has substantial originality may be entitled to a broader scope of protection than a design which is close to designs which had been published before it. If only small differences separate the registered design from the designs which precede it, then equally small differences between the impugned article and the registered design should be sufficient to avoid infringement.

Expert evidence is admissible to point out similarities and dissimilarities, what is common to the trade, and what has been disclosed in previously published designs.

Where a registration relates to the features of shape and configuration of a product, the exclusive right is accordingly for the product as a whole and infringement must rest upon imitation of the shape or configuration as a whole not just a part of the design.[94] Where the design is limited to the shape or configuration of the article, the plaintiff must show similarity approaching identity.[95]

## 13.  Actions for Infringement[96]

### a)  Jurisdiction

An action for infringement of a registered design may be brought in any court of competent jurisdiction by the proprietor of the design or by an exclusive licensee of any right in the design, subject to any agreement between the proprietor and the licensee.[97] The proprietor of the design must be a party to such an action.[98]

The Federal Court has concurrent jurisdiction to hear and determine any action for the infringement of an exclusive right; and any question relating to the proprietorship of a design or any right in a design.[99]

### b)  Limitation Period

The *Act* provides that no remedy may be awarded for an act of infringement committed more than three years before the commencement of the action for infringement.[100]

---

94. *Benchairs Limited v. Chair Centre Limited* [1974] R.P.C. 429 (U.K.C.A.); *UPL Group Ltd. v. DUX Engineers Ltd.* [1989] 3 N.Z.L.R. 135 (N.Z.C.A.).
95. *Sommer Allibert (UK) Limited v. Flair Plastics Limited* [1987] R.P.C. 599 (U.K.C.A.).
96. See Chapters 15 and 30.
97. Subsection 15(1).
98. Subsection 15(2).
99. Section 15.2 and see Chapter 30, part 11(c) concerning Declaratory Relief.
100. Section 18.

# 14. Remedies

In any proceedings for infringement, the court may make such orders as the circumstances require, including orders for relief by way of injunction and the recovery of damages or profits, for punitive damages, and for the disposal of any infringing article or kit.[101]

## a) Injunction[102]

### i) Interlocutory Injunction

An interlocutory injunction may be granted to restrain infringement until trial.[103]

A plaintiff will be required, before such an interlocutory injunction is granted, to provide to the court an undertaking to compensate the defendant for any damages the defendant may suffer as the result of the grant of the injunction if, at trial, the plaintiff is unsuccessful.[104] On the dissolution of an interlocutory injunction, the defendant is entitled to an enquiry as to the damages sustained by reason of the injunction.[105] If the validity of an industrial design registration is attacked, this may lead to significant financial exposure.[106]

### ii) Permanent Injunction[107]

Infringement may be restrained by the grant of an injunction at trial.

## b) Damages or Profits

The assessment of damages or an accounting of profits is controlled by the usual considerations applying in the case of trademark infringement or passing off.[108]

---

101. Section 15.1.
102. See Chapters 15 and 30.
103. *Slim Line Design Ltd. v. Pacific Northwest Manufacturing Inc.* (1999), 86 C.P.R. (3d) 498 (B.C.S.C.).
104. *Rules of Civil Procedure*, R.R.O 1990, Regulation 194 as amended Rule 40.03; *Federal Court Act*, R.S.C. 1985, c. F-7 as amended, section 44.
105. *Mattel Canada Inc v GTS Acquisitions Ltd.* (1998), 82 C.P.R. (3d) 57 (F.C.T.D.); *Algonquin Mercantile Corporation v. Dart Industries Canada Ltd.* (1983), 71 C.P.R. (2d) 11 (F.C.T.D.).
106. *Algonquin Mercantile Corporation v. Dart Industries Canada Ltd.* (1983), 71 C.P.R. (2d) 11 (F.C.T.D.), (1984) 1 C.P.R. (3d) 75 (F.C.A.).
107. See Chapters 15 and 30.
108. See Chapter 15.

Punitive damages may be awarded.[109]

## c) Delivery Up

Section 15.1 provides that the court may make such orders as the circumstances require, including orders for the disposal of any infringing article or kit.

## d) Defenses

In addition to the usual defenses to an action for infringement, the invalidity of the registration of the design may be asserted without bring proceedings for expungement.[110] A claim of invalidity may be asserted on the basis that:

(a) the design is not the proper subject-matter for registration;[111]
(b) the design was published in Canada or elsewhere more than one year prior to the application for registration;[112]
(c) the design is not original;[113] or
(d) the registered proprietor was not the author of the design.[114]

In addition, it may be alleged that the plaintiff is not entitled to any remedy, other than an injunction, since the defendant was not aware, and had no reasonable grounds to suspect, that the design was registered.[115] However, this defense is not available if the plaintiff has marked the articles to which the registration relates as required by the *Act*.[116]

109. See Chapter 30.
110. *Clatworthy & Son Ltd.* v. *Dale Display Fixtures, Ltd.* [1929] S.C.R. 429 (S.C.C.).
111. *Canadian Wm. A. Rogers Ltd.* v. *International Silver Co. of Canada Ltd.,* [1932] Ex. C.R. 63.
112. *Epstein v. O-Pee-Chee Co. Ltd.,* [1927] Ex. C.R. 156, [1927] 3 D.L.R. 160.
113. *Clatworthy & Son Ltd.* v. *Dale Display Fixtures Ltd.* [1929] S.C.R. 429 (S.C.C.).
114. *Angelstone Ltd.* v. *Artistic Stone Ltd.,* [1960] Ex. C.R. 286, 33 C.P.R. 155.
115. Section 17(1).
116. See part 8 of this chapter.

# Table of Cases

# Index

Author name change/suppression,
in copyright, 344
Authors of copyright
author, definition of, 227
computer-generated work, 228
first owner of, 227

Bad faith in domain name disputes,
definition of
in CDRP, 176–77
in UDRP, 170–71
Badges of fraud, passing off, 131
Bankruptcy
copyright, reversions of, 257
licenses, 255–56
property of bankrupt, 255
proposals, 256
*Bankruptcy and Insolvency Act*, 256, 257
Benchers of the Law Society, 297
Berne Convention, in Canada, 2–3, 266
Broadcaster's communication signal, 209
copyright, first owner of, 211
in live event, 211
protected work, 209
rights associated with, 209–11
*Broadcasting Act*, 210, 306

Canada Customs and Revenue Agency
(CCRA), 141
Canada Gazette, 206, 210, 351, 353
Canada-United States Free Trade
Agreement, 306
Canadian Intellectual Property Office
(CIPO), 12
Canadian Intellectual Property Office,
Wares and Services Manual, 60
Canadian Internet Registration Authority
(CIRA), 165
CDRP WHOIS Privacy Policy, 177–78
Certificate of registration, of trademarks, 58
Certification mark definition of, 12–13
Certification mark, 61
Charitable bodies, performance by, 311
Cinematographic works
contracting out, 203
under *Copyright Act*, 188, 189–90
maker, concept of, 240
rights in, 190
terms of protection, 221
CIRA Domain Name Dispute Resolution
Policy (CDRP)
applicable disputes, 173–74

bad faith, 176–77
confusingly similar domain name, 174–75
history of, 173
no legitimate interest, 175–76
procedure, 177
WHOIS privacy policy, 177–78
Civil remedies, for infringement of
copyright, 316–319, 325, 329–337
Collective society, and copyright
General Regime, proposed tariffs filing of,
358–59
Performing Rights and of
Communication Right Societies, duty
of, 351–52
private copying, 364
retransmission, 360–62
Collective works, in copyright ownership, 236
Commissioned work, in copyright
ownership, 232
Commissioner of Patents, industrial designs
application requirements, 375
design definition of, 369
originality of, 372
registration of, 379
term of, 380
Common law rights, 5
Common law trademark, 168
Communication signal, and copyright, 210,
222, 240–41, 318
*Companies' Creditors Arrangement Act*,
257n36
Compensation, acts done before recognition
of copyright, 366
Compilations, under *Copyright Act*, 183, 237
Computer programs
definition under *Copyrights Act*, 186
exception in copyright of, 301
Concurrent rights
under common law rights, 133
registration of trademarks, 71
Confusing trademarks
degree of resemblance, 102–3
from bilingual perspective, 96
famous trademarks, 100–101
inherent distinctiveness of, 97–98
from mythical consumer perspective, 95
nature of trade, 101
nature of wares, services, and business,
99–100
other circumstances, 103
statutory framework of, 94–97
usage duration of, 99